CRUISE CONTROL

CRUISE CONTROL

WENSLEY CLARKSON

BLAKE

Published by Blake Publishing Ltd,
3, Bramber Court, 2 Bramber Road,
London W14 9PB, England

First published in hardback in 2003

ISBN 1 85782 546 2

British Library Cataloguing-in-Publication Data:

A catalogue record for this book is available from the British Library.

Design by ENVY

Printed in Great Britain by CPD (Wales)

1 3 5 7 9 10 8 6 4 2

Papers used by Blake Publishing are natural, recyclable products made from wood
grown in sustainable forests. The manufacturing processes conform to the
environmental regulations of the country of origin.

Pictures reproduced by kind permission of Rex Features.

Every attempt has been made to contact the relevant copyright-holders, but some
were unobtainable. We would be grateful if the appropriate people could contact us.

To Toby, Polly, Rosie
and Fergus

CONTENTS

ACKNOWLEDGEMENTS

The idea of using a leaden, dispassionate word like 'Acknowledgements' for this section cannot begin to express the depth of my feelings for the many individuals who have made this book possible. I owe them my deepest and most heartfelt gratitude.

First to my publisher, John Blake, without whom this book would never have happened. His support and guidance have been very much appreciated.

Then there are: Victor Escandon Prada, Mark Sandelson, Shaun Redmayne, Father Aldric Heidlage, Caroline Mapother, Father Hilarian Kistner, Roger Fristoe, Julie Borders, Jeff Bayers, Bill Ellison, Warder Harrison, Bill Schwartz, Kale Browne, Mario Marcelino, Graham Berry, Henry Darrow, Andre Tabayoyon, John Stockwell, Mrs John Shiels, Mrs William Vesterman, Angelo Corbo, John Voskian, Jonathan Margolis, Anthony Bowman, Louise Frogley, Joe Poalella, Peter Wilson, John Bell, Martin Dunn, John Glatt, Bill Lewis, Rosie Ries, my great friend Rodriguez in Maro, Jorge and his friend Victor and every other person who agreed to be interviewed for this book. A number of them requested that I do not reveal their identities either in the text or on this page. My eternal thanks also to the reference libraries at Globe, Mirror Group Newspapers, Associated Newspapers, News International and the Academy of Motion Pictures in Los Angeles.

In addition, *Top Gun – The Films of Tom Cruise* by Edward Gross (Pioneer Books Inc., 1990) and *Tom Cruise* by Joelene M. Anthony (St Martin's Press, 1988) provided some invaluable information about Tom Cruise and I am extremely grateful to them. Other books that have been helpful include: *Coppola* by Peter Cowle, *Totally Uninhibited* by Lawrence J.

Quirk, *Martin Scorsese: A Journey, Levinson on Levinson* and *Fade Out* by Peter Bart, *Paul Newman* by Elena Oumano, *Scorsese on Scorsese* and *Paul and Joanne* by Joe Morella and Edward Z. Epstein.

But my biggest debt of gratitude must go to Dr Dillon Mapother, who agreed to help me with invaluable background material on Tom Cruise's family history.

Wensley Clarkson

You gotta have a dream,
If you don't have a dream,
How you gonna have a
Dream come true?

RODGERS AND HAMMERSTEIN

PROLOGUE

He's bigger than Jack, bigger than Pacino, bigger even than Arnold, Kevin or Mel. Tom Cruise is the most successful movie star in the world. His last two films garnered an international gross of well over half a billion dollars. In fact, although a few of Tom's movies could be termed disappointments, it would be a stretch to call any failures. The closest was the Irish epic *Far and Away* – and that raked in more than $100 million worldwide.

For years the public has seen Tom as a fresh-faced wonder boy, the all-American quarterback. 'The guy all women want to date and who doesn't threaten any guy,' says one Hollywood producer who has worked with Tom.

Like Schwarzenegger, Tom has been careful to maintain a public image of the quintessential innocent, the good-looking guy who's just enjoying the ride of a lifetime. And, as with Schwarzenegger, any hints of a deeper, more fearfully controlling ego have been blamed on overzealous publicists.

Experience is the name everyone gives to their mistakes, but in Tom Cruise's case there have been few errors in his entire career. Although the Hollywood producer who has just signed up last year's has-been may tell you otherwise, there is only a handful of genuinely bankable box-office stars – names who can 'open' a film regardless of its quality.

That list tends to change virtually every year, but Tom Cruise's name is always present. Ever since his first surprise hit, this actor has guaranteed that he can eliminate all risks at the box office, just so long as you can afford fees that start at the $20 million mark.

Tom Cruise is the only person from his generation of actors who is equipped to step into the shoes of Gary Cooper, James Stewart, Tyrone Power and Clark Gable. Already considered a great movie star in the United States, Tom is the great American hero to the rest of the world. People stop him in the street to tell him how proud they are of him and he has been credited with the revival of true, old-style movie-star ideals.

Usually prologues stick to a very traditional format, but in this case I am going to present this introduction to Tom Cruise in a way I think he would appreciate, by providing a highly focused, point-by-point guide to what lies behind the phenomenal success of an actor whose films have grossed a figure approaching $2.5 billion worldwide, an astounding achievement in a time when more and more people are staying away from the movies.

Family background

Tom's difficult childhood has provided him with inner strength and the will to succeed – something that a person from a happier home might never have been capable of matching.

The theme of fathers and sons regularly appears in Tom's movies and indeed the issue of manhood is a common thread. Tom's father was not around much and he grew up having to prove something on his own. It turned out to be something of a catalyst. It drove him further into new areas of life experience. He was constantly proving to himself that he could do it.

Workaholic tendencies

The one through-line in Tom's films is the way he fixates on his work. It's reminiscent of Robert De Niro, only without the tics. He doesn't just get into character, he plunges right into the shaping of the entire project.

Everyone who has ever worked with Tom concedes that he is completely and utterly work-orientated. After completing *Rain Man*, his equally perfectionist co-star Dustin Hoffman proclaimed: 'He's a demon. He gets up early, he works out, he goes home early, he studies, he watches his diet like he's an old fart, he doesn't drink and he always wanted to rehearse. It affected me emotionally, being in his presence during that time.'

Tom is obsessed by preliminary research. He's flown jets, mixed drinks, used a wheelchair, shot pool and raced cars, all in pursuit of the perfect performance.

Tom's co-star in *A Few Good Men*, Kevin Pollack, enthused: 'He has a work ethic the like of which I've never seen. I can't believe I'm saying this, but this guy really works for his $15 million.'

The winning formula

Somehow, Tom has found a diverse series of winning formulae that have stretched across all the movies he has made to date. Let's break them down for a moment: in three movies he plays a young man haunted by the shadow of his deceased father (no doubt helped by his own painful real-life experiences). In another four hit roles he plays a soldier. Then, in two films, he is a Harvard-educated lawyer. In five movies he even lip-synchs to golden oldies. In another five roles he has affairs with older women (again, his real-life first marriage was to a lady some years his senior). In two roles he plays a nerdy type who romances wealthy socialites. In two other parts he spends much of his time on a motorcycle. In virtually all of his movies to date, he wears Ray-Bans. Then there are five films' worth of the classic, cocky young Tom being put on an even keel by a mentor.

Sometimes one has to wonder if Tom, in his early forties, is in danger of becoming a prig. The idea first surfaced for me when watching his 1987 blockbuster *The Color of Money*. There were twenty-two different kinds of grins, each a magical money-in-the-bank moment, suggesting that the actor knows precisely where his biggest strengths lie.

Undoubtedly, Tom is sometimes very reluctant to break the mould. He rejected the lead in *Edward Scissorhands* (too weird?), the title role in *Bright Lights, Big City* (too much drug taking), *Rush* (similar reasons) and *Backdraft* (presumably because there were so many other stars in that film).

Tom's decision to take on the highly controversial and definitely androgynous role of the vampire Lestat de Lioncourt in Neil Jordan's *Interview with the Vampire* was very brave indeed. Many Hollywood observers believe that this is yet another example of Tom's near obsession with not being predictable, even though the author of the book upon which the film is based was outraged by the casting of so-called squeaky-clean Tom in the main role.

No one really knows what makes a movie work. The whole enterprise is make-believe; a triumph of fantasy over fact. It's what makes the job exciting. A film out of nowhere, with a nobody star, can send people out happy – and make movie producers very rich men.

In Hollywood fifty years ago, the ceiling was lower and the floor more secure than in today's boom-or-bust industry, where there is no safety net – no majority of compulsive movie-goers – to catch the weaker films. Every star, every studio, stands like a colossus on a fault line. If a star like Tom Cruise wants $20 million a picture he'll get it – and he'll earn it.

Cruise control on the set

Tom denies he is a control freak, but there is a lot of evidence that points towards this being the case. His ideals of what each role actually represents often turn him into an incredible perfectionist.

Even on the set of *Born on the Fourth of July*, he regularly bugged mega-powerful director Oliver Stone about shots he felt were not quite right and scenes that did not, in his opinion, work properly. Tom, then twenty-seven, was never shy about exerting his Hollywood clout if it was required.

Later, on *Far and Away*, crew members were warned not to speak to Tom as it might affect his concentration. The same was said to be true on the set of *Mission: Impossible*. While on his most famous hit of all – *Top Gun* – he made the movie's scriptwriter go back and redraft the screenplay at least fifty times before agreeing to the role.

Years earlier, when Tom complained bitterly about his co-star on one movie, he was told he would have to fire her himself. The star – then just twenty-one – had a passionate affair with her instead!

Religion

When Tom was fourteen he seriously considered becoming a priest and it became clear in later years that he needed a church to attach himself to as a kind of security blanket after all the lonely years of his childhood. That seems to be how he became involved in the highly controversial Church of Scientology.

Along with a handful of other Hollywood stars, Tom has spent hundreds of thousands of dollars on training courses inside the church. He often spends days at the church's base camp in the middle of the Californian desert.

For years Tom would not admit he was a Scientologist until confronted during a US television interview. The actor later even persuaded some film-makers he worked with to use a sound system invented by the Scientologists.

Some Hollywood observers believe that Tom's association with Scientology has helped him maintain his highly focused work ethic and greatly assisted him in dealing with stardom.

Others find it more difficult to accept. The fact that members of the church apparently believe in things probably isn't a big deal. Who in California doesn't?

When I began making enquiries into the dealings of the church and Tom's links with it, a flurry of legal threats were made to me personally as well as to a number of associates who have helped me with my research into Tom's membership of the Scientologists. At one stage the church traced my home address and unlisted phone number. There was an overriding impression given by the tone of the letters that I should not continue my enquiries.

The entourage

In many ways Tom lives in his own, carefully cultured world. Few people are privy to his personal habits. There are a splattering of showbiz friends like Sean Penn and Emilio Estevez, but these relationships are not exactly regular. Tom can go for a year without speaking to either, but at least a bond of comradeship is apparently retained.

In Hollywood, CAA chief Mike Ovitz and billionaire David Geffen – the two most powerful players in all of moviedom – are very close to Tom and they have probably done more to help guide his career than anyone else.

Corporate Hollywood adores Tom because he is such a finely tuned work-track individual. Some who have met him describe him as having the work ethics of a fifty-year-old managing director of a large company. He takes every job deadly seriously and he is surrounded by wall after wall of advisers who try to take many of the minor decisions for him.

It is a strange existence, but although Tom sometimes tries to get back into the real world, there is no way that he can lead life like the majority of us. From the high walls and sophisticated alarm systems of his vast Los Angeles mansion to the pairs of bodyguards who tend to shadow his every move, he now has no choice but to grin and bear it.

Restricting the media

Over the years Tom has evolved into the most powerful actor in Hollywood, thanks partly to his complete control over all information regarding himself. Journalists are regularly asked to sign contracts forbidding the use of his words outside certain areas. Furthermore, Tom virtually never gives interviews that last longer than one hour.

'It is almost as if he is trying to stop anyone from finding out exactly who the real Tom Cruise is,' says one experienced showbusiness journalist.

When I first tried to contact Tom to request his co-operation in the writing of this book, three faxes were sent to his PR woman, Pat Kingsley. There was no response to any of them.

Then, when Tom's representatives discovered I had been contacting people involved in the Church of Scientology, a letter arrived at my publisher's office from Mr Bertram Fields, a renowned Hollywood attorney well known because of his representation of Michael Jackson during the flurry of accusations against the singer.

Mr Fields wrote: 'I represent Tom Cruise. I have been advised that you intend to publish a biography of Mr. Cruise. I believe that your book may contain numerous false and defamatory statements about Mr. Cruise. I urge you to check your facts very carefully before publication, since it is certainly Mr. Cruise's intention to institute an appropriate action should your book contain such statements.'

The publishers of this book immediately responded to Mr Fields's letter by urging him to ask his client to meet me in order to ensure that every statement in the book was entirely accurate. Neither Mr Fields or his client agreed to the request.

However, these demands are right in character for Tom, an intensely private person who sculpts his public image as carefully as he does his biceps. For example, almost until the day of their separation in January 1990, Tom insisted that his marriage to Mimi Rogers was perfectly happy.

Tom sometimes fails to turn up at press junkets to promote his latest movie. On one occasion his no-show was accompanied by an ingenuous note complete with photocopied signature, explaining how sorry Tom was not to be there.

When Tom did some TV interviews for *The Firm*, his list of conditions were very tight. He refused to let one reporter interview him until he had seen a videotape of that journalist. Just before the release of *Cocktail* in 1988, Tom learned that a particular writer had written something critical of his then wife, Mimi Rogers. The writer was barred from the press junket for the movie.

Occasionally Tom has hinted that his mistrust of the press stems from early bad experiences at the hands of journalists. But it must be said that there is no evidence of that in anything I have uncovered. It seems far more likely that he simply does not enjoy dealing with the media.

The family man image

By all accounts Tom's first marriage to attractive older woman Mimi Rogers was just a regrettable mistake. After their divorce Mimi Rogers hinted at some elements of marital discord. It was a rare, behind-the-scenes glimpse of the real man, as opposed to the screen hero we all know and adore.

Tom's second marriage, to Nicole Kidman, seemed to have got that image back on track. The adoption of two babies completed the perfect family scenario, one that Tom was ever anxious to present to the world.

There seemed to be another highly understandable motive behind Tom's quest for family togetherness. He genuinely wanted to bring up a family that stayed in one piece as opposed to the fragmented version he grew up with.

Tom and Nicole were up there with the legendary couples of Hollywood like Gable and Lombard, Tracy and Hepburn. In fact, they were probably a more powerful force as a duo than any other couple in La La Land history. Then disaster struck…

Extreme generosity

It has to be said that there is another side to Tom Cruise that rarely gets hinted at in public. The stereotypical work-driven 1980s ultimate yuppy-style figure emerged in the 1990s with a softer, more generous side to him.

Kevin Pollack – his co-star in *A Few Good Men* – tells this story: 'One day I was admiring a pen that Tom was using. I mean, this was a gorgeous pen. Tom explained that you could only get it from one place and so on. On my birthday, Tom gave me one of these pens, which came in a beautiful wooden box. I had it on authority that it was a very expensive pen.

'So a few days later, Tom sees me using a pen that's not the one that he bought for me. I told him that I was scared to use it because, I dunno, I might lose it or something. Again, a few days later, I am in my trailer and one of Tom's assistants knocks on the door. He has another wooden box with a second pen. He told me that Tom had wanted me to have it.'

Tom did not hesitate to fly the entire cast of *A Few Good Men* in his private jet to Las Vegas for dinner and an evening of gambling. A few years earlier Tom splashed out $25,000 for his *Top Gun* producer to attend a racing-car school with him.

So, with precious little stage experience and no workshop or acting-class background, Tom has indeed grabbed Hollywood by the balls. Now he has Tinseltown in a vice-like grip.

The key to Tom Cruise is that he knows exactly how to read situations and people. The adaptability that comes with moving constantly as a child, always being the outsider, and the burning need to rectify the sins of an absentee father have served him well as a performer. He is skilled enough to know how to elicit certain responses, which buttons to push.

Some say he is reminiscent of the young John Glenn from Tom Wolfe's famous account of the packaging of the astronauts, *The Right Stuff*. Always smiling, courteous and ineffably self-confident, Cruise is, as Oliver Stone, his director on *Born on the Fourth of July*, once put it, 'a kid off the Wheaties box'. But he is also, as Wolfe described Glenn, 'a true believer and a half ... a guy with a halo turned on at all times'.

Nicknamed Laserhead, he has a gaze that is all focus – no irony, no sarcasm, no cynicism. Total attention. With the help of Scientology, Tom Cruise believes wholeheartedly in the persona he's invented. I hope this book will demonstrate why.

1

It's a morally superior position, people think, this idea of being driven to be the best. Especially in America. The myth is that good people are driven, and bad people are lazy, and mediocre people are just swimming in the middle somewhere. As if it's all a matter of choice.

JEANNE MARIE LASKAS

Louisville, a town born in war on the turbulent western frontier of the United States of America, became, in the nineteenth century, the antebellum 'Gateway to the South'. Its proud inhabitants, who came from diverse ethnic, cultural and economic backgrounds, carved their city from the rugged Kentucky wilderness and welded it into a dynamic metropolis of driving civic pride and fierce hometown loyalty.

Founder George Rogers Clark had no way of knowing what would mushroom from the tiny enclave he carved in the Kentucky countryside in the summer of 1778 when he settled with 150 volunteer soldiers and twenty families on tiny Corn Island, a short distance upstream from the falls of the Ohio River.

The soldiers were seeking a base to launch an attack against the forts in the British Northwest Territory, which were suffering from increasing Indian attacks along the Kentucky frontier. English, Scottish and Irish families in the party that had floated down the river in flatboats with Clark were looking for fresh land where they could make a new beginning.

Realising that the island was not suited to be anything more than a temporary stopping point, Clark sent soldiers to the mainland to establish a more defensible fort, which they constructed on the edge of the Ohio River. News of Clark's victories in the north-west rapidly lured settlers to the region the following summer. Three hundred arrived in the spring of 1780 alone and in May that year the Virginia Legislature passed an act establishing the town of Louisville. The name was in honour of Louis XVI, King of France, for his aid in the Revolutionary War.

Soon the town assumed the character of a commercial trans-shipment point and the portaging of cargoes around the rapids was a main activity. Boats filled with goods were unloaded, carted overland and then reloaded for the continued journey up or downstream.

By the mid-1800s a canal had been constructed around the falls and soon 1500 steamers and 500 flatboats and keelboats, bearing 300,000 tons of cargo, were entering the canal annually. Louisville's population was edging towards the 30,000 mark and the city's strategic location as a river-rail crossroads gave it a role in America's great push to the west. Railroads connected Louisville with the cotton states to the south, with St Louis to the west, Pittsburgh to the east and the Great Lakes to the north.

The city was bursting with pride by the middle of the century, and this pride had been fuelled in 1848 when Zachary Taylor, who had come to Louisville as a baby and lived there for more than forty years, was elected twelfth President of the United States.

It was in 1850 that surveyor Dillon Henry Mapother arrived in Louisville from south-east Ireland, seeking a new life away from his famine-ravaged homeland. He was the younger of two sons and felt there was little future for him in the Emerald Isle. He felt the need to escape and the new, promised land of America seemed the perfect place to head for.

The name Mapother had, according to family legend back in Ireland, originated when a male child was born to Queen Elizabeth I of England and her lover, the Earl of Essex, hundreds of years earlier. The infant was banished to Ireland with a handful of royal servants, among them a woman who brought the child up as her own. That woman's children referred to the infant as 'my brother', which, in a Gaelic accent, sounded like 'Mapother', or so the legend goes. Thus was Tom Cruise's family name born.

Within months of arriving in Louisville, Dillon met, fell in love with and married a lady named Mary Cruise. The Mapothers became known in Louisville as a caring, happy family. Even the onset of the Civil War, with Louisville being officially named the port of entry for all Union armies in the West, did not affect their happiness. After the war the city soon recovered by diversifying the output of its manufacturing plants and the post-war period become yet another era of growth for the area.

The *Louisville Courier-Journal*'s first edition was published on 8 November 1868. Its headlines that day referred to how race riots in Savannah, Georgia, had resulted in 'radical negroes' taking control of the polls and driving away white men.

Dillon and Mary had two sons, Dillon E. and Wible Lawrence, born in

1872. However, tragedy cruelly invaded the Mapother household in the mid-1870s, when Dillon Henry was struck down by a severe case of food poisoning and died almost instantly. The family was naturally shocked by this unexpected death. Overnight Mary Cruise Mapother became a single mother trying to exist in a bustling, tough town with virtually no social services to support the recently bereaved. For the first time – but by no means the last – a strong woman was in charge of the Mapother clan. Mary took on part-time jobs and held on to the family's house by pure determination and the will to survive. Her bravery and single-mindedness would be passed down through many future generations.

Then she met and married another Irishman, called O'Mara, and on 29 December 1876 the couple had a son. For some reason which has never been clearly explained by the family, that child was christened Thomas Cruise Mapother. It has been a matter of conjecture within the Mapothers of Louisville ever since, because some of them do not consider themselves to be directly related to Tom Cruise's side of the family.

Thomas Cruise Mapother's half-brother Wible stole much of the family thunder by becoming the youngest-ever President of the Louisville and Nashville Railroad. He lived in a lavish mansion in one of Louisville's most sought-after neighbourhoods.

Thomas. I was, perhaps not surprisingly, the apple of his mother's eye. After surviving so much heartbreak, she could not help being especially loving to Thomas – after all, he was her youngest child. She showered him with books and gifts all deliberately intended to encourage him to study hard at school and then college. Thomas reacted well to his mother's encouragement and in his mid-twenties became one of Louisville's youngest lawyers.

Mary Cruise Mapother gracefully accepted Thomas's bride, Anna Stewart Batman, into her home when they married in 1907 and was delighted to become a grandmother when Anna gave birth to a bouncing baby boy called Paul. Their second child, Thomas Cruise Mapother II, was born in 1908. Caroline Mapother, who still lives in Louisville, was their first cousin by marriage and remembers them well. 'They were a good solid family. Pillars of Louisville society and very loyal and dependable,' she explained.

Thomas Cruise Mapother I even became a Jefferson Circuit Court Judge. He was a highly respected member of the Louisville and Kentucky State Bar Associations. A Republican, he served as Judge on the Second Common Pleas Division from 1928 to 1934. He once said that the happiest moment of his life was the occasion when he was presented with a portrait of himself which has hung in Louisville's Second Commons Pleas Court ever since. He was an inveterate walker and a student of Shakespeare, as well as being a member of the Knights of Columbus. Most notably, however, he gained a reputation as something of a loner within the Louisville legal fraternity, as he always worked in practices without a partner. He died unexpectedly of a heart attack in April 1939 as he walked with his son, Thomas Cruise Mapother II, and his wife near their home on Lakeside Drive, Louisville. He was sixty-two.

In later life his widow, Anna, frequently made quilts for the Queen's Daughter annual bazaar in aid of a local orphanage. That was typical of a Mapother wife. Always there, always dependable, always solid. She died in the early 1960s.

Thomas Cruise Mapother II excelled at St Xavier's High School, went on to St Mary's College, Marion County, and then to the University of Louisville and the Jefferson School of Law. He married Catherine (Tom Cruise's sister Cass is named after her) and became a highly respected Louisville lawyer known as Tom to all his friends and family. He also worked as local campaign chairman for the Republican Party in the city and in 1951 led the backing of Judge Eugene Siler as Governor of Kentucky after telling prospective voters bluntly: 'If you don't want Harry S. Truman and his political cronies inflicted upon this country for the next four years, vote the Republican ticket on 6 November.'

Tom and his wife had two children, Thomas Cruise Mapother III, Tom Cruise's father, who was born in 1934, and William, born in 1938.

William continued the family tradition of there being at least one lawyer in each generation of Mapothers. He became a judge at the Louisville Juvenile Court at the age of twenty-nine and showed an intriguing level of compassion when dealing with young offenders. Once he turned to a girl facing criminal charges and told her: 'And you are going to go to school. You are going to have to do something too – not just your parents. You have to help make a happy, stable home. Girls don't run away from happy, stable homes.'

Later William became police chief for the Louisville suburb of Windy Hills and was partly responsible for the introduction of radar scanners for the volunteer police force in 1973 after much encouragement from his brother Thomas Cruise Mapother III. William also became president of a local organisation called Planned Parenthood, an interesting choice considering Tom Cruise's later attitude towards children.

Tom Cruise's father attended the University of Kentucky and excelled at his engineering studies. The Mapother tradition of hard work, leaving little time for play, was being kept up. Thomas III was by all accounts a bit of a boffin, who was more interested in studying the latest laser technology than going to a college dance.

Then he met Mary Lee Pfeiffer, who had been born and raised in the slightly poorer Highlands area of Louisville. It was love at first sight and the wedding in Louisville, in the mid-fifties, was attended by every relative from both sides, including cousin Caroline Mapother.

The long-standing schism that had split the family all those generations earlier was made even more apparent when the happy couple decided to marry in a Catholic church, even though many of Thomas III's relatives were actually Church of Scotland regulars. Cousin Caroline later recalled that 'despite the differences it was a nice wedding'. But the underlying tensions exist even to this day. 'Tom Cruise and his side of the family are not really true Mapothers because Mary Cruise adopted that name for her son Thomas I and we have always been made well aware of that,' explained Caroline Mapother.

Shortly after his marriage to Mary Lee – an attractive brunette with a friendly smile and a warm disposition – Thomas Cruise Mapother III joined General Electric as an engineer and ended up working alongside Caroline's husband.

Working as an engineer for GE was a highly sought-after position. Thomas III was expected to move around the country to wherever research projects were being undertaken and his wife had to follow him and set up home. At this time Thomas III was immersed in the development of light-emitting solid-state lasers. During those first few years of marriage he became somewhat of a workaholic, but this was no surprise to the rest of the family as hard work, some say obsessive, was second nature to the Mapothers.

'He was fascinated by the technological developments of the day. He spent every waking moment working on new projects,' explained cousin Dillon Mapother, a former engineer.

Thomas Cruise Mapother III hardly looked up and noticed when Mary Lee gave birth to Lee Anne, in Louisville. Then, after they moved to Syracuse, New York State, another daughter, Marian, was born, followed on 3 July 1962 by a boy, later christened Thomas Cruise Mapother IV. Baby sister Cass came along three years later. Life at General Electric had become one long round of research projects and Thomas III was starting to dream of life beyond the restricting surroundings of a large corporation. He wanted to put his knowledge to the ultimate test in a free-market economy and start trying to develop his own inventions. He imagined that if his own, personally developed laser system could be properly marketed, it might make him a millionaire many times over.

Tom Cruise later described his father as 'complex. Extremely bright. Artistic'. That sounds like shorthand for not an easy person. But then it takes all sorts to make a world.

And, of course, there was Mary Lee, an energetic, gregarious woman with more than a passing interest in acting and the theatre. She was already carrying most of the responsibility for bringing up the Mapother clan, just like all the Mapother women before her.

Mary Lee also relied on her strong sense of religion, which prevented her from getting too swept up with all her husband's impressive talk of million-dollar deals and luxurious lifestyles. She put all those thoughts of wealth and success behind her and looked for other ways to channel her energy.

Life was pretty quiet in Syracuse, one of those medium-sized cities partially based around a state university. Its main industries were farm equipment and typewriters. It is not a hick town, but it is hardly the cultural mecca of the western world.

Soon after Tom Cruise's birth the family moved yet again.

When Tom was about two and a half years old he sneaked out of the house and disappeared for so long that his mother had to call the police to track him down. When he was found wandering nearby, she asked Tom where he had been and he replied: 'I went on an adventure.'

So she said: 'Next time you want to go on an adventure, why don't you get me and we'll go together.'

A few days later Tom's mother was scrubbing the floor when he went up to her and said: 'It's time.' Mary Lee got up, gathered together Tom's three sisters and they all walked down the street, following Tom. He took them to a pond in the middle of some nearby woods and Mary Lee was shocked to discover that the place her tiny son had been going to alone might well have led to his drowning.

'What do you do here, Tom?' she asked.

'Oh, I just sit and think and throw rocks in the water.'

The family continued to find themselves in and around ever-shifting influences and environments. But throughout all this moving, one thing remained the same – wherever they went, Mary Lee would sniff out the local playhouse. At one stage she even founded her own amateur dramatic group. It was inevitable that her obsession with the theatre would rub off on her impressionable youngsters.

Many years later Mary Lee recalled proudly that Tom had displayed promise as an actor when he was still under ten years of age. He would love to play imaginary games featuring soldiers, policemen and other characters. Mary Lee was as impressed as any proud parent would be and encouraged her only son Tom to continue his play-acting.

Part of Tom's repertoire involved imitating two of the great icons of cartoon history: Woody Woodpecker and Donald Duck. He was also especially fond of W.C. Fields. Tom was already becoming someone who preferred to be in a world of his own. It was like a training for his eventual success, with lots of difficult bridges to cross.

Tom moved so much from school to school that he was always trying to adjust. It was as if he was picking up a part, playing a role along the way. He later explained: 'If we went South, I'd pick up a little Southern accent, because having a Canadian accent wasn't cool.'

Tom was by all accounts a bit of a dreamer at this stage in his life. 'I was always the kid who forgot to take the garbage out on Tuesdays. I would be in the backyard staring at the clouds, daydreaming. I was the kind of kid who wanted adventure. I craved it. I'd go around the backyard, dreaming up monsters and dragons. It was all about needing adventure. I had an active imagination. My mother thought, "If you have all this imagination, why can't you take out the garbage!"'

Around 1967 the Mapother family took off for the even colder climate of Ottawa, Canada, a relatively sophisticated and populous region of the Great White North. Other temporary hometowns were in Missouri and New Jersey, the family moving a total of seven times during the first eleven years of Tom's life.

Inevitably, sport provided an outlet for Tom's natural aggressiveness, no doubt brought on by the continued frustration of never settling in one place. It lent him some self-esteem – esteem that he didn't usually get in the classroom because of his reading difficulties, the result of dyslexia. He began to play baseball at an early age. By the time the family moved to Canada, his father noticed that Tom could skate backwards just as well as local boys who'd been doing it all their lives.

These days Tom can look back on his hectic childhood and, in retrospect, accentuate the positive elements to be gained from non-stop moving. 'It gave me the range to play different types of characters. I have a lot to draw on,' he says. But, at the time, the family must have been desperate to stay in one place long enough to settle down.

The moves were punctuated by visits to Louisville, the only place the Mapothers could truly call home. A host of old friends and relatives lived in the area and this, combined with the slow and easy pace of the city, helped the Mapothers to feel more settled after all their hectic travelling.

But beneath the surface of those apparently happy trips back to Louisville lay a long-standing problem between Thomas Cruise Mapother III and Mary Lee. They were increasingly drifting apart. Thomas was completely engrossed in his obsession with becoming a self-made millionaire. Mary Lee just wanted a simple, contented life without all the frustrations and disappointments that so often dominate the professional life of talented people. She was also fed up with having to carry the full weight of moving the family from town to town like gypsies. The children were undoubtedly affected, especially the two older girls, who seemed to be forever saying goodbye to their school friends.

Young Tom was feeling it too. He became more withdrawn than most of the kids in his class, not bothering to make close friends because he knew that, sooner rather than later, he would have to say goodbye to them, most probably for ever. It seemed easier to him to immerse himself in his own games at home and quietly study at school without any emotional entanglement.

Inevitably, his best friends were his three sisters. The elder two doted on him like stand-in mothers whenever Mary Lee was not around.

Lee Anne's girlfriends all adored and mollycoddled cute little Tom with his sticky-out teeth. On one occasion she invited a couple of friends over and they proceeded to test out their kissing skills on her eight-year-old brother.

But those constant moves were having a serious long-term effect on young Tom. He'd spend all his time getting into the right clique at school and finally buy the right pair of sneakers, and then the family would move. He got into a lot of fights. The school bully would come over and kick the hell out of the new kid. So Tom learned that either he had to fight back or the next guy was going to come over and pound him as well. It was sink or swim time. Tom chose to swim.

2

You know women have dreams of having
careers and being whatever? I had a dream
of raising children and enjoying them and
having a good family life.

TOM CRUISE'S MOTHER

Any twelve-year-old who moved around as much as Thomas Cruise Mapother IV would have developed a sixth sense about certain things. The house in the little town outside Ottawa must have been the sixth or seventh home he'd lived in, and the town was just yet another spread of bricks and mortar to the youngster. Through it all, at least he had the love and support of his family – his mom to comfort him; his dad to stick up for him when things got especially rough. But he had known that something was up for quite some time.

On that particular day his parents sat their four children down and told them what Tom had suspected all along: that their marriage was breaking up. Around the room the flow of tears that followed the news was uncontrollable. It was, Tom later recalled, as if someone had died.

A few minutes later Tom's father took him outside to hit a few baseballs, but sport was the furthest thing from his mind that day. Tom cried so hard in the backyard that he could scarcely breathe. The knowledge that this time his father was leaving for good left the boy with one great fear echoing in his mind: 'What's going to happen to us now? What next?'

Many theories have been advanced to suggest how movie stars are formed. It is frequently found that a large number of them lost a parent in childhood, and many were deprived of love in their early years. As a result, they demonstrate the most powerful drive for attention and affection and are often abnormally sensitive, reserved and isolated.

Some of these traits may apply to Tom Cruise; he is his mother's son by nature if not name, although he has added the steel of ambition. But he rarely mentions his father even today.

During Tom's early days he had been just a hard-working father of four trying to earn an honest living and provide for his large family. Tom always regretted that they were not closer. He also had a feeling that his father was a little eccentric. But there was another aspect to his father which Tom Cruise might not want to talk about. His father was an alcoholic.

The problem was not that noticeable when Tom was a young boy, but by the time the family began to fall apart it had become obvious. Thomas Cruise Mapother III would go into irrational temper tantrums, mainly caused by alcohol. He would often drink secretly before arriving home from his work as an engineer.

After the family broke up, Tom tried to piece the whole sad scenario together and realised that he had first became aware of his father's problem some years earlier. Because the family was in a more stable state then, it did not seem so important. After the break-up, the Mapother kids grew up never actually being able to agree on how much of a drink problem their father had.

Some of Tom's sisters did not accept that he had a real problem. As children, all of them had shut themselves off from the situation. Even now, Tom has great difficulty in talking about his father, let alone conceding that there was an alcohol problem.

Tom's father's drinking became more of a problem after his divorce from Mary Lee. He would wander off to California for months – in one case years – at a time, hardly ever bothering to contact his ex-wife or children. 'He never really accepted he had a problem. Instead he just kept on the move. But back in Louisville there were a lot of worried family members,' explained one relative, too scared to be identified for fear of harming Tom's Hollywood image.

Today Mary Lee will only refer to the split with her husband as 'a time of growing, a time of conflict'. It was also a time of great poverty. With precious little income, she did what Mapother women do best – she fought her damnedest to keep the children fed and clothed. They returned to Louisville and tried to start their lives again.

'You know women have dreams of having careers and being whatever,' Mary Lee says. 'I had a dream of raising children and enjoying them and having a good family life.'

Mary Lee worked at a series of jobs to keep the family afloat: hosting electrical conventions, selling appliances at Stewart's Department Store, anything. One Christmas there was no money to buy gifts, so the family wrote poems to one another and read them out loud.

At first they moved into a low-rent house just off Taylorsville Road in Louisville, and Mary Lee's brother, Jack Pfeiffer, and her mother, Comala Pfeiffer Kremer, helped the struggling family stay in one place.

Tom was feeling emotionally drained by the stress and strain of what had happened. He was in a daze, unable to grasp the reality of the situation because no one outside his immediate family could be told what had happened. He felt especially vulnerable then, but he did not dare tell any of his classmates what he was going through. When he was older he realised that he had missed all the love, motivation and sense of self that comes from having a father. But at that time he didn't stop and say, 'My dad's not around – I've got to learn how to handle it.' He just felt very, very insecure.

That first winter was one of the coldest to hit the area in more than thirty years, but Tom got up every morning at dawn and slogged up and down the nearby streets delivering newspapers.

'Nothing could stop him. He'd go out in the snow bundled up like an Eskimo,' recalled Granny Pfeiffer years later.

Some mornings he even used to sneak out and do his paper round in his mother's beaten-up car. At 4 a.m. his two elder sisters would help their pint-sized brother push the car out of the drive so their mother would not hear it being started up. She would have been furious if she knew he was using it.

Thankfully, one aspect of Tom's life remained partially consistent – his involvement in athletics. He played hockey over the Kentucky border in Indiana, with kids older and bigger than him.

'He was so fast they couldn't keep up with him,' recalls Mary Lee proudly. 'One guy finally got so exasperated that he picked Tom up by the scruff of the neck and the seat of his pants and moved him outside the boundary. I laughed.'

Tom not only pitched in financially by doing that paper round, he also helped out in other ways too. Every night he'd come home from school, bathe his mother's tired feet and then massage them for half an hour. Mary Lee remembered: 'This went on for six weeks, then Easter came and went, and the Monday after Easter I came home from work expecting the same treatment. And he said, "Hey, Mom, Lent's over."'

Tom has rarely talked publicly about his parents' divorce, but he opened up with surprising frankness to *Rolling Stone* journalist Christopher Connelly in an interview in June 1986. 'After a divorce, you feel so vulnerable. And travelling the way I did, you're closed off a lot from other people. I didn't express a lot to people where I moved. They didn't have the childhood I had, and I didn't feel like they'd understand me. I was always warming up, getting acquainted with everyone. I went through a period after the divorce of really wanting to be accepted, wanting love and attention from people. But I never really seemed to fit in anywhere.'

School in Louisville became a disturbing trail of problems featuring narrow-minded teachers and rigid rules and regulations. Tom acknowledged his dilemma and tried to help himself and his sisters adapt to their new life. One day when he was walking to school with them during a particularly difficult time, he said: 'Let's just get *through* this. If we can just get through this somehow...'

He found it extremely lonely without a father. Cruise Senior had moved away from Kentucky and did not even pay any child support. He was rarely, if ever, in contact with his children.

Things got so tough for Tom and his sisters that they frequently wore their cousins' hand-me-down clothes. That meant running around in tennis shoes that were too big and wearing baggy sweaters, but no one minded just so long as Mary Lee kept her family together.

Tom was now the man of the house and he took to his role like a fish to water. He enjoyed the responsibility and played an increasingly active part in the household. His clear ability to adapt was typical of those born under the sign of Cancer. They have an innate ability to fit in under trying circumstances. Poised on the edge of adolescence, Tom was facing a daily barrage of essential issues that confront teenagers. He had his mother to turn to, but there were certain questions that only a father could answer.

In his early teens Tom made a decision that was very mature for his age: he reached out to his mother and sisters and returned their love in a warm and sensitive way. All five developed a truly remarkable kinship that went beyond the traditional confines of male/female roles.

'My mother is very giving, very open, and really loves being around people. She's a great listener. My sisters are very much like her – very strong women,' explained Tom years later.

The family knew it had to pull together because they were on the verge of abject poverty.

Mary Lee was (and still is) a very proud woman. She did everything she could to hold the family together and keep it going. But even Mary Lee had to bow to the financial pressures that were making life so difficult to maintain.

Once, when she went to get food stamps, she took one look at all the people waiting in the social security office and couldn't cope with the shame, so she turned around and walked straight out, determined that she would make enough money to feed the family on her own.

All five family members worked. Lee Anne, Marian and, later, Cass took their turn as waitresses in local restaurants. Tom doubled his paper round and mowed every lawn in sight. Unlike other children on his block, his goal was to help the family survive, not fritter his earnings on comics and footballs.

'It wasn't a bad time,' remembered Tom. 'There was a lot of love and laughter... We all supported each other, although it was tough on my mother because she wanted us to have the best and she couldn't always give it to us.'

Tom also learned another important lesson from watching his mother struggle through those lean years. He witnessed the raw deals women get in the business world. He saw his mother's trials and tribulations as classic examples of sexual harassment, job discrimination and the dozens of other smaller problems faced by women every time they take on a job. Those experiences undoubtedly helped shape his attitude towards his co-stars when he later made it to Hollywood.

'Women to me are not a mystery. I get along easily with them,' is one of his favourite replies to anyone asking about the females in his family. To this day, it is even said that Tom prefers the company of women. 'I trust women easier than men.'

However, life in the Mapother household was no bed of roses. There were fights between Tom and his sisters and he usually ended up the loser. But all that was to be expected in any big family.

Yet another school – this time St Raphael's in Louisville – was notable only because Tom made probably his best friend ever in Jeff Bayers, a fellow thirteen-year-old.

Jeff, who is still in touch with Tom and understandably nervous about upsetting his famous friend, admitted that Tom was 'kinda lonely' when the two first linked up at St Raphael's. 'He'd only been in town for a few days but we hit it off immediately and soon became best friends,' explained Jeff.

He has followed Tom's career in movies very closely and cannot get over how similar many of those roles have been to Tom's real-life experiences. 'It's funny how true to life those roles have been. I guess it must have helped him.'

Jeff, ever the loyal friend, would only concede that Tom was 'very complicated about his father'. The two friends still exchange Christmas cards each year and Jeff keeps in touch with Tom's sister Lee Anne.

At St Raphael's, which had taught Mapothers for four generations, the principal, Paul De Zarn, refused to even comment on Tom Cruise's time there. 'I would have to have some sort of written authorisation from the Cruise family. The Mapothers have a long history with us...'

While at St Raphael's, Tom apparently enjoyed creating entire childhoods to tell the other students about. He would happily hide his true persona behind a mask of tall tales about adventures in the Rocky Mountains and a never-ending stream of other fiction. As the perennial new boy in town, he found it easy to get away with such outrageous stories.

At the time, Mary Lee and her children lived in a comfortable but relatively modest house in a lower-middle-class suburb of Louisville. Number three Cardwell Way was a rented property, but at least it was a quiet street with other kids to play with, although Tom did not mix much with the local children.

One resident still living in the street today recalled Tom as 'the one who would sit on the steps of his house playing the guitar. Real quiet. Seemed like a loner.'

Neighbour Bill Lewis remembered when Tom knocked on his front door on St Valentine's Day 1976 and asked if he could mow the lawn. Bill and the lonely, sad-faced boy from up the street soon formed a strong bond of friendship, no doubt influenced by young Tom's desperate search for a father figure following the departure of his own parent.

'No job was too dirty or difficult for Tommy, as long as it paid money to help his mom out. While most other kids were out raising hell, he had his nose to the grindstone and was working day and night. He was an unusual lad. I told Mary Lee she should be awfully proud of him,' recalled Bill fondly.

Tom soon began regarding Bill as a true father figure. He craved a man's help and advice. On the day of Tom's school graduation, he went over to Bill's home with his necktie in his hand and sheepishly explained that he didn't know how to tie it and neither did his mom and sisters.

Bill – then in his fifties – and young 'Tommy' would sit on the wall outside Bill's house and sup a bottle of non-alcoholic birch beer together. Often the talk centred around Bill's experiences as a Marine during World War Two.

Bill also remembered that Tom didn't even once mention the existence of his father throughout the time he knew him. 'It was as if his father had been wiped from the face of the earth. But I didn't want to pry, so I never asked him what happened to him.'

For a few months during the middle of 1976, Bill became a father substitute to the desperately lonely teenager. Tom even called him 'sir', just like every well-brought-up kid in the South has done for generations.

'I was a fatherly figure to him,' remembered Bill. 'I was always very good to him and we really had something going, the two of us. He was one hell of a nice kid, hard to get to know at first, but full of warmth and energy once you got beneath the surface.'

Tom's friendship with Bill came to a close in just the same way as every relationship Tom had in those days. He turned up on Bill's doorstep one blisteringly hot summer day and told his friend that his family were on the move once more and he wouldn't be able to mow the lawn any more.

It still brings tears to Bill's eyes when he thinks about his young friend. 'I have very fond memories of Tommy. I'd love to get ahold of Tommy now and tell him how proud I am of what he turned out to be.'

He once wrote a heartfelt letter to Tom, years after his career skyrocketed him to movie stardom, but he never got a reply.

Bill Lewis had another reason to remember Tom, because the thirteen-year-old astonished him by talking about his intention to become a priest, even admitting he had decided to join St Francis's Seminary, near Cincinnati, later that year. Bill was surprised to hear a young boy talking in such serious terms about being a priest. 'I found it especially hard to advise him because I was a Protestant, but I did tell him that he should do whatever would make him happy,' he recalled.

A few weeks later Tom headed off to join St Francis's Seminary, almost 100 miles north of Louisville. There was no entrance exam to get into the school and the priests who ran the seminary did not want to make it too strict in case it put any prospective members of the priesthood off joining. At first the notion of leaving his mother and sisters for boarding school scared young Tom, but then it dawned on him that the seminary might be a way to forget the problems of the previous few years and just be a kid again. He had already surprised some friends by talking in fairly sincere terms about taking up the priesthood. It could be the perfect escape for a teenager still reeling from the anguish of seeing his family split in two.

Tom was well aware that the main reason for the existence of St Francis's was to train would-be priests. In fact, most of the funds used to run the school were collected through Catholic charities determined to try to reverse the constant decline in the number of men entering the priesthood. School fees were charged only to those who could afford them. In fact, the seminary had a policy of never asking for more than $800 a year, no matter who the pupil was. Surprisingly, there was no uniform.

The Franciscans are a religious order founded by the Catholic saint St Francis of Assisi in 1209. According to legend, St Francis was the son of a wealthy Italian merchant who turned from a frivolous, hedonistic life to become the God-fearing, devoted and selfless friend of the poor and sick. He went from town to town to preach, dressed in sackcloth, and lived on the alms he could beg from passers-by.

When Tom turned up for his first term at St Francis's, in the autumn of 1976, the school had been reduced to just a hundred pupils. However, there were distinct advantages in small numbers. It meant that each student would receive extra individual attention – something that larger schools could never manage.

Headmaster Father Laurian Rausch welcomed Tom and the other freshmen to the imposing gothic mansion set in dozens of acres of lush countryside about ten miles outside Cincinnati. Prefects from the older classes were appointed to each table in the refectory to keep the younger boys in order, and faculty members were allowed to punish the boys if they misbehaved. The most regular punishment was writing lines, but sometimes physical punishment was handed out by certain priests. That year one of the boys was given a severe beating with a paddle after being caught drinking. No one in Tom's class dared step out of line after stories of the injuries to that boy circulated in the seminary.

The monks who ran St Francis's were proud that at least twenty-five per cent of the boys who attended the school eventually entered the priesthood. By enrolling their sons, parents were clearly implying that their children were considering a life of celibacy. 'We did not expect a permanent commitment from them, but we did expect them to seriously contemplate the priesthood,' explained Father Aldric Heidlage.

The seminary had also become an ideal place for children from broken homes. At least one-third of the boys who were there during the same year as Tom had just been through the heartache of seeing their parents split up.

Life at St Francis's was quite tough and regimented compared with the many schools Tom had attended during his travels around North America. The boys would be awoken by a clanging bell at 6.40 a.m. and then be expected to be in the refectory by 7 for breakfast. At 7.45 a study period was held to ensure that the previous day's homework was properly completed, followed by classes that started at 8.30 and finished at 11, so that everyone could attend mass. At noon, lunch was eaten, immediately followed by more classes, then sport. At 4.30 p.m. there was a study period once again, then supper, with lights out at 9 sharp.

Tom found himself in dormitories sleeping upwards of twenty boys. Each bed was set in a makeshift cubicle with boarded walls on three sides, plus a curtain for privacy. At night the coughing and farting of some children would spark a round of giggling and sometimes the boys would whisper to one another, but much of the time there was complete silence until the wake-up call the next day.

That first term at the seminary, Tom missed his sisters and mother terribly. With only three family visiting days from September until Thanksgiving at the end of November, he found it especially hard. The remarkable bond that existed between him and his family had been cruelly broken, if only temporarily.

Thanksgiving that year was not easy. Tom, allowed back to Louisville for just two days, must have wanted to stay longer with his family. But for the moment Mary Lee knew that St Francis's was a better environment for Tom than the streets of Louisville, where a lonely teenager could get himself into real trouble.

It is not clear how strongly Tom really felt about his religious calling; he is reluctant to be drawn into any conversations about such subjects. 'For me, religion is a very personal thing,' he confessed. He has also said that although he was, and still is, a believer, he did have other motives for enrolling at the seminary: 'We didn't have any money for school ... it was a free education. They even clothed you.'

Tom tried desperately to find some focus in his life during his time at St Francis's. But even there, he felt so different from everyone else. 'I went through a period of really wanting to be accepted, wanting love and affection,' he later recalled.

Although Tom missed his mother and sisters, he also felt reasonably comfortable in the presence of the Franciscan brothers although life in the seminary was pretty basic. At least he got a solid education, probably for the first time in his life. Certainly, young Tom was heavily influenced by the teachings of the brothers and, until the end of his first term at St Francis's, he was seriously considering a life in the priesthood.

Tom was remembered as being the shortest basketball player in the freshman year. Father Aldric recalls him despite the fact that he dropped out of St Francis's after only one year. He says: 'Tom was a rather weak student. He certainly did not make a *big* impression on us.'

Meanwhile the teenager's mind was starting to focus on something altogether less serious than the priesthood. Tom was very shy and was afraid girls wouldn't like him because he was so short. He even asked one of the priests: 'When will girls be interested in me?' The idea of celibacy was not so appealing, after all.

By his second term at the seminary, however, Tom was sneaking out to the homes of local girls. 'We'd go to a girl's house in town, sit around, talk, play Spin the Bottle, and I started to realise that I love women too much to give all that up,' he remembered years later.

Every weekend Tom and his pals would be allowed out to the Springfield Road shopping mall, just a short walk away from the seminary.

On one memorable occasion, Jeff Bayers, Tom's best friend from his brief stay at St Raphael's, in Louisville, turned up at the seminary and the two boys had a great afternoon out in the local town, talking about their old friends back in Louisville.

Jeff never forgot how upset Tom still was about his parents' divorce. 'He wasn't real open about his family problems,' said Jeff. But Tom was more revealing about his intention to become a priest and told Jeff that he 'really wanted to join the priesthood' despite his frustration over how to handle the local girls. Jeff just hoped it would all be a passing phase.

Mass was held every day at the seminary and Father Kistner, who was spiritual director at the time, had to counsel pupils about their religious thoughts and knowledge. Most of the boys saw him at least once during that year, but Tom did not seek his guidance at all.

But not even St Francis's was completely free of the sort of problems that have plagued most schools in the past twenty years. During the year Tom attended, one of the boys was expelled for buying drugs from a peddler who had a menial labouring job on the school grounds. The whole incident was covered up by the priests at the time for fear it might put parents off sending their sons to St Francis's.

The seminary closed as a school in 1980 because the numbers of students dipped below fifty and it simply was not economical to run it as a school. However, most of Tom's teachers still live and work in the imposing building. The hierarchy at St Francis's believes that over the past twenty years many children have led such a wealthy, luxurious existence that they feel no compunction to live the simple, relatively uncomplicated life of a priest.

Father Kistner is still disappointed by Tom's lack of interest in the seminary. In 1988, while Tom was filming *Rain Man* with Dustin Hoffman, the film's makers almost used the seminary for a number of scenes. But in the end they decided to film at a nuns' convent in nearby Crescent Springs and the sisters told Kistner that Tom was very quiet with them, unlike Hoffman, who was happy to swap tales of his Hollywood life with the sisters.

For Thomas Cruise Mapother IV, one year at St Francis's was more than enough, although he later described it as 'the best year I ever did in school'. He appreciated the solid education that the seminary provided for him at a very difficult time in his life.

For much of the summer after leaving St Francis's, Tom would 'borrow' his mom's car most evenings and go out cruising for girls in the early hours. He tended to hang around playing pinball at the Bashford Manor Mall but, not surprisingly, there were few girls to be found at such a late hour.

During this period Mary Lee was trying to rebuild her life and she had met someone who she believed could help strengthen her existence and that of her four children. He was, she felt, someone strong and dependable – a rock of stability who would bring her loving contentment for the first time in her life.

Mary Lee met Jack South at an electronics convention; Jack worked in plastics. They got married when Tom was sixteen. At first Tom felt threatened by his stepfather. There was a part of him that was consumed with love for his mother and he found it difficult to accept another man in the household.

The underlying bad feeling between Tom, who for four years had been the only male influence in the Mapother family, and Jack was apparent to Mary Lee and her daughters. Tom was grouchy and sullen, like most teenage boys. Jack, desperate to make a good impression and painfully aware of the anguish suffered by Tom and his three sisters, knew he could never replace their father, but at least he deserved some respect.

To make matters worse, following his return from the seminary, Tom was sent for a brief time to live with his aunt and uncle – the Barratts – on the other side of Louisville. Mary Lee could no longer afford to rent a house and had to move into her mother's home, which was much smaller, so sending him to her brother's home seemed to make sense.

But Tom felt desperately lonely with the Barratts. He missed his mother and sisters terribly, and knowing that Jack South was on the scene did not help make him feel any more secure. For her part, Mary Lee fully realised that if Tom and Jack were to form a solid relationship she would have to get Tom back as quickly as possible. So she took on an additional job and allowed Jack to start providing a little for them, and, within a few months, Tom was back in the fold. They were all together once again – and that was all that really mattered.

3

He has a charisma that needs exercising.
OLIVER STONE

Tom's first taste of real romance came when he met his first real girlfriend, a pretty sixteen-year-old called Laurie Hobbs, who attended the nearby Sacred Heart School in Louisville. It was October 1978 and Tom – also sixteen – had never even had a proper girlfriend before.

'Tom struck me as being shy, sort of uneasy around girls,' recalled Laurie, now a housewife still living in Louisville.

After weeks of brief exchanges in the street near Tom's home, Laurie found herself with no choice but to make the first move. She marched boldly up to his house, knocked on the door and asked the pint-sized teenager: 'Are you going to take me to the school dance or what?'

Laurie recalls: 'He was cute, but not what you'd call cool. And he had a chipped tooth that embarrassed him so much that he decided to have it fixed.'

The night of the dance, Tom and Laurie went to a friend's apartment and opened a couple of bottles of wine to loosen up. But, as Laurie later explained, Tom was so shy they hardly touched each other that first night and even conversation between the two teenagers was strained. The dance was a similarly frosty experience, but Laurie was not easily deterred.

A few nights later she and Tom got high on champagne and once again she had to make the first move.

'I got things going by casually dropping a hand on the couch beside him. I can hardly describe how excited I was when he got hold of it at last and started playing with my fingers. Then we lunged towards each other, sort of kissing, only we didn't seem able to get our mouths in the right place at first.

'My head was spinning and I could hardly breathe. I could hear my heart banging away in my eardrums. First kisses are like that – you think you're going to faint. Once or twice, I opened my eyes to make sure his eyes were closed, and they were, so I knew he meant it.

'After that it was like we had just made love and could talk about anything. All we'd done was kiss, but a great obstacle had been removed. Things then got pretty hot and heavy. Hands shaking, knees knocking, you name it. My head was spinning and I could hardly breathe. I remember thinking how surprised I was that he could kiss like that.

'We just floated along clinging to each other. I even had to tell him to keep his hands to himself.'

As they kissed and cuddled, Laurie thought to herself: 'There is no way this guy is ever going to be a priest.'

Later she confessed candidly: 'I feel pleased with myself when people find out I dated Tom. But we were both only young and I was a Catholic girl. Although I might have let him slip a hand inside my dress and hold it there.'

Laurie – who lost touch with Tom years ago – also added: 'I often wonder what life would be like if Tom and I had got married. I guess maybe we'd probably be divorced by now. But now and then I flatter myself that I actually taught the world's sexiest male to kiss.'

Tom was still hiding the full pain and anguish of his parents' divorce, so being romantic was a kind of diversion – although he remembers that time with a definite note of sarcasm. 'I was going through puberty, that thrilling time we all remember as such an easy experience, particularly with the opposite sex. Who doesn't feel that way? You think, "If that girl just looks at me, my day is made." I was scared to death of being rejected and I was shy unless I got that look or that smile.'

Throughout all this period, Tom tried hard to keep in contact with his father's side of the family, despite the obvious complications created by Thomas Cruise Mapother III's decision to abandon his young family. On one occasion Tom – then fifteen – and his cousin William, aged twelve, accompanied Grandpa Thomas Cruise Mapother II on a sightseeing trip to Washington DC. It was an important event for young Tom as he and his sisters had long felt a little like the odd ones out as far as the rest of the Mapothers were concerned.

Grandpa Mapother later chuckled as he recalled to other family members how he had booked into an expensive hotel with the two boys and sent them out to get some lemon drops, only for them to return three hours later after 'getting lost' in the nightclub in the basement of the hotel, where they stood entranced by the sight of some pretty teenage girls.

Tom and his sisters were understandably disturbed by the initial intrusion of Jack South in their lives through his romance with their mother. It was difficult to cope with this stranger who had suddenly swept Mary Lee off her feet, and they were suspicious of his motives. But the girls – ever sensitive – soon started to appreciate how important Jack was to their mother. And gradually it began to dawn on Tom that here was a guy who loved his mother in a way not even his own father had.

There was also another aspect to Jack's relationship with Mary Lee. He was prepared to take on a ready-made family and that took some courage. Gradually the children came to appreciate it.

Jack started to take Tom to bet on football games, although he was a terrible better. Tom ended up making lots of money – and on that a bridge of friendship was built.

When Tom had completed his sophomore year of high school at St Xavier's, in Louisville, Jack moved the family to Glen Ridge, New Jersey. This time, Tom and his sisters thought, we might actually have time to make some real friends.

Glen Ridge is a small community of neat, tree-lined streets tucked in the centre of some of the rougher neighbourhoods of New Jersey. This highly residential town is best known for the quiet glow of the Victorian gaslights which have become its trademark. More than ninety per cent of the imposing houses in Glen Ridge were built between 1870 and 1930, making it an area steeped in history compared with many of the surrounding districts.

Violent crime is not a problem in the area and the local *Glen Ridge Paper* tends to favour front-page stories about graduation days and noisy parties. It is the sort of place where drinking alcohol – except on very special occasions – is frowned upon.

Jack South rented an imposing clapboard house on Washington Avenue. It was by far the biggest house the family had ever lived in and for the first time in years Mary Lee and her brood felt that they were leading a normal, happy life.

At Glen Ridge High School, Tom decided to take up wrestling because he reckoned it might help him get some new pals very quickly.

'He joined to meet other kids. He was a very nice, polite sort of kid. Very Southern type of boy. Always saying, "yes sir, no sir",' recalled Glen Ridge High's wrestling coach, Angelo Corbo.

Tom also proved useful at soccer. But his coach, Doc Voskian, later claimed he was a very one-dimensional type of player.

Essentially, however, Tom remained very quiet and reserved at Glen Ridge High, despite his efforts to mix with the other pupils. Corbo was struck by his pupil's close-knit family. He also noticed they were having a problem fitting into the upmarket community. 'This is a very affluent community here. If you're from money you fit in. If you're not … then it can be hard,' explained the wrestling coach.

The wrestling team consisted of twelve boys and Tom tended to rate about number eight in actual wrestling ability. He wasn't one of the best, but he wasn't the worst either. However, Corbo conceded that the main reason he was in the team was that there was no one else in his weight limits of 115 and 122 pounds.

Mary Lee and Jack often turned up to cheer the youngster on. Mary Lee was particularly good at getting involved in the school activities of her children because she was convinced it would help to make them feel more readily accepted.

On 18 January 1979 Tom Mapother, as he was then known, made his newspaper debut when his photo was published in the *Glen Ridge Paper*. A caption under the photo of a very skinny Tom read: 'Tom Mapother has full control over Jefferson Township wrestler in his JV match.'

A week later, on 25 January, Tom's photograph was featured yet again, this time as he wrestled his first-ever varsity match against Hillside School. He might have been a mediocre wrestler, but he certainly had an ability to catch the eye of any cameraman present.

Years later some of Tom's old team-mates in the wrestling side were surprised when the multi-millionaire actor did not reply to a request asking if he would be willing to donate $5000 for a new wrestling mat.

'It would have been nothing to him and we would have put his name on it as an everlasting tribute to his generosity but we never got a response,' recalled Angelo Corbo. 'It would have shown that he cared about the area. He probably could have had the key to the town if he'd made the effort to come back here.'

But Corbo also says that Tom's reluctance to return to Glen Ridge is understandable since the town has made little effort to commemorate the fact he spent the happiest days of his youth there. 'It's typical of Glen Ridge. He's just about the most famous person to come out of the area, but there's no plaque up outside his house and no one seems to care.'

Towards the end of his final term at Glen Ridge, in the early summer of 1980, Tom found himself exactly one pound overweight for his wrestling class. In order to lose that decisive pound he dashed home to do a Rocky routine on the stairway. He ran up and down repeatedly, determined to sweat it off. Nearing his final lap, he slipped on a pile of homework papers his sister had inadvertently left on the stairs, and tumbled head over heels down the steps. To his horror, the fall left him with pulled knee tendons. Not only would he miss the match, he would be sidelined for the remainder of the semester. Tom was sorely depressed. His injury meant he could not handle any other sport. What was he to do with himself for the rest of the term?

Tom was desperate to just focus in and do *something*. He knew he had the energy and creativity. Mary Lee told Tom in no uncertain terms not to mope around the house but to find a new channel for his boundless energy. As it happened, he found an old one – one he'd forgotten all about. He floundered briefly, but then the inconspicuous miracle took place. He decided to turn his misfortune around and asked coach Corbo what he thought about him trying out for the school play *Guys and Dolls*. 'Why not?' said Corbo, privately well aware that his student would not have done that well in the wrestling anyway.

He listened patiently as Tom talked about his acting aspirations. To the wrestling teacher they seemed just a pipe dream. But to Tom Cruise those ambitions were about to become the driving force in his life. He had carefully and quietly nurtured a fondness for acting instilled by his mother, but, always the odd one out at school, had never told his classmates about his interest because that would have singled him out as being different from everyone else.

Corbo obviously enjoyed a close affinity with Tom and he has often considered showing up on location where the star was appearing and saying hello. But he privately admits he does not know if he would actually have anything to say to the new Tom Cruise. 'It probably would have been easier to talk to him when he was younger and did not have any money. Now, I don't know...'

Taking his teacher's advice, Tom attended the auditions and somehow landed the part of Nathan Detroit (the scheming gangster played by Frank Sinatra in the 1955 movie of *Guys and Dolls*, which also starred Marlon Brando) and took to the stage like a monkey takes to a banana plantation.

Mary Lee has never forgotten the glow of pride she felt as the family attended the opening night of the school play: 'It was just an incredible experience to see what we felt was a lot of talent coming forth all of a sudden.' Even back in those days, Tom's mother never had any doubts about her only son's abilities.

A showbusiness agent who happened to be in the audience came up to Tom after the performance and declared him 'a natural'. The agent strongly recommended that he consider acting as a serious career, and Tom needed little encouragement. With his characteristic energy and commitment, he jumped headfirst into his new-found passion. Daydreams of embarking on a hitchhiking tour of Europe or enlisting in the US Air Force (shades of *Top Gun* to come) were unceremoniously dumped. With professional encouragement on his side, he approached his parents with a new plan.

After the show Tom arrived home and said he wanted to talk with Jack and his mother. He asked them for ten years to give showbusiness a try. They were stunned. Jack had genuine – and understandable – misgivings. Shouldn't he try to get a profession first, just in case the acting didn't work out? Mary Lee explained: 'My husband's thinking, "What's this gonna cost me? Ten years of what?"' She howled with laughter. 'It's kind of a joke in the family. Sort of a joke and not a joke.' But Tom was persuasively reassuring, and his enthusiasm was virtually infectious.

Mary Lee remembered years later: 'Tom said, "Let me see. I really feel that this is what I want to do." We both wholeheartedly agreed, because we felt it was a God-given talent; we gave him our blessing – and the rest is history.'

Tom himself was very happy at the reaction of his classmates to his performance in *Guys and Dolls*. They were really impressed. 'All the guys came and saw it and said, "Whoa, we didn't know that you could do that." I felt good about it. Not just the fact that they saw it, but I felt good about it in my heart,' he later enthused.

He was hooked. For the first time in his life he found he could express himself in a way he had never experienced before. 'I felt I needed to act the way I needed air to breathe.'

Graduation Day at Glen Ridge High School was a difficult occasion for Tom and his family. He had already announced his intention to skip college and make a go of it as an actor, so the programme that started with the national anthem, followed by the 'Pomp and Circumstance' march and an invocation by the Reverend Lester Smith of Christ Episcopal Church, probably went straight over young Tom's head.

As if to illustrate his role as an outsider at the school, when the senior poll came out, Tom did not even get a mention. The list – which featured the best-looking, most intelligent, best-dressed, funniest, biggest flirt, best athlete, most talented, most versatile, most likely to succeed, friendliest, worst driver, cutest, quietest, best personality, to name but a few sections – did not rate Tom worthy of a single mention. It just goes to show how wrong people can be!

But he did join in with the strictly non-alcoholic house parties with a Disneyland theme that were held that summer at various pupils' homes in the expensive neighbourhood near the school. Local police officers even glided past some of the houses, taking snapshots as a gentle warning to students not to misbehave – that was the sort of place Glen Ridge was proud to be. By this time Tom's appetite for girls had taken on healthy proportions. As his classmate Bobo Ahmed put it so delicately: 'Tom was a ladykiller. He had a different girl every week.'

Tom conceded a few years later: 'It's a small place. You weren't allowed to date two girls at the same time but had to go steady with one.'

Tom admits he was a jock in those days – a serious-minded, slightly humourless character probably only a few degrees away from being a redneck. 'I was a jock and I sang in the chorus. Jocks don't do that, so I always felt challenged. I always tried not to fall into that mould, not to judge people on where they came from or what they wore,' he recalled.

Later that summer Tom held his own open party for his classmates at his family home. Without any of the inverted snobbery that seemed prevalent in the Glen Ridge area, he insisted that everyone from his year was welcome. 'I couldn't stand parties to which some people weren't invited. Everyone in school knew about my party. Everyone who wanted to come came. We had a big yard and around two hundred people turned up,' he explained years later. It all went off without any problems.

Tom was incredibly protective towards his sisters. One time he was working as a busboy at a country club near Glen Ridge and he noticed a man looking at his sister 'the wrong way'. He immediately stared hard at the man as if to say 'You son of a bitch.'

Another time he was talking to a kid at school who told him that he really wanted to kiss Tom's sister Cass. The youngster was really shocked by this admission and immediately told the other boy: 'If you touch my sister I will kill you.'

A few days after graduation day, Tom, his mother and stepfather attended a special dinner for all the senior varsity athletes from the Glen Ridge High Class of 1980. Tom, who, along with more than fifty of his classmates, received a senior letter award for sporting achievement, listened to Bruce Harper, running back for the New York Jets football team, tell the audience that his own short height – he was just five feet eight inches, which is considered very short in professional footballing terms – had not held him back because he always had the determination to succeed.

Tom, still only about five feet seven inches at the time, took due note of his sporting hero's advice. He had already set himself a goal in life that would not be affected by his short height. Even with unemployment in the United States running at more than seven million people that summer of 1980, Tom did not seem worried about finding a job.

Later he explained that all those schools and the difficult years had made him feel vulnerable a lot of the time and somehow that had manifested itself in his desire to become an actor. 'I was constantly having to put up these guards to take care of myself. You didn't sit around with the guys and talk about, "God, that really hurt my feelings." What you said was more like, "Yeah, let's go out, have some beers and kick some ass." That was really frustrating to me.'

After Tom left Glen Ridge High in June 1980, Cass continued the family involvement in wrestling by becoming team manager. Brother and sister were very close and her interest had been sparked by watching Tom the previous year.

Eventually the Mapothers moved from Glen Ridge and none of them ever returned. Even when Glen Ridge High became the focus of attention across the United States in 1989, after the arrest of a number of students who were later charged with a sexual assault on a retarded girl, Cruise refused to be drawn into the controversy.

For most of his teens Tom hardly ever saw his father, Thomas Cruise Mapother III, but occasionally he would hear about his movements from Catherine, his grandmother on the Mapother side, during visits to their large house on Smithfield Road, Louisville. Tom has never openly talked about what his father was doing through these so-called missing years before his return, like the prodigal son, to Louisville in the mid-1980s.

Cousins Caroline Mapother and Professor Dillon Mapother say that Tom III 'went a little strange' during that period. He married a lady called Joan soon after his divorce from Mary Lee and continued to harbour a misguided conviction that one day he would make his millions from some crazy invention or other. 'Thomas Cruise Mapother III's behaviour towards his children was appalling. I don't think anyone normal would go off and abandon a wife and four children like he did,' says Caroline Mapother.

Childhood friend Sue Downey, who knew Tom during those difficult years in Louisville, said she had heard that the boy's father had a terrible temper and Tom was often so unhappy about his parents' split that he would cry himself to sleep at night.

Family members later revealed for the first time that Tom III was virtually leading the life of a hobo between the mid-seventies and mid-eighties. He seems to have spent much of his time travelling the highways and byways of Southern California.

He virtually vanished for a few years. His parents were besides themselves with worry. His parents, Catherine and Thomas Cruise Mapother II, regularly sent their wayward son letters and cheques but they would be returned to the family home in Louisville with 'Not Known' stamped on them. It seemed that Thomas Cruise Mapother III rarely stayed more than a few days in one place.

On one occasion, according to Caroline Mapother, his parents made an ill-fated trip to try to meet their wandering son in Las Vegas. 'They had got word he was in Vegas and wanted to make sure he was all right. They found out he attended a particular church that gave out food and bedding to transients and so they headed over to it. But by the time they got there, Tom had gone. He just didn't want to see them,' explained Caroline.

The few relatives who did get a glimpse into Thomas III's life at this time report that he grew a long beard and had his hair in a ponytail for much of the time he was wandering California and the far west of the United States with his new wife. He had basically become a man of the road, unable to cope with normal family life.

Caroline Mapother has noted with interest Tom Cruise's later claims in interviews with journalists that he had a deprived childhood living on the wrong side of the tracks. 'These claims make me angry. His grandmother did everything she could to try and help support those children especially after Tom III went off,' she said, adding: 'Tom Cruise has implied he was born into a blue-collar family, but everyone around him was from very respected backgrounds.'

She remembered hearing about Tom's story of the Christmas when the family were so poor they recited poems to each other instead of giving gifts. Mary Lee's pride may well have prevented them from going to the Mapothers for assistance. Caroline, a crusty, straight-talking lady in her mid-seventies with a strong Southern drawl, added, 'Sad as it is, Tom Cruise comes from a broken family and that does not exactly make a pretty picture.'

Whatever the truth behind the real feelings between Mary Lee and her in-laws, it is perfectly understandable that she might feel a little uncomfortable going begging to her husband's family. After all, she came from a poorer background, growing up on the other side of Louisville, where families like the Mapothers were considered the landed gentry of the area.

Meanwhile, for Tom Cruise, the struggle continued.

4

To the outside world Tom Cruise is bright, witty, successful, talented and handsome. But beneath that veneer lies a man in conflict with himself because of an invisible handicap – something that can be, at the very least, debilitating and, at worst, crippling. It is a common handicap which has become much more clearly recognised over the past twenty years. For Tom Cruise has suffered all his life from the learning disability called dyslexia.

As one of the United States' most famous dyslexics, Thomas Alva Edison, explained: 'I remember I used to never be able to get along at school. I was always at the foot of the class. My father thought I was stupid, and I almost decided that I was a dunce.' The fact that one of the nation's greatest inventors should be labelled an idiot at school provides the perfect insight into how Tom Cruise suffered as a child travelling from school to school across the country. Those never-ending changes must have made his 'problem' even harder to recognise because none of his teachers ever got to know him for long enough to help him over his disability.

Dyslexia is a very complex and confusing learning problem – one that educationalists are only now beginning to come to grips with. Along with other so-called learning disorders, such as attention deficient hyperkinesis and hyperactivity, dyslexia is responsible for making life miserable for tens of millions of children and adults across the world.

This invisible handicap comes in many guises, and the case histories are endless. There are children who cannot understand their parents' commands, fathers who cannot even read bedtime stories to their kids, people who have trouble distinguishing between bank notes of different denominations. Then there are the thousands of people of all ages who have to think before tying their shoes, who get lost or disorientated easily, who cannot read a menu or a road sign, or have constant problems articulating their thoughts.

All these problems come from one common cause – a learning-disabled person's brain doesn't assimilate information in the same manner as a healthy brain. Every second of the day the brain is bombarded with information; when this information becomes scrambled, a person is thrown out of step with the rest of the world. Some dyslexics even have trouble analysing facial expressions. It's almost as if there's a link missing from their chain of thought.

Tom's dyslexia made it difficult for him to do his schoolwork. He couldn't remember which way 'c' or 'z' went. Letters would magically switch themselves around and entire words and sentences appeared fractured and backward. It was frightening, disorientating and, above all, frustrating.

'I was put in remedial reading classes. It was a drag. It separated you and singled you out,' he explained later. 'I didn't know whether a "c" or "d" curved to the right or left. That affects everything you do – how you deal with letters and which way they go, the way you pronounce things, your reading comprehension ... everything! My spelling was terrible. Fortunately, I was able to train myself to see letters the way they really were, but that took a lot of work ... and a lot of support from my mother.'

Tom's difficulty was usually interpreted by teachers during his early school days as evidence that he was dumb or unco-operative. Sometimes both. Some recognised there was some sort of problem but failed to establish precisely what it was. 'People would excuse me: "He's the new kid. We'll just help him through this year." I had to train myself to focus on attention,' he later explained.

Typically, at home Tom's confusion over which way to draw his letters did not alienate him from the rest of the family. It actually brought him even closer to them because it is considered almost certain that dyslexia is inherited. Mary Lee eventually spotted the condition in her son because not only did she suffer from it, but so did his three sisters. Gradually she began to take decisive steps to help her son.

Not only did Mary Lee appreciate the anguish Tom was going through, but she also had professional expertise. She had worked with hyperkinetic and dyslexic children and she knew that, with patience and understanding, she could coach Tom and his sisters. Every evening she would carefully check their homework for major blunders, and she gently coaxed the children through numerous crises of confidence sparked by their learning disability. Cass apparently had the worst problems and required almost constant attention just to get her through the most basic written work.

In time Tom learned how to work around his dyslexia. It will never be completely cured, but it is not now a problem that gets in the way of reading either for business or pleasure. However, there are still occasions when Tom finds reading the small print of a screenplay painful.

They say that people with learning disabilities learn to compensate. A man who has trouble communicating verbally or otherwise may pick up a pencil or a paintbrush and become a great artist. It is suspected that Leonardo da Vinci suffered from some sort of learning disability. Tom compensated at school in his own way by turning to athletics.

Sport helped Tom fit in, especially in his teens. It gave him a focus, something that people with his handicap surely need. Tasks that are taken for granted by other children, like thinking about what they would like to do when they grow up, had to be considered in a different light. At one point he thought about being an astronaut, but, with his problems, how could he throw himself wholeheartedly into such an ambition? 'I had to set goals and force myself to be disciplined, because I always felt I had barriers to overcome. I was forced to write with my right hand when I wanted to use my left. I began to reverse letters, and reading became difficult. I was always put in remedial classes. I felt ashamed.'

For Tom, sport provided short-term relief based on physical prowess and the kind of mental alertness that has nothing to do with telling the difference between a 'b' and a 'd'.

During the past twenty years the general public has become much more aware of people with learning disabilities like Tom's. It is now estimated that at least ten per cent of all schoolchildren may have the same kind of handicap and the problem is now more easily recognised. Tom was lucky because he was diagnosed as a small child and that gave him ample opportunity to work on his weak spots. Other dyslexics are not so fortunate.

In recent years Tom has played a role in bringing worldwide attention to this learning disability. By talking openly about it, he has given many dyslexic children the hope for a successful future, and, even more importantly, he has constantly stressed the need to recognise and deal with the special requirements of dyslexics. In 1985 he received an award for Outstanding Learning Disabled Achievement. Along with other honourees – performers Cher (more about her and Tom later) and Bruce Jenner, businessmen Richard C. Strauss and G. Chris Anderson, and artist Robert Rauschenberg – Tom travelled to Washington to receive his award from the Lab School, which teaches both children and adults to deal with their learning handicaps. The six recipients met Nancy Reagan at the White House and the awards were presented by the then Speaker of the House, Senator Tip O'Neill.

At the Lab School, Tom was a huge hit, willingly posing for photographs with a long line of predominantly female students and answering their questions. 'Reading before the class was the most frustrating thing for me... I felt like I was dumb. I was real embarrassed ... my teachers were upset because I made my "z's" backward and I didn't know the difference between "b's" and "d's",' he told the assembled group.

Tom then watched with a definite glint in his eye as the superstar Cher told everyone that she didn't recognise her dyslexia until her daughter, Chastity, was diagnosed. Wearing her trademark of the moment, an enormous black wig, she explained the nature of her impairment and its effect on her life. 'I'm a terrible reader. It took me a long time to be able to write cheques. I have a hard time dialling phones. For me, it's very annoying but in another kind of work it would be devastating. If I read a script, I read it very slowly and memorise it the first time I read it,' she told the White House audience.

Tom's problem with dyslexia had a happy ending, but he'll never forget the battle he fought or the millions of people out there trying to win the war, as he was later to prove.

5

Nothing great was ever achieved
without enthusiasm.
RALPH WALDO EMERSON

When Tom set off for New York to make both his bread and butter and history, it was with $2000 saved from his various part-time jobs and little else but ambition and a prayer. He could well have just blown the cash on a train pass and hitchhiked around Europe like many of his classmates back in Glen Ridge. Instead he bit the struggling-actor bullet and took odd jobs unloading trucks and working as a waiter at places like Mortimer's restaurant. When he could afford to spare a moment, he'd audition or attend a workshop at the Neighborhood Playhouse.

Before even graduating from high school, Tom had managed to approach a manager who had been recommended by a classmate who had appeared in some commercials. A few weeks before his departure for the big city, Tom persuaded his mother to drive with him to New York in a dirty-green Ford Pinto he had bought for $50 a few months earlier. Their mission was to get Tom signed up by that manager. Driving through thick traffic, Tom had a huge argument with Mary Lee, no doubt brought on by the tension he felt over this first-ever meeting with his first manager-to-be. It got so bad that they stopped talking and sat in the car in crawling traffic in complete silence. Tom was angry because he knew that, at seventeen, he could not get a manager unless his mother co-signed a contract with him.

He was hardly well prepared for the most important meeting of his young life. He did not even have any photographs of himself. By the time they got to the manager's office, they were running late so Tom jumped out of the Pinto and barked at his mother, 'Just park the car somewhere', while he went up to meet the manager, a part-time New York actress.

Seconds after Tom arrived in her office, she had him do a brief reading of a Hershey's commercial script. As Tom later explained: 'It was one of those "Yeah, yeah, yeah, babe, you're beautiful, I'm going to make you a star" sort of situations.'

By the time a flustered Mary Lee turned up, Tom had signed on the dotted line. His new manager was convinced she had discovered a potential star.

Just a few weeks later Tom had landed his first role: the character of Herb in a dinner-theatre presentation of the musical *Godspell*. Although both the role and the production were minuscule, they nonetheless validated his talent and brought him his first professional experience in front of an audience.

Inside a month, however, Tom had fired that first manager because she had him doing errands for her. Nobody was going to get in his way. He decided an agent was quite sufficient for a young actor at that stage of his career. There was no need for a manager. Even then he did not mind flexing his muscles if necessary.

Tom presumed he'd be stuck juggling and struggling with day jobs and small productions for some time to come, but he was also confident that his determination would earn him a breakthrough in the major league before long. He never saw himself doing odd jobs for the rest of his life. 'Otherwise, I wouldn't be striving to be an actor, would I? I'd be a professional waiter,' he said later.

As a child, Tom never excelled in any particular one of his many athletic undertakings; flitting from town to town and sport to sport left him no time to develop true expertise in any one area. But after enduring all the shifts of scenery, as well as dismissing ideas of becoming an athlete, joining the Air Force or taking priestly vows, he had finally found his true calling. 'I *wanted* to be an actor,' he insisted. 'I *want* it, *wanted* it very badly. I was *hungry*. I'm *still* hungry.'

Life in New York was a whole new experience for Tom. He managed to find a room mate to keep his outgoings down, but regularly hitched or took a bus back to Glen Ridge for some of his mother's tasty home cooking.

One actor who encountered him at that time described him as 'very New Jersey, less polished than he is now ... he was like a greaser – he had big muscles, he had his hair greased back. He had an angry edge to him.' The truth was that Tom was still painfully shy and slightly overawed by New York, so he was hiding his thoughts behind a seemingly angry exterior. He also believed that as an actor he had to fulfil a role in life, and he clearly saw himself as a tough little guy with a good set of muscles and a cool hairstyle to match.

But there was another aspect to Tom that others noted. 'He was handsome, and those who saw him then recall an urgency in his performing that was hard to dismiss,' says movie expert Chris Connelly.

That urgency was born out of a desperate need to succeed at all costs. Tom had given himself ten years when he announced his intentions to Mary Lee and Jack, but privately he reckoned he would have to make it as an actor much faster than that.

Tom's wrestling coach at Glen Ridge High, Angelo Corbo, got a rare insight into what Tom was like just after he left the school, when he offered the teenager a ride in his car after spotting him standing on a corner in the town of Blomfield, near Glen Ridge. He drove Tom to where he could get a bus into New York City. Tom was full of enthusiasm for his new-found profession. He bombarded Corbo with exciting-sounding stories about life in the Big Apple.

'He said he'd got hooked up with an agent and was trying out for loads of parts. Frankly, I couldn't believe him. It had only been a few months since he'd left school. It seemed incredible that his career could be taking off so fast,' explained Corbo.

Then the fresh-faced Tom astounded his slightly sceptical teacher by announcing with childish fervour and a sly grin: 'I'm doing a movie with Brooke Shields.'

'I really thought he was spinning a yarn when he said that,' Corbo recalled. 'I laughed out loud and told him, "I hope you make it, kid." Frankly, I didn't give him much chance.' The straight-talking Italian–American chuckled as he told the young Tom: 'When you make it, Tommy, remember me, I'll drive your limo.'

Corbo explained later: 'I remember driving away thinking it was all a pipe dream. His parents didn't even know anyone in the acting business. He had absolutely no connections. I just couldn't see it happening.'

Although Tom Cruise's rise to stardom was eventually to be incredibly swift, first of all he had to learn to deal with the rejection of going out on readings for insignificant parts. Somehow he even managed to turn that often demoralising experience to advantage. 'I felt that the people rejecting me were there to help me in the long run. Sometimes it hurts, but I truly believe that there are parts I'm supposed to get and parts I'm not supposed to get and something else is going to come along,' he later recalled.

Tom initially got turned down for dozens of small TV parts as well as a number of television commercials, which often provide struggling actors with a cash lifeline when the 'real' work dries up. A number of directors complained to casting agents that the fresh-faced New Jersey kid was far too intense. What none of them recognised was Tom's driving ambition and utter obsession to succeed. In a teenager it was interpreted as intensity.

Yet within a few months of his arrival in New York there was an inexplicable buzz circulating about this young man who had dropped the Mapother part of his name – something he did mainly because it was less of a mouthful but also to pay tribute to the women who had steered those Mapother men through so much troubled water over the previous five generations.

This period in Tom's career is shrouded in mystery. It is known that he started out in New York by sharing a tiny loft with a male room-mate and worked as a waiter at Mortimer's. Within a couple of months he managed to cut his living costs down even further by becoming an assistant-handyman to the superintendent of an apartment building on the West Side – a part-time job that brought with it free accommodation. But it is impossible to find out who it was that helped guide his career so rapidly.

To all who met Tom at this time, he was nothing if not thoroughly focused. He loved to tell anyone who would listen about his auditions, his agent, his manager, the free flight for a movie test. He had just passed his nineteenth birthday and he was already frighteningly single-minded about his profession. Nothing and nobody would ever get in his way.

It was the beginning of the 1980s – a decade that was marked by big wages and self-motivated people driving onwards and upwards, taking few prisoners along the way. That was how Tom Cruise was starting to sound to his old friends. But there was nothing offensive about his attitude – he was simply a kid with a mission to succeed.

'I focus on my craft, my work. That is the most important thing to me. And what people say, if I let it bother me, I'm going to be in a lot of trouble. I just focus in on what I want and what I want to do, and everything outside of that is just there, and it happens. Whatever,' he told one of the first journalists ever to interview him, eighteen months later.

The reference to Brooke Shields, which his wrestling coach Angelo Corbo had dismissed as a joke when he gave him a lift in his car one rainy afternoon, turned out to be accurate: just five months after settling in New York, Tom bagged a small role in the film *Endless Love*.

Tom Cruise's movie debut turned out to be a seven-minutes-in-heaven type of thing. Not that you'd miss him if you sneezed, but you might miss him if you left the room during the first half of the film. Tom wasn't disappointed by the brevity of his appearance. In fact, he felt fortunate to get a break so quickly and equally fortunate that the movie was not a vehicle for his talents since it flopped in grand style at the box office.

Tom was still just eighteen, fresh-faced, determined and full of vitality. His superfit physique helped gain him many admirers, both male and female, and he kept up his training by working exhausting hours as a busboy in restaurants.

Franco Zeffirelli, the director and driving force behind *Endless Love*, had made a name for himself in the United States thanks to his flamboyant spectacular *Romeo and Juliet*, which starred two teenagers unknown at the time. Despite this, Tom Cruise did not have a clue who Mr Zeffirelli was. In some strange way this complete and utter ignorance on the part of the young actor led to a blissful conclusion because Tom sailed through his brief audition, not a butterfly in sight. Zeffirelli reportedly exclaimed a breathy '*Bellissimo*' after watching Tom in action. Already the young actor was having that soon-to-be-renowned effect on men and women alike.

Tom's character, Billy, was not exactly provided with the sort of dialogue which would help Tom make a worthy impression in his big-screen debut. Basically, he was a young, gregarious jock who is a good friend of the leading male character. Billy did not even merit a surname, although the few lines that Tom uttered so profoundly did determine the course of action for the entire second half of the movie. Tom had a role that might just about get him noticed if it was handled properly and carefully. Meanwhile another member of the cast was grabbing most of the attention.

'I think she is the most beautiful person I've ever seen in my life. A miracle of nature,' gushed Zeffirelli in reference to *Endless Love*'s leading lady, Brooke Shields. At that time Brooke had become a national obsession; a teenage millionairess, the veteran of seven films and a string of Calvin Klein commercials. She had posed nude as a fourteen-year-old and some of her movies, including the highly controversial *Pretty Baby*, had dealt with adult subjects like prostitution and underage sex.

Miss Shields had caused great outrage in Middle America, especially when it was revealed that she was managed by her mother. *New York* magazine put mother and daughter on its cover with the declaration: 'Meet Teri and Brooke Shields. Brooke is twelve. She poses nude. Teri is her mother. She thinks it's swell.' Enough said.

At this time Brooke Shields was really 'hot' in Hollywood terms. She had just completed another titillating effort called *The Blue Lagoon* and, through her outspoken mother, was used to getting exactly what she wanted. Even the fact that the *Endless Love* script revolved more around the male lead than Brooke's role was duly noted and immense pressure was put on Zeffirelli to alter it accordingly, otherwise Miss Shields might contemplate pulling out. It must be pointed out that Zeffirelli tried very hard to find an unknown actress to cast in the lead, but after a huge casting call he decided on Brooke because none of the other girls had been as beautiful. The sixteen-year-old got $500,000 and five per cent of the first $5 million in video rentals.

The male lead, Martin Hewitt, was almost as wet behind the ears as Tom Cruise. He had graduated from Claremont High School in 1979 and gone on to the American Academy in Pasadena. When he noticed an advertisement for auditions in the entertainment section of the *Los Angeles Times*, he was still a student earning some money by working as a parking valet. His starring role came about through sheer luck. He was not hired from the film's actual auditions, but after Zeffirelli noticed him while watching a TV programme made by entertainment reporter Rona Barratt about the business of auditions. Suddenly the director had his male lead.

The screenplay was based on Scott Spencer's novel *Endless Love*. It was an extremely complex book, full of unusual characters and competing thematic eddies and swirls. The movie script was a very watered-down version and a number of characters were added, among them Tom's Billy, who was inserted to eliminate some of the tangled web of people and plot.

Zeffirelli has admitted that just before completing each of his movies he was tempted to throw the entire film in the bin and start again. Most who saw *Endless Love* say he most definitely should have done that in this case.

The movie centres around a teenage couple who rush blindly into an obsessive and dangerous relationship. David Axelrod (Martin Hewitt) is the child of two left-wing lawyers whose overwhelming concern for their fellow man leaves them little time for their son. When David falls in love with Jade Butterfield (Brooke Shields) he becomes embroiled with her entire family, who seem so relaxed compared with his own parents, but there are some familiar problems lurking beneath the surface of this seemingly happy family.

Tom Cruise enters briefly as Billy the friendly jock who inadvertently suggests to David that he set fire to his girlfriend's family's home after they turn against him. Tom's portrayal of Billy offers an important contrast because he is animated, enthusiastic and boyishly gleeful. Seen next to David's sullen depression, Billy highlights the leading man's distress. The final twist in this story came not in the depressingly uninteresting tale itself but when Zeffirelli proclaimed what a great star Brooke Shields was about to come. Nobody present realised that the film's biggest star-to-be was the attractive young man with less than a hundred words of dialogue.

And Tom himself later admitted finding the entire process, which amounted to just one day on the set of *Endless Love*, bewildering. 'It was a hell of an experience. The director kept grabbing at my chest. I wondered what was going on around here. He did it a couple of times, feeling me, and I walked away. It was all pretty strange. I was so naive. I didn't understand.'

Tom has never fully expanded on those comments and it is difficult to interpret precisely what they mean. Is he talking about his own repressed fear of homosexuality or is he referring just to the physicality of the part and the method by which Zeffirelli directs his actors?

Meanwhile *Endless Love* suffered from bad word of mouth even before the movie was released in July 1981. A leak from someone who saw a sneak preview reported that many in the audience booed for the last fifteen minutes because it was so corny. Most of the shouting was reserved for Brooke Shields.

'When she would deliver a line like "I'm hurt" or something like that in a heavy love scene, she came off like a little six-year-old with a boo-boo on her knee or something. The audience was just cracking up,' said that previewer.

In *TV Movies and Video Guide*, the film was labelled a 'bomb'. The magazine continued: 'Scott Spencer's deservedly praised novel ... is thoroughly trashed in a textbook example of how to do everything wrong in a literary adaptation. Rightfully regarded as one of the worst films of its time.'

Sheila Benson, of the *Los Angeles Times*, complained: 'Zeffirelli has turned the catharsis of the novel into a dreadful sickly sweet sheen... All of Zeffirelli's renowned lushness works against a story of dead-ahead urgency. But it may still have a happy ending – it may make thousands of new readers for Spencer's astonishing book.'

Even movie guide books are less than enthusiastic about *Endless Love*, and verdicts like 'an overheated melodrama with unbelievable and unlikeable characters' stand out. In the *New York Times*, the infamous Janet Maslin insisted that 'Zeffirelli and his screenwriter have bitten off so much more than they can chew that their film is virtually unintelligible'.

Zeffirelli himself was clearly in complete denial about the movie's dismal portrayal of young love, telling one journalist: 'I never think of anything I do in terms of financial success. The emphasis is not on sex, it is on the awesome power of love – and there's a difference.'

After invitations to the film's glitzy opening party were sent out, an impressive array of stars, including Elizabeth Taylor, Diana Ross and Liza Minnelli, showed up. But no one had bothered to ask the kid from New Jersey. Tom had definitely lucked out. He had spent enough time on the screen to be noticed, but he didn't have a big enough part to be associated with a flop on his first time out.

Stage one of his plan to become a star had worked out very satisfactorily.

6

Life itself is a very humbling experience.
So that keeps you honest.

TOM CRUISE

Tom Cruise's life on the West Side of New York City was not much more than an extension of the difficult years following his parents' break-up. He was juggling jobs and failing auditions with alarming regularity. Instead of a 4 a.m. newspaper round, he was getting out of bed at all hours of the day and night to repair leaking pipes and broken locks in his starring role as the handsome teenage handyman in the apartment block where he lived.

But for Tom, not yet nineteen, there was one big difference from those painful times a few years earlier and he kept reminding himself of it – he was doing what he wanted more than anything else in the world. The more he tried to succeed the more confident he got. As one old New York acting friend recalled: 'There was no stopping that kid!'

So, when director Harold Becker held a huge audition in May 1981 for two thousand young men ranging in age from prepubescent to late teens for his latest movie project, *Taps*, Tom went charging in with all guns blazing.

'I guess *Taps* was where it all started for me. When I read for Harold Becker, I remember, I literally didn't have a dollar to my name. And even though I didn't have the role yet, I felt really good about the interview,' Tom recalled later.

Next Tom had a meeting with the legendary producer Stanley R. Jaffe (*The Bad News Bears* and *Kramer vs Kramer*, to name but two of his films) and the director. He explained: 'It was like a two-minute meeting – you know, pull your hair up, read this line. And that was it. I walked out of the meeting. I was going to see my family in Jersey, but because I didn't have a dollar to take the bus home, I hitchhiked.'

Later, walking up the driveway to the family house in Glen Ridge, Tom noticed his mother talking on the phone through the window. She seemed very excited. When Tom let himself in with his front-door key, Mary Lee rushed into the hallway and put her arms round her son. 'It's your agent. You got the role.'

Although he hadn't landed one of the two leads, Tom had managed to grab a reasonable part as a friend to one of the leading characters, David Shawn, an aggressive young Marine. Not bad for only his second movie appearance.

Tom considered the part a fantastic opportunity, but when he met the actor cast to play David Shawn, his enthusiasm reached new boundaries. Director Becker – a master craftsman who broke his teeth as a director of highly rated television commercials – watched the sparks fly virtually from the first moment Tom was introduced to the other actor. For the teenager had gone to the trouble of transforming himself into a chunky, physically intimidating rookie soldier. His role might have been small, but Tom was going to give it everything he had. The nightmare for that other young actor had only just begun.

According to Sean Penn, who starred in *Taps* with Timothy Hutton, the other unfortunate thespian was completely overawed by Tom's infectious enthusiasm. Penn, who has repeatedly been accused of excessive behaviour both on and off the set in pursuit of his character's essence, watched the almost fanatical Tom Cruise focus in on his aims with cold, professional intensity, the likes of which he had never witnessed before in his life.

But there was no question of Tom deliberately setting out to destroy his rival, who was playing the supposedly meatier role of David Shawn. That was not the way a well-brought-up kid like Tom behaved. There was no backbiting on his part – he just looked, felt and smelled right for the part. Simply put, he completely overshadowed the other actor from the moment he stepped out for rehearsals.

Becker noticed what was happening instantly and found himself swept up by Tom's electrifying interpretation. He immediately halted proceedings and conferred with the movie's producers. They pored over the script for hours, trying to work out if something could be done to enlarge Tom's character, for everyone present knew that this was too big an opportunity to miss out on.

Then Becker came up with a solution; he proposed that Tom should take over the role of David Shawn. The teenager appeared horrified and embarrassed. He immediately went to the producer and insisted that he could not take over the part without the original actor's blessing. Sean Penn witnessed all this with a wry smile on his face. Here was an inexperienced actor being offered the chance of a lifetime and he was worried about hurting another actor's feelings.

Penn explained: 'Tommy had to get the part. Very intense, two hundred per cent there. It was overpowering – and we'd all kind of laugh because it was so sincere. Good acting, but so far in the intense direction that it was funny. The producers told him, "Look, buddy, if you don't want to do it, leave. We want you for this part, but we're not going to beg you." It was incredible how innocent and naive he was when he came to do *Taps*.'

But what Penn, who had been brought up in a Hollywood family, did not appreciate at the time was that Tom's motivation had always been governed by what was right and what was wrong. In Tinseltown there might have been no guidelines, but where Tom came from there most certainly were.

Tom explained: 'I said, "Thank you very much but I don't want to play David Shawn." I was in a small role and that's the way I wanted it to be. I was learning so much just being around, watching everything that was happening.'

However, there is no doubting the fact that Tom's behaviour was extraordinarily naive. After all, no actor worth his salt would admit to his 'second' that he was a better man and graciously turn over his role. The most intriguing aspect of this entire incident was that not one person present believes that Tom deliberately set out to steal that starring part. Only he knows the true answer to that question.

Anyway, Tom's apparent innocence did not prove a lasting hindrance as he finally accepted the larger part and became David Shawn, leader of Bravo Company. Tom had put on fifteen pounds deliberately, thanks to a few gallons of high-density milkshakes. He more than made up for his lack of inches by making himself resemble an aggressive bulldog, much to the delight of Becker, who wanted David Shawn to fill the screen with unmitigated bodily chutzpah.

And, just like a bulldog, Tom now had the bit between his teeth and had no intention of letting go. The moviemakers were so inspired by his portrayal that they continued to expand his role in the screenplay as filming progressed. The character eventually grew into the classic raving-lunatic cadet and Tom ended up appearing in more than eighty per cent of the finished movie. His career was taking off after only his second celluloid outing.

Tom was ecstatic. 'I felt like it was a chance for me, and a beginning. Me and Penn, I really don't know if we ever slept during that movie.' The two new friends would stay up all night just talking about the movie and their roles. There was little time to exchange the sort of information that one would expect two virile, good-looking young men to talk about. It was work, work, work. 'We were really scared and nervous and excited – we didn't know what was going to happen,' Tom explained. 'It was a special time in my life because it was my first proper movie and it was Sean's too. You just felt that something special was happening.'

As producer, Stanley R. Jaffe had nurtured and carefully developed the script with a painstaking attention to detail. While other similar Hollywood producers of his stature tended to turn out two or three movies every year, Jaffe had averaged one every other year. He was a character who liked to be involved from conception to fruition. 'I buy the material. I work very, very slowly on it. I don't even bring in a director until one or two drafts of the screenplay have been completed,' he explained with studied understatement.

Taps also boasted some very high-brow talent in front of the camera, including veteran performer George C. Scott (who played the general himself in *Patton,* winner of seven Oscars, including one for Best Picture) and Timothy Hutton, who had walked away with an Oscar for Best Supporting Actor for his impressive work on his first-ever movie, *Ordinary People.*

Even though at twenty he was only a year older than Tom, Hutton was streets ahead of him in career terms. And he was finding life as a celebrity tough to handle. Even the small matter of finding a suitable date seemed a nightmare scenario. During *Taps* he explained in graphic terms a situation that would ring a few bells of recognition with Tom only a year later. Hutton said: 'It would be wonderful to meet someone who doesn't know who I am. One girl said I made her feel good because I never take advantage of anyone. I said, "You got me all wrong. That guy on screen isn't me! What if I did take advantage of you?"'

Hutton even took a chance on a blind date, only to find that the girl knew in advance who he was. 'Everybody at the party knew,' he said with exasperation. Tom noted Hutton's frustration and decided that whatever happened to his career he would make sure he avoided any such problems.

Taps was based on a series of tragic events at a military school, so the actors were sent off by Becker to the Valley Forge Military Academy for four weeks and told to familiarise themselves with the tough, gung-ho lifestyle of real cadets. 'This film had to be founded in reality, every movement in it, every word in it,' the director later explained. 'We needed the environment to draw on and that became, as far as I'm concerned, our greatest single resource.'

Tom and his fellow actors soon found themselves submitting to the school barber, a little initiation routine experienced by every new recruit. Then followed a fitting for a smart, tailored uniform with shiny brass buttons. Becker expected Tom and the rest of the cast to live their parts to the full so that they could reflect the reality when they started shooting the movie. This also included appreciating – and experiencing – the stringent rules and regulations facing every new recruit on entry to the military school, such as back-breaking physical discipline with no immediate rewards. *Taps* was turning out to be the nearest to the real thing any of the actors had ever experienced.

'I'm a great believer in rehearsals. In my other films we've had long rehearsal periods and in this movie I wanted it to be dedicated to turning our young actors into cadets,' explained Becker. The director, a soft-spoken, highly articulate man, saw *Taps* as having a strong message for the society of the early 1980s. 'Any kind of closed situation is a dangerous one. The fictional school in *Taps* is also a kind of closed society, one that treats itself as a military post. Is that a suitable lifestyle for young boys who are enrolled at such a school?' It was a heavy, intense interpretation from Becker, but that was the way he was and it had a profound effect on Tom. The young actor took the director's every word literally.

However, dress and discipline were not the only reality-based activities; there were daily weapon drills, parade procedures and every detail of military protocol. The regime included rising at dawn and stomping around in constant formation. Many of the actors moaned and groaned as they became immersed in the disciplined environment. But not Tom – he loved every minute of it. This was his means to an end. If he had to eat dirt he would do it if it made him a better actor.

All these hardships were merely part of a day's work for him. In any case, it provided a perfect outlet for his energy and enthusiasm as well as legitimising his conviction that complete immersion in a role was essential for a good performance. 'To make the character as real as possible I have to find out how I can relate to the character personally,' explained Tom to one journalist after completing *Taps*. 'I have to find out what is "real" in the character that you do ... there are going to be some points where you're going to have to be like a part of the character in terms of yourself, or else your character won't be real.' Tom could talk for hours about his art to anyone who would listen.

In *Taps*, Tom took a huge step forward in terms of his status and ability as an actor. The character of David Shawn was not an easy one to pull off because a delicate balance between Shawn and the other principals had to be maintained for most of the film. Considering the instability of Shawn, this was akin to crossing a tightrope in an all-terrain vehicle.

The role would have been a stretch for actors with ten times more experience than Tom, but somehow he reached inside himself and pulled out a manic, dangerous characterisation – obviously something that had been lurking deep within him for much of his life. 'David Shawn ... is also a part of me, even though he was psychotic... I pulled different things to different extremities, of course,' Tom explained a few months later. He had somehow got a handle on the fact that Shawn was driven by two main emotions – fear and anger. Using those ingredients, Tom brought a startling, almost frightening reality to the role.

Yet Tom never once resorted to the sort of eye-rolling and drooling that so often stereotypes many movie madmen. His eyes became like angry slits, perpetually filled with hostility. He was like a ticking time bomb, humourless and cruel, waiting to explode.

Filming took place entirely in Pennsylvania, in the area around Wayne, in Delaware County. Local businessmen were delighted by an estimated $5 million in revenue brought in thanks to the presence of the movie technicians and actors. And at least five hundred local people were hired as actors, extras, carpenters and drivers.

A Twentieth Century Fox Film Corporation handout detailing the film incorrectly gave Tom's age as seventeen at the time of shooting. He was, in fact, nineteen, but it is believed that the movie's backers thought it might be advisable to give the impression that he was somewhat younger in order to attract a young audience.

Tom was as enthusiastic as ever in the Fox press release, where he was quoted as saying of his experiences at Military Academy: 'I got into it the minute I got there. Being at the Academy and making *Taps* has made me stronger. It's helped teach me endurance.' And he meant every word.

Intriguingly, paperwork uncovered almost thirteen years later shows that Tom did not get a look-in when it came to the traditional Hollywood game of 'star projection'. A Fox legal document gives George C. Scott a 100 per cent guarantee of having his name above the title or in the last position reading: 'and GEORGE C. SCOTT as General Bache'. Tim Hutton was given a 100 per cent guarantee that his name would never be used in a size smaller than any other cast member. Tom Cruise's name is not even mentioned on this document – something that did not go unnoticed by the young actor as his performance in the finished product was considered head and shoulders above everyone else. The situation was intriguingly reversed more than ten years later.

The movie won praise in some quarters, although Z magazine declared: '*Taps*' plot has more than its shares of holes and contrivances ... but its remarkable cast is nearly flawless.' Other critics were also not too quick to hail the movie. *Time* pointed out: '*Taps* takes far too long to reach its bloody, predictable conclusion. Its big guns are loaded with nothing more lethal than Hollywood nerve gas.' *The Motion Picture Product Digest* seemed to get a better handle on what the movie was intended to be: '*Taps* starts out as if it's going to be a larkish movie – just the thing for the holiday season – about some students at a military academy who barricade themselves inside the campus grounds to prevent the 125-year-old institution from being shut down entirely by its trustees and the property converted to a lucrative condominium project.

'All too soon, however, this amicable notion is dispelled, and it is made clear that the film-makers have more grave and didactic intentions in mind.

They are out to deliver a pacifist, anti-military message, and the deeper they get into this element the more ponderous and shrill they become.

'*Taps* turns out to be such a downer, in fact, it's hard to imagine it winning over a large audience at any time of the year – much less than during a period when the paying customers are in a festive mood.'

However, film-industry insiders who had predicted that *Taps* would bomb badly and never make back its original $18-million budget had to eat their words and were looking for all sorts of excuses. Veteran producer Jaffe explained: 'There were three things that nobody understood about *Taps*. First, they didn't understand the magnitude of the star quality of Timmy Hutton. Second, they did not understand that this was an unusual Christmas season in that an inordinate number of the movies were adult-orientated, which meant that a picture which could be sold to youth could break through. And third, they did not understand the considerable anxiety about military matters which has gripped draft-age youth in the wake of the return of deft registration.' Note that not once was the name Tom Cruise mentioned – not that that bothered the young actor.

Tom was delighted by the reaction to the film; it had put him on a pedestal with two famous Oscar winners and introduced him to an up-and-coming talent called Sean Penn, who was to become a great friend. Tim Hutton and Sean were both in his peer group in terms of age, potential and, most important of all, personal commitment to professional excellence.

Tom did not even receive an invitation to the gala premiere of *Endless Love*, but now the young actor was one of the guests of honour when Marvin Davies, owner of the backers of *Taps* – Twentieth Century Fox – hosted a glitzy bash at the AVCO cinema in Westwood, Los Angeles. Even so, it has to be pointed out that Tim Hutton was still being hailed as the hero of the proceedings.

For much of that premiere Tom was in a daze. He could not quite believe that he, a gawky nineteen-year-old kid from a broken home, was there among the rich and famous, in the company of Ali MacGraw, Michael Douglas and Dabney Coleman, to name but a few. At the gala dinner afterwards he sat quietly with his other great friend, fellow *Taps* actor Sean Penn, at a back table beautifully decorated with mirrors, black clothes, white orchids and tulips, feeling awkward in his tuxedo. The next day Tom's name did not even get more than the merest mention in the showbusiness trade papers.

Later, articles in magazines like *New York* claimed that Tom, Sean and Tim were founder members of what became known as the Brat Pack – a play on words on the Rat Pack, a group composed of Frank Sinatra, Sammy Davis Jr, Peter Lawford and Dean Martin, who worked together and rampaged through Hollywood and Las Vegas in the 1960s.

Taps was earmarked as the first Brat Pack movie. It was certainly a landmark movie in that it blazed the way for a more substantial type of youth-orientated film and featured a new type of young star. It is also widely acknowledged that those fresh, young faces helped *Taps* manage to bring in a very healthy $20.5 million at the box office.

After the gruelling shooting schedule on *Taps*, Tom headed off to his grandfather's log cabin on Lake Cumberland, in southern Kentucky, to unwind and 'do some fishing'. He was desperate to recharge his batteries and spend some time alone, thinking through the next step in his career. He had always felt the need for some peace and solitude and the cabin, with its stunning views, was the perfect place. There was no phone, no people – just lots of water and forest.

But there was another reason behind Tom's self-imposed exile after *Taps*. The young actor was emotionally drained after playing that role. He had mentally beaten himself up to such a degree to play a highly strung, aggressive character that it was in danger of spilling over into real life. Years later Tom admitted to friends that after *Taps* wrapped he was 'the most unpleasant person to be around'. His family told him to cool down and learn to relax. They genuinely feared that he would burn out before he reached his mid-twenties if he wasn't careful.

So Tom chilled out by the lakeside and tried to get back to reality. His jaws ached from the tension of his performance on the set of *Taps* and he could not stop nervously tapping his leg. A month or so in the middle of nowhere was essential if he was to retain his sanity.

A few months later his new-found success brought an interesting response from the young actor following the release of *Taps*. 'I have worked very, very hard for everything that has happened to me,' he said carefully, then laughed, 'But Geez, I do get lucky!'

After *Taps*, Tom went to his agency and told them he was not interested in doing commercials or television – that after his experience in *Taps* he only wanted to make movies. The word was already out – Tom Cruise was a hot young property and he was about to learn that there were a lot of people out there who wanted a chunk of him.

7

*I would be shocked if this guy ever sells out
what I perceive as a strong sense of purpose
about the craft of acting, about being true
to certain personal values.*

ROBERT SCHEER

After his performance in *Taps* the Hollywood buzz about Tom Cruise was phenomenal. Even before that movie was released in the Christmas holiday period of 1981, the teenager was signed to a two-picture deal with a Canadian production company. Tom had amply demonstrated that he could take a minor role and expand it until its celluloid power was tangible and undeniable. The next challenge was an out and out starring role ... and such a part lay just around the corner, or so it seemed.

For no sooner had word got out about his *Taps* performance than he was facing that age-old movieland problem – typecasting. 'After *Taps* everyone said, "Okay, now we've got a good psychotic killer,"' Tom observed a few years later. He was being offered countless vicious bruisers, but he felt certain his potential was being ignored. He might have only one major role under his belt, but he knew where he was heading and he wanted to break the mould before it took over his career.

'I needed something that would be in sharp contrast to the brutal cadet on *Taps*,' Tom asserted. As fate would have it, he got what he wanted, even that all-important top-billing status – but, after it was over, he realised what a terrible error he had made. For his next film turned out to be, in his own words, 'the most depressing experience of my life'.

Losin' It was originally entitled *Tijuana* and Tom came on board the project shortly after *Taps* had wrapped. He read the script closely and even asked his pal Sean Penn for his advice – they both concluded that it was in severe need of a rewrite. But the two producers behind the project were a charming, enthusiastic pair and they convinced Tom that *Losin' It* would end up being the next *Breaking Away*. As is the case in probably ninety-five per cent of all movies, the good intentions could never be matched by the actual product.

Tom tried in vain to explain why he did the film, but his excuses sound a little weak today. 'Coming off *Taps*, I felt like, hey, everyone wants to make a great movie. Everyone who's doing this loves their work. It's too hard a line of work to not love it. You work as hard as you can and get everything and something has to work out. Then I did *Losin' It*. When I first read it, it was worse than the released film. I had this small agent at the time who said, "Do it. Do it." I worked hard, but it was a terrible time in my life.'

Losin' It told the story of four Californian high schoolers who head way down south for a weekend on the loose in Tijuana, just inside Mexico, near the border crossing. Dave (Jackie Earle Haley from *Breaking Away* and *The Bad News Bears*), Spider (John Stockwell) and Woody (Tom Cruise) intend to visit a local brothel. Wendell 'The Wimp' has coerced big brother Dave into bringing him along so he can buy illegal firecrackers for profitable resale in the United States. Wendell is played by John P. Navin Jr, an actor Tom met on the set of *Taps* and recommended for the role. Along the way they are joined by a renegade wife named Kathy (Shelley Long in a pre-*Cheers* performance), who is Tijuana-bound to secure a quickie divorce.

The plot was based on a formula that typified the mentality of the early-eighties state-of-the-artless teen flicks. *Spring Break* director Sean Cunningham defined the narrative outline of such films as: 'Kids get drunk. Kids get laid. Kids go home.' Dubbed 'the dumb formula' by *Los Angeles Times* critic Peter H. Brown, it was, with minor variations, the essence of the teen movie. Unfortunately, *Losin' It* fitted in with this class all too well.

The movie's gist is Woody's virginity and how he loses it. He accompanies his pals to the bordertown bordello to rectify his condition, but finds the brothel atmosphere, with its ageing whores and dirty linen, an intimidating turn-off.

Kathy and Woody, both traumatised by the day's events, find solace in each other's company and cling together in the carnival of carnality the director depicts as Tijuana. Over a bottle of tequila they grow woozy and cosy until, driven by different needs, they end up renting a little motel room. There they fulfil each other's romantic longings. When they emerge, Woody has lost his virginity and Kathy has regained her pride and self-confidence.

The movie certainly didn't do the same for Tom. 'You know you're in trouble when it's a comedy and everybody making the movie is miserable,' he recalled.

But while *Losin' It* is probably the least exceptional of Tom's movies, it was not a completely lost cause. There is definite evidence of some sort of socially redeeming value beneath its cheesy exterior – an underlying theme of prejudice versus tolerance is hinted at in the contrasting ways the four teenagers respond to their adventures in Tijuana.

From the minute the opening credits begin to roll, the difference between Woody and his companions are drawn out. Unlike Woody, Dave and Spider are painted as sexually and racially obnoxious; both betray a biased arrogance against their south-of-the-border neighbours. The usually sullen and loutish Spider comes from a squalid and apathetic household – he stole funds for the big trip from his mother's wallet. Dave is a vain slob who stuffs his crotch with a rolled-up sock and keeps his money cache hidden inside a girlie magazine.

Woody, on the other hand, is sensitive to the feelings of others and is true blue to his more vulgar friends. Even a touch of discriminating taste is suggested when he pulls his hidden money from a copy of the erotic masterpiece *Lolita*.

Dave and Spider stink up the movie with their condescension and bigotry, doing things across the border they would never try back home. Dave attempts to seduce a local girl by slipping some bogus Spanish fly into her lemonade. He learns first hand that he's dealing with real people who are sick of being taken advantage of when the Mexican girl's brother defends her honour by abducting Dave and threatening his manhood with a blowtorch. Hoisted up on a crane, the helpless Dave is a captive audience to the enraged protests of the Mexican boy as he shouts out that Tijuana is corrupt and dirty because outsiders like Dave have dirtied it with their sordid intentions and prejudices.

Losin' It's gestures against intolerance aren't enough, however, to disguise the fact that it's yet another lurid and trivial teens-amok movie. The producers tried to have their cheesecake and eat it too – by making an exploitative film about exploitation.

But, in the middle of all this misery, Tom became close friends with another young tearaway of an actor called John Stockwell, who later appeared with the star in *Top Gun*. Both were just twenty years of age, and Stockwell has provided the first-ever insight into the other side of Tom Cruise at this important stage in his career. 'Certainly lots of things happened on *Losin' It* but I just know he would not want these things disseminated. I have nothing against the guy – it is not to my advantage to say anything bad about him,' explained a nervous Stockwell during an interview at his West Hollywood home in the spring of 1994. 'Sure, it would be more fun to say something bad about him. Who needs to hear all that stuff about what a great guy Tom Cruise is yet again?'

Now a movie director as well as an actor, Stockwell stated that he was very worried that anything he said about Tom could create big problems for him with the hierarchy that rules Hollywood today and includes a certain Thomas Cruise Mapother IV. But he still managed to drop some pretty strong hints about the star's behaviour while on *Losin' It*. 'The stuff I know is wild, behind-the-scenes stuff, but unfortunately I know he would not be too happy to hear it.'

Stockwell said that he and Cruise became good drinking buddies the moment the *Losin' It* production hit the border town of Calexico, where more than fifty per cent of the movie was shot. 'Tom definitely knew how to relax. The problem is that if this ever got out, you know, the kind of things I could talk about could only have come from me. It was crazy out there, we were just kids.'

Another actor who got to know Tom during the making of *Losin' It* explained to me: 'Off the record? Tom was into girls and booze just like the rest of us. He had a healthy appetite and sure enjoyed himself during *Losin' It*.'

That same informant spoke in graphic detail about an incident Cruise got involved in at the notorious Club Lingerie in West Hollywood, when the *Losin' It* production team were shooting in LA after the Calexico location had been wrapped. 'Tom and a couple of buddies were in the Lingerie one night and things got a little out of hand. The club was filled with girls. The atmosphere was electric.

'Anyway, Tom was knocking back the beers like the rest of us and he got dancing with this fantastic-looking Asian girl. She was gyrating all over him. As Tom danced closer and closer to the girl, he leaned down and whispered something to the girl and the next moment she pulled a gun on him!

'We couldn't believe our eyes and Tom was terrified. She started shouting and swearing at poor Tommy. He was completely out of his depth. She kept waving the gun in his direction. We grabbed Tommy and got the hell out of that club as fast as possible.'

This story is interesting because it shows that even career-obsessed Tom was capable of unwinding when he felt like it, although the incident does seem a rather ominous mirror of the role he was playing in *Losin' It* at the time!

Back in Calexico, according to John Stockwell, the young women from the Mexican border town were forever throwing themselves at the handsome young actors starring in *Losin' It*. 'There were young girls everywhere. It was typically silly young men's behaviour. We got into everything.'

Up until that point and, in fact, for many years afterwards, rumours of Tom's lack of interest in sex circulated. But back in those swinging days of the early eighties, Tom was far from celibate. 'He was hardly a virgin!' said Stockwell.

Interestingly, Stockwell – one of the few people who knows Tom on a personal level to ever speak out – says that the actor has a side to him that 'always knew he would become a star. Even at the point where he had done nothing he was very aware of fans and treating people well.'

Along with Stockwell and the other main stars of *Losin' It*, Tom had been staying in a scruffy two-star hotel throughout their earlier stay in Calexico. Tom had the annoying habit of challenging Stockwell and the other young cast members to wrestling competitions when things got a bit tedious during the long, boring evenings. 'He was always challenging you to wrestle. He was very good at it and you'd always end up on the grass somewhere trying to put each other into headlocks or squeezing the life out of each other.'

Stockwell's opinion of both himself and his soon-to-be-very-famous co-star is refreshingly unaffected. 'We were all so deeply superficial. We were typical actors who thought everything we were doing was incredibly important. It is all a mystery how anyone gets to become a huge star. There is no rhyme or reason.'

While he was very careful about revealing too much of Tom's personal life, Stockwell did describe his old pal's performance in *Losin' It* as 'awful'. 'I would have disowned that film if I had been him. It was a misguided project although at the time he was very serious about it and actually thought it was going to be a really important movie. He was very earnest about the way he approached it.'

One of the biggest surprises about *Losin' It* was that it was directed by Curtis Hanson, a highly regarded up-and-coming director who went on, in 1991, to direct *The Hand That Rocks the Cradle*, which grossed more than $100 million. 'But it doesn't matter how good the director is, if you've got a lousy script you may as well get a ten-year-old kid to direct – it's cheaper,' said one cast member on the movie.

Another, slightly older actor on *Losin' It* – he was thirty-one at the time – was Central American Mario Marcelino, who had just signed a lucrative contract to appear on the popular soap opera *Falcon Crest*. He got a completely different impression of Tom during the location shoot in Calexico. 'I talked to him one time and all he could speak about was his career, his agent. How he'd got his agent to put him up for some movie and how he was about to fly back to New York to do publicity on *Taps*. I felt as if I was in the presence of a whirlwind. I had never met a kid so intent on making it,' explained Mario.

He said that Tom kept to himself and only hung out with the much younger actors. He also noted that Tom never once mentioned his own personal life. 'It was as if it did not exist. His energy and drive was apparent from the start but what depressed me was that his focus seemed more important than his acting skills. Here was a kid who was a lucky guy because he was not that good. Everyone will tell you the same thing.'

Fellow actor Kale Brown was just as stunned by workaholic Tom's outlook during the *Losin' It* shoot. 'The kid was so focused. He was doing press-ups on the floor with that killer look in his eyes whenever there was a break in filming. I hope Tom has remained sane because it is so easy to get screwed up and insulate yourself. That's what stardom is all about. You form a wall around you and feel messed up.'

The film's makers had decided to dress up the normally dreary town of Calexico and transform it into Tijuana because the logistics of filming in the USA were considerably easier. Mario Marcelino was outraged by the way many of the cast and crew treated the local labour who streamed across the nearby border in the hope of picking up a day's work on the big Hollywood movie that was the talk of the town. 'They treated the locals pretty badly and paid them just $15 a day to work as extras. I was appalled. These people were very poor. They were not used to it. I thought the film ended up giving a lousy impression of Mexicans and that deeply offended me.'

Tom had learned the hard way that you never really know how low you can sink until you've hit rock bottom. Now he'd plumbed the depths of teenage schlock and could use his new-found wisdom and experience to future advantage. He admitted the importance of his one bad career move when he said: 'I can look at it and say, "Thank God I've grown." I thought anyone could make a great movie; all you had to do was knock yourself out. I didn't know anything about anything.'

He promised himself never to make another film like *Losin' It*. 'It was a real eye-opener. It made me understand how you really have to be careful … you've got to examine all the elements of a project. I learned a great lesson in doing that movie. I realised that I'd have to learn how to survive in this business and not let it eat me up. I knew that the kinds of films I wanted to work on from then on had to be made by the best people. There I was, with the opportunity to be a working actor, and I remember thinking that this wasn't going to last forever.

'Money was never a factor with me – I wanted to learn on a film. Money goes, but what you learn can't be taken away from you. Even though the film wasn't as bad as it could have been, it still wasn't the kind I wanted to be involved with.'

Tom was so determined not to get lost in the non-stop Hollywood shuffle of talent and end up being a disposable, average teen idol that he turned down $70,000 and a first-class plane ticket to do a horror film, simply because it wasn't something he wanted to be associated with. He wanted only the best and he was prepared to wait, however long it took.

Picking himself up by the bootstraps, Tom decided to try again. Having witnessed mediocrity, he decided his next serious project was not his next movie role – it was to find the right agent. Within weeks he met Paula Wagner, not much older than himself and on exactly the same wavelength as far as commitment to work was concerned. He outlined his career aspirations to Paula: to grow as an artist, to work with the best people and not to care about money. She took him on and he soon found himself returning to the fold with a new serious commitment to acting, along with a determination not to make any more sacrifices of his pride.

8

*I know where I am. I do my work,
and that's the important thing.
I'll let it speak for itself.*

TOM CRUISE

While *Taps* might well have gone down in Hollywood history as the first Brat Pack movie, Tom Cruise's next appearance on the big screen was considered the classic of its genre. *The Outsiders* went far beyond the usual parameters of the traditional teen flick. It was a sensitive, panoramic drama, devoid of cheap shots and naked cheerleaders. Its box-office success was negligible, but it is still considered a youth-market classic and the movie's overwhelming popularity as a video proves its durability. It is even reckoned that thousands of converts joined the ranks of old fans each year to watch the movie time after time.

It was around this time that Tom became aware of the fact he was being described as a senior member of the Brat Pack – and he was singularly unimpressed. 'I think I was in New York. Someone told me about the Brat Pack and that's when I realised I was a brat. "I'm a brat, Mom." "Girls, I'm a brat." What are you going to say about something like that? I mean, how do I get lumped with that?'

What angered Tom was that he believed that being lumped together with a group of other actors could seriously damage him professionally by encouraging the sort of typecasting he was desperately trying to avoid. 'The thing is, there really isn't a community of actors. I mean that is false, absolutely false. There is not a community where we get together and sit down. The term "Brat Pack" is a bunch of crap, a lot of bullshit.'

Although *The Outsiders* hardly rated one decent review from the critics, it was an undisputed hit with its intended audience. For once, the quality of a film's ingredients – a classic story, a legendary director and a collection of talented young actors – won the day.

The movie also expressed an attitude towards teenagers rarely displayed in any facet of the media. Perhaps twelve-year-old Todd Camhe, who reviewed it on its release put it best: '*The Outsiders* is the first movie that's just about kids and their problems. I think that's important ... most movies and shows with kids in them are about senior proms and high school and buying convertibles. *The Outsiders* is a lot more realistic. The kids all have flaws. They're not the usual stereotypes.'

But then this was a rare movie project for other reasons as well. The novel upon which it was based was located in classic Middle America – Tulsa, Oklahoma. Tulsa is a typical Midwestern city, with a heavy concentration of oil and agricultural industries. It's a sometimes uneasy blend of rural and urban, and when the novel's author, Susie Hinton, was growing up in the sixties, the populace mainly defined its social order in monetary terms. In areas where religious and racial groups are fairly consistent, social conventions are usually reduced to one main definer – the 'haves' and the 'have nots'.

The Outsiders was inspired when one of Hinton's 'have-not' school friends got a severe beating at the hands of several 'haves'. The poor kids formed a gang called 'The Greasers' and the rich kids were labelled 'The Socs' (as in 'socials' and pronounced 'So-shez'). Soon Hinton's initial essay had grown into a best-selling novel, published in 1967. She even used the gender-concealing pseudonym S.E. Hinton so as not to alienate young male readers who didn't normally gravitate towards female writers.

It became, quite simply, a book that millions of American kids read. *The Outsiders* had a broad-based appeal that was obvious to publishers, but for years it went unnoticed in Hollywood. Many later theorised that there simply was not anyone 'in touch' enough to appreciate the novel's youthful message. In the end, it arrived on the big screen via extremely unusual circumstances.

Jo Ellen Misakian, a librarian at the Lone Star Elementary School in Fresno, California, noticed that many of her students seemed to idolise *The Outsiders*. She began to wonder why the book had not been scooped up by Hollywood years previously and after much consideration decided to put the idea to Francis Ford Coppola, the executive producer of another student favourite, *The Black Stallion*. Soon Misakian had managed to get up a petition signed by her students and sent it off to the master director with a copy of *The Outsiders*.

Coppola immediately responded, recognising the novel's movie potential and assigning one of his producers, Fred Roos – who made *The Black Stallion* with him – to buy up the book rights and begin the process of getting a screenplay written. Susie Hinton asked for the not unreasonable sum of $5000 for an option to film her book, but Coppola's company, Zoetrobe, was in so much trouble at the time that she was persuaded to take a down payment of $500. Coppola, director of such movie masterpieces as *The Godfather* series, had originally intended to hand the movie over to another helmsman to direct, but as the months of negotiating and writing progressed he found it impossible to let go of the project.

So, after much soul-searching and a little criticism within the media that Coppola, in his mid-forties, was too old to handle such a youth-orientated subject, he officially got the movie green-lighted. Hinton herself was welcomed on board the pre-production team. As a consultant, she would verify the authenticity of the settings, surroundings and general feel of the movie's backgrounds. She also insisted on having a substantial input into the casting, especially the hiring of handsome Matt Dillon to play one of the leading roles as Dallas Winston.

Word of *The Outsiders* reached the ears of young Tom Cruise during the Christmas holiday period of 1981. Bitterly re-educated about Hollywood, thanks to his awful experiences on *Losin' It*, he had already taken decisive action to rectify his career by hiring new agent Paula Wagner. The pair had agreed to look for quality rather than quantity. 'I learned the things I wanted and I didn't want,' he explained.

The Outsiders instantly struck a chord with Tom because it was one of the few novels he had read in his youth, his reading having been curtailed by his dyslexia. He had started to cope with scripts by reading slowly through them and conjuring up visions of what he read. But *The Outsiders* had opened up his perspective on life, as it had done for an estimated three million other young readers. He had been profoundly affected by the book.

Ironically, another agent who was touting for Tom at the time had laughed when Tom told him of his aspirations to appear in a Coppola movie. 'Francis! He's not going to pay you anything!'

However, Paula Wagner had a savvy eye for good projects and she had gelled so instantly with Tom that he felt complete and utter trust in her judgement. She seemed to be able to second-guess his opinions and the magical mental shorthand they shared made young Tom feel much more secure. Once again a female was leading the way for him and he felt perfectly comfortable in that knowledge. Paula was already becoming like a fourth sister to him.

The go-ahead pair planned the actor's assault on Coppola with military precision. Tom was absolutely and utterly determined to get a part in *The Outsiders*. He had felt like an outsider for most of his life and he was not about to let such a wonderful opportunity slip from his grasp. Paula suggested he pay for his own airfare from New York to Los Angeles and fly into an audition that was to be held the following week. He wasn't even necessarily after a big role – Tom just wanted any part in that movie. He called his new friend Emilio Estevez on the West Coast and begged a free bed for his entire stay in Hollywood. Emilio had already been virtually assured of a major role in *The Outsiders* and was naturally keen to encourage his pal to join him.

'I didn't feel I could carry a film. I hadn't learned enough and I felt that I would be eaten alive,' Tom later explained. After the initial audition, he pulled Coppola aside and pleaded: ' Look, I don't care what role you give me. I really want to work with you. I want to be there on the set and watch. I'll do anything it takes; I'll play any role in this.' It was a brave move – and it worked. Tom ended up with the relatively small role of Steve Randle. But the part as one of the 'have-not' Greasers suited him down to the ground. 'I took *The Outsiders* over a lot of other things. It was a small role ... but I was ecstatic to get that role because, at nineteen, I was going to work with Francis Ford Coppola.'

Tom could easily relate to the role of a poor kid rejected by most of his peers. 'Being the new kid in town was very intense. The cliques, you know. You've got your Democrats over here, your Republicans over there, your country-club kids, the athletes, the writers all over the place. And then there was me. I didn't fit into any group.'

Those experiences had also given him a self-destructive edge – an ideal ingredient for any angry young actor. Tom saw himself as 'reckless'. 'I'm still that way, but in a more specific way. My recklessness goes through to my work. I was always looking for attention. I'd get into fights. I think it was out of a need to be creative because if you can't create, you eventually start to destroy yourself.'

Tom had the perfect background. Not for the first or the last time, he was fully intending to use his real-life experiences to help him gain invaluable momentum on a particular acting role.

When casting was finalised and contracts settled, the names lined up to appear in *The Outsiders* read like a millionaire boys' club or a roll-call of future American film-makers: Tom Cruise, Emilio Estevez, Rob Lowe, C. Thomas Howell, Matt Dillon, Ralph Macchio and Patrick Swayze. And, amazingly, all these hot young names were apparently more than happy to share the limelight. It all seemed too good to be true.

'It was very chaotic,' explained Rob Lowe. 'But that's what was so great about it. Francis is like a giant chef. He'll say, "I need a little more of this and little less of that." He doesn't know exactly until he tastes.'

Coppola launched his mega-name production in Oklahoma in March 1982. For location filming, he insisted there was no substitute for the Midwest's wide-open spaces and gigantic skyscapes. Like an artist painting a canvas, he used the colourful sunsets and clear skies as an allegory. As is traditional for Coppola, his explanation for such film-making was masterful: 'Even as we look at a sunset, we are aware that it is already starting to die. Youth, too, is like that: at the very moment of perfection you can already see the forces that are undoing it. *The Outsiders* takes place in an enchanted moment of time in the lives of all these boys. I wanted to catch that moment; I wanted to take these young street rats and give them heroic proportions.'

As with *Taps*, preparations for actual performances were very intense. Susie Hinton laid out meticulously detailed explanations of her characters' backgrounds and motivation to avoid any actor's interpretation ending up being flat and stereotyped. Pounds of pomade were coated on to Tom's dark locks as that was the Greasers' battle flag, waved by kids too poor to express themselves in any other material way. It was their identity, their version of the varsity letter.

'I remember feeling very good, building up confidence in my own instincts on acting. And understanding more on each level; learning more about film acting and what I wanted to do,' said Tom. He took on the task at hand with his customary intensity, even though his role ended up amounting to less actual screen time than anything he had done since *Endless Love*. His relentless determination to give 120 per cent, combined with his off-screen antics, managed to attract a healthy handful of publicity. His hair already doused with grease, Tom also removed the cap from his chipped tooth (a little souvenir he received during a hockey match) and avoided showering for the majority of the next nine weeks. He was probably not a very desirable dinner companion, but he certainly made his presence felt.

Increasingly, method acting motivated Tom's madness and he was delighted to find in 'Mr Coppola', as he called him deferentially, a firm supporter. For the director was an avid believer in rigorous character analysis. He insisted that his actors digest their roles with incredible thoroughness. Coppola even created a specific environment, including stringent Nautilus, gymnastics and tai chi ch'uan workouts three times a day, to shape the Greasers' bodies to perfection.

Typically, Coppola took this attention to method one stage further by insisting that the 'haves', the actors playing the Socs, stay in fancy hotels, receive their scripts bound in leather, be paid generous daily allowances and generally be pampered and spoilt. Meanwhile the Greasers – who were the real stars of the movie – got absolutely nothing. They had minuscule rooms with no maid service, crumpled, stained scripts and a pathetic amount of pocket money.

Coppola was determined to create real antagonism and he succeeded with ease. His face lit up with delight when he attended a weekend football match between the Socs and Greasers which nearly ended in a real-life bloodbath as tempers frayed and fists flew. Then it was time to start shooting.

Tom wasn't the only actor doing his homework. Virtually everyone seemed to be playing 'Let's pretend' off and on screen and at one stage it got so bad that people seemed to have completely forgotten the golden line between fact and fantasy. The most notorious episode occurred when Coppola suggested to Matt Dillon that he needed a little practical experience as a shoplifter. A camera actually followed at a discreet distance as Matt and two other Greasers wandered ever so casually into a local store, snatched some cigarettes and exited without being noticed by the store keeper.

Co-star C. Thomas Howell recalled later: 'Francis sent Matt Dillon, Ralph Macchio and myself to steal the cigarettes. He followed us with a camera. We stole the cigarettes and left, but didn't know what to do with them. So we went back in and said, "We stole them." They threw a big fit, but when they saw that we were actors, it was okay. We got away with it ... actors have so many excuses.'

It is interesting to note that Tom Cruise was not involved in this escapade. One insider on the set said that he preferred to internalise his character by sitting alone for hours rehearsing a tough Greaser voice over and over again. In any case, Tom's honest upbringing by Mary Lee would never allow him to steal, even in the name of his art.

Heart-throb Rob Lowe was sent off to work in a real gas station to get into his character as a high-school dropout who works with Tom's character, Steve Randle. But that was only the beginning. Tom and the other Greasers were requested by Coppola to vacate their dingy motel rooms and spend a week with the real Greasers who were featured in Hinton's book.

'Of course now they're adults,' explained a bemused Lowe. 'We'd talk with 'em... I mean it was kind of a strange situation. I'd never met these people before. "Hi, I'm here to spend a few nights with you. Coppola arranged it." "Oh yeah, sure, come on in." A little bizarre.'

One day Coppola even herded his young charges into a crowded restaurant and encouraged them to act like the ultimate vandals and troublemakers. The guys harassed the waitresses, flung food everywhere and caused non-stop trouble while Coppola sat at another table a safe distance away and observed like some master controller witnessing the antics of his slaves, a sly grin on his face and the occasional raised eyebrow being the only evidence of his approval or disapproval. This was serious stuff on the method-acting front, but some of the youngsters, including Tom, felt uncomfortable acting as hooligans in real life. Tom believed that the true sign of a professional actor was his ability to get into a specific role, not perform for others before the camera even started rolling.

But Coppola (many of the cast referred to him as 'Father Film') clearly enjoyed the danger. It was as if he was reliving his own youthful fantasies through the outrageous actions of his cast. He had a special attachment to teenagers. 'I had been a camp counsellor when I was younger,' he told one journalist after shooting wrapped on the movie. 'I always got along very well with kids. I like being with kids rather than adults.' Papa Coppola was always available to any of the actors if they sought advice or wanted to go over the details of a specific scene.

Tom felt more at home with the cast of *The Outsiders* than on any other movie he had worked on. There was a comradely spirit, a feeling that they were all in it together. Egos had been dropped in favour of old-fashioned friendship.

After keeping a low profile at the start of the shoot, Tom started to gain confidence and come out of his shell. After all, he was there among true soulmates – actors with whom he could talk all day and all night if necessary. His dream had come true. Now he could relax among friends and a new Tom started to emerge, someone who could match any of the wildness on display.

In one extraordinary scenario, he put honey on co-star Diane Lane's toilet seat and inscribed 'Helter Skelter' on the mirror of her hotel room. The actress's response is unknown but some inside *The Outsiders* production felt it was a particularly tasteless episode and confirmed that Tom still had a lot of growing up to do. However, some of his young friends were full of admiration and pleasant surprise – they had thought Tom was pretty square and not capable of any skulduggery.

Within a few days of the honey-on-the-toilet-seat episode, Tom's great new friend Emilio Estevez retaliated by rubbing human faeces on his doorknob. Papa Coppola had wanted real louts and now he had them.

All the stars faced a barrage of about five hundred lusting teenage girls each time they stepped outside the Excelsior Hotel. According to one witness who spent some time at the location, there was, besides the horseplay and beer guzzling, a lot of sex between some of the visiting celebs and local girls. Even the computer games Coppola had installed in his production offices weren't enough to cool off the hot libidos.

For much of the production, unit publicist Beverly Walker played mother hen and she was even responsible for killing the first set of still photos taken for publicity purposes because there was too much 'crotch posing' by Tom and the boys – great for gays and wishful females but not the class act one expects from a Coppola production. Ultimately, the crotch-posing incident highlighted a problem for the movie's makers. Whether they liked it or not, they had a cast filled with heart-throbs out of the pages of *Sixteen* magazine.

In the end a happy medium was found in which actors gave both serious and trivial interviews for the sake of the film.

Overall it was a happy set. Coppola enjoyed the kids and they got an equal kick out of him. He paid them the ultimate compliment by treating them just like grown-up actors, encouraging their input, allowing them to improvise dialogue, letting them devise details to bring their characters to life. Emilio Estevez even dreamed up his own hairdo, a grotesque Vaselined ducktail with a front flip that no professional hairdresser could ever (or would ever wish to) get just right. Furthermore, given the unlimited amount of beer Tom and the others were allowed to guzzle after each day's shoot, the kids didn't even mind the long work days, which sometimes lasted eighteen hours. Then there was Coppola's home-made pasta. Often he would cook up some tasty dishes for the assembled youngsters and watch them hungrily devour every morsel. *The Outsiders* was certainly not the traditional Hollywood movie.

About halfway through the shoot Tom invited his cousin William R. Mapother Jr to join him for a few days on the set. The young Louisville resident had a great time hobnobbing with some of the world's most exciting young actors. He played racquetball with Rob Lowe and found Matt Dillon 'a really nice guy. He usually plays a redneck but he's not like that at all.' William, one of Tom's closest confidants, later joined Tom's production company in Los Angeles as head of film development.

Tom's own part in *The Outsiders* was always small, but plainly something was missing in the final version of the movie. There are even several scenes where Tom is in the background but doesn't participate in the action. Unfortunately, much of the action ended up on the cutting-room floor, along with a large chunk of other footage, including much of Rob Lowe's performance. Coppola was overruled by studio executives who, having spent $10 million on the production, did not approve of the version he presented to them. Even so-called powerful directors like Coppola often lose control of the final cut of a film if the producers have retained the power to make artistic decisions.

Meanwhile, within weeks of wrapping *The Outsiders*, Coppola was planning to launch another tough production, this time of a project called *Rumble Fish* and based on another S.E. Hinton novel. Tom, along with many of the cast and crew from the recently completed film, was approached to appear in the new movie, but he had already lined up something very special that he had kept under wraps from everyone on *The Outsiders*. Reluctantly, he rejected Coppola's offer of another film. Since then the director has rarely given Tom a mention when talking about his experiences on *The Outsiders*, although he does regularly refer to Matt Dillon as 'one of the best young actors to emerge since the Brando–Dean era'.

Not surprisingly, *The Outsiders* opened to mixed reviews after being deliberately moulded with an adult audience in mind. *Time* said it all in one headline: 'Playing Tough, Going Nowhere'. Peter Rainer, writing in the *Los Angeles Herald Examiner*, called it a 'gutsy, overblown vacuum'. Vincent Canby, in the *New York Times*, labelled it as 'spectacularly out of touch ... as if someone had handed Verdi a copy of "The Hardy Boys Attend a Rumble" and, holding a gun to the poor man's head, forced him to use it as a libretto'. There were even stranger reviews, like that of *New York* magazine's David Denby, who dubbed it 'the cinematic equivalent of purple prose'. However, John Engstrom, in the *Boston Globe*, hailed it as 'a small, sincere and nearly perfectly realised film about adolescence in Oklahoma' and praised Coppola's 'cool restraint', while *Variety*, often a down-to-earth judge, regarded the production as being like a 1950s drama about problem kids.

The most damning review came from Andrew Sarris, in the *Village Voice*. He complained: 'Coppola has treated very slight material with an excess of emotional display that is embarrassing to watch with a straight face. Much of the dialogue is so yearningly "sensitive" that many of the lines sounded like song cues, and many of the images are so blatantly homoerotic, that I was tempted to look in the final credits for Kenneth Anger's name as a consultant.' Hell hath no fury like a critic scorned.

But at least the young actor's tens of thousands of lusty young female fans were satisfied. As Tom's cousin William explained after attending the movie: 'The majority of the audience was seventh- and eighth-grade girls, who were screaming and yelling over Matt Dillon and the other guys. When one of them took off his shirt, they really freaked out!' When asked his own opinion of the movie, William tactfully replied: 'Well, I'm not a movie critic, but I thought some parts were good and emotional and other parts could have been acted better. The movie ended on a depressing note, not upbeat.'

Todd Camhe, the youngster whose review is still considered the most worthwhile, made what many consider to be the correct interpretation of the movie. 'Most of the critics are looking at the kids in the movie as characters with problems, but they don't really identify with them because they don't care. I don't think it's true that kids never talk about poetry or sunsets. The kids in the movie are talking to their best friends, so they don't have to worry about acting cool or tough ... the reviewers have been saying that *The Outsiders* is only for kids, but I think it's for grown-ups as well. People over fifty probably won't like it, but they don't like many movies anyway.'

Tom Cruise was perfectly happy with his performance in *The Outsiders*. 'It was never a main role, but I created something. That was where I learned I had a sense of comedy. I still want to work with Francis again.' He felt it had put him back on track and he and agent Paula Wagner had already secretly cast around for the perfect starring vehicle to help lift his career towards superstardom.

9

The dream is always the same.
JOEL GOODSEN IN RISKY BUSINESS

Tom's eye for the main chance had proved itself when he managed to slip quietly out of Oklahoma to fly to Los Angeles during the later stages of filming *The Outsiders* to read for a leading role that was to catapult him to superstardom.

Young writer-director Paul Brickman had originally fought strongly against having the young actor even come in for an audition for his teen-orientated movie project *Risky Business*. After seeing him play the crazy rookie in *Taps*, he believed that Tom was 'too much of a psycho'.

The director had in mind someone altogether more gentle and charming for the lead role in his carefully nurtured project. The character he was thinking about constantly was called Joel Goodsen, a basically nice teenager who ends up in a heap of trouble after his parents decide to leave him home alone for the weekend.

Brickman seemed flat, almost uninterested when Tom turned up at the audition. But the young actor and his agent Paula Wagner had seen the script and they both knew the movie was the perfect starring vehicle for Tom. Up until then his potential as an actor had been barely tapped – the roles he played had either been too small or lacked the depth needed to demonstrate his capabilities.

Over lunch with producer Steve Tisch, Paula Wagner had come up with an outrageous ruse to get Tom into the casting meeting. 'The idea was,' explained Tisch, 'that he'd drop in on me as if we were old friends and I'd take him to meet Paul Brickman.'

And that is precisely what happened. Cruise and Tisch even persuaded Brickman to agree to meet them at 5 a.m. on a Sunday morning, much against his better judgement. To make matters even more dubious, Tom looked about as far removed from a pampered teenager as one can get because he was still tattooed and greasy, as well as bearing the sinuous muscles of the street brawler he had been playing in *The Outsiders*. A flash of that famous smile even revealed a chipped tooth. This was going to be an uphill struggle.

Tom's extraordinary appearance did nothing to dispel Brickman's apathy; he was completely pumped up physically and still talking in an Oklahoma accent when the reading began. But once Tom settled down and began adjusting his reading of the *Risky Business* script, the director sat up and began to take notice. 'When he read for the part, he stopped himself halfway through and said, "Wait, I think I can go in this direction," and started over again,' recalled Brickman, who saw this as a courageous thing for a young actor to do. But, as he explained: 'Tom is a courageous guy. He's got a will for excellence.'

It's a telling testimony to the expressiveness of Tom's acting ability that he managed to convey Joel Goodsen's warmth and candour despite his hard-edged appearance. When Tom returned for a final tryout his schedule was just as tight – he flew in at 1 a.m. for another early-morning appointment and had to get back to the set of *The Outsiders* in Oklahoma by ten o'clock that evening.

This time he looked even worse than before – his hair was greasy and he was wearing a preppy Adidas shirt. He was stunned to find his co-star, Rebecca De Mornay, sitting there! She had already been cast and the director wanted to be absolutely certain that the two had a certain chemistry. Somehow Tom got over that hurdle as well.

'We were after that combination of youth, beauty and talent,' recalled casting director Nancy Klopper. She was particularly on the lookout for a young Dustin Hoffman who would have the innocence and naivety for that side of the character as well as the sex appeal and pizzazz that young girls would find attractive.

For his part, Tom felt completely at ease with Brickman the moment he saw the look in his eyes following his decision to start reading all over again. The director could have been impatient, fed up with the indecision. Instead he was impressed that this kid from New Jersey had the nerve.

Later Tom explained: 'My best work comes when I'm really communicating with the director and I work great with Brickman.'

The interesting thing about *Risky Business* is that it was essentially, like

Losin' It, about a teenager who loses his virginity. However, there was an edge to it, a sophisticated approach that would put the movie on a much higher pedestal than the sort of ghastly teen-flicks produced since the phenomenal success in 1982 of *Porky's*, which took in a staggering $160 million at the US box office alone. Since then a torrent of similarly mindless sexploitation flicks had flowed unabated, threatening to submerge popcorn-munchers from coast to coast in North America.

Before finally fulfilling Brickman's vision of the perfect actor to play Joel, producer Steve Tisch and Jon Avnet had found the perfect actress to play the role of Lana, the prostitute who transforms Joel's life. They were all healthily besotted by blonde Rebecca De Mornay, who just happened to have made her most memorable screen debut in Francis Ford Coppola's *One From the Heart*, a sentimental, highly stylised and extremely expensive fantasy of Las Vegas nightlife which bombed appallingly at the box office. Rebecca's one and only line in that entire movie was the immortal utterance: 'Excuse me, those are my waffles.'

Rebecca had an interesting background. She was in a rock 'n' roll group at fifteen and starred in a Bruce Lee kung-fu movie only a few years later. She had just the right balance of inaccessibility and cunning. As she herself put it so aptly: 'Lana isn't exactly Miss Warmth. So that's what I gave him.' Combined with Lana's growing sense of attachment and love for Joel, these emotions added to her depth, shading her enigmatic and erotic allure.

Tom, meanwhile, plunged himself head first into his own part as Joel by travelling down to Florida to jog off fourteen pounds he considered that his character simply would not be carrying. 'Florida's hot, really hot,' he explained breathlessly. 'I wanted to sweat as much as possible and I also wanted to get away, to focus myself.' That old familiar word 'focus' was coming into the frame yet again.

After reaching his weight goal, Tom stopped exercising 'so I could put on a little layer of baby fat'. He explained very matter of factly: 'He's a vulnerable person. I didn't want any physical defences up for him. No muscle armour at all.'

Tom also immersed himself in the part of Joel by going to LA's Highland Park area, where the film was located, and hanging out with the local rich kids for a few weeks, getting a feel for their dress code, sense, speech and mannerisms.

The preparation was half the fun for him. 'I enjoy the pressure of making a movie. It's like getting psyched up for a wrestling match – but with higher stakes. I thrive on it.'

Joel is basically an average all-American kid who just happens to have wealthy parents who want him to attend the prestigious Princeton University. To a lesser degree he shares that desire and the movie chronicles what happens after the parents head off for the weekend, leaving him in charge of the house.

Everything goes fine until Joel's sexual urges convince him to contact a call girl, played by Rebecca De Mornay, whom he invites around to the house. Eventually this leads to a clash between Rebecca and her pimp, and later Joel's father's Porsche is accidentally wrecked.

Meanwhile Rebecca makes Joel an offer he can't refuse. If he'll let her and her call-girl colleagues use the house for one weekend as a brothel, he could work as their pimp and use the money to pay for the damage to his father's car. It sounded like the perfect plan, but in Hollywood movies such schemes always end in disaster – unless you happen to have Tom Cruise in the lead role.

In the young actor, Brickman found a perfect embodiment of Joel. In developing this complex character, the director used his scriptwriting expertise to the full, enlivening the character with a wealth of autobiographical touches. For example, Highland Park, where filming began in the autumn of 1982, was where Brickman had spent much of his youth. This gave Tom an excellent opportunity to dig into Brickman's persona for his inspiration.

Risky Business had two sequences that stand out more than any others. The first is when Cruise plays air-guitar to Bob Seger's 'Old Time Rock & Roll'. Tom later explained that this was nothing more than a brief description saying, 'Joel dances in underwear through house', until the confident young actor decided to put his own personal stamp on it.

'I tried it a couple of ways where it didn't work, so I put on my socks, waxed the floor and then put dirt around the area so I could slide right out to the centre of the frame. Then we did the thing with the candlestick – using it as a microphone – and made it into this rock and roll number.'

Moms and daughters alike would swoon at the wondrous sight of Tom coming on like a junior member of the Chippendales as he made his entrance clad only in sweat socks, BVDs and a pink, button-down shirt. Tom improvised all his dance moves on the spot, delivering his impression of a strutting, rocking cock o' the roost. He was dancing and bouncing off the living room furniture, even shimmying on the couch and doing 'the worm'.

The only person on the set not surprised by Tom's off-the-cuff routine was Paul Brickman. 'Tom is able to bridge innocence and heat. It's a difficult range, but he'd got it naturally.'

Single-handedly, Tom transformed a somewhat banal scene into one of the most memorable movie sequences in modern movie history. He later revealed that he got his inspiration from watching disco movies like *Saturday Night Fever* back in Louisville. 'If you couldn't dance you couldn't pick up the girls. All the girls loved to go dancing on Saturday night. I used to watch

American Bandstand and *Soul Train* all the time and I'd rehearse dancing, so that when I showed up at a disco, I could ask girls to dance. I taught myself how to do the robot, spinning and stuff like that. That's what acting is. Finding yourself in roles and bringing aspects of yourself to life. Not being afraid to do that.'

Tom's gyrating in his underwear garnered much attention on its own; TV viewers were treated to it daily in a television ad for the movie and a rock video for Bob Seger's big hit also featured in the clip. It was no mean accomplishment and would no doubt have delighted Joel himself. Enthused Tom: 'With kids, to be a rock star is the ultimate. When their parents leave, they turn the music up. Dancing with your pants off – it's total freedom.'

The second sequence that raised temperatures and consolidated Tom's image as a teenage heart-throb came when he made love to Rebecca's character, Lana, aboard a train – it is almost surrealistic in its erotic imagery. Tom and Rebecca enjoyed a love–hate relationship during the shooting of *Risky Business*. It was a situation that eventually led to a long-term, real-life, live-in love affair. But at the time of filming this controversial scene it seems that love was the furthest thing from both of their minds.

'I remember it was uncomfortable,' recalled Tom with classic understatement. 'A love scene can really step over the line sometimes. I don't mean that I step over the line or that the other person steps over the line – it's just, how far do you go? And although it may be exciting and romantic for the audience – you hope it is, otherwise you're doing it for nothing – it's just kind of uncomfortable.'

The movie proved very popular with the so-called MTV generation as it turned out to be a hell of a ride, a real standout within the teenage comedy genre. In fact, it ranks among the top three, the other two being Rob Reiner's *The Real Thing* and John Hughes's *Ferris Bueller's Day Off*. As *Risky Business*'s producer, Steve Tisch, explained: 'The teen audience has a finely tuned antenna for being hyped. The interest from the studios waned because they could not design movies that worked for that audience. These movies can't be ordered like you order a pizza. It's just as difficult to make a good teen movie as a good thriller or action movie.'

Tom made sure that Joel never became a caricature, always managing to make the character a real one. Rebecca De Mornay proved the perfect sexpot, but a great deal of the credit for the movie's success rightly went to Paul Brickman, who refused to compromise and take the easy path of gratuitous sex or sophomoric humour.

Tom knew that he and Rebecca had pulled off a performance that he could display with pride. 'Hurrah!' he proclaimed. 'Finally there's a love scene with some taste that teenagers will see.' He keenly defended the open sexuality of the movie: 'It's not a woman-being-exploited movie, a T-and-A film with girls' bras popping open and stuff like that. I feel the scenes were shot in a very stylish way and young people appreciate that.'

Somehow Tom even managed to find he shared something in his background with Lana, the prostitute: 'As an actor what do I do except sell myself? I am hired to put my soul on the line. My self. Bring myself into character.'

Within days of the film being edited, rave word-of-mouth praise started to circulate about *Risky Business*. It was what is known in Hollywood terms as a 'sleeper' – a movie that no one expected to be a big hit when it was being made.

Tom was certain *Risky Business* would provide the perfect step up the stardom ladder in Tinseltown. 'It is the first film I carry. It has given me freedom, opened up doors. I'm getting better scripts, a wider variety of characters to play. Producers and directors don't feel like it's a risk letting me star in a film. They trust me.'

His risk-taking had paid off handsomely. Before *Risky Business*, he explained, 'I'd go into a meeting and have to work hard to make them see me, do my juggling act, prove myself to them. Now they say, 'I know he can do it.' They tell my agent, "I'd like to meet him."' Strutting his stuff in a lead role, Tom had proved to the world that he was every inch a star.

As with all good Hollywood movies, there was a major battle over the ending of *Risky Business*. Originally there was a big emotional scene in the restaurant in which Rebecca sits on Joel's lap and it just ends at sunset with Joel stroking her hair as she rests her head on his shoulder. The scene then cuts back and forth and Joel exclaims, 'Isn't life grand?'

But the producers, Geffen Films, wanted the movie to end on a more upbeat, commercial note. At one point Paul Brickman threw a tantrum and refused to film the new ending. The Geffen producers started casting around for a new director to finish off their very expensive investment.

However, Brickman had a keen supporter in Tom Cruise. The young actor was determined not to see his character, Joel, sell out at the end. Finally a compromise was reached which left director and star content if not exactly enthusiastic. 'Joel has to know in his heart that this woman is more important than money. That's what I wanted to get across. A lot of people, when I discuss the ending of the film with them, say Joel didn't sell out – some say he did. It's a subtle film and you walk out with what you want to walk out with. It has so many different levels.'

Risky Business paid off big for everyone concerned. Geffen Films had backed the movie on a budget barely exceeding $5.5 million and it had gone on to gross more than $60 million at the US box office. It also made millions more on cable TV networks and in video sales.

David Geffen, head of Geffen Films and his own highly lucrative music record division, had made tens of millions of dollars from musical megastars like Don Henley and John Lennon. But his previous attempts at film-making had ended in heavy financial losses. *Risky Business* made him personally at least $5 million because of the complex nature of the financial backing of the movie. Geffen, who has been for years a very powerful figure in Hollywood, never forgot the actor who made all those millions of dollars of profit possible.

Ironically, Tom had not been given any percentage share of the profits from *Risky Business* as he had signed for the lead role at a time when his box-office viability was unknown. His fee was understood to have been in the region of $200,000. But then no amount of cash could have bought in the kudos that came with the success of *Risky Business*. On the other hand, Geffen became an overnight fan of Cruise and would have a very substantial influence on the young actor from that moment onwards.

After the film's release, Tom still insisted that starring vehicles were not his only aim in life. 'I am not interested in just starring roles. I'm still interested in character roles. Good films. If I am going to carry a film, I want it to mean something.' He was even insisting that he had been turning down other lead roles because of his wish to do only quality projects.

Despite its heavily pro-youth slant, *Risky Business* got relatively good coverage from the movie reviewers.

Perhaps the least-expected success story resulting from *Risky Business* was the phenomenal boost in sales of RayBan's classic Wayfarer sunglasses. Sales of this model, first introduced in 1952, tripled after audiences got a peek of Tom sporting them in the movie. He dons the shades halfway through the film, transforming Joel into a not-so-naive, slick-talking guy.

The whole art of wearing sunglasses took on new social significance. According to New York fashion consultant David Wolfe, if you're wearing RayBans 'you look like you know what you're talking about'. Tom Cruise helped make Wayfarers RayBan's second-best-selling sunglasses. The Aviator shades he wore in *Top Gun* are rated number one by the company.

With the success of *Risky Business*, a sequel would have seemed an almost certain proposition. But producer Steve Tisch killed the idea stone dead when he told the *Los Angeles Times* that he 'never felt we needed to selfishly capitalise on the success of the movie by rushing out and doing a sequel'.

It seemed very commendable, but there may well be an even simpler answer – Tom Cruise never does sequels; well, not yet anyway. As far as the brand-new star was concerned, money-spinning follow-ups were to be frowned upon because they would divert him from his predestined goal of becoming the world's most successful actor. 'My agent handles the money. I'm interested in the characters. What's important for me now is to keep in focus, keep my mind straight. Right now, we're building a firm foundation for a career. We're looking for growth,' he said with great maturity for one so young.

It all sounded more like the business plan for a major corporation rather than a highly talented artist on the edge of incredible success. But that was the way Tom wanted it to be.

Top left: Tom's great-grandfather, Thomas Cruise Mapother Jr, in 1948.

Top right: Tom's great-grandmother, Mrs Thomas Cruise Mapother, then aged 80, at a bazaar in Louisville in 1957.

Bottom left: Tom's great-great-grandfather Dillon Mapother, who emigrated to Louisville from Ireland in the mid-1800s.

Bottom right: The impressive eight-bedroom mansion near the centre of Louisville, where Tom's great-great-uncle Wible Mapother lived when he was one of the most powerful figures in Kentucky.

Top left: Tom at the St Francis Seminary.

Top right: Tom looking chubbier, and featuring a chipped tooth, in a photograph taken shortly after his parents separated when he was 12 years old.

Bottom: Tom (*second from right*) dressing up for some improvised theatre at his home when he was just 11 years old.

Top left: Marian, one of Tom's two elder sisters.

Top right: Tom's first ever girlfriend, Laurie Hobbs, aged 15.

Bottom: Tom in the Glen Ridge soccer team (*third from left, back row*).

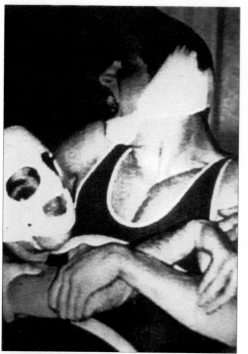

After his exciting first period pin in his last bout, senior Tom Mapother unfortunately suffered multiple muscle injuries before Wednesday's match, and will be sidelined for he remainder of the season.

Top left: Tom in action for the Glen Ridge wrestling team.

Top right: The beautiful mansion on Washington Avenue, Glen Ridge, New Jersey, where Tom moved with his sisters after his mother met Jack South.

Bottom: An excerpt from Tom's first ever appearance in print in the *Glen Ridge Newspaper's* report of a school wrestling match.

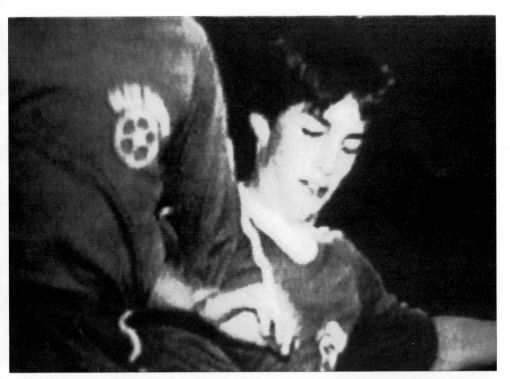

Top: Tom in soccer action at the St Francis Seminary.

Bottom: St Xavier's School, in Louisville, which Tom attended following his parents' divorce.

Tom displaying his powerful good looks – even at the age of 15.

Top: Tom in the Glen Ridge High soccer team.

Bottom: Tom with a classmate at Glen Ridge High.

Top: The imposing St Francis Seminary as it looks today.

Bottom: The Mapother family plot at the Calvary Cemetery in Louisville.

10

Joel always has the brakes on, but Tom
always has his motor running.

PAUL BRICKMAN

The nightclub was virtually steaming with atmosphere. Beautiful women of all sizes, colours and shapes seemed to be lining the walls. Throbbing salsa music was coming from the dance area. The constant hum of conversation, combined with the clink of bottles and glasses, dominated the dining section.

As the two handsome young men tried to make their way through the crowds, every female pair of eyes within range locked on their hunky targets. Tom Cruise and Sean Penn had just arrived and word was spreading through the New York nightspot like wildfire. Pairs of women whispered in each other's ears. There were admiring glances from others, unashamed looks of sheer passion from the bold ones. Then a gasp: Robert De Niro and Mickey Rourke were following just behind the younger stars. This was turning into most women's fantasies all rolled up into one.

Tom was probably the only one that night who felt just a little uneasy at the sight of all those pouting lips and lusting hips. He was more used to cooking himself some pasta at home and sitting back to watch videos of his favourite films, *Casablanca*, *Women in Love* and *Annie Hall*. He looked away each time any of these sensual sirens caught his eye, while Bobby and Mickey just soaked up the atmosphere and the beautiful bevy of women who went with it. The evil grins on their faces said it all. There was a confidence in their swagger that said they had been down this path many times before.

By the time this Hollywood foursome got to their table everyone in the nightclub knew precisely where they were seated, such is the power of being a celluloid hero. Sean Penn tried to relax his young friend. He had known ever since the pair become close pals during the making of *Taps* that beneath the arrogant, confident, ever-focused exterior lay a shy, complicated character who was in reality still a 'short-assed kid from Jersey'. *Risky Business* had just been completed and the word in Hollywood was that it would be a smash hit and its star was going to get a million dollars for his next movie without any difficulty.

Each of the stars ordered a beer and swapped titbits of conversation as the older, more experienced of the foursome, Rourke and De Niro, let their eyes casually drift around the room before locking on to some delightful-looking woman. Tom, meanwhile, kept his eyes locked on the table in front of him and his three companions.

Suddenly, out of nowhere, a well-manicured finger tapped him on the shoulder. He nearly jumped out of his skin. He turned to find a truly magnificent-looking girl, with gorgeous olive skin, leaning towards him. Her tight black mini-dress seemed to grip every curve of her body.

'Hi,' she said ever so calmly. This was the sort of club where old-fashioned etiquette about men only trying to pick up women had long since disappeared.

'Hi,' came the superstar's slightly hesitant reply.

'Mind if I sit down?' This girl had guts and she did not mind showing them.

'Sure,' Tom mumbled, not quite sure why he even responded, but still taken aback by her forwardness.

The following five minutes were taken up by what can only be described as harmless tittle-tattle; polite conversation.

Sean Penn was the only one of the other three men who witnessed what happened next. Mickey and Bobby had long since become immersed in some shapely piece of femininity.

Tom's new best friend leaned over especially close and whispered something in his ear about him coming back to her apartment to continue their in-depth conversation. The young actor's eyes turned instantly to steel.

'I have a girlfriend I'm in love with,' he exclaimed.

Sean Penn heard every word and was astounded. It was also the first time Tom had ever publicly referred to the fact that he was living with Rebecca De Mornay, his beautiful young blonde co-star in *Risky Business*.

'That girl just wanted Tom for his body and she told him, "You should have told me that five minutes ago!"' explained Penn.

This was a significant moment in Tom's career for another reason. By rejecting the girl's advances he was putting on record his determination never to become embroiled in the seedier side of superstardom – something that his three companions that night had enjoyed more than a brief taste of over the years.

For Tom's attitude towards women had been shaped by his admiration and love for his mother Mary Lee and his three sisters. They had guided him through the poverty and heartache, as well as countless awkward teenage moments. Tom could never treat women as mere cattle to be traded up – or traded down – on a whim. He had total and utter respect for the female species and watching them all lined up, waiting to be wined and dined in that New York nightclub, was almost offensive to him.

Tom has never doubted his own tastes and preferences where women are concerned. He deeply values mutual challenge, respect, commitment and independence. 'I like bright, sexy, very sexy women,' he has explained in the past, 'and strong, someone whom I'm not going to run over, someone strong enough to stand up to me.' Tom has great admiration for self-sufficient women with their own careers and personal goals. He sees this quality as an essential ingredient in all relationships. His idea of the perfect woman – even in those far off days when megastardom was still around the corner – was someone stable, but not boring.

'I don't get into habits with someone, the same thing every night,' he confessed. 'I want someone extremely bright and creative. That kind of woman is likely to be pursuing her own vision in life, which for me is ideal. I don't want someone … depending on me for everything, because I do need a lot of time alone.'

The key word for Tom is 'independence'. His lonely childhood, drifting from school to school, made him very self-sufficient and he cannot abide people who are in desperate need the whole time. There were also the classic problems of being in a relationship with someone who might spend three-quarters of the year away from home.

In his terms, a successful relationship required some very special preliminary 'clauses'. He explained: 'You can't say, "Okay, let's keep that thought – I'll be back to you in a couple of months when I finish this."'

Those ideal ingredients seemed to be possessed by Rebecca De Mornay, Tom's first serious girlfriend. Yet no one present during auditions and the first few weeks of shooting *Risky Business* would have guessed there was an iota of passion between them.

Their first encounter came when Tom – still in Greaser mode for his role in *The Outsiders* – turned up for his second audition for *Risky Business* director Paul Brickman. Tom later admitted he took one look at his prospective co-star Miss De Mornay and his libido sounded a red alert. 'I walk in and see this stunning gorgeous woman sitting there looking at me and I'm thinking, "Oh my God,"' he later recalled.

Brickman did make some revealing comments about the sex scenes in

Risky Business which provide ample evidence that true love was always lurking somewhere in Tom and Rebecca's hearts. 'We were able to make the sexual scenes work because of the trust we had in each other. To begin with, I cleared the set except for the cameraman – even the sound people weren't there. I wanted to make it as private for Tom and Rebecca as possible,' he explained. 'If you want to know the truth, those sex scenes were hard work. It was hard to get them [Tom and Rebecca] started, but it was harder to get them to stop!'

Around the time of Tom's alleged attempt to get her removed from *Risky Business*, he bumped into Rebecca in a 7–11 convenience store in West Hollywood. They got talking and, as they say, one thing led to another. They didn't – as was claimed – move into a hotel suite together instantly, but the relationship began to grow into something special.

Rebecca was stunned by the change in Tom's attitude. All their on-set difficulties seemed to have disappeared. He saw it a totally different way; that was business, this is pleasure. In other words, his on-screen tension was solely connected to his work-orientated, highly competitive nature. He saw nothing strange in becoming good friends with someone from a movie they were starring in together. Such is the mind of a highly focused, incredibly ambitious film star like Tom Cruise.

As the couple became reacquainted Rebecca found herself being inexplicably drawn to the vulnerability that Tom had hidden so carefully during work hours. They discovered that they had so much in common. Both had survived the spectre of painful parental divorce and the hardships of growing up without a father. Rebecca's father – well-known Californian right-wing talk-show host Wally George – had separated from her mother, Julie, when she was just an infant. Julie had remarried, but then Rebecca's stepfather, Richard De Mornay, died only two years later.

Rebecca later described her mother as a bohemian. But that lifestyle only took over for Rebecca and her little stepbrother Peter when her then recently bereaved mother decided to embark on an extensive journey through Mexico, Jamaica, Bermuda, England, Germany, France, Spain, Italy and Austria. The young Rebecca learned to adapt to the ever-shifting customs and languages of her many homes. 'I was desperate to fit in ... so I'd adapt a local accent as soon as possible,' she explained. 'I learned to speak German with a perfect Austrian accent.' It sounds like shades of Tom Cruise's upbringing.

Rebecca also become fluent in French and the Queen's English as opposed to the American version. 'When we lived in England the children used to mimic my American accent, so I wound up speaking like a cockney.'

When Rebecca returned to the United States, she felt as disorientated as Tom had by the time he reached Glen Ridge, New Jersey. 'I've always been an outsider trying to fit in,' she explained. 'I worked hard to be accepted.'

But Rebecca harboured no regrets or bitterness about her unorthodox upbringing. 'It was a great learning experience. I'm very American in the way I look at things, but I do know there's another world out there.'

That was where Rebecca differed enormously from Tom. He had not been any further than Mexico and Canada when they first fell in love. However, he found her strong personality and individual resourcefulness very attractive. Soon the couple were dating very regularly, and within months they were living together.

'Rebecca was my first serious girlfriend,' Tom said. 'Living with her was fantastic. She's bright and talented.' For her part, Rebecca described Tom as ' a pure person ... there's something earnest and virtuous about him that's quite rare.' The contrast in descriptions is significant. In Tom's eyes, Rebecca was a wildly extrovert, exciting girl. To Rebecca, Tom was solid, dependable, almost safe.

She had this interpretation of why their relationship evolved. 'There's definitely something different about kids who come from broken homes. They have this sort of searching quality, because you're searching for love and affection, if you've been robbed of a substantial amount of time with your parents. I think that's true of Tom.'

Rebecca also had a very sympathetic understanding of Tom's learning disability because she had a nephew with dyslexia. She constantly helped Tom with script reading and when he got overworked and stressed out – a condition accentuated by dyslexia – she would take extra-special care of him.

Tom, in turn, spent hours poring over various nuances of acting technique to help get even better performances from Rebecca. He taught her to polish and repolish every sentence until it was absolutely perfect. There were no half measures with Tom Cruise.

'She is so strong and honest. I'm already a better person and a better actor because of our relationship. She has a true understanding of what I'm going through, and I also know about the room she needs. Being in the same business can be difficult, though. I go to a movie and see Rebecca doing a love scene with another guy, telling him that she loves him. I'm always facing my fears.'

Tom's stardom – and the intrigue of his relationship with Rebecca – turned up the flame of public interest. *People* magazine asked the couple to pose for a cover; paparazzi stalked them outside their New York hotel. The public started discovering how wholesome, gracious and kind Tom could be. But there were still areas of his life he hadn't yet come to terms with.

One day he stayed on the set of a movie entitled *The Slugger's Wife*, in which Rebecca was starring, and helped her perfect a Southern accent. Cast and crew were astonished to discover Rebecca and her lover going over her lines again and again late one night.

During the latter half of filming on *Risky Business* what had started as a tense battle of egos had transformed into a lovey-dovey hand-holding scenario which had very good side effects for Paul Brickman. For Tom and Rebecca's sizzling train sex scene near the end of the film was made all the more authentic by the couple's real-life love affair.

The biggest test of their relationship came when Tom shipped himself off to London for *Legend*. The film hit major technical difficulties and he spent the best part of a year stranded in England, although Rebecca, who had many old friends in London, did travel over a couple of times.

Ironically, it was after Tom's return to New York that their relationship suddenly began to flounder. They discovered that they had little left in common and parted. It was all done quietly and discreetly – not one word appeared in the press for months.

There was no denying that Tom and Rebecca's break-up was very painful. For Tom it was probably the most emotionally difficult period of his life since his father had walked out ten years earlier. For years afterwards Tom refused to even refer to Rebecca. Later he did refer to the split by saying: 'It wasn't like, "Hey, shake hands. It's been great, baby, let's have lunch." When you care about someone that deeply, it's always difficult, but it wasn't ugly.'

Rebecca was more open about the problems. She hinted at creative difficulties between her and Tom. Certainly a clash of egos would not be surprising in the circumstances. 'There's the potential threat of competition, there's a continual threat of long separations, of major love scenes, of adverse publicity, and of the transitory nature of the business itself,' she explained with remarkable coolness. But then she cited one vital factor that might well have been missing, ultimately, from her relationship with Tom. 'Total understanding of what each other does.'

As far as Tom was concerned, the competitive edge between himself and Rebecca was perfectly healthy. Both were successful, ambitious actors. Surely they could continue to separate work from their home life? But it's never as easy as it sounds.

Tom hinted at the situation when he explained: 'You have to have the strength to separate. People are more prone to stay together for the security, which is something in my life that I have really not done ... if something's not working you've got to face it and move on.' And that was precisely what Tom did.

The break-up was done in a highly civilised fashion. No plate throwing; no bitter fights over possessions; no hurtful jibes in the tabloids. The parting of the ways for Tom and Rebecca took place in a very cool, controlled atmosphere – just the way Tom liked running his life.

Years later he was positively gushing in his praise of Rebecca. 'Living with her was fantastic. She's bright, talented.'

However, Rebecca did say later, rather coldly, when asked if they had stayed on friendly terms, 'No, we're not friends. But we're not enemies either. Tom is a lovely guy, but success caused too much friction. We were both ambitious and hard-working. I'm afraid the ending was not very amicable.'

Tom was relieved – even pleased – that he had avoided being accused of behaving like his lady-killing fellow Brat Packers such as Emilio Estevez, Rob Lowe and, of course, Sean Penn.

But all that changed in 1985, when Tom, then twenty-three, went to the White House for a special dyslexia fund-raiser for the Lab School and ended up meeting singer Cher, aged thirty-nine. The event was overshadowed for Tom by the spark that ignited instantly between the two stars. Tom, wearing a 1920s gangster-style suit, looked positively conservative in comparison with Cher's black and grey gabardine outfit, complete with a vast, jet-black punk-style wig.

At that time Tom was already being hailed as a major star, following the phenomenal success of *Risky Business*. Even his demeanour – which had earlier been that of a slightly baby-faced, chubby-cheeked boy rather than a man – had changed. A butterfly had emerged from the gawky, unformed cocoon and the new Tom Cruise was strikingly handsome and full of confidence and inner assurance.

Cher was riveted from the first moment she saw him. To her, he was handsome in a manly kind of way, yet with oddly boyish expressions and mannerisms. She had also suffered the same sort of chaotic early life and within minutes of meeting at the White House, they were comparing notes on their dyslexia-blighted early years. Later conversations between the pair were to have little to do with learning disabilities.

'Cher was truly mesmerised by Tom at the beginning,' explained one of his former business partners, Stephen Clark. 'She said, "I can't take my eyes off the guy. He's so damn handsome all I want to do is stare at him. Have you ever seen a man with a face like that? And a body like that?"'

At first Cher devoted herself to Tom because she did not believe in going out with more than one man at a time. Her previous lover – movie executive Josh Donen – was pushed aside and Tom and Cher spent long evenings together talking and watching old movies in his New York apartment. The singer told one friend: 'He drives me wild!'

On other occasions during the relationship, Cher would cook Tom meals at her Malibu home, so that they did not have to go out in public and risk being photographed together. At the time, the romance was one of Hollywood's best-kept secrets. Tom even met and got along well with Cher's children, Chastity, just eight years younger than Tom, and Blue, then nine.

Cher and Tom dated off and on for several months. Cher spent a lot of time at Tom's New York apartment, hanging out there for days at a time when he was on the West Coast. Reports that Cher had moved into his place were sparked by sightings of her at the entrance to the apartment block. But she was actually taking advantage of Tom's offer of free use of the apartment while he was away. They never lived together.

In fact, Tom started also seeing another older woman – an actress called Mimi Rogers – at this time but he never considered he was being disloyal to Cher because he did not look on the relationship with the singer as serious. However, Tom's romance with Mimi was so slow to develop that he managed to keep it a secret for months.

Inside Hollywood stories about Cher and Tom began to circulate because they were getting into juicy kissing scenes at Tinseltown parties such as one gathering hosted by Paul Newman. But it should be pointed out that neither was married at the time, so there was nothing morally wrong with what they were doing. It was just considered a little immature, especially on Cher's part.

Tom actually went to the trouble of denying the romance in public. He insisted to *People* magazine: 'Cher is funny and bright and we're good buddies and that's it.'

Cher looked on Tom as a good, handsome young catch at the time. 'But it is debatable whether she ever took him all that seriously as a lover,' explained one Hollywood insider.

And later she even admitted that one of the risks about dating younger men is that they often fall for someone else. 'When you date younger men you gotta be prepared that they might want to try other experiences. It's the risk that you take.'

When it did end, Tom was a little guilt-ridden about his romance with Cher. During their relationship he felt a little embarrassed by the fact that he was dating such an obviously older woman, but he was attracted to the fact that she was so independent. She did not need him, and in a strange way that made him feel more secure. When the affair ended he was also genuinely worried that he might have upset Cher when she later found out about his relationship with Mimi Rogers.

After the break-up it was suggested by friends of the singer that Cher was so crushed by Tom's rejection that she has never got over it and that she compares every man she dates with her 'lost, beloved Tom'. But the truth is probably far simpler – they had a passionate fling that taught Tom how to handle older women and Cher got to date the man who went on to become the world's most successful movie star.

There was never any question of Cher planning anything serious with Tom. Her ego might have been temporarily damaged when Tom chose to get into a relationship with Mimi Rogers, the actress who later became his first wife. In retrospect, what really drew Tom and Cher together was their dyslexia and the memories of a difficult childhood.

Years later Cher proved she had no hard feelings towards Tom by saying she felt genuinely sorry for him when he failed to get the Best Actor Oscar for *Born on the Fourth of July.* 'He deserved it so much!' And she went on in reference to her own Oscar win: 'But I got one eventually – and so, I'm positive, will Tom!'

Other relationships that did reach the popular press included rumours of a hot romance with actress Daryl Hannah. Tom laughed that one off when a friend asked him what she was like when they went on a date. 'I did?' Tom asked incredulously. 'How was I?' He'd never even met Daryl Hannah. 'I don't know why people think I'm running around with everybody.'

Top Gun director Tony Scott – himself something of a ladies' man – described Tom as 'a magnet for women'. But the truth was that even then the young actor was desperate to settle down. Casual relationships were not his favourite way of life.

One time Tom – dressed 'inconspicuously' in RayBan Aviator shades and a bomber jacket – was dining on romantic chilli dogs with a date at the New York celebrity hangout Serendipity 3 when he became increasingly unnerved by a quartet of giggling girls standing nearby gawking at him. When the waiter intervened and told the girls to stop annoying Mr Cruise, Tom rewarded him by paying the $17.50 bill with a $50 note and instructions to keep the change.

But another, much more serious incident really freaked out the young star. It occurred when he was living in a classic New York loft on the West Side. Over a number of days and nights he started to notice that someone with a set of binoculars was spying on him from another apartment block across the street. At first Tom thought that maybe they were not actually aiming their spy gadgetry at him and he ignored it. But, by the third night, Tom was convinced that their binoculars were trained on him.

In a remarkable piece of one-man detective work, he calculated which apartment the spies were using and confronted the bewildered owner of the flat that same night. The man had no idea that his two young daughters had set up the ultimate peep show for their friends. The shocked – and deeply shamed – father immediately offered to board up the girls' window and grounded the young peeping toms for a month. But Tom came up with his own solution, which seemed completely out of character with the shy, reserved young man most knew him to be. He told the father he would take the girls to lunch if they promised not to spy on him ever again. Naturally, they agreed.

Following the split with Rebecca De Mornay, he was also in a rather confused state about whether it was better or worse to date women inside the entertainment industry. His earlier opinions had been tainted somewhat by his most recent experiences and he even went to some lengths to go out with women outside the industry, like lawyers, writers and artists.

'I'm not really sure whether it is an advantage to be with someone in the business. I know I need someone who is adaptable, someone who can go from one extreme environment to the next and not go crazy. Sometimes I get up in the middle of the night and want to work. Other times, I can sleep for days,' explained Tom.

By the middle of 1987 Tom was topping just about every eligible bachelor list in America and Britain. One issue of *US* magazine had a cover featuring Tom, Charlie Sheen, Corbin Bernsen, John Kennedy Jr and Jon Bon Jovi as a few of the country's hottest single men. The viewers of the popular American television show *Entertainment Tonight* voted Tom 'Sexiest Man in Hollywood' with more than 27,000 votes (Don Johnson followed with just 19,000).

But in reality Tom was still the same loner he had always been. He told friends at the time that it did not bother him. But it must have had some effect. As he admitted to movie director Cameron Crowe in 1986: 'It's not easy. I spend a lot of time alone. I mean, a lot of time alone. But I've spent time alone my whole life and it doesn't bother me. I feel lonely at times. It takes time to get to know people.'

It was ironic really. On the streets of New York his success in a string of movies had made Tom a very famous face, although he had a great deal of trouble getting used to being stared at all the time. 'I used to think, "Jesus, is something hanging out of my nose?" It took time to get adjusted to it.'

Meanwhile Tom was still waiting for his perfect woman to appear on the horizon. 'In the final analysis, it's just the person, isn't it?' he remarked once while discussing the ups and downs of finding Ms Right. 'Who knows? One day, I'll just be walking down the street and there she'll be.'

11

I didn't become an actor for money;
the money isn't why I work. It's great
to have, though.

TOM CRUISE

The onset of stardom that came with the runaway success of *Risky Business* caught Tom Cruise completely by surprise. Suddenly he was inundated by press and television coverage; an obligatory media blitzkrieg which fuelled the public's natural curiosity about aspects of Tom's private life that he found very uncomfortable to talk about. The questions were never ending and concerned his love life, his childhood and even the pain of his parents' divorce. Tom was completely unnerved by the entire experience. No one had prepared him for it and he did not know how to respond. 'I'd say to myself, "My God, I've never told anyone about these things before in my life."'

Tom was baffled by the media's obsession with him. He felt mightily uncomfortable being asked such intimate and prying questions. 'You know how it is when you're a kid and you aren't wearing the right kind of shoes and they hang you up in the locker room for being a nerd? Well, I was never wearing the right shoes,' was his cryptic explanation.

During his childhood Tom had always been the new kid in town and he had devised a clever routine to make people accept him easily. He would create new personalities and backgrounds to fit each new situation. But this was different. This was the big, wide, grown-up world and there were a lot of inquisitive people out there wanting to know the truth about Tom Cruise. 'When you travel like that, you can make up who you are. But I couldn't do that in interviews,' he explained.

After *Risky Business* there was also the little matter of Rebecca De Mornay. Their love affair seemed like a movie publicists' dream and some cynical members of the press even tried to suggest that the entire relationship had been created to help promote the film. But, as we already know, Tom and Rebecca's relationship had got off to such a rocky start that it would have been impossible to manipulate the affair.

The whole media circus surrounding *Risky Business* terrified Tom and once he had performed his contractual obligations in terms of interviews and television appearances, he jumped off the publicity merry-go-round. 'I had to say, "Listen, guys, for myself, I'm just not personally ready to do this."'

Tom was already starting to shape his attitudes towards the press and its intrusion into his life. He was later to state that he learned a lot of lessons during those early years; lessons that convinced him to try to take complete and utter control of the flow of interviews and photographs about him in a way no other star has ever attempted. He made no secret of his opinion that the proper perspective on the acting profession places integrity in the foreground and publicity way back on the horizon. 'My art, my craft is the most important thing to me. Keeping my integrity is important, keeping my base... When I look at myself in the mirror, at first I think, "Oh God, why can't I do better work?" But then I see I'm really proud of what I've done.'

Tom was getting fairly obsessed about his work. He had even stopped cracking vaguely amusing one-liners during press interviews As he told one journalist: 'I guess I do get very serious when I talk about my acting. But it is very important to me. I hate that word "career". I try not to focus in on thinking of it as a career. "Career" sounds very money-orientated... I just want to keep focused on my craft.' Whatever way Tom said it, it sounded like he had a one-track mind. And that word 'focus' would not go away.

That was Tom's priority even back in those days. The other key word was 'quality' – or at least what he deemed to be quality. However, movies are not won or lost by one person. They are a team effort, consisting of the skills and failings of hundreds of people and, because of that, every actor, director and technician will make his or her fair share of disappointing films during a career.

But at that time Tom sincerely believed that he had learned all his lessons right at the start, thanks to the appalling *Endless Love* and the sloppy, silly *Losin' It*. He insisted on maintaining his integrity and, besides choosing his movie projects with incredible caution, he also completely clammed up, refusing to give any interviews for the next couple of years.

There was some clever thinking behind his decision. Tom's silence helped create an even greater buzz about himself. Hollywood's main-line players don't read the pages of the tabloids, they concentrate on trade papers like *Variety* and the *Hollywood Reporter*, and both those publications were attaching Tom's name to just about every major project in Tinseltown that required a leading man under the age of thirty. The trades also ran daily columns filled with snippets of inside gossip that fuelled that day's discussion at lunches in restaurants like Spago's and the Ivy.

When one columnist reported that Tom's per-picture fee had rocketed to $1 million, producers all over town took that as confirmation that Tom Cruise was the hottest male actor in Hollywood and they presumed his fee would keep climbing. Many of them started swamping his agent, Paula Wagner, with screenplays.

Most of the projects on offer were the sort of teen flicks that Tom thought he had turned his back on since *Losin' It*. Both he and Paula Wagner soon realised that if his career was to develop on a healthy arc rather than adopt a short-sighted money-grabbing mentality like many others before him, then he should throw every one of those lucrative movie scripts in the rubbish bin and wait until something with a little more depth came along.

So, despite his enviable negotiating position, Tom chose as his next film a rather low-key project that he was convinced would test his acting skills rather than inflate his bank account. Choosing the correct film is a finely balanced decision for a movie star, because if the subject is too dense and heavy-going the movie will probably get nothing more than a limited release before disappearing into oblivion. Choose a rip-roaring piece of commercial tripe and you are more than likely to be laughed out of town by the critics.

Unfortunately, Tom agreed to play the lead in a film that was almost certainly predestined to be overlooked by a mass audience due to its sombre, almost depressing overtones, not to mention a complete lack of Hollywood sparkle. *All the Right Moves* featured Tom in the role of Stef Djordjevic, a high-school football star with more than a passing resemblance to *Risky Business*'s Joel Goodsen.

Stef's main characteristics were just the sort of things Tom felt he could relate to: anxious, insecure, honest, forthright, incorruptible but also determined to win no matter what. There were also elements of Stef's family background that mirrored his own. 'There were times when my father was working,' reflected Tom. 'I remember that for about a year we lived in a nice house in a nice neighbourhood. Then, later on, times really got tough. But it was exciting, it was challenging. And there was a sense of teamwork. We all worked together and when the team broke down there were problems. It wasn't easy.

'I think on certain levels I could identify with the guy. But I didn't need the ticket out. I didn't feel that trapped. I was lucky enough to live in places where I could always make the money.'

Tom's ever-improving ability to remould his body and mind to fit any character he was playing resulted in a complete physical transformation for the role of Stef. He underwent an intense weight-training course and exercise regime to regain the kind of hard-edged physique he had when he portrayed Steve Randle in *The Outsiders*.

It seemed as though no detail was too small for Tom's cosmetic scrutinies. He wanted to ensure that his character would fit in perfectly in the grimy, grey town of Johnstown, Pennsylvania, which was transformed by the film-makers into the fictional Ampipe, Pennsylvania. Tom died his hair jet black and took on the demeanour of a pale, scrawny youth to such good effect that if it hadn't been for his bulging biceps he would have looked extremely sick.

The essence of the story is Stef's dream of escaping the steel mills of Ampipe to make it as a big-time football player. His coach, Vern Nickerson, was played by well-known television actor Craig T. Nelson. He is just as keen to escape the drudgery, and the movie builds up to the game that will determine if both of these characters can finally realise their dreams.

In *All the Right Moves* Stef's girlfriend, Lisa, was played by Lea Thompson, who went on to find fame and fortune in movies such as *Back to the Future* and *Space Camp*. It was Lea's first starring role and her preparations were just as demanding as Tom's. She had to go undercover at a local high school in order to absorb the way of life in a tough, gritty steel town. Lea needed to know the dreams and fears of girls raised in such an environment. Lisa has a predicament even more desperate than Stef's: she aspires to study music, but she's painfully aware that only those with footballing talents ever escape Ampipe.

Tom and Lea hit it off as friends from the moment she was introduced to him during a reading, by contrast with his initially antagonistic attitude towards Rebecca De Mornay. They shared very similar views about movie-making and acting and Lea had very strong, forthright opinions about the sort of roles women are expected to play in films. 'I read a lot of scripts and most of them are about men. Women are just there to be cute and look nice in a bikini. Well, that's absurd. Young women have the same problems growing up that guys do and I think audiences are starting to want more strong female parts in movies, young women who are fun and smart.'

Lea's opinions mirrored almost exactly those of Tom's mother and three sisters and he felt very at ease in her company.

Tom was especially attracted to the part in *All the Right Moves* because the director, Michael Chapman, had been Martin Scorsese's cinematographer on *Taxi Driver* and *Raging Bull*, a film that Tom had seen at least five times with Sean Penn when they became close friends during the shooting of *Taps*.

Tom and Chapman hit it off immediately and before actual production of the movie they would meet at Chapman's house to rewrite certain lines of dialogue to suit Tom's instincts about his character. The young actor had very strong opinions about dialogue and he always insisted on altering elements, even without the involvement of screenwriters if necessary. Tom believed, and still does to this day, that ultimately he was the one who would be damaged by sloppy dialogue and he was determined to ensure that every word he spoke would be completely believable. Like a master craftsman, he would sometimes toil for days on the shape of one sentence just because he felt it did not flow correctly.

Chapman and Tom also held little gatherings at the director's house each Sunday night and invited other actors to their sessions to discuss the characters with them and rework other elements of the script as they went along.

Lea Thompson was very impressed by her co-star's analytical approach to acting. 'He's astonishingly smart the way he knows how to break down scenes in a script before playing them.' She was also astonished to discover the full range of Tom's acting talents. 'He can act younger and more innocent than he really is,' she enthused.

Tom related more to the character of Stef than to any other role he had so far played. When the plot called for him to act out the despair and disappointment of being dropped from the football team, he remembered back to the time when he was sidelined from the wrestling team at Glen Ridge High. He also insisted that no doubles be used in the football sequences and – apart from several staged shots – no one was spared the rigour of full-contact play, even if that risked actual bodily harm. Tom relished the physical contact. It was a bit like being back in school, only the big difference was that this time he got to make the football team.

One day, after a series of head-knocking open-field collisions for the camera with fellow actor Paul Carafotes, Tom showed up looking so cock-eyed that Chapman had him sent to hospital, where tests revealed a minor concussion. The film's consultant for these blood-and-guts sequences was local high-school coach Don Yanessa, who said admiringly: 'I think Carafotes went for the hit so hard 'cause it was his job and I think Cruise really liked it!'

Some critics were very generous in their praise of *All the Right Moves*. Noted reviewer and television personality Roger Ebert proclaimed in the *Chicago Sun-Times*: 'It is an astonishing breakthrough in movies about teenagers.' ABC-TV's Katie Kelly declared: 'Tom Cruise proves once again he is an actor to watch. I really like this one.' Kathleen Carroll of the *New York Daily News* wrote: 'Tom Cruise is exceptionally appealing and his sensitive performance more than matched by that of Lea Thompson. It is a gritty, dignified movie.'

The film itself fared poorly at the box office. *Time* magazine noted: 'This was no chic adolescent fantasy, just a drab ring around the blue collar, and suddenly Cruise had lost the big mo he earned in *Risky Business*.' Movie pundit Edward Gross wrote: 'With the exception of its fairy-tale ending where everything works itself out, *All The Right Moves* is a downright depressing film.'

Premiere magazine probably summed up the movie perfectly when it stated: 'For Cruise's career, it was the time. It solidified his now-preeminent position among Hollywood's young actors.'

Tom's gamble with *All the Right Moves* had paid off handsomely because he was establishing himself at the top of his class rather than sacrificing art for money, or so he thought. Reviewers admired his 'accessibility' – ironic when one considers the extraordinary efforts he has made to remain a very private star. Next to him, fellow Brat Packers were coming off a poor second: Matthew Broderick was compared to Walter Matthau in knee pants, Matt Dillon was dubbed a male-model fantasy (despite Coppola's raving admiration) and Sean Penn was simply earmarked as frighteningly intense – and a troublemaker to boot.

'Cruise's dark eyes, jutting cheekbones and nosebone-smooth jaw are natural tools for conveying moods ranging from astonishment to deep hurt to scant amusement,' gushed writer Fred Schruers. His assessment of Tom's image as conveyed in *All the Right Moves* accurately describes the state of his career at that stage. 'Though Cruise is supposed to be a tough guy, he's not allowed to look bad. He may bumble and screw up, but that girlishly attractive face was never meant to get kicked in,' insisted Schruers. 'When some thugs beat him up, he wears an adroitly placed light-blue bruise; smudged with blast furnace soot, he's all the more fetching, and we know that any minute now the story line is going to lift him up where he belongs.'

Just after completing shooting on *All the Right Moves*, Tom told friends he wanted to try his hand at some New York theatre work in an effort to stretch his acting skills even further. Home at that time tended to be a Samsonite suitcase, but the young star insisted that his 'emotional base' was strong and that was all that mattered.

Amid all the adulation and stardom, Tom's emotional base came crashing down in late 1983 when he learned that his father, Thomas Cruise Mapother III, was seriously ill with cancer. The prognosis was bleak. While Tom had been making *All the Right Moves* his father had been operated on, but doctors had found that the disease had spread to other parts of his stomach.

Since their father had walked out of their lives ten years earlier, Tom and his three sisters had received only the barest snippets of information about him, and to this day Tom has, understandably, remained very sensitive about the subject. It is not even clear if he actually knew anything about his father's travels across the United States in the years after he and Mary Lee separated.

'The family were very protective about the fact that Tom's father had disappeared and I couldn't even broach it during my interview. It was a very sensitive issue,' explained Louisville journalist Roger Fristoe, one of the first people to interview Tom following his early successes. Indeed, Tom's grandmother, Catherine, explained in whispered tones to Fristoe that Tom's father was 'an area she did not think anyone in the family would talk about'.

Throughout this period Tom's cousin Caroline Mapother was a confidante to Catherine, so she gained a unique insight into the whole sad scenario. She says that after the split Tom Sr 'just vanished'. He remarried and drifted across the western side of the United States with his new wife, picking up odd jobs wherever he could still harbouring a dream that one day one of his inventions would earn him a fortune. 'He was a drifter. I felt so sorry for him. He obviously regretted what happened between himself and Tom's mother,' explained Caroline.

Tom's cousin Dillon Mapother, self-appointed family historian, said: 'He was living a hand-to-mouth existence. It was very sad.'

Some time during his travels, Tom Sr parted with wife number two and then became ill, so he finally abandoned his tinpot ambitions and headed back home to Louisville. It was a sad homecoming. The city where his family had always held their heads up high and had enjoyed political and legal influence for at least four generations did not exactly welcome him back with open arms.

Tom Sr's parents, Thomas Cruise Mapother II and Catherine, were naturally relieved to see their wayward son finally come home to the fold. However, his wanderings had turned him into an eccentric character not really capable of blending back into a society like that of Louisville.

With some financial backing from his parents, he rented a small, cheap apartment at the Crestview complex, on Brownsboro Road, a tatty block on a busy main road. Then he persuaded his family to provide financial backing for a book he intended to write on how to invest money wisely – an ironic subject considering his own chaotic working life.

Shortly after that he met and fell in love with Jill Ellison, the wife of a local newspaper executive, and caused another mini-scandal in the tight-knit community by moving her into his apartment. Jill was in her early thirties while he was close to fifty. The cancer was already spreading and he realised that his decision to move back to familiar surroundings was rather fortunate.

Tom Sr was hale and robust right up until the end and he was just as reluctant to talk about his son as Tom was of him. He did not deny that he had failed to keep in touch with his son and he never once tried to take any credit for Tom's success. As for criticising his son's films, he would never have dreamt of doing that. He felt he did not have the right to since he had failed so badly as a parent.

Caroline Mapother says she doesn't know how much Tom is aware of his father's last few years of life. 'Maybe he doesn't know about it all. It's all so sad.'

Bill Ellison, the husband of the woman that Tom's father took up with, said he had no idea where his former wife was now living. Mr Ellison, who works as an editor on the *Louisville Courier-Journal*, said: 'I don't feel this is something I can talk about. I don't know where my former wife is now but I can tell you that she never actually married Mapother. It was a very difficult time for us all.'

One of his colleagues reiterated: 'It is a very delicate matter.'

Caroline last saw Tom Sr shortly before his death when he hosted a book-signing session at the Hawley-Cooke book store in Louisville for his self-published *Winning Through Intimidation*. He steadfastly refused to even attempt to cash in on his son's famous name and insisted on writing under the pen name of Thomas May. Tom Cruise did not show up at the signing.

'He was very ill even then,' explained the manager of Hawley-Cooke. 'His woman friend at the time did all the negotiating for him. She seemed very supportive.'

The book was geared towards the money-grabbing 1980s. 'The theme was somewhat aggressively saying that you should save yourself first, look after number one. It was a pretty aggressive tone, as I recall,' said store manager Bill Schwartz.

A year later, shortly after Tom Sr's death, his girlfriend called the store manager and asked if he wanted to buy some extra copies of the book that Tom Sr had kept. The store manager put them out on his bargain book counter but virtually none of them sold. The book, sadly, was a complete flop.

The Thomas Cruise Mapother III that cousin Caroline met that day at the book signing was a mere shadow of his former self. He had a long, flowing beard and hair, was wearing scruffy jeans and, as Caroline explained: 'He looked like he had, as they say in Kentucky, come from the country and was in trouble. I suppose you could call him a hippy really.'

After news of Tom Sr's illness got out, Tom and his sisters rushed to their father's side; it had been almost five years since he'd last seen his dad. Tom Sr knew his own failings as a parent, but he could not help feeling proud of his son and, having seen his photo in so many newspapers and magazines, he longed to see him one last time. The boy he'd read about seemed so different from the twelve-year-old kid he had abandoned. He feared that their meeting might be acrimonious, but when they were reunited his fears evaporated and all the bitter regrets of the past were forgotten. For Tom, the overwhelming emotional impact of seeing his father that last time would be indelibly imprinted in his mind for ever.

Father, son and daughters cried without shame. The children showed a level of forgiveness that is admirable and they probably made their father's last memory of them a happy, loving one. For Tom Sr had never really expected to ever be reunited with them again.

Tom Cruise was understandably torn apart by the reunion. But at least it cleared up a few of the many unanswered questions about who his father really was and why the family had fallen apart in such tragic circumstances ten years earlier. Tom knew that his father felt deep remorse for what had happened and he greatly regretted that his father had not been a bigger influence on his teenage years.

Caroline Mapother remembers being stunned by the news of Tom Sr's death and the fact that so little was mentioned at the time of his illness. 'It was as if the memory of Tom's father was just wiped from the face of the earth,' she said.

Tom Sr's funeral was a very quiet, very small affair. It is not even clear whether Tom and all his sisters attended the graveside at the Mapother family plot at the Calvary Catholic Cemetery on the outskirts of Louisville.

Today the grey gravestone is virtually unreadable because of the overgrown plants surrounding it. It reads simply: 'Thomas Cruise Mapother III Oct 15, 1934 Jan 9, 1984.'

In 1986 the coffin containing Tom's grandfather, Thomas Cruise Mapother II, was lowered next to that of his son following his death on 17 January that year. Officials at the cemetery said they had rarely seen Tom visiting his father's or grandfather's graveside.

His father's death was Tom's first experience of the death of a loved one and he wondered how he would have coped if he had not had a serious multi-million-dollar career to throw himself into. Just before his father died he had agreed to star in the $30-million movie *Legend*, to be directed by British helmsman Ridley Scott, a man reputed to be capable of painting truly vivid images with film following his fantasy-world epics *Blade Runner* and *Alien*. Tom knew it was going to be a tough, slow process to make the film, but gallantly refused an offer from agent Paula Wagner to get him out of his commitment to the project. He felt he had made a promise and could not break that pledge to Scott and, because of his father's death, he explained later, 'I had this thing, like I had to go through with it.' Tom wanted to re-focus his mind away from the heartache and anguish that he had left behind in Louisville.

Legend also seemed the perfect opportunity to prevent Tom from being pigeonholed in any particular category.

At the beginning of 1984 Tom found himself in London for the *Legend* shoot, cut off from his support system: his family, Rebecca De Mornay and the US movie-making community. To pass the time he began hanging out on the set for hours on end, even when he was not needed by meticulous master craftsman Scott, a gritty Geordie who had already amassed a multi-million-dollar fortune by directing some of the most significant television commercials of the sixties and seventies.

Scott fully appreciated what a gamble the role was for Tom. 'For him to do this movie is very brave … as a career step it's very challenging. Suddenly, he's stepping out of the usual kind of role that a twenty-three-year-old guy is going to do, and into a much more theatrical situation.'

This was a very difficult time for Tom. He took long walks by himself around Hyde Park to try to relieve the boredom and isolation. Uncomfortable thoughts of his father still drifted back. Certainly, Tom liked to be alone, but not all the time, and he found London a cold, grey place where people were not always as instantly friendly as in Kentucky or New Jersey. As usual, he tried hard to immerse himself in the character he was about to play. 'He's very unassuming. He doesn't judge people. He has a great capacity to love. And he's magical, which is nice,' he explained.

Legend's elaborate sets at Pinewood Studios, near London, looked like a sensuous fairy tale, similar to Disney meets Cocteau's *Beauty and the Beast*. The main stage was on the set originally built for the Bond film *Moonraker* and even the extras were having to submit to four-to-five-hour make-up sessions to transform them into elves and fairies. Scott, a former art school student and artist, refused to shoot until everything was absolutely perfectly set up, so the actors, including attractive Mia Sara and Briton Tim Curry, and the crew endured painfully long gaps between camera set-ups. Sometimes a scene that might last thirty seconds in the film would take a week to shoot.

Then, to make matters even worse, halfway through filming Tom injured his back and spent the following few days bent over like Quasimodo. There was also the cute little fox that Tom had to cradle in his arms for one scene, which merrily scratched the skin off Tom's legs while he had to sit there looking tranquil. Then came the bird who flew towards Tom, supposedly to land on his hand, yet kept on going. The whole crew was mobilised into shimmying up the walls with nets in search of the errant fowl. It seems the trainer had decided to economise and it was the only bird they had.

By the time Paula Wagner and her husband dropped in on the *Legend* set during a honeymoon trip to London, the young actor was feeling at a fairly low ebb. It was the first time Paula had ever visited her precious young client on a film set and the couple took Tom off for lunch, hoping to raise his spirits.

While they were eating, a phone call came through to the restaurant to say that Ridley Scott's pride and joy – *Legend*'s multi-million-dollar fantasy-world set – was engulfed in flames. Two stagehands and four firemen were injured tackling the blaze and an estimated $3 million worth of props went up in smoke. Things were definitely going from bad to worse.

Somehow Tom managed to find a light side to this disaster. He turned to Paula – by this time probably his closest, most trusted confidante in Hollywood – and said: 'I hope you'll understand when I ask you never to visit a set of mine again.'

Tom rushed back to the set to inspect the damage and was devastated by the charred remains of the elaborate forest that had been created. Suddenly, across the burnt set, he spotted Ridley Scott wandering in a daze among the ruins and called to him: 'Rid...' But he did not know what to say. Scott looked up at Tom, who was by now terrified that he might have encroached upon his director at an awkward moment, and said: 'Well, I'm going to go play some tennis. How about meeting me for dinner later? Does that sound fine to you?' Tom was stunned – and then mightily relieved. From that moment the two became firm friends.

The fire put Tom in a very difficult position. The shoot was seriously delayed and he had dozens of other top-quality scripts waiting for him to green-light back in Los Angeles. 'I really had to make a choice. When the set burned down, it was like, "What are we going to do now? Where does this take us?" I said, I can sit here and feel shitty and wallow in my frustration, and banging your head against the wall, you say, "Okay, that happened, now what do we do? Let's go ahead."'

Tom saw his experiences as yet another test of character and determination. Every mountain was there to climb. No peak would get in his way, however high. 'I mean, I always had that ability to just deal with things. My whole life has been like that: "Okay, what do I do now?"'

In *Legend*, Tom's character of Jack O' The Green – who wears a green outfit and resembles the son of Robin Hood – spends a lot of time talking to unicorns. You could safely say it was something completely different for the young actor. Tom said he was grabbed by the character of Jack after watching Ridley Scott develop the character through a poetic script. This time Tom's traditionally thorough, muscle-obsessed research required a new type of intensity. He carefully wrote up a background for his character, to create a sense of history, and then practised his backflips and grew his hair long.

Scott, a man of few words, said admiringly: 'It's always good if a large amount of input comes from the actor. He's the person doing the work. If Tom can get inside the role and brings to it something that I hadn't thought of, then that's the best way to operate.'

Tom was rather noncommittal when asked about the movie's box-office potential. 'I can't predict what is going to be box office and what is not. I think anyone who says, "This is going to be a hit" before the thing is made really doesn't know. Nobody knows. So you'd better do something you believe in and you love, because if it's not financially successful, you'd better walk away with something.' It almost sounded as if Tom already knew how *Legend* would fare.

In fact, at one point studio executives seriously considered not even releasing the movie and cutting their losses after they received reports that audiences who sneak-previewed the trailer laughed at Tom's hair. (Just two years later long hair for men came back with a vengeance!)

Legend opened in America as that week's top-grossing film and then promptly sank without trace. Hollywood interpreted this to mean that Tom had become such a box-office pull that even a film as poor as *Legend* could open well because it had such a magnetic name in the starring role. All his pre-production handiwork had certainly helped him salvage a decent performance even if the movie itself was very disappointing.

The critics were united in their dismissal of the movie. Richard Corliss wrote of it in *Time*: 'Landscapes too remote. Quests too familiar and special effects too rudimentary.' Kevin Thomas, in the *Los Angeles Times*, said: 'According to Ridley Scott, legends are born of the eternal struggle between the forces of light and darkness. Perhaps so, but it's hard to imagine his *Legend* living up to its name.'

Tom himself even admitted later that he had been 'just another colour in a Ridley Scott painting'. But he publicly insisted that all the delays had not affected the movie's final outcome.

The truth was that there were a lot of post-production problems. Scott had made a fairy tale, something he believed was a breakthrough visual film, whereas the project's main backer, Twentieth Century Fox, thought the whole piece was a little too romantic, and so Scott had to go back and re-edit the film to give it a harder edge.

Tom later described *Legend* as a 'tortuous experience' which he never wanted to endure ever again. 'Making that movie was exhausting.'

All in all, the making of *Legend* was a severe test of his patience and ability to enjoy his work. When he got back to Los Angeles he had already decided that his next project would be the complete and utter opposite of that lengthy, heavy-handed experience. It would be something filled with comic-book heroes and adventure.

12

I feel the need, the need for speed.
'MAVERICK' IN TOP GUN

The first thing you pick up on is the sound – the ear-splitting, brain-busting, bone-shaking rumble, the rumble that shatters as though it were the end of the world. Tom heard the sound and turned away from his lunch break directly towards its source, an F-14 Tomcat roaring down an adjacent runway. His concentration broke and a smile slipped through lips so tight they seemed on guard duty. As the jet screamed into the atmosphere, the smile took on an afterburner's glow. 'Ah,' sighed Tom, searching the sky through RayBan Aviator lenses, 'the sound of freedom.'

Throughout the trials and tribulations of making *Legend* for the best part of a year in London, Tom somehow held his relationship with Rebecca De Mornay together. But on his return to New York the couple found that actually having to live together for any length of time was not the pleasurable experience it had been before Tom's departure to Britain. It was, as they say, by mutual consent that Tom and Rebecca decided it was time to call it a day and the actor – still only twenty-four at the time – immediately committed to a project that was to accelerate his career more than any other single movie before or since. He needed his freedom in a big way.

The film was called *Top Gun* and it had been carefully developed by two of Hollywood's sharpest young producers, Jerry Bruckheimer and Don Simpson. The project's conception occurred when Bruckheimer was skimming through a copy of *California* magazine in their office and spotted an article by writer Ehud Yonoy entitled 'Top Guns'. The piece was an in-depth look at a flight school for the US Navy's best fighter pilots. Bruckheimer was immediately hooked. 'I thought, "This looks like *Star Wars* on earth,"' he later recalled. 'I flipped it over to Don, who read the article and said, "We've gotta buy this."'

Within two months the dynamic duo were presenting their movie idea based on the article to Pentagon top brass in an effort to recruit the US Navy to their cause. Simpson ad-libbed a story outlining the film he wanted to make and the admirals gave it their enthusiastic approval and promised to lend their considerable technological muscle to the project. The Navy's thinking was pretty basic: they knew that an action-packed hero flick would enormously help the Navy's image and breathe life into the recruitment slogan: 'Not just a job, but an adventure.'

Simpson and Bruckheimer then visited the Miramar Naval Air Station, in San Diego, California, ninety miles south of Los Angeles. They encountered pilots who looked as if they had just walked out of central casting – charismatic, young, sexy, confident characters with wild monikers like Snake, Jambo, Mad Dog and Jaws. These were guys who really lived life on the edge.

The 'rock 'n' rollers in the sky', as Bruckheimer dubbed them, would provide perfect raw material for a supremely popular movie. And the two producers were just as convinced as to who would make their perfect leading man. 'From the first time we went to Miramar,' recalled Bruckheimer, 'even before the script was written – we said, "These guys are Tom Cruise!"'

Added partner Simpson: 'He represents the all-American, straightforward, proper young man.'

(What Bruckheimer did not say was that before Tom came into the frame for the role, the actor's old friend Sean Penn had been the producers' favourite.)

In Hollywood terms, Tom had already established himself as the archetypal, high-profile, clean-cut, all-American performer. He was up there with Harrison Ford, Warren Beatty and Arnold Schwarzenegger even though he had yet to make a really huge, blockbuster hit movie.

Simpson and Bruckheimer were old Hollywood hands and had proved themselves a very astute pair capable of delivering hugely successful films. They grossed a massive $270 million with their very first effort, 1983's *Flashdance*. The following year the incredibly popular *Beverly Hills Cop* made $350 million, thanks to a blend of Eddie Murphy's sassy comic routines and a fast-paced cops-and-robbers drama.

The two producers were as flamboyant as they were rich by the time they started developing the *Top Gun* project. Hollywood mansions, Rolls-Royces and a penchant for the good life complemented their reputations in movieland. A very powerful team who tended to follow their instincts, they insisted on overseeing every aspect of film production and few people were ever allowed into their carefully managed world.

Simpson told *Life* magazine that he and Bruckheimer 'like pictures about triumph'. His partner then chipped in, stating, with uncharacteristic modesty: 'What we like, other people seem to like.' With a $15-million budget, including an allowance for vast amounts of jet-fighter fuel that cost $8000 an hour, *Top Gun* was going to be an expensive route to reality.

So, with screenwriters Jim Cash and Jack Epps working around the clock to come up with a script that would meet their approval, Simpson and Bruckheimer approached British director Tony Scott, who happened to be the brother of Ridley Scott, with whom Tom had worked in London on *Legend*. Previously Tony had made only one movie, *The Hunger*, and that had been panned by the critics and failed miserably at the box office. After its failure Tony, who like his brother had amassed a fortune by making lucrative TV commercials, had a hard time bouncing back on to the feature-film market. He even confessed at one stage he 'couldn't get arrested', let alone find a new project.

In 1984, while accompanying his friends Simpson and Bruckheimer on a perilous raft trip down the Colorado River, Tony heard all about the *Top Gun* project, which the pair had already earmarked for another director. He was disappointed as he could see what a potentially great movie it could be. So, for months nothing was mentioned about *Top Gun* until the two producers called Tony out of the blue and offered him the movie. 'I jumped at the chance. Who wouldn't?' he said later. The producers never explained what caused them to change their minds about their original choice of director.

The pair also informed Tony that Tom Cruise was attached to the project. The director had no objection; he had even met Tom during the actor's lonely stay in London during the making of *Legend*. 'I felt he had just the right arrogance in the best sense of the word,' explained Tony, a more flamboyant, gregarious character than his older brother.

The initial draft of the *Top Gun* script was actually first shown to Tom for his approval before *Legend* wrapped. It seemed a welcome piece of light relief compared with the British-based project. 'I was hungry for it,' said Tom later. He found the coincidence of working with Ridley Scott's brother 'weird – I feel like a member of the family'.

Tony Scott had an interesting take on Tom. 'Tom is frighteningly polite. He's so nice he's sick,' he said with more than a hint of healthy British cynicism.

The project should then have gone rapidly forward to production, except that Tom Cruise was about to prove he was no ordinary movie star. He had studied the script very closely and was very unhappy about how it was shaping up. It is worth remembering that Tom had long since decided that he would make all the demands he felt necessary if a screenplay seemed substandard.

Tom wanted the writers to go back and rethink certain important aspects as well as improve the way the main characters were being projected. 'It was important to me that we made a movie about characters and the human element – not just a war picture.' Tom wanted the emphasis to be on 'competition, not killing'.

Scott, Simpson and Bruckheimer might well have told certain stars where to get off at this stage, but not Tom Cruise. They all knew how much they needed his name in their project and they were also well aware of his reputation for meddling in scripts. But they conceded that he had a very good point about the script not being right. Tom, for his part, had been intensely involved in rewriting *All the Right Moves* and he felt he had the experience to influence the direction of the screenplay.

The two producers then made an unusual arrangement with Tom, of a kind that few actors in the world would have the clout to achieve. They agreed to let him have two months to work on the script and develop the character he was being asked to play, and then he would sign a contract to perform the lead role.

It was a remarkable agreement because Tom was basically saying that he preferred to risk investing his precious time in extra work that might not result in a deal, rather than be stuck with an unsatisfactory screenplay or an underdeveloped role. He was fully aware that the two producers had nothing to lose because they would end up with a better script and an opportunity to attract all sorts of big names if Tom pulled out. But the development of the *Top Gun* script was probably the most savvy thing Tom had done up to that point in his career.

However, at first Simpson and Bruckheimer were not keen on Tom's proposal, because they presumed there would be a non-stop battle of egos over the size and structure of his role. Explained Simpson: 'I was against it, because I like to run things. To me, an actor is generally a hired hand. But we talked at great length and he proved himself to us.'

When that particular meeting was over, Tom stood up, shook both producers firmly by the hand and told them: 'Gentlemen, I'm on board.' He was already sounding more like a 'Top Gun' than an actor. Later he even managed to get the producers to allow him to have approval of his co-stars. Tom was welding awesome power for one so young. 'I've got a strong point of view and I like to get it across in the films I do,' Tom explained. 'Everything that I've done to get involved in this was to benefit the piece itself.' That naturally included benefiting the character he was playing in the movie.

As Simpson later admitted, the script-development sessions with Tom were 'terrific'. 'He would show up at my house, grab a beer and we'd work five or six hours on the script. Sometimes we'd act scenes out. The guy doesn't see things from just a couple of perspectives – he can really wrap his arms around something and see it from all angles. We had a lot of fun.'

As was becoming traditional for Tom, his research into the lead role in *Top Gun* was meticulous. He went to the Miramar naval pilots' school three months in advance of the shoot to soak up the heroic real-life characters. He went to 'Top Gun' classes and 'what I discovered was a group of men who enjoy flying above almost anything else you can name'.

However, Tom's stint at Miramar was hardly a bed of roses. As he later explained: 'These guys took one look at me and said, "We are going to kick your ass."' Somehow Tom turned them around and within days he was eating, drinking and sharing the lives of these brave pilots. To get a chance to tag along on one of the F-14 fighter-plane flights, he had to prove he was physically and mentally capable of withstanding lightning-fast changes in the environment. He put on weight deliberately and trained himself to a state of physical fitness comparable to that of the pilots.

To prepare for the film's spectacular dog-fight sequences, Tom and the other principal actors had to go through several days of psychological testing for F-14 certification, learning how to withstand high G forces, eject and escape an ejection seat in water. It was, as Simpson later said, 'literally a crash course'.

Tom ended up being taken up in an F-14 three times. They turned out to be unforgettable highlights of his life. 'Those jets rip through the clouds,' he later recalled. 'It's very sexual. Your body contorts, your muscles get sore, and the straining forces blood from your brain. You grab your legs and your ass and grunt as sweat pours over you. It's just thrilling. I had this grin on my face that wouldn't leave.'

But there is no doubting that Tom was swept up by the patriotic fervour and adrenalin-inducing lifestyles of the pilots he encountered. As one naval commander said, 'They're the last of the cowboys. Back in 1836 they would have been gunfighters squaring off against the bad guys. A century earlier they would have been pirates. Even earlier, they would have been gladiators fighting in the arena amidst the sawdust, playing for the big chips with no way to walk out unless you win.'

When Tom finally delivered his version of the *Top Gun* script, Simpson and Bruckheimer were delighted. He had introduced elements no one had ever thought about and tightened up the action. The gamble had worked and now it was down to Tom and director Tony Scott to make sure it all held together on celluloid when shooting started in June 1985.

Scott's first concern was the photography. As a former art director and meticulous maker of TV commercials, he had a definite eye for the light and colours that help to make a movie look beautiful. He was determined to make sure the cinematography was the closest most people would ever come to actually being in the cockpit with those pilots, and that is precisely what was achieved.

Tom's character, Pete 'Maverick' Mitchell, opens *Top Gun* in the middle of an emergency with his partner 'Goose', played by dashing Anthony Edwards. The two actors worked perfectly together. Edwards, whose other films included *Sure Thing* and *Gotcha!*, proved to be an independent, easy-going character with a healthy, down-to-earth attitude towards movie stardom. 'For a lot of actors, movies and publicity are a way of life. Me – I'd rather go sailing,' he said proudly.

In the film, Maverick and Goose are supporting fellow fliers 'Cougar' and 'Merlin'. Cougar was played by John Stockwell, Tom's old drinking pal from *Losin' It*. More than three years had passed since that low point in Tom's career and Stockwell noticed a big change in his personality.

'In *Top Gun,* Tom was clearly a star and much more careful about what he did. He was much more reserved, much more aware. Those good old days were over and he was very careful about preserving his image,' explained Stockwell, who revealed that Tom kept well away from the crazier actors – himself included – who still liked to head off for some fun once the day's shooting wrapped. Sometimes Tom would join them for a beer in a bar but then disappear the moment 'things got raunchy', said Stockwell. 'He never got involved.'

Tom's Maverick is so volatile that he turns on the heat without hesitation or forethought and he is constantly battling against his main rival and personal nemesis, the aptly named Tom 'Iceman' Kazansky, played by Val Kilmer, who went on to marry the beautiful British actress Joanne Whalley, as well as star in movies such as Oliver Stone's *The Doors* and deliver a highly acclaimed performance in *Tombstone* in 1994.

Tom and Val – both intensely in favour of the method school of performance – did not exactly hit it off. As sworn enemies on the screen they both decided to continue their bad relationship off duty as well. There was speculation that the fact Val had enjoyed a fling with Cher two years before Tom met her at that White House fund-raiser for dyslexia might have caused a little friction between the two stars.

Kilmer graciously sidestepped the issue when confronted about it years later and in fact has said little about what really happened on the set of *Top Gun*, although it is clear that he felt the movie was not exactly a healthy stepping stone for his own career.

After meeting Tony Scott, he was bluntly critical of the *Top Gun* project and told the director: 'Frankly I don't like this.' He explained later: 'I loved what I had seen of Tony Scott's work but I just didn't want to do that movie. Tony said, "Don't worry, your hair will look great." He thought that would make a difference. He was infectious that way.' It is worth remembering that while Kilmer might not have really wanted to be in *Top Gun* with Tom Cruise, Tom himself felt the opposite way about Val since he approved Scott's casting of the young actor.

Later, reflecting on his experiences in *Top Gun*, Val explained: 'I have very definitely had a different kind of career than Tom. You never know if a job has commercial success written all over it. I just think life's too short to worry about that.'

Tom and Val's rivalry on screen put two very exciting talents in direct competition. Besides pitting their strengths against each other in the air, they also take part in a no-holds-barred volleyball match, which was criticised by many as being a flimsy excuse to titillate the audience with muscular torsos and bronzed skin. Tom insisted this was not the case when he later said: 'It shows that to fighter pilots, physical prowess is very important. Plus the scene shows the constant competition between these guys – how they compete on every level.'

Tom was privately infuriated by the accusations that he was purely a beefcake star of *Top Gun* – and this was before shooting had even been completed. As a result, he insisted that shots of him topless could not be used to help promote the film once it was released. 'If you notice, none of the *Top Gun* TV commercials or stills being released show me with my shirt off. And you don't see posters of me like that. Any poster that's ever been made has been black market – I've never authorised anything,' he said later.

The character of Maverick had attracted Tom for all sorts of reasons. The actor loved the fact that he was completely unpredictable. 'He doesn't do anything by the book,' he said. 'He's kind of wild and he experiments with different ways of flying. The film is about a guy who has an absolute passion for something, a guy who wants to live at one hundred and fifty per cent afterburn all the way.'

But the aspect of Maverick that really pulled in Tom was that the character's father had died after his plane was lost during a mission twenty years earlier. Losing a father was certainly something that Tom could closely identify with in real life. He openly acknowledged that bond with his character by saying: 'Obviously my father wasn't a fighter pilot and didn't die a hero, but I think a lot of the gut-level, emotional stuff – the love of father and the conflict in that – is there.'

Tom's love interest in *Top Gun* was played by blonde actress Kelly McGillis as the civilian instructor Charlotte 'Charlie' Blackwood. Maverick gets off to a bad start when he tries to seduce Charlie in a bar without even realising who she is. The slightly sick-making sequence involved Tom crooning 'You've Lost That Lovin' Feelin'', and some said the relationship smacked of cradle snatching.

Kelly was Tony Scott's first choice for the part, although Tom, Simpson and Bruckheimer definitely played a part in selecting the actress. The director explained: 'I think she's just right. She had to be a mature-looking actress to fit the role.'

Initially, stories of the casting session circulated in Hollywood, suggesting that Tom had vetoed Demi Moore in favour of Kelly because he was infatuated with her. That could not have been further from the truth.

Kelly radiated a certain mysterious femininity yet retained a lot of strength and independence. She herself modestly scoffed at such praise, saying: 'It's all luck. I think I'm the least appealing cinematographically. I'm not Kim Basinger. I don't think about those things. I can't and I don't want to.'

Naturally a brunette, Kelly bleached her hair blonde and the scenes featuring her and Tom literally sizzled on screen despite criticism from reviewers who complained that they found the relationship between Maverick and an older woman 'unbelievable'. The public certainly did not seem to mind.

Off screen, rumours of a romance between Tom – now single again after breaking up with Rebecca De Mornay – and Kelly persisted and spread like wildfire. The outspoken actress was flattered but incredulous. 'It's just not true!' she protested. 'But it's fascinating how people love to pin the leading man and the leading lady together.'

The true situation between the two actors was that Tom was having great difficulty 'relating' to Kelly because she was a blunt, carefree character who approached her acting in a very different way from him. At one stage things got so frosty between the two actors that there were serious worries that it might affect their respective performances. Ironically, it was later claimed that this was a deliberate policy on the part of the two stars because they wanted to instil some sexual chemistry in their on-screen relationship. It certainly worked! Not since Tom's early clashes with Rebecca during the making of *Risky Business* had he had such a breakdown in communication with a leading lady. This time, however, they were not destined to turn the situation around.

Kelly was dating handsome actor Barry Tubb – known in Hollywood as the most famous non-star in Tinseltown. He played 'Wolfman' in *Top Gun* and Kelly would walk straight off the set at the end of a hard day's shooting right into his arms. Some months later the *New York Post* spotted Tom and Kelly dining in the same restaurant in Manhattan – on opposite sides of the room. Tom wore dark glasses and chatted with family friends and their children while Kelly was huddled with a guy on the other side of the restaurant. They never even acknowledged each other.

But all this friction did not prevent Tom and Kelly from pulling off some very steamy scenes together on the set of *Top Gun*. Tony Scott even shot an extra love scene between the two co-stars. Shot in a lift, this was considered so steamy by most Hollywood insiders that the producers were lucky to get the movie the all-important PG rating in America that would enable all those teenyboppers to queue up and see their idol.

Many of the movie's action scenes were shot 'live' and that meant dicing with danger for Tom and the rest of the cast and crew. When the movie's most dramatic rescue scene was shot, Tom had to bob about in icy waters off Point Loma, California, for hours while being picked up by air-sea rescue helicopters. As he leaned out of a small lifeboat and yanked what was supposed to be his colleague Goose from the water, the lines of his parachute entangled with his watchband. The chute, heavily saturated with sea water, caused Tom to lose his balance and he became trapped in a chaos of ropes before being pulled beneath the choppy waves of the Pacific Ocean.

The production crew tried frantically to free him and, fortunately, two real-life Navy divers were on hand to tackle the emergency. The divers leapt into action and Petty Officer 2nd Class Darryl Silva was the first to reach Tom. 'He was three feet under water and I grabbed the shoulder strap of his flight suit, but couldn't lift him, so my partner also grabbed the strap,' he explained later.

Silva then went back under the water and started desperately trying to untangle the parachute lines from Tom's wrist. It was a battle against the clock. Silva managed to haul Tom into the raft, where the young actor was spitting up huge quantities of salt water and coughing. The officer administered mouth-to-mouth resuscitation, something that millions of women throughout the world would no doubt have liked to do! Tom came round and muttered thanks to Silva for saving his life and an hour later he was before the cameras once more, proving himself the ultimate professional.

Tom also proved he was determined to stay with the project every inch of the way – even after the shooting of *Top Gun* was completed. He sat in on much of the post-production process and had some fairly harsh words to say about the rough cut – the first, roughly edited version of the film. He told *Premiere* magazine: 'In the rough cut the aerial story just didn't work. Tony Scott had miles and miles of aerial footage. He had to go back and tighten it up, define the story more. I always try to look at a rough cut like, "The movie's not out yet – you can fix it."'

Behind the blunt words lay a complex scenario because Tom was undoubtedly participating in the film-making process more than virtually any other actor in Hollywood. But then he already had the clout to do so because director Tony Scott, plus Simpson and Bruckheimer, knew that he was the key to their success. Normally, they would have told an actor where to get off for daring to pass an opinion on such matters as the editing process.

Tom was helping guarantee that the end product was as near to perfection as one could get. 'Once a film comes out,' he elaborated later, 'they say, "Oh, of course, that's why he took it. It's a commercial movie; a hit! Why wouldn't he want to do that?" People don't understand the risk factor. It didn't start out as a commercial movie. Nothing is a sure thing! And if you looked at the script beforehand and saw what might have happened...'

Tony Scott saw Tom's active interest in all aspects of the film as the actor being 'like a terrier, he locks on and hangs on'.

Another aspect of the lead-up to the movie's release was Tom's wholehearted decision to go out on the road and actively help promote *Top Gun* following his self-imposed silence of more than two years after the problematic work he did to help promote *Risky Business,* which turned into a stressful situation for the then press-shy Tom. It wasn't as if he had now decided that he loved the media and did not mind revealing his innermost secrets to them. He had simply grown up considerably since *Risky Business* and now appreciated that giving hundreds of banal interviews was an important part of the movie-making process if he was to maintain his newly acquired position at the top of the Hollywood pile.

Tom's coverage for *Top Gun* was truly awesome. He did his first 'grown-up' cover for the arty New York magazine *Interview* (up until then he had only been featured on hundreds of teen mags). There were also persuasive pieces to be found in *Rolling Stone, People* and *US.* He schmoozed with newspapers at a New York junket. In Los Angeles he did interviews with *Associated Press, New York Times Syndicate, Knight-Rider Syndicate, USA Today* and some radio. There were also TV appearances on *Good Morning America, CBS Morning News, Entertainment Tonight,* the *Movie Channel* and *CNN.*

The younger, inexperienced Tom had found it virtually impossible to deal with prying questions about his parents' divorce and other personal matters. But for the *Top Gun* publicity roadshow, journalists seemed more interested in finding out how much money Tom was getting – and that was something he found easy to cope with. 'I make it my policy not to talk about money,' he would respond coolly. 'In choosing a role, money is not an issue if I want to do something.'

In all interviews he remained the essence of politeness and seemed overly concerned about making sure each journalist was being looked after properly. While there was no doubting Tom's good manners, in reality he was undoubtedly hiding his true feelings about the press, as he would later prove. But for the moment he had a major movie to promote and if that meant being pleasant towards a bunch of blood-sucking journalists then so be it.

Even when reporters pressed Tom about the fact that many movie-goers perceived *Top Gun* to be a blatant exploitation of handsome young male bodies, he kept his cool. 'I don't take my shirt off to sell tickets. The way I look at it is, let a good movie bring the audience in,' came his ever charming reply.

Top Gun opened with a winning $8.2-million take at the US box office in its first week of release. But the public's relish for the movie did not exactly match critical acclaim. Most reviewers sneered at its excessive commercialism. '*Top Gun* is little more than a glitzy, superbly photographed recruiting movie for the US Navy flight school. It is also a visually stirring if somewhat aimless movie,' was about the best of a bad bunch from *Video Review* magazine, and reviewer Jeffrey Lyons summed up: 'It's trite, it's hokey, it's manipulative, but *Top Gun* is perfect for unchallenging, exhilarating entertainment.'

Movie historian Edward Gross got a slightly better grasp of the subject matter when he wrote: '*Top Gun* is a full-length cartoon, though a highly effective one.'

There were also some highly personalised attacks on Tom by the reviewers, among them the *New York Times*'s Walter Goodman, who wrote that 'Cruise brings little but a good build to the role'. *USA Today*'s Jack Curry went one step further by proclaiming: 'Supposed to be a super flyboy, he comes across more like just a fly or a boy.' *Newsweek*'s David Ansen did at least concede: 'The likeable Cruise is simply miscast. He's not the dangerous guy everyone's talking about, but the boy next door.'

Tom was deeply hurt by some of the more personal attacks on him. He knew perfectly well that the movie was a highly commercial comic-book-style adventure but he could not understand why the critics were taking it all so seriously. However, inside Hollywood those who sneered at 'beefcake' were more than muted by the cold, hard fact that the film's phenomenal success – it went on to make more than $170 million in the USA alone – had firmly established Tom as the world's biggest box-office attraction at the age of twenty-four.

The public did not seem to care about the critics' objections either, because the movie became the biggest-grossing film of 1986 and then went on to be the first blockbuster theatrical hit to surpass its box-office take on videotape, resulting in a total gross of over half a billion dollars.

Obviously the question on everyone's lips following *Top Gun*'s success was: when is there going to be a sequel? But Tom had other ideas on the subject. It wasn't a matter of when, or even if. He told friends he had no intention of making a second version of the movie. Every few months articles would appear in either the tabloids or the industry press suggesting that Tom was about to sign up to replay the role for some vast sum of money ($25 million at the last count). Simpson and Bruckheimer held on to the sequel rights, and they were as keen on making 'Top Gun II' as Tom was opposed to the idea.

But then, in 1992, there were reports that Tom has secretly purchased the sequel rights from the two producers for in excess of a million dollars. These claims have never been officially confirmed, but according to Hollywood observers Tom planned to either sculpt the perfect script for a sequel or he deliberately bought the rights so as to prevent Simpson and Bruckheimer from ever making another *Top Gun* movie.

In August 1993 it was reported that location scouts were out looking for good sites to film the sequel and Jack Epps, who wrote the original *Top Gun*, was said to be hard at work putting together a script for the sequel. But by the following summer the movie project had still not materialised.

While Tom was well and truly perched on top of the fame mountain, his love life was going from bad to worse. Rebecca had gone and the few dates he did have time to go on just did not work out. On one occasion he went to a celebrity bowling session at New York's Madison Square Garden and ended up snapping at a photographer and staying only ten minutes. The fact that old flame Cher was among the other famous faces in attendance that might well have had an influence on his decision to leave in a hurry.

Tom later admitted that this was a very lonely period in his life. He had all the trappings of power and success but no one to share them with. His problem was a classic symptom of the 1980s, when wealth and success so often had priority over happiness. Tom knew he was getting more and more sucked in by the Hollywood system and all he really wanted was someone uncomplicated to share his life with.

The extraordinary success of *Top Gun* actually forced him into even more of a social shell. A simple trip with his sister and her baby to the Smithsonian Institute turned into an horrific experience when hundreds of fans started pointing at him and staring, and then some began demanding autographs. Tom felt responsible for his sister and niece, so he ordered them out of the building and slipped out of the back entrance. That experience simply fuelled his desire for solitude, even though he was still as desperate as ever to find someone to love.

Top Gun's success and Tom's very intense involvement in the entire film-making process finally persuaded him to open a production company to develop projects specifically for him. TC Productions was given a very loose development deal at Columbia Pictures and soon dozens of scripts were pouring in every week. Tom had been very careful in the preceding three years to try to get a feel for every aspect of film production, from development through to distribution, and he brought in his cousin William Mapother as head of development in the first of many moves to install his own family members in positions of trust within the Cruise empire.

A few years earlier, efforts to write, with his friend Emilio Estevez, a screenplay based on a novel by S.E. Hinton, who wrote *The Outsiders*, floundered mainly because neither actor really fully understood the screenwriting process. Now Tom would hire his own screenwriters to convert his ideas into movie scripts before adding the sort of finishing touches that helped turn *Top Gun* into such a huge success.

Tom even toyed with the idea of starring in the lead role of a screen adaptation of Jay McInerney's novel *Bright Lights, Big City.* 'It's an interesting role, but I'm learning that I can't just jump into something. I like to take my time and make sure I feel good about it.' Eventually Tom rejected the project because it dealt explicitly with excessive drug-taking among New York's rich and successful. Tom – the homespun boy who had never even been near a cannabis joint – was concerned that such a role might damage his image.

Now he was adhering to a game plan in which the role – and the project – was the main priority. He actually believed that his popularity was not his concern. 'I've got enough just to deal with what I have to deal with. Let someone else figure out who's hot and who's not and all that kind of thing. I'll be happy just to work.'

13

I don't like my part too much,
it's just an okay part, but I can learn so
much from those two guys.

TOM CRUISE

Actors who make films in which their good looks are amply displayed are, more often than not, demeaned by hostile critics as 'just another pretty face'. Tom Cruise had already suffered his fair share of such accusations and, twenty-five years earlier, another matinee idol, Paul Newman, faced precisely the same sex-idol label. Just as Tom had steadfastly navigated around the pitfalls of beefcake and Brat Pack pigeonholing, so Newman had faced up to similar battles during his early career.

'My fame came with a beefcake stereotype,' admitted Newman. 'All people asked about was my blue eyes – ladies still ask me to remove my sunglasses so they can see them.'

In 1961 a tough, young pool player named 'Fast Eddie' Felson provided movie-goers with a precise demonstration of the game's finer points when *The Hustler* was born – and provided Newman with an escape route from those hunky roles. In 1986 he did the same thing for Tom when he picked him to star in the better-late-than-never sequel, *The Color of Money*.

Newman brought Fast Eddie back from beyond, but with him came the youthful warrior, a true contender for the throne: Vincent Lauria, to be played by Tom Cruise.

The inside story of how Tom came to be paired up with one of Hollywood's most respected stars began late in 1984, when Newman approached director Martin Scorsese (*Mean Streets*, *Taxi Driver*, *Raging Bull*, to name but a few) to discuss the possibility of directing *The Color of Money*. But there was one problem: Scorsese never directed sequels. He preferred to avoid them like the plague they had become. But there was something about this particular project that was special and irresistible. 'I love Paul Newman's work – especially *The Hustler* – and I like the ambiance of that film,' he explained.

This was to be a very special project indeed. The screenplay had been carefully developed by Newman through writer Walter Trevis, the author of the novel upon which the movie was based. Then Scorsese, ever the perfectionist, threw that draft out and insisted on starting again. As his collaborator he chose Richard Price, an experienced New York author best known for his tales from the dark side of life in lower Manhattan's Little Italy, where both Scorsese and his great friend Robert De Niro grew up. Price shared the director's predilection for heroes with a twist. 'Marty and I like mean things,' he explained. 'The meaner the better because the greater the shaft of light at the end.'

Both men knew they had to get the script absolutely right otherwise a complex financial and distribution deal in place with Disney's Touchstone Pictures might collapse.

When Paul Newman inspected Price's early efforts he got very concerned because Scorsese's slant seemed to be making hero Fast Eddie extremely dark and twisted – qualities that no self-respecting movie star likes to see dominating their character too much. 'One thing I was sure of – if I ever made a sequel, it was damn well going to be better than the original,' he insisted.

From that moment onwards Newman decided to attend every single script session to make sure his baby was going to be reborn in exactly the way he deemed right and proper. It was during one of these meetings that he started to notice that Vincent Lauria – the young hustler who was Fast Eddie's protégé – was starting to bear an uncanny resemblance to the young star he most admired: Tom Cruise. 'He seemed innocent and sweet, the kind of character this boy would be,' noted Newman.

Scorsese was not impressed with the suggestion at first. He had been hoping to sign the lesser-known up-and-coming New York actor Vincent Spano, who had starred in *Creator* and *Alphabet City*. But this was Newman's project and he put his foot down firmly. Scorsese, who had met Tom when they shared a pizza in a Los Angeles restaurant in 1983, gave in because he had been impressed by his performance in *All the Right Moves*.

There was a problem when Tom turned down Newman and Scorsese's first indirect approach to him because he feared *The Color of Money* would turn out to be a Newman vehicle which would leave him looking like a redundant hero. Tom had a naturally cautious streak in him as well as being slightly overawed by the prospect of working on a movie with two of the biggest names in film history. But Newman knew that Tom was his man and he pursued him relentlessly, finally persuading him to attend a meeting. 'When we met, we hit it off from the start,' he explained.

One associate described the relationship perfectly: 'They are genuinely fond of each other. They have a nice, jokey sort of rapport and I think it's one of those good, solid exchanges that's going to go on.'

Secretly, Tom's stomach was turning cartwheels at the prospect of starring opposite Newman. He later confessed to feeling sick with nerves during that first meeting, but the professional side of him knew that *The Color of Money* was a superbly scripted project. 'I'd be a liar if I said I felt totally confident and relaxed,' he conceded later. 'But the screenplay was so well written and we had a two-week rehearsal period. Newman really took the time to make everyone feel comfortable – he's very supportive and generous with his time as an actor and a person. We became good friends.'

Tom quickly recognised the potential in his role and the fact that it presented him with a unique opportunity to take his career in yet another direction. 'I want to go all the way,' he proclaimed. 'Look at Newman, look what this man has created as an actor and a human being.' While there is no doubting Tom's words, it has to be noted that Newman received a much smaller, sub-million-dollar fee for his starring role in *The Color of Money* and both Newman and Scorsese put up one third of their salaries each to help guarantee the film got made.

Newman was certainly impressed by Tom. 'He's prepared to hang himself on a meat hook. He'll hang himself out to dry to seek something. He's not afraid of looking like a ninny. He doesn't protect himself or his ego. And he's a wonderful experimenter. Of course, like any actor, when the material is poor, he falls back on his successful mannerisms: the happy kitchen. I don't know that he's a great mathematician or a theoretical physicist, but he has what he needs to be a good actor.'

The movie had not even begun shooting and the Newman–Cruise team were already sounding like a mutual admiration society.

Tom threw himself into researching the role of Vincent Lauria with his customary enthusiasm and began cruising the pool halls of New York to get a feel for his character through some of the real-life Fast Eddies. He especially enjoyed watching the hustlers trying to hustle each other, by telling tales of sprained wrists and failing nerves to guys who had used the same stories themselves a hundred times, all for the joy of pulling off a good one. 'It's not the money for these guys; it's the hustle,' Tom explained. 'One day they're up a hundred thousand dollars. The next day they'll go to the track and blow it all. They justify it, the morality.'

But Newman did have one distinct advantage over Tom – he knew how to shoot pool. So the younger actor went on a crash course to learn the finer points of the game and he was soon potting everything in sight. Michael Sigel, the professional hired to squire the two actors turned pool sharks around the table, was very impressed by his youthful pupil and Newman too was amazed by Tom's skills on the felt. 'It took me a long time to get okay. It took him very little time to get very good.' The two actors even kept their skills polished by constantly playing for bets between breaks in rehearsals and the actual movie shoot, which was to be a tight, forty-nine-day schedule shot mainly in Chicago.

Newman even leapt to Tom's defence publicly when a Chicago newspaper slammed the younger actor's pool technique. The veteran star personally wrote to the editor insisting that Tom was a fine player in his own right.

The movie was painstakingly shot as master craftsman Scorsese began fitting all the pieces of the filmic puzzle together. 'I worked day and night for months,' Tom recalled later. 'For one shot, Marty told me, "Okay now, the camera's just going to follow you around the table, and you got to clear off the whole table. You think you can do that kid?" I go, "Yeah," and I went home, and I was just sweating. So I really had to learn how to play. But for me, that's exciting. The more I learned about playing pool, the more confident I became. I love pool now.'

For the first few weeks after their first meeting, Tom insisted on calling both Newman and Scorsese 'sir'. It was a classic example of Tom's good upbringing and it made tough New Yorker Scorsese feel very uncomfortable. Eventually a meeting was organised with the express purpose of persuading Tom to stop doing it. He eventually obeyed their command, but continued to find it very difficult not to show great respect for the two movie-making giants.

An important priority for Scorsese was to ensure that *The Color of Money* could stand on its own and not be judged purely as a sequel to *The Hustler*. That meant he was constantly trying to imprint his own unique film-making stamp on it. He explained: 'We wanted this movie to stand on its own. The only link to *The Hustler* is the character of Fast Eddie. He's no longer a pool player. He's now on the outside of the game looking in, and with a whole new prospective.

'Our movie is about a man who goes on a journey towards self-awareness. A man who changes his way of living, changes his values. The movie is about a deception and then a clarity – a perversion and then a purity.' From these words one can tell why Scorsese commented later that the finest compliment he could ever receive would be to be described as an artist. On *The Color of Money* he had another reason to be satisfied, for he managed to come in $1.5 million under the film's original $14.5-million budget. That's the sort of stuff sainthood is made of in Hollywood.

For much of the movie Tom's character, Vincent, has with him his girlfriend, Carmen, played by Mary Elizabeth Mastrantonio. The two actors had to perform a number of steamy bedroom scenes, but, despite these, for once Tom was not romantically linked with his attractive co-star.

In August 1986 there was a sneak preview of *The Color of Money* at a cinema in Paramus, New Jersey, not far from Tom's old home in Glen Ridge. Paul Newman, his wife Joanne Woodward and Tom drove down together from Connecticut, where Tom had been staying as their house guest. Scorsese came from New York. Audience reaction to the movie was good, and Touchstone executives, plus the stars and director, decided that perhaps the movie's release date could be brought forward. As a result, it was scheduled to open in the USA in mid-October rather than December.

Meanwhile Tom – dateless and feeling a little left out in the romantic stakes – went off to a Bruce Springsteen concert in New Jersey to unwind after his exhausting year. The concert proved a welcome opportunity to recharge his batteries in more ways than one. For Tom enjoyed a brief encounter with Patti Sciafla, who went on to become the mother of three children by 'The Boss', who was still married to his first wife at the time.

Cruise, Newman and Mastrantonio all received enthusiastic praise for their performances from many reviewers following the release of *The Color of Money*. Richard Schickel, in *Time* magazine, took note of Tom's duality: 'There is something funny about his knot-headed exuberance and something unsettling and dangerous about it, too.' He continued: 'There is a ferocity in Cruise's flakiness that he has not previously had a chance to tap. That, in turn, gives Newman something to grapple with. There is a sort of contained rage in his work that he has never found before, and it carries him beyond the bounds of image.'

Newsweek's David Ansen touched all bases when he wrote: 'At the improbable age of sixty-one, the old bull – arguably America's best loved male movie star and certainly the most durable – has come down from the ridge in Westport, Conn., to play an aging but still hustling Eddie. The casting of Newman and Cruise is more than just the casting coup of the year. Anyone who doubted Cruise's seriousness as an actor will have to think again after seeing this whirlwind display.'

In Britain, reviewers were just as supportive. Neil Norman, writing in *The Face*, said: 'The moral dilemma of competitive motivation – play to win or play for money? – means that Scorsese's film is littered with human digressions. This is the most satisfactory aspect of the film as it allows actors ... to create flesh and blood characters without the constraints of a thematic straitjacket.'

All this high praise had one very important knock-on effect besides naturally helping *The Color of Money* succeed at the box office. The Academy

Awards were only a few months away and word about the movie was gaining momentum and building into a deafening media roar. In plain Hollywood terms, there was a powerful Oscar buzz accompanying the movie. Newman's name on anything was enough to guarantee attention because he had already been nominated six times for Best Actor – and lost every time. Now the media was pushing hard on his behalf, believing that the Academy could not turn him down a seventh time.

'The Newman–Cruise combination is irresistible to editors,' explained *Newsweek*'s David Ansen. Soon Paul and Tom's smiling faces were appearing on covers of *Newsweek*, *Life*, *USA Today* and the *New York Times Magazine*, to name but a few. In the *Life* spread, the cover photo was shot two different ways, with Newman and Cruise lying in opposite directions on a pool table in Newman's Connecticut home. In deference to equal billing, *Life* distributed in the western half of the United States had a cover with Newman upside down and Tom facing the other way; for the other side of the country, the positions of the actors were reversed. In an experiment to see which version would sell more, *Life* displayed the alternative covers side by side at twenty selected newsstands. Tom Cruise won with fifty-five per cent of sales.

On the Oscar front, Paul Newman seemed to be out in front as the leading contender for Best Actor. *The Color of Money* had become a highly acclaimed movie which grossed $6.4 million in its first weekend in the United States, earning an average of $10,000 per screen as it opened in 635 cinemas across the country. An array of celebrities attended the New York premiere at the Ziegfeld Theater and the bash after the screening was thrown downtown at the Palladium nightclub, where 1200 guests danced the night away beneath hundreds of billiard-ball balloons. Tickets for the event had sold at $250 each and raised more than a quarter of a million dollars for the Actors Studio, then in serious financial trouble.

Tom was very proud of *The Color of Money*. 'As long as people keep hiring me,' he said, 'I'm gonna take a lot of chances and make some really good movies. And some not very good movies – hopefully, not too many.'

Many Academy insiders confidently predicted that Newman would win the Oscar simply on the basis of his past acting achievements and because he had been so unfairly overlooked before. The experts were absolutely right and he was awarded, *in absentia*, the Oscar for Best Actor.

But what the tens of million of film fans watching the ceremony across the globe did not realise was that Newman had been racked with guilt about his nomination because he believed that Tom equally deserved the award for his performance in the film. Before the ceremony, Newman secretly sent Tom a telegram of condolence when he learned that the younger actor had not even been nominated for Best Supporting Actor. He assured his young friend that he did deserve a nomination and added: 'If I win, it's ours as much as mine because you did such a good job.'

Tom was moved to tears when he received the telegram, which he had framed to hang on the wall of his New York apartment.

Newman would tell anyone who would listen about Tom's great talents. 'Tom has such instinct – he knows a lot more at his age than I ever did. He's got guts too – I called him "Killer" because of his tremendous courage. He's always saying, "I'll give it a whack!"'

Behind Newman's praise lay the foundations of a very special friendship between the two actors. The veteran had become a virtual father figure to Tom, giving him advice and encouragement whenever it was needed. For Tom the bond was especially close because he genuinely saw the older actor as someone he could turn to. In many ways Newman became the father Tom had so desperately needed since the age of twelve. They built up a touching rapport of a kind that exists between very few actors in their league.

'Paul is very easy. Very down-to-earth,' explained Tom. 'Really open. We would go over and eat at his place; he'd cook. We all got so fat – oh yeah, I would go over to his trailer, and we would have lunch every day, dinner every night. It was like this family working together. Gained about a hundred pounds. We had a blast. He is an extremely bright man, very eloquent, gracious, generous, knows how to tell a good joke.'

Tom took in everything Newman told him about Hollywood. He duly noted his warning that movie audiences had a fickle attention span. 'They're like Romans, forever looking for a fresh Christian to feed to the lions.' Newman also disclosed his own low opinion of the movie industry as a whole. 'Success is measured by one thing: box office.'

Tom admired Newman more than any man he had ever met in his entire life. 'He lives a normal life. He's got several businesses, a wife, a family. That's good for me to see,' noted Tom, who one day intended to emulate his hero in every way.

Tom's only consolation for not being even nominated for the Best Supporting Oscar came when he received the 1835th star on the Hollywood Walk of Fame. The ceremony took place on Hollywood Boulevard, near the corner with Orange Avenue, amid a twinge of controversy caused by some Tinseltown stalwarts who claimed that Tom was far too young to be given a star on the pavement. Unfortunately, in 1990 it was discovered that Tom's star had been virtually completely removed by fans who had been helping themselves to chunks of it as souvenirs. It was the first time in the Hollywood Walk of Fame's thirty-year history that anyone had ever vandalised a star.

However, there were times when the father–son relationship between Newman and Tom was reduced to something that made them resemble a pair of childish adults playing silly pranks. During the making of *The Color of*

Money, both indulged in endless silly pranks, like the time Tom gave Newman a suspender belt and bra for his sixty-first birthday.

But the biggest influence Newman had on his younger co-star was to pass on his own fascination with the high-speed thrills of car racing. This passion for speed was, it seems, highly infectious. As Newman explained: 'I asked Tom if he wanted to try my car and he said, "You bet!" Now he's hooked and he's very good.'

Tom rapidly graduated from racing lessons to car clubs and then to his first professional race: the Road Atlanta series, held in Brazeltown, Georgia. Newman raced in the same series and finished fourth with $4000 in prize money. Tom's debut was marked by several mishaps, including a near miss during a practice run in his Nissan 300ZX. Then, during the actual race, he fishtailed twice, forcing one contestant off the track, and then went into a complete spin-out when negotiating a tricky turn.

Despite all this, Tom emerged unscathed from his trial by fire and commented nonchalantly: 'Smooth as silk.' When asked some pointed questions about his disaster-prone first effort he replied: 'I drive faster going to work.' Tom ended up finishing a reasonable fourteenth out of forty-four entries – not bad for a neophyte.

By taking a youngster like Tom under his wing, Newman could not have been unaware of the inevitable presumptions that he was working out his parental feelings by 'adopting' a surrogate son to share his acting and racing career. There was a genuine bond holding the two of them together, aside from the young actor's desperate need for a father figure in his life and the fact that Newman had lost his only son through a drug overdose. In each other the two stars had found the same profound respect, trust and caring that many long for, whether famous or obscure, young or old.

14

If you marry, you will regret it.
If you do not marry, you will also regret it.

SOREN KIERKEGAARD

One week after the glamorous launch party for *The Color of Money*, Tom went down to Georgia for the Valvoline Road Racing Classic of 19 October, joining his recently acquired best friend Paul Newman to indulge in his new-found passion for motor racing. What made this event so significant was that he decided to bring along his new girlfriend, an actress called Mimi Rogers. It was her first public outing as partner to the world's number-one movie star.

The couple had first met across a crowded dinner table at the home of mutual friends in Los Angeles more than a year earlier. Mimi had been dating an associate of Tom's.

Mimi – a statuesque woman with a thick halo of soft, auburn hair and a polished, modulated voice – had recently finished a very serious, long-term relationship with Tom Selleck. At one stage she had been set to marry the six-foot-four-inch star of *Magnum*, and the moustachioed heart-throb had even told one friend: 'She's the main woman in my life.'

The couple openly smooched on the set of movies and generally seemed at ease together. Then something inexplicable occurred between them and they were no longer an item. Mimi never revealed what it was that caused her split with Tom Selleck.

Back in Georgia that afternoon with Paul Newman, Tom Cruise and Mimi held hands constantly as they greeted Newman with a good-luck floral arrangement, complete with a card that read: 'These are for your garden. Go get them. Love Tom and Mimi.'

Encouraged by Newman, Tom took a one-day driving seminar at Georgia's Chestnut Mountain racetrack with Newman's Nissan team-mate and Road Atlanta's chief driving instructor, Jim Fitzgerald. Newman even rented a half-mile track for him and his Hollywood pal to do a little race practice on. 'He took me out and spent a lot of time talking about it,' Tom later recalled. 'I've always loved cars and motorcycles and stuff. Racing is one thing I said I wanted him to get me into.'

As Newman gushed about Tom's 'star status', the young star never strayed far from Mimi's side. Meanwhile racetrack officials were predicting big things for Tom. 'As far as Tom is concerned, he shows a lot of ability and potential as a racer,' said Road Atlanta operations manager Janet Upchurch. 'He's a smart young man and we're hoping he gets into road racing. He seems to enjoy it very much.'

Mimi, an impressive lady with a million-dollar smile and a curvaceous body to match, looked on intently as her young lover and one of Hollywood's elder statesmen indulged their mutual admiration. She seemed completely unfazed by the press attention her visit was provoking and even insisted: 'I've never given it much thought. It was never an issue with us.'

Mimi's first break had been in television's hugely successful *Hill Street Blues*. But her next two series didn't do so well. There was a starring role in the eminently forgettable *Paper Doll*, an ABC-TV pilot that Mimi was ever so relieved never went into a full series. Her following project was a series entitled *The Rousters*. That also failed miserably, although Mimi, ever the resolute professional, bounced back with a highly acclaimed play called *The Last Prostitute Who Took Pride in Her Work*. This was followed shortly afterwards by a major feature movie entitled *Gung Ho*. Director Ron Howard – once Ritchie Cunningham in *Happy Days*, who went on to become a director of such popular pieces as *Splash* and *Cocoon* – chose Mimi to play the role of Michael Keaton's girlfriend in the 1986 comedy about cultural differences between a Japanese company and its American workers. *Gung Ho* was later made into a short-lived TV series without Mimi in the lead.

But Mimi's best movie part to date had been playing Christopher Reeve's girlfriend in the movie *Street Smart*, a vastly underrated production that elicited some fine all-round performances from a number of actors, including Mimi and Christopher, but particularly Morgan Freeman, who later gained worldwide attention through *Driving Miss Daisy*.

'Mimi was a smart, sexy lady who had lived life to the full. You could say she was more than a match for Tom,' explained one member of the *Street Smart* crew. They vividly recall watching Mimi squeeze into a variety of very shapely outfits for her role. 'She is the kind of woman who sticks out in any crowd. There is something about her – she exudes a certain type of sensuality. It is quite remarkable.'

Tom had never forgotten how impressed he had been by Mimi's intelligence and stunning good looks at that dinner party a year earlier. But he had done nothing about it at the time because well-brought-up boys like Tom do not steal girls off other guys.

Mimi's most vivid recollection from that first dinner party meeting was simple: 'I guess we both thought we were kinda cute. You just know.'

Tom's self-confessed penchant for bright, attractive girls meant that when the couple bumped into each other nearly a year after that dinner party, twenty-four-year-old Tom and thirty-one-year-old Mimi instantly clicked as a couple. The thing that really swung it for Tom was that Mimi had been a child when her own family split up. It was as if he could only relate to people who had experienced some of the same sort of personal anguish as him.

Mimi, born in Coral Gables, Florida, told Tom how her parents got divorced when she was just seven years old. Her mother had moved across state, leaving her father to look after both her and her younger brother, Paul. Then followed many years of annually moving with their father – an engineer, like Tom's father – to wherever his work took him. Mimi learned to be a chameleon, fitting in wherever they went – Tucson, Washington DC, Detroit, Los Angeles, the Bay Area. Mimi, a science whiz in school, skipped grades twice because she was so intelligent. But her unconventional childhood made her more of an outsider than most kids, except for Tom Cruise.

Tom did not even give a moment's thought to the age difference between them. After all, this was the mid-eighties and Hollywood was well used to women being wooed and won by younger men. Adding to her mystique, Mimi refused to discuss her age in all press interviews after she met Tom and estimates of her age varied enormously. She seemed to be between six and ten years older than him, depending on which newspaper you read.

Besides Tom Selleck, Mimi had also been romantically linked with the likes of Ed Marinaro and Bobby Shriver – a member of the Kennedy clan. The moment the press got wind of Tom's relationship with Mimi, a vast trawl of her background was ordered by the notorious US tabloids.

Mimi, 'the older woman', was painted as some sort of sexual siren who would teach Tom a thing or two about love making. In fact, the two enjoyed an immensely equal relationship in the early days of their love affair. There is no doubt that Tom looked up to Mimi (she was an inch or two taller than his five feet nine inches!) but she enjoyed the warmness of their friendship and the fact that Tom was not one of those brutal macho characters who would throw his masculinity in her face all day long.

It has also been suggested that Paul Newman – the nearest thing to a father figure in Tom's life at the time – was instrumental in getting the couple hitched. One night Paul and Tom were out at dinner when Tom made a real point of mentioning how much Mimi meant to him, and how the age difference did not really matter to him one bit. He told Newman he was confident that she was a good, strong.

He even admitted: 'When you don't feel like getting married, marriage is just a piece of paper saying two people own each other... I have a very cynical attitude about it.' Tom's outlook was hardly surprising, considering his parents' divorce. But then he remembered his sisters and added: 'They're married and happy.' In some ways it would have been easier for Tom to say 'no way' to marriage if the debris of matrimony was scattered all around him.

Newman listened carefully to Tom's comments and then recounted his own personal experiences. Mainly, there was his own thriving marriage to Joanne Woodward, which had neither damaged his sex appeal nor lessened his status as a serious actor. Newman urged Tom to set a date for marriage to Mimi.

Tom took note of his friend and father figure. No one had ever spoken to him on this sort of subject before. He began to realise just how much he missed not having a father to bounce such things off. Newman made Tom realise how important marriage was. Tom knew all along that his friend was right, but he just had to hear it from Newman before he realised it himself.

There was another motive behind Tom's decision to marry Mimi. He sincerely wanted to try to ease up on his enormous workload and actually start to enjoy life instead of dashing from one movie to the next without ever pausing for some fun. 'I know it's not the norm to be my age and this successful. I can't say I felt totally great about it in the beginning, but then I thought: "Tom, this is where you want to be,"' he explained.

'You see some people destroy themselves because they become successful and feel guilty about acknowledging it – and then it goes away. Now I'm trying to enjoy myself and what's happened to me. I think I've settled in a little more. Even after the financial success of *Top Gun* I have trouble enjoying it instead of taking the moment to say: "Hey, this is really amazing."'

On 9 May 1987 Tom took Paul Newman's advice and married Mimi in a secret ceremony that, ironically, Newman could not get to because he was premiering his next movie, *The Glass Menagerie.* But then a lot of people did not show up to the ceremony because the couple hardly told a soul. Unlike his great friend Sean Penn – whose marriage to Madonna had been eclipsed by a media circus that included helicopters hovering overhead and boats bobbing about on the ocean – Tom succeeded in marrying without any member of the media knowing about it.

Even the so-called well-informed gossip columnists like Liz Smith of the *New York Daily News* were left red-faced and empty-handed. She complained in her column: 'Why didn't any of my thousands of spies out there bother to tell me Tom Cruise was marrying Mimi Rogers last weekend?'

Tom even kept Andrea Jaffe, the publicity agent for both performers, in the dark about their marriage plans. Two days after the ceremony she admitted: 'Guess what? I got a phone call today telling me. I didn't get any details. I don't even know what day it was.'

The secrecy surrounding Tom's wedding to Mimi was just another example of the young actor's increasing obsession with privacy. He might have owed his multi-million-dollar salaries to the public who flocked to see his movies, but that did not mean they owned a chunk of Tom's personal life. In the few days leading up to the wedding, Tom decided not even to tell some of the Hollywood associates who had grown close to him, for fear that the news might leak out and he'd face the sort of chaotic scenes that greeted Penn and Madonna. He told the people who were invited that he was having a 'Spring Bash' at the house and did not reveal the marriage plans until after everyone had arrived.

What few facts can be gathered about the ceremony are as follows: best man was Emilio Estevez and Tom's mother, Mary Lee, later conceded to *People* magazine that the wedding was 'very small, intimate and beautiful'. A short Unitarian service was held in a large Victorian house that Tom and Mimi were renting in Bedford, New York State. Besides Emilio, the only non-family members in attendance were a girlfriend of Mimi's, who acted as bride's attendant, and the Unitarian minister who presided over the union. Initial reports that actors Judd Nelson and Charlie Sheen were among the guests were later denied emphatically.

The couple and their guests dined on food prepared by Tom's mother and his sisters. Even the wedding cake – chocolate with white marshmallow icing – was baked by one of Tom's sisters.

'I couldn't be more blessed,' exclaimed Mary Lee.

Tom and Mimi were said to be too busy to even consider a honeymoon of any sort; instead they combined business with pleasure and headed for Los Angeles to visit friends, including Mimi's best friend, actress Kirstie Alley, and her husband, Parker Stevenson. So much for Tom's intention to reduce his workload. It was disappointing for Mimi, whose romantic image of marriage considerably differed from Tom's real, ambitious aims, which could not be effectively watered down by his wedding.

Just before the marriage ceremony, Mimi said optimistically: 'If I were offered an unbelievable role that was shooting in Tunisia for three or four months and Tom couldn't go ... well, Tunisia would have to wait.' Mimi even talked in glowing terms about having children with Tom and insisted that he was 'as committed as I am. This is for real.'

But, whether he liked it or not, Tom's career was feeding too many mouths in Tinseltown for there to be any let-up in his work commitments. Hollywood wanted its pound of flesh and personal happiness was not going to get in the way of making movies. Mimi herself took a rather dim view of those who live for the glare of publicity: 'I want to work but the pure concept of fame is not the point with me. Being famous is not all that great,' she insisted. There were obviously a lot of fundamental differences between Tom and Mimi and they were only just beginning to surface.

Hollywood was hardly in a state of shock about Tom's decision to marry. His relationship with Mimi was perceived to be solid and gracious, with just a touch of spice because of their age difference.

Mimi's magnetism was undoubted. 'There's a little something about her that appeals to an awful lot of men,' explained her old family friend former San Francisco 49er quarterback John Brodie. Everybody did better whenever she was around them. Tom Cruise certainly did.'

Mimi was just as committed to the idea of a wedding, as she explained: 'Beforehand you don't think it's going to change things, but it does. There's just a deeper sense of responsibility and commitment and it's great.'

Friends of the couple recalled that they were 'heavily into each other almost to the point where the rest of the world did not exist'. Mimi admitted that she and her new, young husband were 'very much mutual boosters'. She explained: 'We rely on each other to tell the truth. I guess we're very lucky and I think he's very talented and he thinks I'm talented.'

Shortly after the wedding, Paul Newman and Joanne Woodward even made up for not showing up at the ceremony by taking Tom and Mimi out for dinner at a trendy New York restaurant on York Avenue called Wilkinson's Seafood Cafe. And in late 1987 *Cosmopolitan* even awarded Tom and Mimi its coveted 'Couple of the Month' award.

Before their marriage, Tom and Mimi's relationship had been noted as one of the happiest in Tinseltown. By all accounts no one had ever heard them even raise their voices to each other. Mimi – with her ample bosom and penchant for showing off her figure in a subtle sort of way – seemed to complement the conservative image of Tom. They were known as 'the perfect couple'.

But slight cracks began to appear shortly after their wedding and alleged tiffs were reported with glee in the US and British tabloids. Their first row concerned Tom's speedy driving. It was claimed that Mimi asked Paul Newman to have a talk with him, but no one could ever quite fathom out whether Newman actually talked to his young protégé or not.

When Tom luckily escaped serious injury after his Nissan 200SX hit a wall during the Sports Car Grand Prix at Ponoco International Raceway in Pennsylvania in August 1989, Mimi felt her nerves becoming frayed. Tom got out of the car himself and walked to an ambulance. He was taken to the infield hospital and released. Tom's only comment: 'I wanted to improve on my second-place finish... I was following a team-mate into turn one, and I lost the draft.'

Another major long-term problem for the couple was that Tom was planning to continue living in his recently acquired $3-million apartment on New York's East 13th Street, while Californian Mimi seemed intent on remaining in Los Angeles. In the first few months after the wedding they tried hard to see as much as possible of each other, but it wasn't easy.

Mimi did not particularly like New York as a place to live because she had been brought up in hotter climates. Tom's apartment, in one of the most sought-after blocks in the city, enjoyed fantastic views and celebrity neighbours, including Rolling Stone Keith Richards and Phil Collins. Tom even tried to make the apartment more homely by getting a highly paid interior decorator in to make some adjustments, including the installation of some $5000 sofas which caused a major traffic jam in the narrow street outside when they had to be delivered by crane because they were too big to go in the lift.

The couple laughed off constant claims in the tabloids that Tom was jealous of Mimi's love scenes and vice versa. Tom was consistently linked with every leading lady he starred alongside, but the couple managed to make light of all the outrageous claims in a way that Tom seemed unable to do later in life. In Tom's Los Angeles office he even had a favourite absurdity framed and hanging on the wall. The headline read: 'Wife Jealous.'

Mimi went off and played the steamy lead in *Someone to Watch Over Me*, directed by Ridley Scott, who had worked with Tom on *Legend*. Some of the sex scenes with co-star Tom Berenger were fairly explicit and there was some speculation that Tom was upset by them.

However, after completing *Someone to Watch Over Me*, Mimi announced that she definitely still believed there was a lot more to life than making movies. 'I want to go through the whole Museum of Natural History and read everything. I love the gems and natural minerals exhibit and the whale. It always amazes me that something could be so big.' Her focus was definitely not on the same objectives as Tom.

The couple did look as perfect as ever when they attended the premiere of *Ishtar*, starring Dustin Hoffman, who had been slated to appear with Tom in his next project, *Rain Man*. And Mimi seemed to revel in the company of Tom's young, glamorous Brat Pack pals, although Tom's friendship with Sean Penn had cooled a little after his marriage to Madonna because Penn had become much more inaccessible.

There was also talk in Hollywood that Tom wanted to start a family with Mimi. At one stage a friend of Tom's was quoted as saying the star had told him: 'I've always loved kids and Mimi is the one that I want to have them with.'

However, by the summer of 1988 reports alleging that Mimi was having problems getting pregnant had started to circulate. The *Sunday People* in Britain claimed that Tom had dismissed fertility experts called in to try to find a way of ensuring Mimi got pregnant. The report alleged that Tom and Mimi had been keeping to a strict love-making schedule in order to pick the most fertile times of the month. The article ended by quoting a friend as claiming that after Mimi failed to get pregnant, Tom had said: 'We'll leave it to God's will.'

That report was followed up almost a year later by one in the US tabloid the *Globe* which claimed that Mimi had been seeking advice from Kirstie Alley, who was also having problems conceiving. The report alleged that Mimi and her best friend had been 'giving each other a lot of moral support. They talk all the time about how badly they want a baby.' About a year after his marriage to Mimi, Tom made a fascinating comment about his. 'At times I look to see if I'm doing what I set out to do,' he explained. 'I'm always finding out new things about what's going on with a character. Making a movie is like a chess game. It's about constantly changing patterns, adapting to new things. It's not just black and white. Every day something happens and you think, "That's terrific, let's shift with this."'

15

Tom reminded me of those guys you see in boot-camp films, doing push-ups, and the sergeant is saying, 'One more! One more!' And Tom is not only the guy doing the push-ups, he's also the guy saying, 'One more!'

DUSTIN HOFFMAN

The bowling alley was crowded with families enjoying an American-style classic Saturday night out. No one noticed the two shortish men aiming their bowls with deadly accuracy. They could have been father and son.

The two men were then joined by a family of four, including a clearly autistic child and his brother, and continued their bowling. Still no one spotted them. Tom Cruise was out on a research field trip with Hollywood icon Dustin Hoffman.

The two actors were trying to gain some real-life experience for the characters they hoped to portray in *Rain Man*. For Tom, it was like a dream come true to find himself slated to appear opposite Hoffman. The project appeared to be on the verge of production and he could not believe his good fortune in moving from his classy role in *The Color of Money* to an even more impressive part opposite a truly legendary name.

It seemed that Tom was on a creative roll following the acclaim he received after the release of *The Color of Money*. Still only twenty-four, he had clearly mapped out his future with great precision and had been casting around very carefully for the perfect next movie when the *Rain Man* project fell into his lap. Tom was absolutely determined not to take any retrograde steps in terms of his career. If that meant waiting months, even years, for the right sort of project to come along, then so be it.

When Tom's agent, the ever-loyal Paula Wagner, had earlier slipped her client a script of *Rain Man* that was circulating in Hollywood, she already knew that it would appeal to him, but her first approach to Hoffman's people got a polite rebuff because the star of such classics as *The Graduate* wanted comedian Bill Murray to co-star alongside him. But then Murray started making big demands and, within days, Tom and Hoffman had teamed up and the project seemed to be on the verge of being green-lighted.

Tom could not believe his luck. Only two years earlier he and Sean Penn had driven past Hoffman's Beverly Hills mansion and dared each other to go and knock on the door of their acting hero. Neither had the courage to do it.

The stories about Hoffman were legendary. In Hollywood everyone knew his reputation: Dustin Hoffman is a perfectionist; Dustin Hoffman demands absolute accuracy and won't proceed until he gets it; Dustin Hoffman even held up the shooting of *Marathon Man* for hours because the scene called for his character to jump out of bed and grab a flashlight, but Dustin knew that his character wouldn't keep a flashlight by the bed.

Dustin Hoffman was the sort of perfectionist that Tom Cruise wanted to be. He felt they would be soulmates even before they actually got to work together.

But then *Rain Man* became caught up in what is known as development hell. Several versions of the screenplay were written and rewritten and numerous directors attached at one time or another, and it became clear that *Rain Man* was no nearer actual production than the first day it was devised.

What makes this all the more surprising is that among the cluster of directors involved was Stephen Spielberg – the most powerful auteur in Hollywood and surely someone who could get a movie green-lighted at the flick of a finger. Unfortunately, this was not actually the case. In movieland no project – whoever is attached – gets financial backing until a studio says 'yes' and, in the case of *Rain Man*, studio executives were having very big problems coming to terms with the subject matter: an autistic man's reunion with his criminally inclined brother. Hollywood just did not feel ready or able to cope with dealing with mental retardation.

A year had passed since Hollywood's most powerful talent agency, the awesome CAA, decreed that Dustin Hoffman, who had just starred in a miserable failure of a movie entitled *Ishtar*, should be teamed up with Tom Cruise. The notion of a Hoffman–Cruise movie sent Tinseltown into paroxysms of excitement – rapidly followed by total confusion. The age gap between the two stars was twenty-eight years! How could they be believable as brothers? *Rain Man* was supposed to be a story about an idiot savant, not about a biological accident. The casting of Tom and Hoffman would require a massive restructuring, yet another rewrite...

CAA – under the auspices of Mike Ovitz and his most trusted foot soldiers – completely disagreed. They argued that although Hollywood might be cognizant of the age gap, the great viewing public wouldn't even notice. The charisma of the actors would carry the day.

With the project back to swimming around in development hell, Tom decided to commit to a film called *Cocktail*. If ever it was true that every two steps forward require one step back, then this project was definitely the proof. While there is no reason why Tom should make his every film choice serious and dramatic, people inside Hollywood were rather puzzled as to why he picked a movie like *Cocktail*.

One theory is that Tom had waited around so long for *Rain Man* to be green-lighted that he felt he needed some light relief. *Cocktail* could certainly never be classified as anything more.

The plot was simple: Tom played a Manhattan barman who falls in love with a wealthy woman (played by Elizabeth Shue) and the film chronicles their relationship and the one between him and his mentor, played by Australian actor Bryan Brown. The result was a movie that's all flash and no substance.

Before even starting the shoot, Tom got a light-hearted reminder from his old mentor and father figure Paul Newman not to take life too seriously. The veteran star sent Tom a six-pack of beer with a note attached that read: 'You're always working. I want you to sit down. I want you to take a weekend. I want you to drink all these beers.'

Tom thought long and hard about that note from Newman. He knew what the older actor was trying to tell him: slow down or you'll burn yourself out before you get into your thirties. A few years later Tom reflected: 'I've thought about that a lot. And I have slowed down. Some...'

Tom did his usual thorough research on *Cocktail* but this time it was a little more convivial than usual. For the best part of a month he hung around in some of New York's best-known bars and was even spotted mixing drinks behind the bar at John Clancy's Seafood Restaurant before flying to LA to take bartending classes with Glendale barman John Bandy.

Tom's character in *Cocktail*, Brian Flanagan, was brash and flash, and Tom found himself defending his image during press junkets in the lead-up to the movie's release. The public was getting the impression from *Cocktail* that Tom was a 'cocky bastard'. He was keen to pour scorn on that notion. 'I feel a responsibility to bring the truth to the character that I play. This is not Tom Cruise. This is Brian. But people often misinterpret it.'

Tom was even publicly criticised because his character jumped in and out of bed with a host of different women – and never once wore a condom. He had a clear response: 'I don't think it's my job to educate people on safe sex. Do I have to wear a condom in my scenes on the screen? This is an R-rated film. People under seventeen won't get in without their parents. This is the eighties. There is AIDS. There is alcoholism. People should be able to figure it out for themselves.

'Images of how people perceive you can't control your life, so I just do what I'm doing. I'm a working actor who feels fortunate to be where I am and to do what I've done.'

Behind the scenes, shooting in glamorous locations like Port Antonio, Jamaica, turned into nightmare scenarios when four days' worth of shot film was found to be overexposed and had to be reshot. Tom was joined by Mimi for a few days in Jamaica and the rest of the cast and crew noted that the young actor hardly ever mixed with his colleagues off the set. Instead, he and his wife would wander off along the beach for long walks away from the crowds.

One of the few good things about *Cocktail* was Tom's beautiful co-star, Elizabeth Shue. A native of South Orange, New Jersey, just a stone's throw from Tom's old home at Glen Ridge, Elizabeth also came from a broken home. But there the similarities ended. The two actors were enormously polite to each other, but there was no off-screen friendship.

The recently married Tom proved more than a handful in the sex-symbol department during the making of the film. He was not keen on exposing his assets on the big screen. As director Roger Donaldson, a straight-talking New Zealander, admitted: 'Tom was very concerned about showing his ass.'

Tom was reluctant to perform a crucial love scene with Elizabeth Shue. Many believed his increased shyness had been caused by his marriage to Mimi. Others were convinced that he simply did not believe a star of his stature should have to do gratuitous bedroom scenes.

'Love scenes make me nervous,' Tom insisted on the set. 'It's very strange to get in bed with someone you don't really know. They're embarrassed and I'm kinda going, "You okay?"' He then laughed as he said: '"Right then, let's do it." It's no fun at all. You have to be professional about it. You respect the other person's feelings. There's a line to cross. I don't do it and it's never been done to me. That's the way it is.'

Shue, a very attractive, bubbly blonde, had shot to fame in *Karate Kid*, a movie that did incredibly well at the box office despite having no stars in it and nothing more than a rather weak plot line. She tactfully remained silent about her steamy kissing scenes with Tom and even refused to comment on them when one tabloid incorrectly tried to suggest that Tom had a real-life romance with her.

Cocktail eventually proved an interesting testimony to Tom's pulling power because it took more than $70 million at the box office after its release in July 1988, even though it was dubbed one of the worst movies of that year. One angry reviewer wrote damningly that Tom 'doesn't even try to act'. Highly respected TV critic and Chicago-based writer Roger Ebert wrote stingingly: 'This is the kind of movie that uses Cruise's materialism as a target all through the story, and then rewards him for it at the end. The more you think about what really happens in *Cocktail*, the more you realise how empty and fabricated it really is.'

Tom insisted that the mistakes he made during *Cocktail* would help his next performance. Typically, he was managing to turn a cinematic disaster into a learning experience.

When the *Rain Man* saga resumed at the end of the *Cocktail* shoot, the latest director attached to the project was Steven Spielberg. But, rather than being overly impressed by Spielberg, Tom let it be known that while he was delighted to hear about the master helmsman's interest in the script, he was far more concerned about keeping Dustin Hoffman and himself attached to the project.

When Spielberg's interest also faded, Tom started to genuinely worry about whether it would ever actually get made. One day he phoned Hoffman in a state of virtual panic. Tom recalled: 'I said, "Listen, it doesn't look good, but I wanna make this movie," and Hoffman said, "You wanna make this movie?" I said, "Yeah, I wanna make the goddamn movie." And he said, "Then we're gonna make the film. Hang tight, Cruise: we're gonna make this movie."'

Later, when told of Tom's account of what happened, Hoffman agreed with everything except he insisted he never called Tom by his last name.

Then in stepped director Sydney Pollack, whose films included *Tootsie*, starring Hoffman, and *Out of Africa*. He had already passed on the project once before because 'it had been around a long time and everybody was having problems with it'.

Initially, fellow director Barry Levinson was asked by super-agent Mike Ovitz to help Pollack try to knock the project into shape. As is surprisingly often the way in Tinseltown, Levinson did not mind helping out a rival director, as he would no doubt be expected to return the favour some day.

By this stage neither Tom nor Dustin Hoffman had even faced the reality that they might act together in a film, because neither believed the project would ever get off the ground.

Then Levinson, a quietly spoken man with shoulder-length grey hair, got a call from Ovitz telling him Pollack had dropped out of *Rain Man* and asking if he would like to do it. Levinson accepted and then found himself in a desperate scramble to rewrite the script before principal photography was scheduled to start just seven weeks later.

Before Levinson climbed on board, Dustin Hoffman had done extensive research into autism and he felt very committed to trying to portray an autistic correctly. Levinson backed his actor all the way because he was convinced that Hoffman's character, Raymond Babbitt, would provide the main thrust of the film. Tom was more than happy to play second fiddle to

Hoffman because he acknowledged that he was in the company of a true master of his art.

Levinson was no pushover either. The former writer had a formidable directorial reputation (*Tin Men, Good Morning, Vietnam*) and while he liked everyone to suggest new ideas, he was not afraid of telling interfering actors where to get off – and he was in the company of two of the most notorious in modern Hollywood history. He explained: 'If an actor wants everything to be the way he wants it to be, then it's best to say, "Look, get your own fucking movie and do it yourself." But if you are working on collaboration, that's terrific, because if you are exchanging ideas you may find a better one that takes you to a higher level. That's what gives you adrenalin; it's what drives you and stimulates you.'

The director then cast beautiful Italian actress Valeria Golino as Tom's character Charlie Babbitt's girlfriend, Susanna, and the movie got under way in Cincinnati. Within days the attractive brunette actress was experiencing Cruisemania at first hand. 'Once, after Tom and I shot an outdoor scene in which we hold hands, a trembling girl came up to me and tried to kiss my hand because it had just been in Tom's. Things like that happened all the time with his fans. It was amazing,' she explained.

Valeria and Tom also became the subject of endless rumours of a love affair which, the notoriously inaccurate US tabloids claimed, was threatening to break up his marriage to Mimi. Nothing could have been further from the truth. There was no affair. In fact, Valeria and Tom hardly mixed off the set.

Hoffman, known as a bit of a movie-set maniac, was full of praise for his young co-star. 'He's a demon,' he marvelled. 'He gets up early, he works out, he goes home early, he studies, he works out again at night ... and he always wanted to rehearse.'

Tom then got a few words in and it all started to sound a bit like a mutual admiration society. 'What you get from great actors like Newman and Hoffman is where to focus your energies and what to worry about and what not to worry about.' Tom even conceded, 'because as a young actor, you're worried about everything'.

In 1984, long before the *Rain Man* project had got under way, Tom had been in a New York restaurant with his sister when they had spotted Hoffman across a crowded room. Eventually the young actor plucked up enough courage to go over and tell him what a great admirer he was. Hoffman immediately insisted that Tom and his sister go and see him at a play that very evening and come backstage afterwards. Tom was astonished because Hoffman knew precisely who he was.

But while Tom and Hoffman might have sounded as if they were going to make the perfect match, others involved with *Rain Man* were not so sure – especially when it came to dealing with Hoffman. The production manager and the assistant director – both veterans from Hoffman's greatest triumph as a sex-swap actor in *Tootsie* – told Levinson's producer, Mark Johnson, that Hoffman had been so difficult that they'd given him bad news or asked for favours only when he was in his full Dorothy Michaels drag; as a woman, they said, he was much nicer.

During shooting, the expected clash of egos between Tom and Hoffman never materialised. In fact, it simply did not exist. 'Dustin was very supportive,' explained Tom. 'I mean he's so shrewd, so intelligent. He's a consummate professional. He knew what was best for the film. He saw the limitations of his role and saw the whole picture. He had the overview to see where the film should go, as if to say, "Look, we've got to set up who this guy is," because I kept saying, "Who am I? What is this guy about? What is going on?"'

Beneath Tom's slightly desperate-sounding words was an actor's genuine concern with his character. He was playing the smooth car-dealer yuppy brother to Hoffman's autistic Raymond and he knew he was going to have to battle to make his presence felt. He cleverly allowed Hoffman to become his mentor to a certain degree. He did not want to make the older actor feel inferior in any way – he also wanted to learn.

Hoffman was very receptive. He gushed about Tom: 'He's a moment-to-moment actor. He's there in the moment. He doesn't have any intellectual idea of what he wants to do – he's coming off the gut, and that makes him a pleasure to play ping-pong with.' Hoffman admitted that by the end of *Rain Man* the situations had completely reversed. 'Tom was as much directing me as I was directing him.'

Levinson was also full of praise for Tom's acting abilities and insisted that his apparently inferior role was in fact the most essential element in the movie. 'I thought Tom Cruise did well because he had to drive the whole movie. He had to be on top of it the whole time, because if he didn't the movie would lie down.'

Both Tom's and Dustin's performances in *Rain Man* were highly acclaimed. Hoffman was incredible as Raymond, developing a twitch of his head, a unique style of walking, an interesting choice of vocalisation and managing to give a terrific performance without the benefit of making eye contact with his co-stars. To an extent, it's almost as if he were acting his scenes by himself.

Tom simply overshadowed any of his previous performances. Under his gifted hand, Charlie is emotionally frozen on the surface but, just beneath, he's a weapon ready to fire – a bit like Tom Cruise in real life. The frustration and barely controlled anger he's feeling becomes a tangible thing for the audience. It's interesting that through these feelings he unwittingly begins to develop an understanding of his brother that might not have been possible at the outset.

Nobody in Hollywood thought *Rain Man* would make any money, not even director Levinson. 'I thought this would be a kind of offbeat piece, even if it did star Tom Cruise. On opening night I drove past one of the theatres and it was half full. So I thought, it's going to do some business, but not do particularly well.'

The movie's backer, MGM/UA, was not a healthy studio at the time, so *Rain Man* had only one preview before release. The usual audience research was abandoned because their reaction to the film was so negative. The audience resented the fact there was no happy ending to the film and many people were upset by Tom's character's cruelty to his brother. But Levinson refused to pander to the audience and stuck firmly to his guns. 'I did not set out to make something that was going to be this great piece of mass entertainment.'

Former studio executive Peter Bart explained: 'The conventional wisdom on *Rain Man* was that it met none of the normal criteria of a "hot picture". *Rain Man* was not sexy. It wasn't especially comedic. Its perspective on humanity was rather dark. The Dustin Hoffman character was not redeemed or transformed into a "normal" person. Indeed the only thing the picture had going for it was that it was superbly directed and performed. And it rang true.'

The analysts' dire predictions were wrong from the start. *Rain Man* was not just a hit – it was indeed a complete blockbuster. In its first eighteen days the film registered a remarkable $42.4 million at the US box office. By the end of March 1988, five months after its release, receipts had soared to $155.7 million, thus passing *Rocky IV* as the highest-grossing picture in the history of United Artists.

Rain Man came in under budget by $2.5 million (the original estimate was $30 million) and went on to gross an estimated $500 million worldwide. Once again a movie featuring Tom Cruise was heavily nominated at the following year's Oscars and went on to win eight Academy Awards, including Best Director for Levinson and Best Film. And once again Tom was overlooked when Hoffman won Best Actor. He found it difficult to hide his disappointment but he felt that, like all the knocks he had faced in life, this was just another learning experience and he would build on it and continue seeking out the quality roles until he got what he deserved.

Movie expert Edward Gross said Tom was perfectly entitled to feel disappointed. 'The feeling of teamwork between the two is obvious in the finished film, for they work together like one complete individual. Hoffman won the Academy Award and the lion's share of the credit for his excellent performance as Raymond. It's disconcerting, however, to see that Cruise was not equally lauded. In his hands, Charlie Babbitt is a flesh and blood human being who goes through a 180-degree transformation due to contact with the brother he never knew existed. Never again would anyone doubt his abilities as an actor.'

Los Angeles Times film critic Sheila Benson wrote: 'No one can argue that *Rain Man* is Cruise's quantum leap, so that it can be said unblushingly that he holds his own with the masterly Hoffman.'

Not everyone was so impressed by the film. New York's *Village Voice* insisted: '*Rain Man* is a small, sweet, unconvincing road movie that overinflates itself on the gaseous notion of a lovable autistic idiot savant "curing" his conventional autistic, that is to say "normal", kid brother in the course of a week-long drive to California.'

The notorious Pauline Kael, in the *New Yorker*, was even harder on the young star: 'And Cruise as a slimeball is just a sugarpuss in Italian tailoring. He doesn't even use his body in an expressive way. His performance here consists of not smiling too much – so as not to distract his fans from watching Hoffman. Cruise is an actor in the same sense that Robert Taylor was an actor. He's patented: his knowing that a camera is on him produces nothing but fraudulence.'

But there were consolations for Tom. Not only did he make a whopping $5 million flat fee for *Rain Man*, but he also made at least $5 million more when the movie topped the $100-million mark because of a complex deal that meant he and Hoffman were making more cash from the movie than the backers, United Artists.

Tom was at least able to bask in the movie's commercial glory. 'People asked after *Rain Man*, "How are you going to match the success of that picture?"' he commented. 'I said, "I can't live my life by what is going to make $20 or $100 million. I don't know what is going to happen to my career. I am going to take a lot of risks and some of it is going to work and some of it is not going to work. Some of it will be trash and some of it I hope will be good. I make the decisions. I pick the scripts. I have only myself to blame if things don't work out. That is why I want to live my life. That is the way I set out to live it at the beginning."'

16

*I think he became middle-aged making
this movie. I think he passed out of his youth
truly into early middle age. He'll never be the same
boy he was before. He knows too much now.*

OLIVER STONE

Like so many American kids of his generation, Tom Cruise came of age after his country's fall in the Vietnam War. Tet, My Lai, Cambodia, Kent State: to Tom they were just names, vague and confusing, devoid of any historical or emotional interest. The war was something that was not among his concerns or in his consciousness. Whatever happened to America after the war, when thousands of Vietnam veterans came home crippled and in wheelchairs, was not high on his agenda. By his own admission, when it came to Vietnam, Tom was a complete innocent.

Then, one night in Manhattan in January 1988, he found himself having dinner with a charismatic man called Oliver Stone. Stone had been a United States Marine who was twice decorated in Vietnam, but Tom only knew him as the brilliant director of films like *Wall Street*, *Salvador* and the Oscar-winning Vietnam movie *Platoon*. Tom listened intently as Stone told him about his next project: a film about Vietnam even more ambitious than *Platoon*, a story that maybe, just maybe, could draw out the core of the Vietnam tragedy and make it a lasting testimony to peace for generations to come.

In vivid detail Stone described the elements that would be portrayed in his film, such as battlefield horrors and confusions, women and children mistakenly killed, the physical and psychological wounds inflicted on a nation that left many GIs so badly injured they would come home with shattered bodies and minds that would stay that way for the rest of their lives. Then would come shots of the veteran hospitals where tens of thousands of soldiers suffered anguish after the rest of the country had turned its back on them. Stone promised too that he would focus on how the war tore America apart at home – the politicians, the anti-war movement and how it attracted many of those very same GIs who suffered so much for their country. That was the second war – the one in their own backyard.

Tom was riveted by the widescape scenario described by Oliver Stone, probably the most influential movie-maker in Hollywood at the time. But when the director started to explain that he intended to draw the essence of Vietnam through the true story of just one man, US Marine Sergeant Ron Kovic, of Massapequa, Long Island, Tom tried not to look too overawed. It was starting to dawn on him that Stone was considering him for the role of Kovic.

To Stone, Kovic was the symbol of the Vietnam War. The ex-Marine even described himself in his best-selling autobiography as a true 'Yankee Doodle Dandee'. Born on 4 July, American Independence Day, Kovic grew up in a working-class Roman Catholic family steeped in the virtues and traditions of God and country, community and flag. His heroes had been John Wayne and President John F. Kennedy. When the call to fight for his country came, he did not hesitate to take his place in the fight to stop the march of communism. He paid for his loyalty by being wounded in action and sent home in a wheelchair. Permanently crippled. Impotent.

As Kovic says: 'I'll never feel the inside of a woman. I can feel the pressure of her body, but I'll never feel her skin against my chest. I'll never really. That whole thing. And the beauty of this woman, holding a naked woman for the first time, and how incredible that is.'

There were, explained the stern-faced director, one or two problems. To start with, he had not lined up an actor to play Kovic and, probably even more importantly, he had little or no money with which to finance the project. At this point Tom would normally have stood up, said a gracious goodbye and gone out through the restaurant door. But he was sitting with no ordinary director; Oliver Stone was a legendary, hard-hitting, blunt-speaking film-maker with a passion for subjects that often proved infectious. And Tom was already hooked.

Stone went on to explain that he had written a screenplay with his old friend Kovic in the late seventies. At that time they had lined up Al Pacino to play the lead but the money had fallen through at the last minute after rumours of creative discord between Pacino and Stone. Kovic had been especially hard hit by the disappointment of not seeing his life story converted to the big screen. Stone's voice lowered to almost a whisper and he asked Tom if he would like the part.

Tom nodded instantly. He was more than ready for a personal declaration of independence after a bellyful of highly commercial Hollywood movies. The biggest other project on the horizon was a sequel to *Top Gun* and he had promised himself he would never do that even if they paid him $100 million.

What Tom did not fully appreciate at the time of that meeting over dinner in New York was that he was about to embark on his own frightening rite of passage, accompanied by two war-torn characters called Kovic and Stone. Tom's decision to go with Stone's project was probably the most important decision of his career. It was a done deal and, with Tom's name and face attached to the project, Stone would get the funds to back it. Not only did Tom enlist with Stone, he also agreed to defer his own fee until revenues started coming in. Stone had made the same arrangement in regard to his own fees, and so another bond was forged, bringing star and director even closer together.

'Our only concern was bringing the film to a certain level, to make it real,' Stone explained. 'I always admired Tom as an actor. I had a feeling about him. And I had known Ron about ten years. When you put them together, you know.

'Both men are motivated by a desire to be the best, to be No. 1. And they both had high self-esteem. In the 1960s, with Ron Kovic that took the form of joining the Marines. And at the end of the day, I sensed with Tom a crack in his background, some kind of unhappiness, that he had seen some kind of trouble. And I thought that trouble could be helpful to him in dealing with the second part of Ron's life.'

Kovic's personal involvement in the project was essential, so it was only natural that Stone's next task was to take Tom to see this man, crippled, confined to a wheelchair, so that the actor could understand the man he was going to bring to life on the screen, so that he could understand the thousands of other veterans who had come home in wheelchairs.

The meeting between Tom and Kovic was a true eye-opener, the two men bonding immediately. 'It was very emotional. If it had been me, back in the fifties, back in the sixties, well, I understand that feeling of country, of wanting to do something good for people and your country,' Tom enthused.

Tom, Kovic and Stone sat on the vet's bed at his modest home near Los Angeles and watched his home movies from his childhood. Kovic was understandably apprehensive. He had great doubts and fears about how the project would take shape. But Tom soon convinced him otherwise.

Kovic was to serve as Tom's guide, confidant and adviser throughout the entire production of Stone's movie, entitled *Born on the Fourth of July*. He became a modern-day Virgil leading Dante through the circles of Hell, showing his young impersonator the pitfalls and the correct way to walk through them. Tom accompanied Kovic to some veterans' hospitals, where he saw at first hand some of the relics of the Vietnam War, destined to remain hospitalised for the remainder of their lives.

Tom became totally immersed in a world of paraplegics and began to discover some startling similarities between his own upbringing and that of Ron Kovic. Both men came from a Catholic background, both knew what hunger was and both suffered from a lack of formal education. Tom became increasingly convinced that fate had landed him the lead role in Stone's megamovie. It made him all the more determined to make a success of the film.

Beneath the surface, Tom was nervous, excited and unable to believe that such a major acting role had come his way. 'There was an element of great challenge, of great emotional commitment. But at the end of it, I didn't want Ron to say, "Oh man, I made a mistake, you shouldn't have played the role."'

Male bonding complete, next came two separate weeks in an army boot camp for Tom. Stone brought in a no-nonsense, straight-talking former Marine captain named Dale Dye to take charge of Tom and a handful of other actors during their training. The first week was at a camp in the USA and this was followed by a trip to the Philippines, where the battle scenes would eventually be shot.

Stone decided that, to make Tom's role look entirely authentic, they would inject him with a special serum that would paralyse him for two days at a time. Tom, by this time completely and utterly swept up with the project, immediately agreed to the suggestion. Anything that would add authenticity to his part was okay by him. It took a very worried movie insurance broker to point out that if something went wrong they would not pay up to replace Tom and start the film all over again. The serum plan was finally abandoned. 'The point is, he was willing to do it,' Stone later recalled.

Tom then spent weeks in a wheelchair alongside his new friend Kovic. It was an enlightening experience, exhausting both mentally and physically. On one occasion he nearly got in a fight with a store owner who objected to him being in his shop in the wheelchair because it might mark his carpet.

When *Vanity Fair* journalist Jesse Kornbluth showed up for a prearranged interview with Tom, he thought the star had failed to show up until he noticed a thin man in a wheelchair wearing a baseball cap with a Southern Methodist University insignia, a cheap checked shirt and jeans. He had dark insomnia smudges under his eyes and a week's growth of beard. Suddenly the man in the wheelchair rolled alongside Kornbluth and said, 'Hey. I guess it's working.' Tom Cruise had arrived for his interview.

Kornbluth asked Tom if he felt torn by the fact that he could actually walk in real life. He could just get up and walk away from that wheelchair.

Tom replied: 'Listen, you talk to people in wheelchairs, they don't want to see me in a chair and they don't want you to feel sorry for them. They work like hell to live and be alive; if they didn't want to be alive, they wouldn't be. But seeing a boy in a wheelchair like that ... it's not easy. It's not easy to go home and say, "Hey, I'm getting it."'

Born on the Fourth of July also starred Willem Dafoe as Kovic's paraplegic soulmate Charlie, Raymond J. Barry as his father, Caroline Kava as his mother and Kyra Sedgwick as his teenage love, Donna. But there was no getting away from the fact that all the pent-up primal feelings throughout the movie were expressed through Tom.

Much of the shooting of the film remains a complete blur: the battle scenes, the wounding, the sense of shame and alienation Ron Kovic felt when he returned to the USA.

Oliver Stone kept to a strict shooting schedule that frequently called for twelve- or thirteen-hour days, often shouting nothing other than 'Action' at the assembled actors, followed a few seconds later by 'Do it!'

Tom's already legendary attention to detail involved challenging everything from a line in a script to the exact shading of make-up. Stone said that while Tom always tried to be decent to the people he worked with, his drive for excellence could get in the way.

Like Kovic, he took himself very seriously, and when characters like that get hot in a culture that is often frivolous or superficial, they can miss a beat. In Tom's case, it sometimes bogged him down in his own intensity. But if Tom came across as a bit serious, well, life can be serious too. As Tom said, at least he could get up out of that wheelchair after each scene; Ron Kovic never could.

Tom found shooting Kovic's hospital scenes the toughest part of all. In real life Kovic had spent four months strapped to a bed in a desperate bid to save his leg. Tom had to try to be that character and deep inside it really hurt. His biggest problem was that as he tried to be Kovic, he started to feel the same notes of desperation, the same disillusionment, the same rage at the government for the way it treated all those injured veterans.

Next came the most visually and psychologically uncomfortable scenes for the audience – Kovic's living hell as an impotent man. A scene in a Mexican whorehouse catering especially for crippled Vietnam vets drove home the point with typical Oliver Stone bluntness. Once again the settings were of filth and degradation, but this time Kovic is trading that against the minute chance that he might be able to achieve sexual satisfaction. He is framed paralysed from the waist down, with catheters running out of his crotch, so lonely that he risks potential humiliation for a woman's touch.

Tom found those scenes harrowing, as he explained later. 'The way I work best is to be totally relaxed. I don't pretend to be the character, I *am* the character. But you know what struck me? Intellectually, philosophically, you sit back and you go, "Well, I'm someone who doesn't feel that being masculine is in my, you know, crotch. There are many other elements to being a human being and a man." But there were moments when I read the script, when it just struck me, WHAACK! to the marrow. Hold it! The realisation of losing that...

'Reading those scenes it was right there in my face: you're going to play this. The loss of manhood. The loss of one's ability to create on a physical level. It's not being just able to feel a woman, to be inside a woman, it's being able to create a family. To procreate is a very important aspect to life. And where does that take you, if you can't?'

Tom sounded as if he clearly understood every one of the torn emotions that Ron Kovic suffered. In later years his own wish to be a father would cause no end of anguish, so perhaps those words have rung in his ears ever since.

In the key bedroom scene in the movie, Tom found himself completely unable to perform for the camera for the first time in his entire career. This time it was nothing to do with immodesty or fears that such a scene was gratuitous. He got up from the set and walked to Oliver Stone's side and muttered quietly: 'I'm just not there. It's just not working.'

Later he explained: 'I remember feeling a lot of anxiety actually. Going, "Why do I feel all this anxiety?"'

Stone looked sternly at his young star and was unrepentant. His reply sounded like that of a battle commander: 'Look. You got it. Just don't think about it. Just do it, man, do it.' Then he shrieked: 'Action! Snap to it, Mr Cruise!'

But still Tom could not do it. He went through the motions for a few seconds before the cameras, then broke down in floods of tears, unable to contain himself for a moment longer. All the memories of his childhood, his father, the pain, the loneliness just came flooding back. 'I was crying and laughing a little, too. It was an absolute relief. Essentially, I just let go.'

What happened in that scene occurred over and over again as Tom drove himself to the edge of his abilities. All that cold, clinical focus that he had always referred to so keenly had gone out of the window. In its place was good old-fashioned emotion. It was this kind of intensity and commitment that brought Tom universal praise for the quality of his performance in the movie.

Ron Kovic himself was reduced to tears on many occasions as he watched from the edge of the set. 'I'm extremely proud of his performance,' he says. 'I truly believe he actually becomes me.'

Just before heading to the Philippines for the final stage of the shoot, Tom started to wonder if perhaps he had taken on too much with the strenuous part. Every night was punctuated by appalling nightmares in which he was being shot in the jungle. The terrifying reality of the dreams helped Tom to take stock of what he was doing. One lesson it taught him was that he had to learn how to loosen up, to move 'in and out' of a role more comfortably so that it didn't dominate his life to an unhealthy degree.

On the last day of shooting Kovic took the Bronze Star he had kept in a box by the side of his bed for twenty-one years and gave it to Tom as a lasting tribute to his performance. 'I told him it was for his heroic performance,' he said. In truth, it was a gesture of thanks from the crippled ex-soldier. Somehow, through Tom's performance, Kovic had exorcised many of the demons that had haunted him since the day he was shot in Vietnam. As a celebration of that, he wanted the young actor – still only twenty-six years old – to have his last actual reminder of the war. In turn, Tom gave Ron a watch that the vet still wears to this day.

Oliver Stone also hailed Tom's performance as heroic. After shooting was completed he told the star he felt indebted to him for standing by his project because it meant that Stone could keep his promises – to himself; to his friend Ron Kovic; and to tens of thousands of fellow veterans who share the wounds of Vietnam. 'We wanted to show America, and Tom, and through Tom, Ron, being put in the wheelchair, losing their potency. We wanted to show America being forced to redefine its concept of heroism.'

Yet the picture's backers, Universal, had fought a raging battle with Tom's publicists to prevent them from releasing still photos of Tom in a wheelchair, for fear of turning off the audience. The studio was concerned about whether the film would attract the folks who had flocked to see Tom in the past. The young star was privately furious at this interference because he genuinely believed that he did not have a stereotypical audience. It deeply offended him even to consider such a thought.

After *Born on the Fourth of July* was released, Tom was proclaimed by many critics to have deftly made the transformation from an attractive screen presence to serious dramatic actor. Oliver Stone summed it up when he said: 'He's not the simplistic cardboard figure many believe. He's very serious. Committed.' *Newsweek* movie critic David Ansen reckoned: 'Cruise has been very smart by taking risks.'

Writing in the *New York Post*, David Edelston acclaimed the movie as 'powerful, bombastic and furiously uneven'. And movie writer Edward Gross said: 'Tom Cruise's portrayal of Ron Kovic is proof positive that he is one of the most versatile actors working in Hollywood today; a presence that will undoubtedly leave others of his generation behind in his wake.'

The movie went on to gross $70 million at the US box office alone, an incredible achievement when one considers how uncommercial the subject matter was.

As far as Tom was concerned, the best news of all to come out of the movie was that he had been nominated for a Best Actor Oscar for his astounding performance as Kovic. Maybe this time he would stand a real chance. Hollywood sneerers instantly started predicting that *Driving Miss Daisy*, a soft, seamless tale of an old lady and her black chauffeur, would overtake *Born on the Fourth of July* in the race for Oscars. Many of the old guard in Tinseltown still felt that Tom had to suffer a few more years for his art before he could truly merit a seat at the top table.

But Tom's millions of fans in the United States thought otherwise. In a poll conducted on the eve of the Oscars ceremony in March 1990, thirty-nine per cent of *New York Daily News* readers reckoned Tom should get the Best Actor award. Some movie experts believed that he would get the statue because he had not even been nominated for *Rain Man* the previous year and the Academy 'wants to kiss and make up'.

Tom was nominated and attended the Oscar ceremonies that year, but had to forgo the Governor's Ball and other post-Awards galas to get back to the set of *Days of Thunder*, which was shooting at Daytona Beach. Universal transported him to Los Angeles by private jet and then back to the location just a few hours after the end of the ceremony.

Although Tom did not win the Oscar that year, he seemed genuinely delighted when British actor Daniel Day Lewis got the award for Best Actor for his work in *My Left Foot*. Tom knew that one day his time would come – it was only a matter of time. Just as long as he remained focused it would happen ... eventually.

After the ceremony he said sportingly: 'It's exciting. Just getting nominated. That acknowledgement from my peers. It's also good for movies. I believe in the Oscars, because I feel it's good for what we do. It's tradition.' And he wanted a part of that tradition – badly. Tom was actually fairly overawed just to be sitting in the audience for the Oscars alongside such luminaries as Anjelica Huston, Jessica Lange, Jessica Tandy and Morgan Freeman.

Then, out of the blue, came a story that rocked Tom more than anything ever published about him before. The *News of the World* in Britain claimed in a huge front-page story that Tom had been secretly rushed to a hospital in Paris because he was suffering from breast cancer. The report went on to imply that Tom's mother, Mary Lee, had confirmed that her son was seriously ill. The article came like a bombshell in Hollywood. Anything that even remotely suggested that the world's biggest box-office attraction might be ill was big news in the movie capital. Soon everyone was saying, 'Have you heard about Tom Cruise?'

Meanwhile Tom's personal publicist, Andrea Jaffe, was juggling hundreds of press inquiries from around the world following the *News of the World* 'revelations'. She insisted that Tom's mother never gave an interview to the British tabloid and went on to warn that Tom's lawyers were considering legal action. 'Believe me,' insisted Jaffe. 'He's fine.'

Claims that Tom was also receiving treatment for the breast cancer at the Cedars-Sinai hospital in Los Angeles were also discounted.

Subsequent articles claimed that Tom had simply been suffering from a heavy bout of flu, but the damage had already been done. Some believe the rumours were started when Tom – in London on a get-away-from-it-all holiday with Mimi – interrupted his peace and quiet to attend a premiere of *Rain Man* sporting a startling shaved head, which had been done for a crucial scene at the end of shooting *Born on the Fourth of July*.

Later Tom seemed remarkably jocular about the rumours, even though they gathered momentum to include a claim that he had developed AIDS. Many Hollywood insiders believe that Tom's *Born on the Fourth of July* haircut was definitely responsible. 'Some bright spark added two and two together and decided he was dying,' explained one Tinseltown source.

Tom saw the AIDS rumours as yet more evidence of the media's attempt to undermine his career. He made a note of the circumstances behind the stories that circulated and promised himself that, as his stardom grew, so would his ability to silence the gossip mongers.

17

This isn't film-making, it's war.

TOM CRUISE

Tom's ever-growing obsession with car racing became part of his Hollywood persona towards the end of 1989. With leading producers Don Simpson and Jerry Bruckheimer badgering him to commit to their sequel of *Top Gun*, Tom came up with the perfect solution – he decided his next movie should be the greatest car-racing adventure ever filmed.

The idea of starring in a motor-racing movie had been tucked neatly in the back of Tom's very focused mind ever since he had driven his old friend Rick Hendrick's Winston Cup cars around Daytona, the most famous racetrack in the world, three years earlier. After just a few laps of thrills and spills he decided he had to make a movie about the profession.

Tom then quietly started his homework on the subject and carefully studied just about every car-racing film ever made, including Paul Newman's own *Winning* and a number of other even less auspicious efforts, like *Grand Prix*, starring James Garner. Tom soon discovered that there had never been a truly great film on this theme. Nor could he have failed to notice that most of these movies were made after stars had expressed an interest in the subject and the films had then been built around their personalities. In other words, the drama had to be created out of nothing, and that was always a bit of a problem.

'A lot of them didn't have a story, just the action. As a result, you felt separated from the movie,' explained Tom. 'I mean, I don't care how much machinery you have in a film. If I can't get involved with the characters, then for my money I'm not gonna enjoy it. I want the racing scenes to punctuate what's happening in the characters' lives.'

Tom wrote a brief outline and took it to Ned Tanen, a Paramount executive and fellow car freak. The studio then recruited screenwriter Donald Stewart to flesh out the young star's treatment. But when a less-than-visionary script came back, Tanen and Tom took Tom's idea to Simpson and Bruckheimer. It was the exact reverse of what happened with *Top Gun*. This time the two savvy producers offered Tom all the advice and encouragement – they clearly saw the project as *Top Gun* on four wheels. The fact that there was not a decent script in sight did not bother them in the slightest. Don and Jerry could fix that easily!

Meanwhile Tom was still explaining to all his friends and associates in Hollywood how he came to be so obsessed with starring in a motor-racing movie.

'I just became caught up with the people, their dedication to their profession and level of intensity,' the ever-enthusiastic Tom told one Hollywood associate.

But starting a new screenplay from that brief outline written with great care by Tom was not as easy as he thought it would be. Tom, Simpson and Bruckheimer hired Warren Skaaren (*Top Gun*, *Beetle Juice* and *Batman*) to write it. That was where the problems began. Tom, always the perfectionist, forced the weary writer to produce dozens of drafts before he burned out and politely pulled away from the project.

By this stage Tom was feeling very frustrated. He actually thought that his idea was so strong it would virtually write itself on the page, but screenwriting is a severe test of patience; a bit like a huge jigsaw puzzle with tens of thousands of pieces to put together. The notion that a writer can go home, sit down and knock out a perfect script is just not true. In reality, he writes a few pages, rewrites them, then rewrites them and so on until he has achieved the basic shape of the story, and then he goes back to the producer – in this case Tom – to be told, more often than not, to start again.

By the time Skaaren walked away from the project, provisionally entitled *Daytona* at this stage, Tom was starting to realise that a producer's role is not as easy as it seemed. He decided that he would try to land a really big name to mould his idea into a winning screenplay, so he went right to the top and hired Robert Towne, a legendary hellraiser and scriptwriter of such classics as *Bonnie and Clyde*, *The Godfather* and *Chinatown*. You couldn't go much higher than that.

Tom was relieved and elated. He completely threw out Skaaren's original draft and got down to work with Towne. And within weeks he was telling anyone who would listen: 'What's great about Bob Towne is that he just came in and understood the world. He focused on the piece. He liked these people. I remember after an hour – we had gone to a racetrack – he said, "I get it, Cruise. I know what you're talking about. This is fantastic." That was exciting.'

Naturally, Tom saw his project as more than just fast, throbbing cars cutting in and out of beefcake shots of himself. 'It's manipulating a vehicle with tremendous power around a track. The level of competition is driver to driver. It's modern-day gladiators. It's a war. There's a tremendous amount of dignity in the characters and in the people I've met just hanging around the circuit.'

Tom believed that racing cars was not that different from making movies. Both professions required complete and utter dedication, working sometimes fourteen hours a day, seven days a week, often for ten months of the year. Just like on a film set, a family is created by this process and everyone goes through the ups and downs together. But those close to Tom at the time say that he became so embroiled even in the pre-production stages of the project that he was perhaps not quite seeing the wood for the trees.

Teaming up with Simpson and Bruckheimer, his old acquaintances from *Top Gun*, certainly made Tom feel more secure about the project's viability. He believed that as long as the two producers were running their side of things, then it would surely end up being a highly commercial film. When *Top Gun* director Tony Scott climbed aboard, the word in Hollywood was that this was one movie that simply could not fail. Tom publicly declared that he liked to work with people he knew, although he was very careful not to give the impression that their partnership would last beyond that actual movie.

Don Simpson was well aware of the comparisons being made between this new project and the successful *Top Gun*, and he didn't mind one bit. He knew that if Tom would not agree to do a *Top Gun* sequel, then this was the next best thing. He also realised that making a movie about racing cars was no easier than their previous outing with those Mach 1 pilots.

'In *Top Gun*,' he explained, 'we shot the ground story, then the sea story, then the air story. It was like shooting three separate movies. This time, we have dramatic scenes, and then all the racing. And the racing is nearly impossible for us to predict or control. But we're going to take the image of stock-car racing as most of the public perceives it and turn it around. We're going to show them how high tech and professional it really is.'

Jerry Bruckheimer commented: 'I don't think there's ever been pressure to produce a big film. What we try to do is make effective films and films that we are real proud of. To satisfy myself, there's always pressure, creative pressure to do something different, unique.'

Apart from *Born on the Fourth of July*, an operation which was completely led by Oliver Stone, Tom had been allowed to have a large say in the casting of his previous three or four movies and in this project – now renamed *Days of Thunder* – he was going to use that clout to devastating effect. His initial insistence on casting Australian actress Nicole Kidman was eventually to change his life.

Then veteran actor Robert Duvall was hired to play yet another father figure to Tom's character, Cole Trickle.

Filming of *Days of Thunder* got under way in November 1989. Within weeks rumours were spreading around Hollywood that the project's actual production costs had soared way beyond the original estimate of $30 million. The studio backing the film had insisted that the movie be ready for an autumn 1990 release, which meant that Tony Scott would have to edit the entire movie incredibly fast in order to complete it on time. Every day new pressures were mounting on the producers and the director.

Then there was Tom. He was starting to spot holes in the script that he had not noticed before shooting began. Bob Towne had to be on hand for the entire shoot to make last-minute revisions as Tom and Scott tried desperately to polish the script even more. The situation wasn't helped by the fact that, as a few people on the set realised, Tom was being completely diverted by his co-star Nicole Kidman. To start with, the pair only exchanged glances and smiles, but it was clearly building up into something much more serious.

In the middle of all this Tom took a spin round the Charlotte Motor Speedway track in North Carolina and set a new track record by averaging 166 mph. It was almost as if he was trying to prove he could do it for real as well as in the movies.

Filming of *Days of Thunder* was hampered for much of the time by foul weather. Unexpected rainstorms and a severe freezing spell made racing scenes especially difficult to shoot.

In January 1990 Tom made the cover of the prestigious *Time* magazine as a tribute to his extraordinary performance in *Born on the Fourth of July*. The background to the article provides a fascinating insight into how it can often help to have friends in high places. Over the years, Tom had built up quite a rapport with *Rolling Stone* owner Jann Wenner and, as a result, had received rather more than his fair share of coverage in the magazine, including an appearance on the cover at almost the same time as *Time* featured him.

Tom was so worried that he might offend Wenner by appearing on the cover of *Time* as well that he personally rang the publisher to explain his decision. 'When Tom first told Jann about the cover, Jann was a little upset,' revealed a source. Then, in an astonishing example of Cruise control at its mightiest, Tom Pollock, chairman of Universal Studios (which had backed *Born on the Fourth of July*), called Jann and appealed to his sense of friendship and the two men agreed that it would be okay for Tom to appear on the cover of *Time*. Ironically, and some would say typically,

Tom still managed to insist on the *Rolling Stone* article being penned by a writer he approved of.

Back on the *Days of Thunder* shoot, Tom, ever the focused one, came up with a novel solution to keep up with the constantly changing script: he taped pieces of the screenplay on to the car's dashboard so that he could recite dialogue while zooming around the track. It was a dangerous habit that diverted his concentration on a number of occasions – not something to be recommended when doing 150 mph on one of the fastest race circuits in the world. Somehow Tom avoided any serious crashes, but there were numerous dented fenders.

Days of Thunder's backers, Paramount, sent teams of executives down to Daytona to make sure that Tom and his co-stars were not taking any unnecessary risks as their insurance policies did not allow for the stars to get involved in the thick of the racing action. Secretly, Tom insisted on doing his own share of stunts because he wanted the movie to look as authentic as possible.

When Paramount decided to bring forward the US release of *Days of Thunder* to the 4 July holiday weekend of 1990, Tony Scott and his team of editors found themselves with just six weeks to complete post-production of the movie – a process that usually takes at least six months. It was even decided to shoot an extra love scene between Tom and Nicole Kidman in a thinly disguised attempt to cash in on the couple's real-life love affair.

Simpson and Bruckheimer tried to avoid talking to Scott towards the end of that day's extra shooting, following heated exchanges between the two producers and their director. They simply did not have time left to allow him to shoot any extra footage. Paramount were putting enormous pressure on the entire production because the film's escalating costs had led to their decision to release it earlier than planned in order to get their huge investment back as fast as possible.

That extra day's shooting actually ended at four the following morning and Tom immediately threw himself into his role in the post-production process by visiting the editing room, cutting, looping dialogue and then taking care of TC Productions business during the evening. It was a gruelling schedule, but Tom relished every minute of it, although, curiously, he did not wear a watch, which played havoc with his timekeeping.

'It's exciting because it really puts you absolutely to the limit,' he explained. No wonder Simpson and Bruckheimer nicknamed Tom 'Laserhead' after finishing *Days of Thunder*. Tom had a simple explanation for his nickname. 'Because when I focus in on something I kinda tear it apart until I understand it. But it takes a laserhead to know a laserhead.'

In the end, *Days of Thunder* knew exactly which buttons to push to keep an audience as finely tuned as one of Tom's cars. Tony Scott's direction was as effective as ever in the circumstances, but the film was missing a heart and soul. It seemed like a classic formula movie without any real punch, and much of the blame was laid at the door of the screenplay. 'The biggest problem with the film are aspects of the screenplay. There's nothing wrong with pure escapism, but many parts of the story are so formula and so much like *Top Gun*, it's annoying,' wrote film critic Edward Gross.

Basically, there were too many cooks involved in *Days of Thunder* and the script paid the ultimate price. Tom, Scott, Simpson and Bruckheimer all wanted a say, and for a writer of Bob Towne's calibre it was a nightmare. He allowed them all to have some input and the result was a hotchpotch of formula ideas.

There were also very strong rumours about the film's ever-escalating budget. By the time of its release, estimates were around $60–70 million, making it one of the most expensive movies ever made. Tom got a fee of $10 million for his troubles.

The reviews were predictably appalling. 'It is one thing to market a film solely on the strength of its star. It's quite another to go ahead and make the film that way,' wrote the icy Janet Maslin, referring to Paramount's multi-million-dollar promotional campaign, launched weeks before the movie's premiere in a desperate attempt to cash in on Tom's so-called star appeal.

Tom even had to grit his teeth and be charming to the media as part of the push to promote *Days of Thunder*. Women writers were literally lining up to take it in turn to do a few laps with him on the Daytona circuit – all in the name of good publicity. Some of them were mightily disappointed. Wrote Jeanne Marie Laskas in *Life* magazine: 'He doesn't look like Tom Cruise. He's a lot smaller than Tom Cruise. Small hips, small shoulders, just plain little. I wonder how they made him look so big in the movies. I wonder why these movie people have lightened his hair and also permed it. It doesn't look good. It looks overdone, exhausted, as if to shout, "Just leave me alone already!" – a sentiment very much in keeping with the mood here today.'

Then followed a terrifying 180-mph tour of the circuit that reduced Laskas to a virtual gibbering wreck as she became queasy and dizzy. After numerous pleas from the journalist to return safely to the pits, Tom finally rolled to a halt with a grin on his face that was subtle evidence that he had just scored a major victory over the piranhas.

Movie critic Marilyn Moss wrote just as damningly as other detractors: '*Days of Thunder* is a minor film with major pretensions, not to mention a major noise factor that barely masks what the story lacks in believability.'

Women reviewers seemed to find the film particularly unappealing. The *Philadelphia Inquirer*'s Carrie Rickey wrote: 'Not only does *Days of Thunder* disappoint on the basic narrative level, it is also a peculiarly thrill-less action movie. Shot from the driver's point of view, the race sequences lose their novelty as swiftly as a video game.'

Soon everyone was on the bandwagon. The *Los Angeles Times* described *Days of Thunder* as a 'fake of a film', while the highly respected *Hollywood Reporter* dubbed it a 'very fast film by its nature with some story wobbles'. Last word to Henry Sheehan of the *Los Angeles Reader*: 'As soon as the screen is empty of speeding cars it is empty of their impact as well.'

In the middle of all this, Tom was highly embarrassed to be voted *People* magazine's Sexiest Man of the Year. Previous winners included Sean Connery, John F. Kennedy, Harry Hamlin, Mark Harmon and Mel Gibson.

Tom rejected the idea that there had been problems on *Days of Thunder* and even talked in glowing terms about it being a so-called 'big picture' and explained why he would continue to make them. 'My favourite thing is to go to a film opening night or opening weekend and sit there and have a group experience. I enjoy films that run the gamut... I'm looking for what's going to have the greatest impact, what's going to communicate. But I look at everything. I just haven't found anything small that I felt was interesting enough for me to spend the time.

'When I'm making a film, it's a year out of my life, I mean, I've been working on *Days of Thunder* for a year and a half, really, and for a year straight of seven days a week. So you have to believe in what you're doing and love it, because there are sacrifices. When I do something, I have to feel a hundred per cent committed.'

Days of Thunder went on to gross more than $80 million at the box office, but it was still deemed to be a failure as the original costs of the movie would have swallowed up all of the profit. It also made the 'worst movie of the year' lists in many publications.

Shortly after *Days of Thunder* wrapped, Tom was by his own admission about ninety per cent committed to a highly controversial role as a drug-addicted undercover policeman in *Rush*, a movie based on the real-life memoirs of a Texan policewoman called Kim Wozencraft. His only dilemma about the part was that he had turned down the lead in *Bright Lights, Big City* and this was another movie that had a very ominous drug-taking content. Tom admitted he was concerned about the project and told producer Richard Zanuck that he would make a commitment to it once he saw the finished script, which was being written by his *Days of Thunder* collaborator Robert Towne.

Eventually Tom turned down the controversial role and it went to Julia Roberts's one-time beau Jason Patric. Around this time Tom found himself being offered another off-the-wall part as the lead in *Edward Scissorhands* for Twentieth Century Fox. *Batman* director Tim Burton was to helm the project and it was described as a modern-day *Elephant Man* yarn. For some inexplicable reason, Tom pulled out of starring in the movie and that role went to teenage heart-throb Johnny Depp instead. Another role that never came to fruition was *The Curious Case of Benjamin Button*, for Universal. F. Scott Fitzgerald's short story had been turned into a screenplay by writer Robin Swincoard and there was speculation that Steven Spielberg was slated to be director. But once again this was a project that faded from sight for Tom. Then came the supposed pairing of Tom with Eddie Murphy for *Out West*, with veteran Walter Hill at the helm. Again Tom dropped out for no apparent reason.

But there would be plenty more offers, and Tom knew he could well afford to wait for the perfect platform.

18

You have to assume there are small-minded or nasty people out there. And for some reason it makes them feel better to think, 'That little no-talent slut, she just looks for celebrities to date.'

MIMI ROGERS

My need to achieve was really great. It took its toll on the marriage.

TOM CRUISE

A few months before starting rehearsals on *Days of Thunder*, Tom went to a private screening of a small-budget but hig acclaimed Australian film called *Dead Calm*. The movie was directed with great skill by Australian Philip Noyce and starred New Zealander Sam Neill, one of the most accomplished actors ever to come out of the Southern Hemisphere.

But it was Neill's co-star who caught Tom's eye. Nicole Kidman was just twenty years old when she played the part of the wife of Neill's character, naval officer John Ingram. The film centred around the couple setting off on a yacht for a vacation following the tragic death of their child in a car crash. Somehow, despite her Pre-Raphaelite, shoulder-length red hair and porcelain features, Nicole managed to be convincing as a housewife, and all who saw her performance proclaimed her as a big star of tomorrow.

Tom was entranced as he watched *Dead Calm*, which featured some harrowing scenes, including Nicole's rape by a man who breaks into the couple's yacht and leaves the husband floating helplessly in the ocean. That girl, he decided, would be his co-star in *Days of Thunder*. So it was that Nicole Kidman landed the role of Dr Claire Lewicki and became Tom's love interest on and, subsequently, off the big screen.

On a number of occasions during those difficult months in late 1989, he frequently moved out of the couple's luxurious house in Brentwood, Los

Angeles, and went to stay with friends – only to move back in with Mimi after a few days away.

Mimi obviously realised that they were having marital problems, but she genuinely felt they could talk it through. She made Tom attend marriage guidance counselling through the Scientologists. But the few sessions the couple attended did nothing to improve the situation. Even a number of secretive dinners together in small Brentwood restaurants ended in angry words on both sides. It was becoming clear to all of Tom and Mimi's friends and associates that the marriage was in deep trouble.

One of the friends Tom went to stay with was actor Emilio Estevez. The two stars had been friends since Tom first arrived in Hollywood. Tom even encouraged Emilio, his best man at his wedding to Mimi less than three years earlier, to date Mimi. No one knows if this was because he wanted his wife to fall in love with another man or because he hoped that Emilio might be able to talk some sense into Mimi and either help mend their broken marriage or – much more likely – suggest that she 'should just let it go'.

It all sounded terribly civilised, but the truth was that Tom felt riddled with guilt about Nicole, even though there is no suggestion that he began a physical relationship with her until later.

In early December, Mimi flew to Florida to be with Tom during the filming of *Days of Thunder*. She still hoped to save their marriage. Within hours of her arrival, Tom asked for a divorce and told the stunned actress: 'I'm with Nicole now.'

Mimi was completely shattered and took the first plane back to Los Angeles. She knew there was no point in trying to make it work. Tom had made up his mind – there was nothing left between them. The end had been sudden and clinical – a bit like a business deal that had gone wrong.

Later Tom told writer James Greenberg that he considered his split from Mimi as 'no different from what other people go through. You've got to confront it and say, "Okay, where do you take it from here?" You handle it and take responsibility for what occurred and move on. It's as simple and not as simple as that. As years go by, it's not even something I think about; after a couple of years you go, "What were those issues?" I'm living now.'

Tom defended his decision to dump Mimi in favour of Nicole by telling Greenberg: 'It just seemed right. I think anyone who has met Nicole would understand. It was like nothing occurred before, and just because you get divorced doesn't mean that's it. I was ready, I was really excited.'

The actor was already blotting Mimi out of his mind like some bad dream.

Tom also told Greenberg: 'My divorce was something that had to be done.' He refused to acknowledge that his own parents' divorce made the split with Mimi even more difficult. 'I think anyone who has been through a divorce can't believe it's happening to them, whether you come from a divorced family or not.'

Back in Los Angeles, Mimi remained stunned by Tom's request for a divorce. Within days his lawyers were in touch. They wanted to hammer out a deal that would make the split as painless – and uncontroversial – as possible. The top-secret negotiations meant the actress would end up with a fortune, including the house in Brentwood, which would leave her wealthy enough never to have to work again. Conservative estimates put the entire settlement at around $10 million.

A reported call from Paul Newman suggesting Tom reconsider ending his marriage got the young actor thinking about whether he was right or wrong to split up with Mimi. Newman told him: 'Time heals all wounds. Joanne and I learned that a long time ago.' Tom was impressed that his friend had found the time to talk to him, but he did not think it was the right advice in the circumstances.

Just before Christmas 1989 Tom forgot his own marital problems and slipped quietly into a hospital in Fort Mill, South Carolina, to give a boost to a ten-year-old girl waiting for a heart transplant. Little Brandi Mason could not believe her eyes when her idol walked in clutching a hat and shirt from *Days of Thunder* and autographed her pillowcase before visiting some of the other sick children in the hospital. It was a pleasant diversion after all that emotional upheaval.

On the *Days of Thunder* set, Tom and Nicole were very careful to keep their friendship out of everyone's sight. Tom did not want anything to upset his carefully laid plans for a smooth and satisfactory divorce from Mimi.

On New Year's Eve, Tom splashed out $13,000 for a party on location in Charlotte, North Carolina, for the rest of the cast and crew. Despite going through one of his regular teetotal stages, Tom was still happy to pay for the bash as it was his way of saying 'thank you' to the team for all their sterling efforts. Wearing a red cardigan over a simple white T-shirt and jeans, he shook lots of hands and talked with many people, but Nicole Kidman was nowhere nearby. That relationship would continue to be kept under lock and key for a while longer. Tom did not want to appear to be rubbing in the fact that he had a new love.

Friends and colleagues on the set of *Days of Thunder* reported that Tom changed into a much more relaxed character after his friendship with Nicole began to blossom. He no longer felt the same level of intensity which had haunted the final few months of marriage. Nicole's motto was: 'Life is for living.' She was about to re-educate Tom along those lines. Nicole was a refreshingly unaffected, down-to-earth, typically Aussie girl, with a spark and vitality for life which Tom had never encountered in Hollywood before.

Even so, at the beginning of January 1990 Tom was still refusing to admit publicly that his marriage to Mimi was in the process of being ended, despite rumours flying around the *Days of Thunder* set.

Back in Los Angeles, Mimi tried to get over the shock of Tom's request for a divorce by being seen out in public with Emilio Estevez. Mimi and Emilio were photographed outside a nightclub by some of Hollywood's infamous paparazzi.

In fact, Estevez persuaded Mimi to fly to the *Days of Thunder* set to make one last appeal to Tom to save their marriage. Mimi held a teary-eyed meeting with Tom on 11 January at the Charlotte Hilton-University Place Hotel, but he told her it was too late.

For once the US tabloids seemed to have been one step ahead with the story. Before any news of the break-up had been officially released, the *Globe* ran a piece from its Hollywood bureau chief that was splashed across an entire page and headlined: 'Wife Gives Cruise the Boot'. The essence of the article was that Tom had split up with Mimi after a huge row. 'The actor has been back to see hot-tempered Mimi on a number of occasions in a desperate attempt to mend the marriage but to no avail,' the piece claimed. The story quoted a source close to Tom as saying: 'The marriage is in serious trouble. They're having big problems.'

But the most intriguing aspect of the article was the claim that the couple felt under a lot of pressure to have a baby. It stated: 'They've had no luck, but Tom is still desperate to have a child. He's almost fanatical about it.'

The *Globe* claimed that, during a discussion about parenthood in October 1989, 'things got out of hand and they got into a real screamfest. Mimi hit the roof and she yelled at Tom to pack his bags and get out of the house.'

References to Mimi being heartbroken about not getting pregnant may not be accurate, but there is little doubt that the couple were feeling under intense pressure to start a family. There was even talk of Mimi seeking fertility treatment.

Just after that final meeting at the Charlotte Hilton-University Place Hotel, divorce papers were secretly filed in Los Angeles. Tom told friends it was the honourable way out of the relationship as he was starting to feel a certain amount of wanderlust and, rather than sneak around behind his wife's back, he preferred to be completely honest with her.

The actual divorce papers were filed on 16 January, citing as petitioner 'Thomas Cruise', and the respondent was named as 'Miriam Cruise, aka Mimi Rogers Cruise'. Petition WED 052576, signed personally by Tom on 12 January after his attorney had flown especially to the *Days of Thunder* set in North Carolina, was for a dissolution of the marriage and gave as the date of actual separation 9 December 1989. It cited 'irreconcilable differences'.

The most interesting aspect of the very brief divorce papers filed at Los

Angeles County's Superior Court of California is the fact that Tom had requested confirmation of the couple's separate assets and obligations and a line had been typed on the form which read: 'All such assets and obligations of the parties have been confirmed by written agreement.' On the following page under a section marked 'Property rights to be determined', his lawyer had typed 'in accordance with written agreement'. In other words, a deal had already been struck splitting the couple's possessions. Tom and his attorneys had managed to get Mimi's complete agreement on a split of possessions before news of the separation was even made public.

The following day, in a tersely worded statement, the couple said: 'While there have been positive aspects to our marriage, there were some issues which could not be resolved even after working on them for a period of time.'

Tom defended his decision not to admit earlier that his marriage was in trouble by saying: 'I felt that to compromise our privacy was to compromise a basic trust. I hope that can be understood.'

Rolling Stone was furious that Tom had sat through the earlier interview without admitting his marriage was in trouble. Writer Trip Gabriel had even asked Tom point blank about his marriage problems. If this was a special relationship with a magazine, then goodness knows how many lies Tom would tell if he did not like the publication, *Rolling Stone* reasoned. Senior editor Peter Travers complained: 'He sort of talked around the issues. We feel misled by what happened.'

Time's film critic Richard Corliss probably summed it up best when he said: 'His was an Academy Award-worthy performance. He gave it to all reporters. Every celebrity plays a game. Tom Cruise was giving one of his best performances by playing Tom Cruise.'

Tom was severely criticised in the media for the role he played in covering up the fact that his marriage to Mimi was in trouble. *Newsweek* even ran a piece on 29 January 1990 headlined: 'The Great Tom Cruise Cover-Up'.

The entire cover-up operation had misfired badly for Tom, who actually thought that his denials would be stored away and forgotten about.

Tom didn't realise that these public attacks on him were the result of what the media perceived to be a deception on his part. He saw nothing wrong with lying to journalists for the sake of his own privacy, but they seemed deeply offended that he should dare to do such a thing.

On 22 January Tom faced the full might of the world's press at the annual Golden Globe Awards ceremony in Los Angeles, where he picked up a Best Actor trophy for *Born on the Fourth of July*. He tried desperately to avoid shouted questions as he left the festivities at the Beverly Hilton Hotel. But, when the press turned their attentions towards his mother, Mary Lee, he looked about ready to explode.

Mary Lee, however, was more than capable of looking after herself. 'It's a personal thing. I have nothing to add,' she told reporters with great professionalism and coolness.

The following month, Mimi – already resigned to becoming an ex-Mrs Tom Cruise – threw a birthday celebration that was described as her 'coming-out party, of sorts'.

For months after the divorce papers were filed, Mimi found it difficult to even mention Tom's name. After all, she honestly believed that they had fallen in love and that their union would last for ever. Now she had a lot of time on her hands and started to do some intense thinking about where the relationship had gone wrong. She even admitted to her friends, in roundabout terms, how difficult her marriage to Tom had been, especially the fact he was a successful actor.

She had the distinct impression that Tom had become such an object of extreme attention that it had, inevitably, made him much more demanding of the people around him. She came away from her marriage to Tom convinced that actors were definitely more emotionally immature than the rest of the world.

Mimi had witnessed at first hand the coddling and cotton-wool treatment, and firmly believed it had contributed to the break-up. She reckoned that success had hit Tom so suddenly that his entire world had turned upside down. Virtually overnight he had become the focus of a tremendous amount of attention. Everyone wanted to be his best friend and no one would dare to say no to him. Mimi felt that perhaps he lost his footing because no one would criticise him. In many ways she wished that his success had come more slowly, as then he would have been able to learn along the way and make adjustments in order to work out what was real and what was an illusion.

Until just a few months before the break-up, Mimi genuinely believed that Tom was someone who was secure enough to open up emotionally. She saw him as very tender and caring, which was just the way she liked men to be. But eventually she noticed that Tom had developed into a compulsive, even slightly obsessive personality, and she found that very annoying. She had always loved Tom because he was not the kind of man who thought emotion was a sign of weakness. But that attitude had changed enormously towards the end of their marriage as the cracks began to appear. Mimi, a strong independent spirit, found it difficult to cope with the changes.

The final evidence of that change came in the months after the separation, when Tom's people insisted on a complex set of rules and regulations that Mimi knew she had to obey. This was all part of the Tom Cruise machinery, now in charge of a carefully orchestrated damage-control operation designed specifically to avoid Tom being embroiled in an unpleasant tit-for-tat divorce with Mimi.

Tom's team of lawyers, movie executives and agents all wanted to preserve that wholesome image of their 'property'. The result was that Mimi was restricted to an oblique interview with *Hello!* magazine in which she had to pretend she was not talking about Tom when in fact the whole world knew she was.

Tom didn't really care that much for the media. At that time one New York paper published a story claiming he had sent one of his two golden retrievers to an animal psychiatrist for therapy. That hardly earned his respect. 'People so easily – blindly – believe what they read. For example, I read the paper and see so many things about myself that are so untrue. When I started out, I'd think, "Those motherfuckers – I am going to go out and get every one of them!,"' he told one startled writer at the time.

As the weeks turned to months, Tom and Nicole started to become a definite item, although most members of the cast and crew of *Days of Thunder* were still only aware of gossip about the couple. On the set, the two were still very careful not to be seen showing each other any sign of affection. After the film moved to locations at Daytona Beach, Florida, the couple dined out regularly at the Olive Garden restaurant and shopped at Publix market for burgers and other cookout fare. Tom even took Nicole skydiving.

The ultimate proof of their blossoming affair came during their first simultaneous parachute jump. As they hurtled earthward at 110 mph – with instructors at their side – speed demon Tom swooped in and planted a kiss on Nicole's mouth. Their union was sealed. Before they left Florida, Tom bought four top-of-the-line skydiving rigs, two for himself and two for Nicole, at a total cost of $10,000. What he did not reveal at the time was that he had been skydiving throughout the making of *Days of Thunder*, behind the backs of the film's insurers.

Tom managed to get himself stopped for driving at 66 mph in a 35-mph zone on 2 March 1990, in Darlington, North Carolina. Fearful of bad publicity if they dropped the charges, officials eventually fined Tom a paltry $125 after city judge Dan Causey reduced the charge to careless operation of a vehicle, which carried no point penalty.

Soon Tom and Nicole were appearing in public in Daytona Beach hand in hand. It was very noticeable because Nicole was a good two inches taller than the world's most macho movie star. Tom was so completely besotted by Nicole that her height seemed irrelevant. Significantly, up until that point in his career, Tom had never once asked for built-up insteps or any other false measures to disguise his shortness.

Days of Thunder co-producer Jerry Bruckheimer also confirmed Tom's complete lack of sensitivity about his height – at a conservative guess no more than five feet eight inches. 'It's not like dealing with Alan Ladd, where they had to stand him on apple boxes. With Tom we don't even toy with camera techniques.' True or false, Tom was proving to be the consummate pro on a film set.

Tom and Nicole took a break from the bone-shattering shooting schedule of *Days of Thunder* and turned up at the 1990 Oscars hand in hand – the final public proclamation of their relationship. Mary Lee looked on proudly at her son and his new lover. Tom had given his mother three $10,000 hand-beaded designer gowns to choose from for the big event. That Easter, Tom took Mary Lee, then aged fifty, for a parachute jump with Nicole and planted a mid-air kiss on both of them!

By April, as the *Days of Thunder* team continued shooting highly complex racing scenes at Daytona Beach, Tom and Nicole were openly romancing each other. Tom's rented white BMW and Harley-Davidson motorbike were frequently parked outside the luxurious apartment leased for Nicole a mile from Tom's place on the exclusive Fly-In resort, complete with its own private runway in the backyard.

In keeping with Tom's unwillingness to strip for movies, he curtly refused to remove his underpants for a shower scene in *Days of Thunder*. Some Hollywood observers speculated that his romance with Nicole was a likely influence on this decision.

Besides seeing Nicole, Tom also spent a lot of time in Florida with actor John Travolta. The two celebrities were both heavily committed members of the Church of Scientology and appeared to have a lot in common.

But it was Tom's love affair with Nicole that dominated his life. He felt as if he had finally found true happiness.

19

*My agent is the only person who
understands what I really want. And my wife.
Other people just don't get it.*

TOM CRUISE

Nicole Kidman will probably loathe the reference, but she really did start living a fairy-tale life from the moment she caught Tom Cruise's eye. She'll loathe it, not only because it's a cliché, but also because it reveals the true perspective of her life. Fantastic things may happen to and around her, but at heart she has, according to friends and family, remained true and unchanged from the bouncy little girl who grew up happy and secure in a big family in Sydney, Australia.

From the periphery, at least, the fairy-tale analogy is hard to ignore. For Nicole, time has done anything but stand still. The young actress had already made a reasonable name for herself in a handful of Australian mini-series and television shows before grabbing the lead in the movie *Dead Calm*, which opened up her world and led her into the arms of Tom.

Nicole left Australia in the autumn of 1989, amid goodbye tears from her mother, father and sisters ... basically off on a wing and a prayer. She had absolutely no idea if her grandiose plan to make it in Hollywood as an actress would work. All her friends in the Australian movie industry warned her that it would be tough and to expect it to take at least five years to get any decent parts. But Nicole wasn't in the least bit worried. She's the sort of girl whose spirit and vitality override any fears of the outside world. If it didn't work out, she thought to herself, then so be it. However, even her eternal optimism could never have foreseen the chance encounters that would lie ahead.

The key to Nicole's character lies in her safe, secure, happy background. It is the exact opposite of Tom Cruise's upbringing in that her family always remained together and they moved about once in her entire childhood.

Tom had learned from his marriage to Mimi Rogers that two likes don't necessarily make a happy union inside wedlock. Even at the pinnacle of his career, there was an underlying current of insecurity in Tom's character. What he really needed was someone who could be outgoing, entertaining and loving, but also capable of accepting him for what he was and providing the security net he so desperately craved.

Nicole's family consists of her father, Dr Anthony Kidman, her mother Janelle and younger sister Antonia. Nicole was born in Honolulu while her father was a student at the University of Hawaii, and thus gained duel Australian-American citizenship, which allowed her later to work in the USA unhindered by visa problems. The family eventually moved to Sydney's northern suburbs, the sort of area where just about any parent would be happy to bring up their children – rolling hills to the west, hundreds of miles of sandy beaches to the east and a climate of safety that would be difficult to match anywhere else in the civilised world.

Nicole knew precisely what she wanted out of life, even at the ripe old age of nine. One former school friend recalled: 'When I was nine I went to her sister's birthday party. Nicole bossed us around and made us play games properly.'

Intriguingly, the young Nicole hated her now-famed curly locks and used to do everything to try to flatten them. The friend explained: 'She used to wash her hair in this rosewater stuff and when she came to class it stank the whole room out. It smelt like rose toilet freshener, it was so strong. She insisted her hair was a perm. She hated her hair and slicked down the curls every morning.'

By the age of thirteen, Nicole had grown to be a gangly five feet ten inches tall and was frequently mistaken for someone in their late teens. Here was a girl whose talent was spotted so early on that she was recruited for her first starring role in the mini-series *Vietnam* while still attending North Sydney Girls' High School.

Actor Patrick Phillips, who met and starred with Nicole in an episode of the Australian series *A Country Practice* when she was just sixteen, recalled: 'Even then, I thought she was incredible. She just had this naturalness and loved the camera. A good personality, Nicole. She's something really special.'

Within weeks of arriving in America, in the autumn of 1989, Nicole found herself being chased by Hollywood's most infamous Casanova, Warren Beatty. The Oscar-winning actor and director met Nicole at a movie premiere and then repeatedly called her up, asking her to go out for dinner with him. Nicole was never tempted, however, because Beatty was not her type. In fact, after meeting Tom Cruise, she claimed that the entire Beatty episode was a piece of tabloid fiction, but in fact, following Beatty's attempt at seduction, she had openly talked about it to people she encountered in Australia. She felt a little embarrassed when it leaked out in Hollywood after her marriage to Tom.

No one knows precisely when Nicole and Tom actually started dating, but back in Australia, handsome actor Marcus Graham was sitting in his luxurious flat in Sydney presuming that Nicole, then twenty-two, would be flying home to see him to continue their relationship – but she never came.

Marcus, hailed as Australia's newest sex symbol at the time, has the sort of looks that makes women sigh. An unruly mop of jet-black hair, strong eyebrows and an intense expression that could melt a female at twenty paces. In other words, he has the same sort of looks that skyrocketed Tom Cruise to the top of his profession.

In 1989, aged twenty-six, the former star of Australia's top-rating soap *E-Street* was establishing himself as a serious actor when Nicole announced her intention to fly to Los Angeles to seek her fame and fortune. The couple had been living together for some time before she announced her plans and, in fact, their relationship had been well documented in some of Australia's numerous teen magazines. They were deemed to be the country's most glamorous young couple – and they were very much in love.

Nic, as she likes to be called by her family and friends, and Marcus had first met a year earlier when he was appearing in a play called *Heartbreak Kid*. They bumped into each other in the foyer and it was, according to Marcus, love at first sight. Soon they became an item in Sydney's close-knit acting circle and Marcus watched admiringly as Nic's career took off. However, the young actor later reflected: 'While I was really happy for Nic, I felt it magnified my own inadequacies.'

The first confirmation of the break-up of their relationship came when Marcus saw television pictures of Tom and Nicole together at the Oscars ceremony in March 1990. The young actor was gutted. He could not quite believe what he was seeing. He tried to call her but she would not take his calls. That was when he knew for certain it was all over.

Nicole's parents took the massive surge of publicity surrounding their daughter's affair with Tom very much in their stride. However, they began to get irritated and took a leaf out of Tom's book when blatantly inaccurate reports started circulating. According to Nicole's sister Antonia: 'When a radio station read out a piece from a newspaper which had Tom Cruise buying Nicole a $50,000 Corvette and a house, Mum demanded and got a retraction.'

Nicole's mother knew it was untrue because, throughout the early months of her affair with Tom, she rang her mother on numerous occasions and, according to Antonia, 'she tells Mum everything'.

Nicole's family found being thrust under the international spotlight rather irritating at times. Antonia recalled: 'In three different stores I used my credit card, which, naturally, has the Kidman name. Every time I was asked if I was related to Nicole. In the end I denied it, not because I don't love and feel proud of her, but because it's easier to pretend that I'm not her sister rather than face a barrage of questions.'

Within months of the relationship being revealed, Tom and Nicole were on their way to becoming one of the most famous couples in the world. Nicole's father, Anthony, a biochemist and stress-management-book author, happily played the role of the most calming influence in the family. While her mother, Janelle, says that Nicole is prone to playing everything down, she did reveal that her eldest daughter sometimes fears that her mother will put her foot in it by being too sentimental.

Throughout those early difficult days of Tom and Nicole's romance, the young actress called her mother every other day to keep her abreast of what was happening. She told her that Tom was an 'intense, energetic twenty-seven-year-old with a great sense of humour and a very nice way of throwing back his head when he laughs,' explained Janelle, who added: 'He's got that American way of not doing things by halves. He works and plays full on.'

Janelle is always introduced to people as 'my mother, Janelle Kidman' after she decided it was 'ghastly' to be referred to as 'Nicole's Mum' when her daughter introduced her to anyone.

Others in Australia were not in the least bit surprised that Nicole's career and love life took off after the release of *Dead Calm*. 'I remember promising Nicole that even if *Dead Calm* didn't make a dollar, it would make her an international film star,' recalled the movie's writer and co-producer, Terry Hayes, long-time friend and mentor to Nicole.

Only a few months after their relationship went public, Tom delighted Nicole and his family and friends by splashing out almost $5 million on a secluded house set in an acre of ground in exclusive Pacific Palisades, just west of Los Angeles, one of the most expensive real-estate areas in the world. Tom purchased the Colonial-style home with electric gates in the name of a trust, to prevent news of the deal leaking out.

Built in the early-1940s, the two-storey house was newly refurbished and contained five bedrooms and five bathrooms in an area of slightly more than 6200 square feet. It also included a dramatic spiral staircase, four fireplaces, a wood-panelled library, a two-storey guest house, a motor court, a swimming pool, a spa and an English garden.

Although the house was immaculate, the couple hired an army of painters and carpenters to transform it into a palace. They added a movie theatre, billiard room and weights room, as well as gold-plated bathroom fixtures and marble and mahogany fire surrounds. The free-form swimming pool has an eight-foot water slide on one end and a jacuzzi on the other.

The house seemed to be Tom's way of saying he was deadly serious about Nicole. Shortly after the purchase he bought her a $200,000 diamond ring, although they were not officially engaged until later.

This had followed the sort of wooing which would put any romantic lead actor to shame. Tom sent Nicole a dozen red roses every day for two weeks, then bought her a $40,000 matching pair of diamond earrings. At one stage during his courtship he even left a folded note on the pillow of her bed at their hotel in Los Angeles, saying: 'My darling Nicole, I chased you and chased you until you finally caught me. Now will you marry me?'

Nicole read the note as she got up and immediately rushed into the kitchen of their suite and flung her arms around Tom and said: 'I will, I will!'

More parachute diving followed, including a high-flier at 25,000 feet, with Tom and Nicole holding hands for the cameras.

With the couple's relationship now definitely in the public domain, they made a very secretive visit to Sydney by private jet from Los Angeles, so that Tom could meet Nicole's parents. During their hush-hush trip, Tom and Nicole went with her parents to a well-known Indian restaurant called the Maharani, in the Crow's Nest district of Sydney. Tom even joined in the spirit of the evening by drinking potent Indian beer, even though he had spent much of the previous five years as a teetotaller. They also went to the opera, met Nicole's old friend and mentor producer-writer Terry Hayes and even managed to help a member of the paparazzi when he tripped over a kerb while trying to take photos of the couple. It all seemed a million miles away from Hollywood.

There was another reason behind Nicole's visit to her homeland. She was missing her family terribly, even though her mother visited her at least three times in the first year she was in moviedom. Nicole admitted to Australian writer Susan Duncan: 'The hardest part is the loneliness. It can get very lonely so far from home.'

Often Nicole's mother would send her daughter a 'care package' containing newspapers, magazines and jars of Vegemite.

There was another downside to this fairy tale for the young Australian actress: Nicole sometimes found that things with Tom were happening so fast she could barely cope. Often she would get up in the middle of the night and wander around the streets, just walking until she felt she had calmed down. She felt a little scared of what was happening. 'It's scary. That's why I can't place a lot of emphasis on it. I mean, you can be hot one day and not the next. One moment you're on the "in" list and the next you're "out".'

On their return to Los Angeles, Tom took Nicole on a weekend to the desert at Palm Springs, to learn how to ride motorbikes in the sand dunes, and then whisked her off to the Bahamas for a couple of weeks of complete rest. The couple went scuba diving and, for the first time in their relationship, actually started to get to know each other properly.

Every now and again Nicole would pinch herself just to make sure it was all still really happening. 'I still feel, "Gosh, I really shouldn't be here." I get insecure. I ring my mum. There is never a time when I don't think the role I'm playing is going to be the last I'll ever be offered. Then I ring my mum again.'

For Tom, being with Nicole was the best thing that had ever happened to him. Sometimes it seemed as if he could not keep his hands off her. When the couple went to an afternoon performance at a New York theatre they started hugging and kissing the moment they got to their seats on the front row of the balcony. When the lights dimmed, a sudden scream pierced the theatre, followed by a thud as an elderly woman collapsed in the orchestra pit.

Tom immediately vaulted the balcony railing and jumped down to the floor below and was the first person to reach the stricken woman. 'Call 911!' he yelled as he comforted the old lady. An ambulance arrived within minutes and the woman was taken away. Meanwhile Tom returned to his seat and resumed kissing and cuddling Nicole.

On 18 December 1990, Nicole's parents and sister slipped discreetly out of Australia for a Christmas break in the United States. Six days later they and only seven other guests, including Tom's mother and his three sisters, attended Tom and Nicole's wedding in the ski resort of Aspen, Colorado. The couple had been secretly planning the marriage for about a month.

However, the wedding nearly did not go ahead when Tom was arrested for speeding by a disbelieving Colorado marshal, Norman Squire, who thought Tom was lying when he announced: 'Hi, I'm Tom Cruise and I'm getting married.'

The cop shot back: 'Sure you are, and I'm Mary Queen of Scots.' Tom wasn't carrying any means of identification, so the lawman told him: 'Take off your hat if you're really him.' It was only then that Marshal Squire believed his celebrity suspect and allowed Tom to continue on his way to the wedding.

On the morning of 24 December, the stately log house was filled with fragrant flower arrangements, including a willow arbour laced with white lilies and red roses. As the sun began to set, Nicole, wearing a white silk gown with a long train, joined Tom, dressed in a black tuxedo, for the start of the thirty-minute ceremony, which was conducted by a civil celebrant.

With younger sister Antonia standing by as her bridesmaid, Nicole peered down at her shorter husband-to-be to exchange their self-written marriage vows. According to Australian actress Deborra-Lee Furness, who was among the guests: 'Both Tom and Nicole, as well as their families, had tears in their eyes.'

It was all in great contrast to Tom's earlier marriage to Mimi Rogers, when both bride and groom had worn jeans and bare feet.

Nicole was given only four days off from filming her latest movie, *Billy Bathgate*, with Tom's co-star in *Rain Man* Dustin Hoffman, for the couple to have a mini honeymoon, although Tom had sent bouquets of flowers to the set in a small town in North Carolina virtually every day in the lead-up to the wedding.

The following day, Christmas Day, Nicole rang the rest of her family back in Australia to tell them the news. Tom even came on the line to wish his new family Happy Christmas. 'Nicole was very happy when she called. She said all the normal things that brides say,' reported her aunt, Linda Fawcett.

The day after Christmas, Nicole called Sydney radio journalist Peter Ford to tell him the big news. 'She was blissfully happy. They are very much in love and Nicole was ecstatic when she called,' explained Ford.

By May 1991, Nicole's parents had become even more active in pursuing inaccurate reports concerning their daughter and her husband Tom. The worst example came when an Australian magazine claimed that Tom had attacked and bruised his wife during an incident on the set of *Billy Bathgate*. The article, headlined 'Nicole – Were Those Bruises Cruise's?', stunned Dr and Mrs Kidman and they immediately filed a complaint to Australia's Press Council, claiming that the story was not presented fairly, did not respect their daughter's privacy and was harmfully inaccurate. The complaint was upheld and the magazine was ordered to print an apology and a retraction. It seemed that Tom's anti-press attitudes were clearly becoming infectious.

The following month rumours that the couple were expecting a baby reached almost epidemic proportions. The *Daily Mail* in London kicked off the stories by publishing a front-page article claiming that Tom was 'bursting with pride' at the news. Newspapers even alleged that Tom had ordered his new bride to take a fertility test before they got married. Tom was also quoted as saying: 'It's a miracle. She's pregnant and I did it. I'm going to be a dad. I can't wait to hold my first-born in my arms.'

Nicole's father was reportedly refusing to confirm the claims, which eventually turned out to be completely false.

No one knows if a sudden, and highly secretive, trip to a Los Angeles hospital in October 1991 was in any way linked to Nicole's alleged 'pregnancy', but her admittance to St John's Hospital and Health Center in Santa Monica, just a few miles from Tom and Nicole's luxurious home in Pacific Palisades, certainly appeared to be dramatic. She was booked into the hospital under a false name after suffering from 'stomach pains'.

Nicole had fallen ill two weeks earlier during the reshooting of certain scenes in *Billy Bathgate* in New York. She immediately underwent tests in New York and then flew to Los Angeles for surgery, described as 'minor abdominal surgery to remove scar tissue that was causing her pain', a source at the hospital revealed. It is not known whether Tom was with Nicole at the time.

Soon after leaving the hospital, Nicole jetted off to see her family and friends in Sydney, without Tom, who stayed behind in Los Angeles after falling from a tree while gardening at their home. Tom fractured a rib and broke the little finger of his left hand in the fall and Nicole had to drive him to hospital, where he was fitted with an elastic chest brace to protect his rib and a sling for his arm.

The visit to Sydney was pronounced a private trip by Nicole's publicists and they insisted she would not carry out any public engagements. Since her marriage to Tom she had become the most famous actress in Australia and everyone wanted to meet her, however briefly.

In the event, Nicole weakened and brought some Christmas cheer and presents to sick youngsters at the Camperdown Children's Hospital in Sydney. She chatted with teenagers and spoke warmly about Tom during the one-hour visit and she promised the assembled crowd she would be back in Australia with him the following February.

Nicole had two special reasons for visiting that hospital: her mother Janelle had at one time worked there as a nurse and she herself felt a special affinity for children which was rapidly manifesting itself as a genuine urge to be a parent.

Tom, back in Los Angeles, kept tabs on his pretty young wife by calling her every day without fail. He started to notice that, after a few days, Nicole's Australian accent had kicked right back into gear. He told her not to lose it 'because it is one of the things about me he really loves,' said Nicole later.

But there was another side to being Mrs Tom Cruise, as Nicole complained during that trip to Australia. 'There is an intense interest in my personal life and I've spent a lot of time building up a career and my first love is acting. When you meet someone – a high-profile person – and you fall in love with them, you don't have any choice. You're suddenly thrown into the limelight.'

Nicole was particularly upset by reports in some US publications which suggested that she got some of her work because Tom had campaigned for her. At one stage rumours circulating Hollywood cruelly suggested that Tom had persuaded Nicole to agree to marriage and a family in exchange for some sort of contract guaranteeing her lead roles in half a dozen movies. It was a nonsensical suggestion, but it hurt the actress deeply.

'As Tom says, "There are a lot of actors around with girlfriends who are actresses who aren't working,"' she told one writer. 'I'm not blowing my own trumpet here, but it makes me irritated because you never get the part unless you come up with the goods. Studios have millions of dollars riding on these movies and they're not going to go, "Let's please Tom and put Nicole in this movie." It just doesn't work that way.'

Although Nicole had fought hard to maintain her own identity, she admitted that the media attention on her marriage sometimes became a heavy burden. 'I have trouble because I'm very honest and if someone asks me a question, I'll usually answer it.'

Her attitude towards the press was refreshingly straightforward compared with Tom's rather duplicitous response. 'It's like a game and we treat it like a game. We haven't had people lurking in the bushes yet. Occasionally we get people following us, but Tom is a very good driver so we can usually get away.'

Then, in an interesting reference to the couple's future plans to have children, she added: 'When I have children, I don't want my children splashed across the cover of magazines and I don't want them put into the spotlight like that.'

Nicole continued to deny the never-ending rumours of her pregnancy. Unlike Tom, she insisted on handling the media's constant enquiries head on with a complete and utter denial rather than a 'no comment', which she believed simply fuelled the speculation. Behind the public façade, she and Tom were getting increasingly anxious to start a family. Watching friends like Dustin Hoffman and Paul Newman, both happily married with children, had convinced them that it should be sooner rather than later.

One of the more intriguing aspects of Tom and Nicole's marriage was that Nicole openly admitted to friends that her husband bought most of her clothes for her and she rarely went with him to choose them. 'He just sees something he likes and brings it home to surprise me,' she told one acquaintance excitedly.

It was almost as if Tom was moulding his young bride into exactly what he wanted, although Nicole was hardly complaining. Tom would often buy outfits from the best designers, like Karl Lagerfeld, and thought nothing of spending $10,000 on a dress for his wife. Another gift from Tom was a bright-red Mercedes sports car with a price tag of a cool $100,000.

Amid all this talk of children, the broody Nicole was presented with a lovable labrador puppy by Tom. It seemed to be wedded bliss. Life inside that palatial mansion in Pacific Palisades did sound rather impersonal, however. Nicole told one friend that Tom, who had started smoking the occasional huge cigar, had taken to frequently listening to Bruce Springsteen on his state-of-the-art stereo system alone in a room that had been designated as 'his'. Meanwhile Nicole spent a lot of the time in different parts of the vast house.

None the less, everywhere Tom went in public he couldn't wait to tell the world what a wonderful wife Nicole was. At the prestigious American Cinema Awards ceremony in Los Angeles in early January 1991, he accepted an award and then proceeded to announce that Nicole had been 'a great source of support... I thank her from my heart.'

To all the world, Tom and Nicole seemed like the perfect couple. But they had their problems, just like everyone else.

20

I'm much more relaxed now than I used to be.
I was much more intense and driven. I had to live all
my life today as opposed to just relaxing and
trusting that I'm going to be here tomorrow.

TOM CRUISE

Tom was feeling a touch uncomfortable, lying there stark naked with his eyes closed, even if there was a bowl protecting his modesty from a young lady. She could not, of course, resist a peek, followed by a smirk, which the camera caught but Tom didn't. 'What did she do?' he yelled, sitting bolt upright in the bed. Tom hates to be left out.

The lady playing peekaboo was his brand-new wife, Nicole Kidman, and the couple were acting out a scene from *Far and Away*, an epic tale of an Irish peasant who hooks up with a spiritual landowner's daughter to travel in America at the turn of the nineteenth century. Hundreds of millions of people were expected to watch the film when it was released, and it was not just Tom's smile but what was underneath that bowl that was expected to bring the punters in.

By all accounts, Tom spent most of the making of *Far and Away*, during the first half of 1991, telling anyone who would listen of his love for Nicole. On and off set the couple seemed to be forever smooching and kissing. Even director Ron Howard admitted it was a bit of a worry: 'There was a lot of kissing going on – all day long. There really was a honeymoon glow. For while they never consummate their love in the movie, it was easy for them to draw upon the awe and mesmerising attraction that was in their recent memory. Tom would look at her sometimes and say: "Isn't she beautiful." Or he'd have his shirt off and be boxing and she'd come by and exclaim: "What a chest!"'

Propman Derek Wallace said that every time the director called 'action' the couple would be passionately kissing in some corner or other. 'Finally one of the drivers threatened to throw a bucket of cold water over them. I've never seen a couple so close – or so ecstatically happy,' he explained. Tom would even bring his wife constant cups of coffee to keep out the cold and regularly bullied her to keep a thick sweater on at all times.

Tom revealed that he just could not help himself. 'I love being with her twenty-four hours a day. She is both my wife and my best friend. The perfect day with Nicole would be when we don't get up in the morning, a room-service day. I'll leave the rest for interpretation.'

What he did not mention was that he and Nicole would regularly disappear into their personalised luxury trailer for hours at a time, no doubt to 'reassure' each other of their mutual love and respect.

Since meeting Tom, Nicole had perfected a mid-Pacific accent, despite her insistence that Tom preferred her Aussie brogue. For *Far and Away* she had to be Irish-American. She perfected it with ease after the pair hired a couple of locals to hang out with. However, Tom continued to have a 'divil of a time' mastering the lingo. In the end he had to sit down with dialect coach Sean O'Casey in an effort to get it right. Most who have seen the film say he still managed to get it badly wrong.

However, nothing would deter Nicole from her passion for Tom. She seemed as full of love for him as he was for her. 'There's a light about him. When he laughs, his eyes crinkle up, he throws his head back; it's contagious and you've gotta laugh too. He's this powerhouse, he sort of fills the room – the energy coming out is amazing.'

In a specially arranged television interview with Oprah Winfrey just before shooting *Far and Away* commenced, the couple giggled and hugged like two school sweethearts when the TV host asked them if they did everything as a couple. 'Yes,' replied Tom. 'We like being together twenty-four hours a day.'

It certainly sounded as if Tom had returned to his favoured mutual appreciation society mode when talking about Nicole. But there was another motive behind his gushing words: he really wanted to avoid the sort of problems that were caused by the long separations during his first marriage, and that was why *Far and Away* seemed the ideal project for the couple to embark on.

The added bonus was that Nicole was as determined to start a family as Tom. She even told one writer that she wanted 'at least three children', with the proviso that they be brought up in Australia 'to keep their feet on the ground'.

The *Far and Away* shoot took place in Montana and Ireland, a country steeped in the history of Tom's adopted clan, the Mapothers. The actor, by now approaching his twenty-ninth birthday, also hoped the luck of the

Irish would rub off on him and Nicole following the dismal failure of *Days of Thunder*.

Tom had to learn how to ride and managed to master the art after only four lessons. Nicole, already an accomplished rider, had no problems whatsoever. During subsequent filming a note of rivalry built up between husband and wife, with Tom desperately trying to ride faster than his wife on certain occasions.

Things got off to a bad start in Montana after a spectacular wagon-race sequence turned to mayhem when a thousand extras and stunt riders, plus hundreds of horses, mules and wagons, hurtled across a desolate plain. According to crew members, a cannon shot, along with noise from a helicopter filming overhead, spooked the animals before the race and out-of-control wagons broke into pieces, hurling animals under the wheels. Several animals were hurt and one horse was so badly injured it had to be destroyed.

But at least Tom and Nicole had their wondrous dressing-room trailer to retire to when things got too hectic. The vehicle was a sort of belated wedding present for Nicole. Valued at $750,000, it came complete with marble floors and was said to be five feet longer than any other star's trailer in Hollywood. The ultimate status symbol.

After wrapping in Montana, the film moved to Dublin and things really started to go wrong. To start with, Tom was warned that he and Nicole – by now probably the most famous couple in the world – were likely victims of a terrorist attack by loyalists from Northern Ireland desperate to upset the peace talks that were in progress between Britain and Ireland at the time. Tom was shaken by the warning and reluctantly agreed to have three bodyguards shadow him and Nicole throughout their stay in the Emerald Isle.

'Tom was very worried by the threats. He took them very seriously and it certainly made the couple feel a little isolated at times,' explained one Irish member of the film crew.

The three armed minders included two former members of the SAS. Two years later one of them was arrested for drug offences after claiming that Thai gangsters had put out a contract to have him murdered. He had a habit of carrying a Magnum around with him all the time.

Tom had realised that he could take no chances while in Ireland. Within days he started to feel like a prisoner in his own hotel suite – he was just grateful to have Nicole with him. Tom and Nicole settled comfortably in a vast honeymoon suite at the Westbury Hotel. Every morning, like clockwork, they would arrive at the set in a chauffeur-driven car at 10 a.m.

Later they moved to Dublin's Berkeley Court Hotel and stayed in the penthouse suite, complete with a marble kitchen, peach bedroom, bathroom with jacuzzi, and a view of Dublin Bay. They played a daily round of squash, their favourite game, at Dublin's Riverside Racquet and Fitness Club.

The couple, accompanied by their bodyguards, even shopped for Irish linen at a small Dublin shop, where Tom bought two queen-sized virgin fleece mattress pads. They then attended a play at the city's famous Abbey Theatre. During their stay in Dublin they also entertained friends like Sean Penn and actor Billy Baldwin, as well as Nicole's parents and Tom's mother.

Tom's friendship with Sean Penn is fairly unique because Penn is the only member of the so-called Brat Pack of the early 1980s whom Tom remained close to. For a while during Penn's troublesome marriage to Madonna the two actors saw little of each other, but once Penn set up home with beautiful blonde actress Robyn Wright, the two stars became good friends again. Wright was involved in a smaller-budget version of *Far and Away* called *The Playboys*, so the two couples had lots of stories to swap about their experiences in Ireland

Halfway through their stay in Dublin, Tom and Nicole sneaked off to Paris for a romantic weekend away from the movie set – and those bodyguards. The couple strolled hand in hand near the Louvre, stopping occasionally for a completely spontaneous embrace. Then they headed back to their $500-a-night suite at the famous Hôtel Bristol. A chauffeur-driven Rolls-Royce was at their disposal throughout the trip.

After ten weeks' non-stop filming in and around Dublin, Nicole, Tom and their minders moved to a rented cottage in the beautiful west-coast town of Dingle, County Kerry. There filming centred on a farmyard set, built on a blustery cliff top near the tiny village of Ventry.

While Irish eyes might have been smiling on them up until then, their luck soon changed fast. Only weeks before their arrival in Dingle, three teenage boys plunged to their death close to where the movie was set. Then filming was halted when Tom nearly took a tumble over the same cliff. He was trying to pull the donkey across the farmyard in a scene and lost control of it. He panicked and as he moved away he slipped and started to fall down the slope. It was all the more frightening because it was exactly the same spot where those poor boys had died.

Two crewman on the movie then had a lucky escape when their helicopter was hit by a freak fifty-foot wave as they were taking low aerial shots of the ocean. The chopper crashed but, amazingly, both pilot and cameraman escaped unhurt, although a $1-million camera sank to bottom of the sea.

Tom and Nicole were seldom seen during their stay on the west coast. But their landlord, Swiss lawyer Dr Albert Schumacher, did play the piano for them at several sing-songs that lasted until 2 a.m. at the little cottage. However, relations between the couple and their landlord soured after only six days when Dr Schumacher claimed he was beaten up by one of Tom's bodyguards after he complained about the heavies wearing wet clothes and shoes in the house. 'I tried speaking to the chief bodyguard, but he took no notice,' explained Dr Schumacher. 'The bodyguards lifted me up and dragged me about forty yards and kicked me for ten minutes.' Dr Schumacher ordered the Cruise party out of his house. Tom, who was fed up with the good doctor by this stage, was more than happy to set up a new base five miles along the coast. Shortly after this, Nicole flew home in a private jet after her part in the movie was completed.

One of the more dangerous scenes in the movie was a bare-knuckle boxing sequence that got fairly ferocious at one stage. Although the bare-knuckle fight scenes were choreographed, Tom still got quite seriously injured during one incident when the stunt boxers tried to make the scene look 'too real'. Suddenly Nicole – watching on the sidelines – screamed out to stop the action because she feared Tom was about to get seriously hurt. She then pulled director Ron Howard aside before being convinced that the action was a vital ingredient for the film. Tom and Nicole were both frequently thrown from their horses during some of the tricky land rush scenes.

After *Far and Away* was finished there were strong rumours that Tom had forced the movie's producers to cast Nicole in the leading female role. The couple became hypersensitive to such suggestions and, during pre-release publicity interviews with the media, insisted on being interviewed separately to make their point. One publicist working on the film said emphatically: 'They're separate people, with separate careers.' Besides that, thirty pages of studio-produced publicity material did not even mention the fact they were married!

The publicity work that accompanied *Far and Away* was exhausting for both Tom and Nicole. At one stage he had to speak to a hundred and fifty newspaper, magazine and television journalists over a two-day period and the one question on everyone's lips was: 'Is Nicole pregnant?'

Even more ludicrous than the pregnancy rumour was a little titbit about Tom having allegedly had liposuction on his bottom. According to one disreputable source, Tom wanted to look good from the back for some of his scenes in *Far and Away*, even though there were no nude scenes in the film. Tom's publicist, Pat Kingsley, flatly denied the rumour.

Far and Away was released virtually simultaneously in many countries around the world, so Tom and Nicole embarked on a gruelling round-the-world promotional trip. In May 1992 they went to the Cannes Film Festival, where the film was featured. Then it was on to London for the royal premiere, followed by Japan for the opening of the picture there. The main feature of the film – besides starring Tom and Nicole – was that it had been shot on 65mm film, which gave it a 'widescope' appearance when shown in cinemas. It was supposed to help capture the essence of the Oklahoma gold rush of 1889 and some of those rolling hills of Ireland, but audiences were not impressed.

The reviews of *Far and Away* were mixed, to say the least. Kathleen Carroll, in the *New York Daily News*, wrote that there was 'surprisingly little passion or electricity in this boisterous period love story'. Caryn James of the *New York Times* commented: 'This film is as much an epic event as sitting at home watching television.'

In Britain, the reaction to the film was no better. '*Far and Away* proves you can lay out a fortune on a film and end up having a film fit only for laying out,' wrote the *Daily Mirror*'s reviewer.

However, the normally hypercritical Julie Salamon was more kind when she wrote in the *Wall Street Journal*: 'Odd as it seems for a film built on such a grand scale, sweet is the operative word here, and that's not meant as an insult.'

The movie's other big problem was that it had been slated as Universal's big blockbuster for the summer of 1992, up against *Lethal Weapon III* and *Batman II*. The other two films fared much better.

Far and Away proved a disappointment at the box office because it did not take the expected $100 million-plus in the United States. Tom, who was said to have been paid a whopping $12 million for his role, took the film's failure philosophically. As usual, he looked on it as a learning experience, and the definite lesson was that, after two attempts, appearing in movies with Nicole maybe wasn't such a viable idea. The couple agreed to go their own separate ways professionally. It had been a bold experiment while it lasted, but from now on they really had to get on with their own acting.

'I keep telling people not to say a movie is going to make $200 million because you're setting yourself up to take a fall. You can't predict,' Tom told anyone who would listen.

Hollywood insiders refused to slam Tom's performance, instead blaming the script. 'Tom Cruise didn't bomb. The movie bombed. If someone came to me now with a Tom Cruise project and a good script, would I want it? You bet I would!' said one Hollywood producer. A Tinseltown agent offered this explanation for the film's failure: 'This is a minor lull in a very strong career. *Far and Away* was too weighty for a summer movie, too ambitious, and selling it as a Tom Cruise picture was a mistake by Universal.'

Libby Gelman-Waxner, a pen name for a very well-known screenwriter in Hollywood, wrote in 'her' *Premiere* magazine column: '*Far and Away* proves once and for all that Americans are right to avoid historical subjects. Tom, you're adorable, but your dental work is circa 1992, if you ask me.'

When the movie was shown at the Cannes Film Festival in May 1992, the audience hooted and groaned and it was dubbed a cliché-ridden epic.

Tom also faced some flak about his reported fee of $12 million for *Far and Away*. In a pre-recorded interview with American TV's *Entertainment Tonight*, Tom insisted that no one in Hollywood would pay him that kind of money if they didn't think he was worth it.

As if to drive home the point that he was really a rather modest kind of guy, Tom's involvement with environmental groups led to him driving around Los Angeles in an electric car – a marked contrast to his black Acura NSX, which could top 160 mph and usually stayed in the garage except on special occasions. Tom was growing increasingly sensitive to criticism about his lifestyle and was determined to show he could be an example for America's youth. His strategy was carefully mapped out. As always, he knew exactly where he was going.

21

*Honour is a very important thing in my life.
I got that in the family, in terms of being true
to yourself and standing by your own truth.
That doesn't mean I'm always perfect.*

TOM CRUISE

It was a clear, chilly night, the kind of early-autumn evening in which your breath comes out in little puffs of vapour. Groups of teenagers clogged the patio of a restaurant across the street from the movie crew. But they were not ordering a thing. They were just waiting.

Suddenly the Chevy approached, pulled up to the kerb and Tom Cruise popped out, strode less than ten paces to the newsstand and bought a magazine while exchanging a few words with a man standing on the sidewalk.

'Cut!' screamed the assistant director. That fifty seconds of screen time had taken hours and hours to shoot, and the crowds watching from across the street gasped with excitement. They had caught a glimpse of their hero, Tom Cruise, in the flesh.

A few hundred yards away in a trailer was Jack Nicholson. But none of the hundreds of fans were there to see him. They all wanted to see Tom, the good guy who always wins in the end.

The scene was a brief, albeit important, one from Tom's next movie, *A Few Good Men*. But it proved beyond a shadow of a doubt that he had arrived as the world's number-one box-office attraction. For alongside Tom in *A Few Good Men* were a glittering array of other big Hollywood names, including Nicholson, Demi Moore, Kiefer Sutherland, Kevin Pollak and Kevin Bacon – all overshadowed by Tom.

A Few Good Men was adapted from an acclaimed stage play by Aaron

Sorkin which took some of America's big cities by storm in the early 1990s. The military courtroom drama about a pair of Marines accused of murder was not just expected to do well. It had to, because all the major stars were being paid huge salaries.

On the first day of rehearsals, the cast of *A Few Good Men* gathered around a table for a first read-through of the script. 'Normally in those situations,' explained director Rob Reiner, 'actors are just marking themselves because they haven't yet found all the colours of their characters.'

But Jack Nicholson came in with a full-blown performance that shook everyone in the room. Everyone, that is, except Tom. He said nothing and did not respond. All the other actors noticed, but said nothing. As Reiner explained: 'It was like the young titan and the old titan going at each other.'

Tom's attitude towards Nicholson was much cooler than it had been with people like Hoffman, Newman and Duvall. He was now thirty years old and a much more accomplished star. There were to be no more 'yes, sirs' and 'no, sirs'. Tom even mastered a superb Jack Nicholson impersonation in front of the older star that had everyone – including the old maestro himself – in stitches of laughter.

In interviews during the run-up to the release of the movie, Tom was full of praise for Nicholson, but it was different from the deferential tone he had used when speaking about other, older male stars. 'Nicholson's a legend. And he's very unpretentious. He knows acting and he loves acting. He was really generous off-camera when I was working. He was right there.'

Besides his huge fee, Tom also received a number of incredible perks during the filming of *A Few Good Men*. His was the biggest trailer on the set, and contained phones, faxes, a TV and a jacuzzi. He had two chauffeurs on twenty-four-hour standby and a luxury jet with full security in case he had to rush back to Los Angeles at a moment's notice. He also had his own personal make-up and hairdresser.

Tom's part in *A Few Good Men* as a callow young lawyer forced to defend two soldiers during a disciplinary action had many familiar elements about it. To start with, the character had to emerge from the legends created by his highly successful late father, and secondly he was playing a lawyer, a career that many previous Mapothers, including his uncle and grandfather, had become very successful at, back in Louisville, Kentucky.

The theme of fathers and sons had been played out over and over again in Tom's previous work. In fact, the issue of manhood had become a very common thread. As his *Days of Thunder* co-star Robert Duvall commented: 'Tom's father wasn't around. I guess he grew up having to prove something on his own. I'm sure it's something of a catalyst. It drives you farther into new areas. To prove some things.'

Certainly Tom's role as Lieutenant Daniel Kaffee in *A Few Good Men* called for more mastery of the English language than any of his previous roles. And mastering complex dialogue was not easy for the actor, considering his past battles with dyslexia.

Co-star Kevin Bacon had become friendly with Tom after the two actors found they both had problems reading their lines. They even started rehearsing each other while being made up before each day's shoot because some of the dialogue was so legally complicated that it was very difficult to remember. 'It was completely foreign to me and, to a certain extent, to him,' explained Bacon. 'It was exhausting, but fun. That's why you act.'

Rob Reiner believed Tom's part as Kaffee was the biggest challenge he had ever faced as an actor. 'He went to work, studied the terminology. He really steeped himself in it,' commented the director.

The most significant aspect of the movie was that all the traditional Tom Cruise ingredients were thrown to the winds. As Reiner explained: 'The character was really a bigger stretch than anything he'd ever done. There were no scenes when he could turn on the charm. There was no romance in the film.'

Even Tom, who usually never conceded that any aspect of his work was difficult, agreed. 'You can always tell when someone on screen doesn't understand what they're saying. I understood everything I was saying. You have to get it right. Like anything, you have to get it right.'

Screenwriter Aaron Sorkin, who became close to Tom during the making of the film, recalled: 'He really had the instincts. The non-wiseass moments, the non-glib moments. There's not a lot of pyrotechnics. For a lot of other actors, it could be a rude awakening, but not Tom.'

Those on the set said that Tom behaved as immaculately as ever. But there was an inner battle going on all the time which no one was aware of. Tom was desperately trying to make his own voice sound more authoritative, stronger, more forceful. In the past, some film-industry experts had pronounced that Tom's voice was 'thin and high-pitched', did not aid his performance and might well have hindered his chances of an Oscar. Tom saw *A Few Good Men* as an opportunity to improve on that problem because his character had to hold his own against older, more experienced men in a courtroom setting. It was not easy by any means.

Tom sought advice from Robert Duvall, who seemed to have replaced Paul Newman as a father figure in his life at that time. In Christmas 1991, Tom gave the veteran Oscar-winning star a $20,000 jumping horse as a gift. Some saw it as a thank you to Duvall for helping Tom and Nicole to seal their love for each other during the shooting of *Days of Thunder*.

Later Duvall said, with just a hint of paternal pride: 'He's got his own world. He may have a small entourage, but mostly it's his wife, Nicole. They hibernate with certain friends and associates. She's quieter than he is. I hope it lasts, because it's tough.' He insisted: 'He's very open-hearted on a certain level. And he's the most genuine and most accessible of that whole group of young actors.'

Probably the single most controversial aspect of *A Few Good Men* was the astronomical fees paid to the three principal actors. Tom was on a reported $12.5 million, Jack Nicholson was paid $5 million for just ten days' work and Demi Moore was on a cool $3 million. Kiefer Sutherland got a relatively modest $1 million and Bacon ended up with $750,000. Tom's deal actually put him firmly at the top of the best-paid actors' league and sparked a furore in the press about overpaid Hollywood stars and directors because *A Few Good Men* would have cost less than half its $41-million budget if it had not been for the huge sums paid out to those actors.

Some accused the stars' agents of taking advantage of the power vacuum at the studios when certain films were being green-lighted only on condition that a specific star became attached. The actual film seemed to be taking second place to the celebrity content. Others in Tinseltown argued that only a tiny percentage of a film's profits were ever returned to the star under the so-called points system, which was supposed to provide an actor with a bonus if his or her movie was a big box-office success.

'No one will complain if Disney make a half a billion dollars because it's a company,' explained movie analyst Jim Logsdon. 'But people will complain about an actor making $15 to $20 million as a person.'

Increasingly, the studios were putting pressure on stars to share the financial burden of certain projects to avoid situations where star involvement gets an otherwise bad movie off the ground and then the film still loses a huge amount of money.

Perhaps the ultimate evidence that Tom had truly arrived as Hollywood's number-one star came when Disney chairman Jeffrey Katzenberg was shown preliminary drawings for his upcoming cartoon movie *Aladdin*. Katzenberg complained bitterly about the low 'hunk' content of the appearance of the *Aladdin* character. Convinced that the way it was drawn would not attract enough older children, the Disney chief ordered his artists to make the character look more like Tom Cruise! The team of experts at Disney immediately bought dozens of photographs of Tom and pinned them up in their production offices and promptly converted the previously weedy *Aladdin* into a Cruise lookalike. The result was a cartoon character who definitely resembles Tom and also proved to have his box-office magnetism, because *Aladdin* went on to become the biggest-grossing cartoon of all time.

The production itself was remarkably trouble-free, considering the number of fragile egos on display. Tom and Nicholson exchanged sickly-sweet compliments about each other, much to the annoyance of petulant Demi Moore, who reportedly threw a few 'temper tantrums' because she felt neglected when the two men were both on set. Later Demi sportingly said of Tom: 'He's very smart about himself. He knows his strengths and his weaknesses and he's not afraid to expose them to get what he needs.' Behind the polite words, she was definitely feeling a little neglected.

The relationship between the characters played by Tom and Demi Moore was – except for a few longing looks – essentially non-romantic. The actress even admitted that her agent was wondering: 'Isn't there at least going to be a kiss?'

But Tom was saving all his passion for real-life wife Nicole, who turned up on the set in Boston and spent much of the time smooching with him in a corner between takes. The couple sneaked off one night to watch a video version of Tom's screen debut, *Endless Love*, in which he had a brief walk-on part. Tom doubled up with embarrassment as Nicole laughed and then told him she thought he was really sexy in it.

Tom also proved there was another side to his work-obsessed persona when he paid for all his co-stars to fly in his private Lear jet for dinner and an evening of gambling in Las Vegas. He even arranged for a special private salon at the Mirage Hotel and Casino where everyone could play blackjack. Demi's outspoken husband, Bruce Willis, won more than $10,000 and there was a minor crowd-control crisis when Bruce, Demi and Tom decided they wanted to play the slot machines in the main casino.

Kevin Pollak said of his co-star: 'I really enjoyed hanging out with Tom. It gave me a chance to see how the other one per cent live.'

A Few Good Men got mixed reviews but proved that there is nothing to beat the sheer pulling power of stars at the box office, by taking in more than $100 million in the USA. *Vogue* magazine described the movie as being filled with 'a great deal of young and not so young and pretty much middle-aged talent'.

Meanwhile Tom's loyalty to his immediate family and friends was becoming increasingly apparent. A few years earlier his close friend and cousin William Mapother had joined TC Productions and now Tom's eldest sister, Lee Anne, came on board as Tom's main assistant. The actor believed that he could trust his close family and friends much more than the rest of Hollywood. After leasing the ultimate status symbol – a Gulfstream jet – he decided to shell out a reported $15 million for the plane.

The success of *A Good Few Men* was yet another lesson in life for Tom. He knew that the time was approaching when he would have to take a vast creative leap into a role that no one would expect him to take. It might not be his next film or the one after that, but sooner or later he would have to find something that would shock and amaze his fans and prove once and for all that he was an actor capable of anything.

When one writer asked him if he could play a junkie or a gay character without damaging his career, Tom answered: 'What do you mean by "could I"? Like, who would stop me?' He continued: 'If I read a character that had some value and he was gay or a drug addict – and it had some payoff ... then you do it. Right now those kinds of things are available to me, but have I read any great scripts where I wanted to do it? I can say right now, "No, I haven't." That doesn't mean that in the future I'm not open to doing it if I find it.'

Tom's ability to look to the future was always apparent and he had one eye on something completely different.

22

*Guys want to be like him and girls
want to be with him.*

JERRY BRUCKHEIMER

Counteracting all the high-tech-effects movies of the summer of 1993
came the action pyrotechnics of Paramount Pictures' *The Firm*, based
on John Grisham's best-selling suspense novel and starring Tom with veteran
actor Gene Hackman.

Grisham's book, besides being a great page-turner, was a parable of greed
in the money-loving eighties. To bite the golden apple, it reminded us, was to
invite poison. This was also the decade that had given birth to the career of
Tom Cruise.

He and Hackman play two members of a Memphis firm which just
happens to be representing the Mafia. Tom is Mitch McDeere, the new recruit
lured into the partnership under honourable pretences; Hackman portrays
Avery Tolar, the veteran lawyer who becomes his mentor.

The film's dynamic ensemble also included Jeanne Tripplehorn (the 'other
woman' in *Basic Instinct*) as Mitch's sceptical but strong-willed wife, Abby;
Ed Harris as FBI agent Wayne Tarrance, who tries to force Mitch to turn over
evidence against his employers; Wilford Brimley as William Devasher, the
gritty head of security for the firm; and Gary Busey in a small, but smarmy
role as an ex-con lawyer who tries to help Mitch while he can. A cameo by
Holly Hunter was also much acclaimed after the movie's release and
eventually helped earn her an Oscar nomination.

But it was *The Firm*'s director, Sydney Pollack, who drew the most intense respect from Tom and his co-stars. After a career in which his movies had earned forty-three Academy Award nominations, including four for Best Picture, and in which he'd been nominated three times, winning once for 1985's Best Picture, *Out of Africa*, nothing could faze him.

The much talked about pairing of Tom and Hackman seemed destined to initiate yet another father–son relationship between the younger star and his more established veteran performer. But Tom was older and wiser and, just as with Jack Nicholson in *A Few Good Men*, he was no longer prepared to bow down to his more senior colleagues.

This change of attitude towards his elders resulted in a new problem that is also an old problem. In fact, it's as old as the hills of Hollywood. For halfway through the movie's back-breaking post-production schedule, reports in the Hollywood trade press suggested that Hackman was furious to discover that his name was not above the title of *The Firm* alongside that of Tom. Sources in *Daily Variety* suggested that Hackman, having just won a Best Supporting Oscar for his brilliant work in the Clint Eastwood-directed western *Unforgiven*, felt that he should get due credit in his next movie, *The Firm*. However, Paramount insisted that only Tom's name should be above the title, because they believed his name could draw big crowds. Hackman was begged to agree but in the end his agents insisted his name was dropped completely from the title credits.

Insiders said Hackman was 'dismayed' to be put in such an awkward position, but Tom had it in writing that his face and name would dominate posters, billboards and print advertisements for *The Firm*. Paramount tried to pacify the older actor by claiming that if both stars' names and faces dominated the film's publicity material, people might think it was a buddy-buddy movie rather than a thriller. But Hackman didn't buy that and he demanded that all references to him be removed. No one knows how personally slighted Hackman felt, but the message was loud and clear: Tom Cruise is the most powerful movie star on the planet and what he says goes!

There was another ego at stake besides those of the two starring actors. *The Firm* had been devised and written as a million-selling novel by former Memphis lawyer John Grisham. In the early 1990s it became virtually impossible to walk more than a few yards without seeing a Grisham book. Tom had first set eyes on this one after a crew member on *Far and Away* sent him a copy.

The rise of Grisham had been almost as phenomenal as that of Tom Cruise. Yet he had written just four novels: *A Time To Kill*, *The Firm*, *The Pelican Brief* and *The Client* – all within five years. *The Firm* had even been sold as a movie to Paramount on the strength of a one-sentence pitch by Grisham's agent. Not one word had been written, yet he landed a $600,000 deal for the movie rights. So while Tom and Hackman each burnt the boards on the acting side, the question on more people's lips was: 'Where's Grisham?' No one knows if this slight diversion away from the movie's main players had any effect on their performance. Probably not, but for the first time in his professional life Tom was actually competing for coverage with a non-actor.

Filming *The Firm* in Memphis in November 1992, Tom seemed more relaxed than he had been in years. One night he paid an entire dinner tab for some college kids who sang Tom's *Top Gun* tune, 'You've Lost That Lovin' Feelin'', at a restaurant. The star also donated $15,000 to a local children's hospital.

Much of the shooting took place in tranquil, tree-lined roads in the city's suburbs. The locals got used to being woken at 5 a.m. as crew members wrestled with the contrivances of film-making, from catering vans, lighting and sound equipment to props and costumes. In Tuckahoe Lane, where Tom's character Mitch lives, neighbours stood on their front lawns craning for a glimpse of Tom and his attractive co-star Jeanne Tripplehorn. Often there early in his leather bomber jacket, waistcoat and white T-shirt, Tom even managed to shake a few hands.

After four wet months in freezing-cold Memphis, the cast and crew of *The Firm* headed for the sunshine of the Cayman Islands. 'The mood in the cabin became religious – like a revival meeting,' said Jeanne Tripplehorn echoing everyone else's sentiments at the time.

The Firm soon became the talk of the islands. Rumours spread about the shoot taking place on deserted beaches and hundreds of locals would show up at some picturesque spot only to discover the gossip was false. Often the most exciting event was the daily visit of the turtles which swim in to be fed their breakfast of dog biscuits by the residents along the shoreline. Local tourist officials believed that all three islands, Grand Cayman, Cayman Brac and Little Cayman, would finally be put on the tourist map by the movie.

In fact, offshore banking and diving drew the characters in the movie to the Caymans. But in real life the actors considered the location a 'real perk'. Gene Hackman even got himself a diving certificate especially for the movie and he and Cruise dived at a picturesque bay called Orange Canyon. Going down to depths of a hundred feet, they proclaimed that the sights beneath the surface were 'spectacular'. Neither actor used a stand-in for any of the film's diving scenes. There was a little friendly macho rivalry between the two stars, although to some it seemed rather more intense.

Meanwhile Jeanne Tripplehorn chased barracuda as she snorkelled in her free time. However, none of the actors was permitted to get a tan because they still had two more weeks of filming the office scenes back in Los Angeles.

The atmosphere in the Caymans was much more relaxed and by the end of that part of the shoot, crew members were begging Tripplehorn to fluff lines so that they could stay longer. Gene Hackman even announced he loved the place so much he was considering buying a property on the paradise island.

Then in stepped a beautiful young brunette actress called Karina Lombard, from Venice Beach, California. The starlet had been cast to play a prostitute who seduces Tom in a sizzling sex scene on the beach. However, she was bitterly rude about her famous co-star after their love scenes together. Because she was a mere nobody playing a small role, no one paid her much attention, and that grated with the twenty-four-year-old actress. When the director yelled, 'Cut!' she complained: 'There were, like, fifty people rushing to clean him up and I'm standing there full of sand, and nobody comes to help me... I thought, "Ewww!"'

She provoked the same sort of reaction to herself when she made an astonishing public attack on Tom's wife Nicole, criticising her for hanging around during the filming of that love scene. Even more revealingly, the young actress claimed that Nicole had flown into the Caymans on the same flight as her and caught the same flight back to Los Angeles after her role was wrapped. If this was true it seemed an extraordinarily jealous way to behave on the part of Nicole, but then she and Tom are both very possessive people, so perhaps it was not so surprising.

Lombard summed it up by saying: 'She [Nicole] was on the set the whole time watching, watching, watching. Everyone stared at me like I had come, I'd see, I'd conquer.'

Later, after a few calls from 'people in Hollywood', Lombard hurriedly issued a 'clarification' of what her remarks really meant, saying, 'Nicole was absolutely not spying on me!' But then Lombard, who was put under ridiculous pressure not to talk following her original outburst, went back on the warpath, claiming that Tom was 'whisked away by his beloved' after each take. 'I was there to do a job,' added Lombard, who lambasted any suggestion that she was a starlet on the make by rightly pointing out that she was happily married to actor-playwright Anthony Crane at the time. Meanwhile Nicole Kidman was quoted in the press as saying that her husband's attractive co-star was 'very rude'.

Others speculated that Lombard was purely trying to generate publicity by her outbursts. But friends of the actress hotly denied it and insisted that she was simply very serious about her work. 'She's terrifically passionate about her work,' explained friend Martine Beswicke. 'There's a wonderful naivety about her.'

Certainly Lombard's background did not suggest she was of the cashing-in-on-a-non-scandal bimbo variety. Born in Tahiti, the daughter of a banking heir and an Indian medicine woman, she was brought up for much of her life in lively, cosmopolitan Barcelona.

It makes her comments about *The Firm* all the more interesting. 'When I think about *The Firm* shoot, it hurts. I was quite lonely.' For the young actress felt that she had been neglected by nervous production people fearful that Tom might think she was throwing herself at him. In fact, Tom never even gave her a second thought, but the army of advisers that surrounded his every move were second-guessing a situation they feared might arise – especially since everyone knew that Nicole and Tom were still behaving like honeymooners most of the time.

Reports in some of the US tabloids claimed that Tom had personally insisted that Lombard be banned from *The Firm*'s publicity rounds just before the film's release. Showbusiness reporters pointed out that there were no photographs available of that sexy beach scene with Tom and claimed that he had insisted Paramount did not release them in the usual press packs that go out to help to promote movies.

Months later Lombard got some subtle revenge when she was asked whom she preferred kissing, Tom or another co-star, hunky Brad Pitt (who went on to appear in *Interview with the Vampire* with Tom). She said: 'They are both great kissers, but since I got along more with Brad I would have to say he was the best. We were kissing a lot longer. There's a lot more heat and I really respect him.'

Interestingly, in the book of *The Firm,* Tom's character Mitch has his fling on the beach but does not tell his wife about it. In the movie version, Tom confesses all to his wife. No one will say exactly who suggested the change, but there was talk that Tom contributed to the script changes.

Jeanne Tripplehorn was allowed to comment about Tom since she played his wife in *The Firm* and the most frequently asked question was: what is it like kissing Tom Cruise? 'Well, he's got some very nice lips, I enjoyed it,' came her giggly reply. At least someone enjoyed kissing Tom!

Tom was married and Tripplehorn was engaged to American TV star Ben Stiller. The actress found her love scenes with Tom especially hard for that reason. 'You have your private life and those you love, and then you're thrown into this very unnatural situation. But you want it to work, and hopefully you find something to enjoy about it.'

Reviews of *The Firm* were fairly good. Respected Kenneth Turan of the *Los Angeles Times* hailed the acting as 'quietly effective' but saved much of his praise for veteran director Sidney Pollack. 'He has not only taken the risk of letting his film run the two and a half hours needed to include relevant characterisation, he has demonstrated how emotional shading and subtlety can be worked into big-ticket items.'

Britain's *Daily Mirror* was not so full of praise: 'Cruise fans may be satisfied by their boy's angst-ridden heroics. The rest of us will have to wait for *The Fugitive* for the real thing.' The paper described the movie as a 'tedious tale' and accused it of not being a real thriller in the traditional sense.

The *Los Angeles Weekly* wrote: 'It's no disgrace that, having held his own with the likes of Newman, Hoffman and Nicholson, he's met his match in Hackman. Cruise is the weakest thing in *The Firm*.'

Tom did get some praise from *The Hollywood Reporter*, whose reviewer Duane Byrge wrote: 'As the tenacious young lawyer, Cruise brilliantly embodies the character's ambitious resolve.'

Tom had played similar roles in *The Firm* and *A Few Good Men*, portraying in both a glib, cocky legal eagle who has just graduated from Harvard Law School. It was undeniable that audiences had flocked to see him, but now some Hollywood observers began to ask whether movie-goers would have reacted with similar enthusiasm if his characters had been associated with less prestigious academic institutions. Or what if he had avoided the legal profession altogether? In effect, they were calling into question the notion that he had some mystical and durable popularity.

Tom, well aware of what was being said about the similarities of the two roles, was already carefully looking around for something completely different. But he couldn't help smiling as *The Firm* toppled Steven Spielberg's epic *Jurassic Park* from the number-one box-office slot in America. The movie made an astounding $100 million within twenty-three days of its US release.

'We expected this to be a big movie, but no way did we anticipate this kind of box office result so quickly,' said the delighted Paramount President, Barry London. Only *Jurassic Park* (nine days) *Batman* (ten days) *Batman Returns* (eleven days), *Terminator 2: Judgement Day* (sixteen days) and *Indiana Jones and the Last Crusade* (nineteen days) achieved the $100-million milestone faster.

Tom surprised the crew on *The Firm* by presenting them each with a glass paperweight containing a miniature replica of the movie's poster. There were some rumblings about a bottle of booze or a production bomber jacket being a whole lot more useful.

The crew's grumblings were not helped when news spread that Tom, director Sydney Pollack and producer Scott Rudin had each been given a $100,000 Mercedes 500SL as a personal thank you when *The Firm* topped the $100-million mark at the US box office. Ironically, Paramount had to fork out a further $50,000 to each of the three after it was discovered that they would have to pay that in tax on the perks. There were also mutterings as to why novelist John Grisham did not get a car, especially since it was reported in the spring of 1994 that Tom was planning to play the lead in a screen adaptation of Grisham's latest blockbuster, *The Chamber*. Paramount paid the writer $3.5 million for the film rights before he had written the first word of the book!

Back in Memphis, a pair of Tom's underpants left in his rented house by accident were sold in a charity auction for $200 as if to compound the fact that Tom was the most sought-after male in the universe.

After *The Firm* wrapped, anxious Paramount executives started trawling around desperately for another project for Tom, aware that the movie was going to be a huge hit and wanting to get Tom into something as quickly as possible, so as to cash in on that success. The only thing they could find that seemed of any interest to Tom was a screen adaptation of *Mission: Impossible*, the TV series that ran on CBS and in Britain from 1966 to 1973. Actor Peter Graves starred in the show and became its trademark across the world. He played the head of a secret government agency called the Impossible Missions Force, but as such he was principally the conduit for interaction among an ensemble espionage group.

At Paramount writers were busily reworking the script, so that Tom could be the main spy. But they were painfully aware that if Tom gave the project the thumbs down, then it could self-destruct in five seconds. A year later, in early 1994, rumours of Tom's involvement resurfaced following the phenomenal success of *The Fugitive*, another project that started life as a TV series.

On *Forbes* magazine's list of the highest-paid entertainers in the USA, Tom came in at number sixteen, $1 million above Arnold Schwarzenegger, with a fortune estimated to be in the region of $35 million, although he was probably worth at least $10 million more than that.

In July 1992, Tom further expanded his Cruise control by setting up a new production company with his agent Paula Wagner, from CAA. Wagner, who had loyally and expertly represented Tom for eleven years, became his producing partner and the pair were in such a strong position, thanks to Tom's immense pulling power at the box office, that they decided to take their time before attaching the company to any one of the big studios. This made a lot of sense as it would allow Tom to pick and choose the projects he wanted to do rather than having the studios dictate to him.

In a carefully worded statement, Tom said: 'For some time I have wanted to create a film company that would give me the opportunity to develop and work on a wider range of films – some of which I would act in or direct, and others which I would produce. I wanted to find the right partner to make it work, and as Paula and I talked about it, it became clear to both of us that we ought to do it together.'

Tom also wanted to ensure that his company had enough muscle to give him the freedom to direct if and when he decided it was time to make their most significant step of all. Tom knew that helming a picture was a whole different ballgame from acting and he was determined to take his time and start with something modest.

Wagner, a former New York actress and playwright, had become one of Tom's closest friends. She and her husband, Rick Nicita, head of CAA motion-pictures department, were regular visitors to the Cruise mansion in Pacific Palisades.

Significantly, CAA mogul Mike Ovitz – one of the most powerful men in Hollywood – stepped up his links with Tom after Paula left his company and CAA continued to handle the superstar. Ovitz and his president, Ron Meyer, even issued a joint statement to the Tinseltown daily bible, *Variety*, about Tom's link-up with Wagner: 'Their relationship has developed into what we know will be a very successful partnership. As their friends and agents, we look forward to working with them and their new company for many years to come.'

Wagner also made a point of stating in the launch announcement that Nicole Kidman was not involved in any way with the newly formed company.

A few weeks after that initial announcement, Tom and Wagner announced they had signed an exclusive multi-picture deal with Paramount Pictures, completely contradicting the pair's intention to pick and choose whatever projects they liked. Hollywood insiders pointed to Tom's close working relationship with Paramount chief Stanley R. Jaffe, who gave Tom his first big chance when he was producer of *Taps*.

Meanwhile Tom and Nicole continued to prove to the world that they were as heavily in love as ever. For Christmas 1992, Nicole contacted the International Star Registry in Ingelside, Illinois, and paid $45 to christen a star for Tom in the Hercules constellation. ISR representative Elaine Stolpe explained that Nicole named the star Forever Tom. The moniker is not recognised by scientists, but for anyone with telescopes the coordinates are: right ascension – 16 hr, 55 min, 48 sec; declination – 47 degrees, 39 min.

Around this time Tom even took his environmentally friendly electric car with him for an interview with a journalist from *Rolling Stone* and ended up having a race up Sunset Boulevard with the writer!

Another movie project that Tom was allegedly attached to was Paramount's big-screen adaptation of Ira Levin's best-selling novel *Sliver*. The actor was rumoured to be set to get his biggest-ever fee, $20 million, but eventually the deal fell through because Tom did not like the erotic content of the film, which centres around the sexual activities of residents in a New York apartment block. If Tom had taken the role he would have ended up cast alongside Hollywood's so-called sexiest actress Sharon Stone, but he was looking for something to really get his teeth into ... and it was lurking just around the corner.

23

*We must ourselves fight on a basis
of total attrition of the enemy. So never get
reasonable about him. Just go all the way
in and obliterate him.*

L. RON HUBBARD

'Scientology is an applied religious philosophy. Its goal is to bring an individual to an understanding of himself and his life as a spiritual being and in relationship to the universe as a whole.

'Scientology provides mankind the means to attain a comprehensive understanding of the human spirit and to achieve the traditional religious goals of spiritual enlightenment and salvation. This spiritual path is the result of almost fifty years of extensive research by the Founder of the Scientology religion, L. Ron Hubbard. The millions of Scientologists and others who benefit from L. Ron Hubbard's discoveries regard him with great respect and admiration.'

This is the official description of the Church of Scientology which appeared in a full-page advertisement taken out in *The Times* of London on 28 May 1994. It cost more than £20,000 and came just a few weeks after Richard Gere and Cindy Crawford took out a similarly sized advertisement in the same publication to announce to the world they were not gay. The Scientologists had decided it was time to tell the world that the United States Internal Revenue Service had finally granted them charity status in America.

However, in Germany on 27 January 1997, the Scientologists received a blow to their credibility that sparked a huge row, pulling member stars like Tom Cruise into the limelight. Bill No. 5.4858.700.124.7 was passed as a new law by the Stuttgart City Government in what the Church of Scientology described as 'its campaign of prejudice against us'. Others saw it as a perfectly understandable attempt to stem the ever-increasing power and influence of the church in Germany. The Church of Scientology was so infuriated it 'recruited' the help of numerous Hollywood stars to help convince the world that its charitable status should not be outlawed in that country.

In the *International Herald Tribune* newspaper, celebrities who were not Scientologists, including Goldie Hawn, Dustin Hoffman, Larry King, Tina Sinatra, Oliver Stone and Gore Vidal, signed an open letter to the German Chancellor, Helmut Kohl, imploring him to 'bring an end to this shameful pattern of organized persecution'. Behind the scenes, members such as Tom Cruise and John Travolta helped the Church of Scientology assemble such an impressive cast of supporters. But the Germans refused to back down. As one German government official put it: 'These people don't understand Germany. We have a special history and have to take special actions to preserve the German way of life.' It was a fascinating about-turn in the fortunes of the Church of Scientology, which is recruiting millions of new members each year throughout the world.

It's not clear exactly when Tom Cruise began to call himself a Scientologist. In 1989 a Church of Scientology publication included Tom Mapother (the Cruise part of his name was left out deliberately) and his cousin William Mapother on a list of people who had just completed basic Scientology training. In fact, Tom was first introduced to the church after he married Mimi Rogers, whose father was a founder member of the Scientologists. Tom and Mimi even attended marriage-counselling sessions at the church when their relationship started to crumble in the summer of 1989.

As a petite fifteen-year-old schoolgirl, Mimi was already a hugely committed member of the church. Mimi insisted that she was never converted to Scientology. 'Rather, that philosophy was simply part of my upbringing. And I think it was an excellent system of belief to grow up with because Scientology offers an extremely pragmatic method for taking spiritual concerns and breaking them down into everyday applications.

'Scientology is controversial because it doesn't deal with traditional concepts of God and people are always threatened by anything that veers away from the accepted norm. However, I've never been disenchanted with Scientology because the basic philosophical tenets I grew up with have proven to be sound.'

The reasons behind Tom's attraction to Scientology might have been just as simple as the fact he craved belonging. Movie critic and screenwriter Michael Medved reckons that artists and entertainers need 'a community, a tribe, a place where they can fit in'. He also explained: 'Part of being in the arts has to do with rejecting whatever the conventional wisdom is.'

Beverly Hills psychologist Dr Eugene Landy, who has treated some of Hollywood's most famous names, explained: 'Religion is just one of those things celebrities turn to.' The need for structure in every life, but especially in a celebrity's, declared Dr Landy, is 'one of the basics of all basics'.

The Church of Scientology itself has always insisted that it was not concerned about the number of famous people who have joined its ranks in recent years, but there is no doubt that such celebrities as Tom do serve a useful purpose. An internal memo dated 26 January 1992 describes them as 'resources to forward the expansion of Scientology through the arts'.

The idea of using celebrities to help promote the church came from its founder, L. Ron Hubbard, who believed fervently in their importance when it came to gaining acceptance in mainstream America in the mid-1950s. Ironically, in those far-off days his efforts with the likes of celebrities such as Marlene Dietrich, Ernest Hemingway, Howard Hughes and Greta Garbo completely failed.

Hubbard wrote the rules by which the Scientologists now operate and they included an incentive to any person who introduced a famous name to the church. 'Hubbard was like a god, he could command the waves to do what he wanted, he was totally in control of his life and the consequences of his actions,' said former Scientology ship officer Hana Eltringham Whitfield.

However, it wasn't until the mid-1970s when *Saturday Night Fever* star John Travolta became a Scientologist that Hollywood began to sit up and take notice of the Scientologists. In 1990 the actor and his wife, Kelly Preston, even insisted that the birth of their son Jett should be held in complete silence, following church teachings that this helps to safeguard the sanity of mother and child.

Kirstie Alley, Travolta's co-star in the phenomenally successful *Look Who's Talking* series of movies, also joined the Scientologists. Other famous members include jazz pianist Chick Corea, actress Karen Black, opera star Julia Migenes, Priscilla Presley and her daughter Lisa Marie Presley. The late Sonny Bono, one-time pop star, later Republican politician and former husband of Tom's ex-lover Cher, even wrote a poem for the Scientologists:

I'm on the first step to the stairway to infinity ... and now I feel the force of something new surrounding me...

But there can be little doubt that Tom is the biggest catch of all. By landing Tom, the church became a heavyweight player, more likely to influence others with its plans for 'peaceful revolution'.

Many Hollywood observers say that Tom's renowned focus and intensity were even more apparent after he became involved with Scientology. 'Essentially, it's enabled me – it's just helped me to become more me. It gives me certain tools to utilize to be the person I want to be and explore the areas I want to explore as an artist,' he says.

Tom has always insisted that his religious choices were an entirely personal matter and his legal advisers frequently react very strongly to any references to his involvement in the Church of Scientology. However, there is little doubt that his faith regularly plays a role in both his work and home life. He is even known by the initials 'TC' to everyone in the church.

Tom has got up to grade six in the religion's controversial auditing technique system.

The church insists it does not cash in on the big-name members, yet it calls its in-house magazine *Celebrity* and its star disciples happily appear to endorse the church's 'message'. In return they are treated with great reverence.

Scientology is based on a concept that involves exorcising 'the painful experiences of your life' that interfere with rational thought. This is achieved through the 'auditing' process, which is performed by an 'auditor' and can involve using an 'E-meter', a primitive polygraph (also known as a lie detector). Basically, Scientology is all about gaining control of one's self and one's environment. For Tom, as someone who certainly suffered from his share of emotional upheaval as a child and then grew into a controlling sort of person, the church offered an ideal base.

The church claims to have eight million members worldwide and centres in more than seventy countries.

Tom rarely refers to the Scientologists directly, but in the summer of 1992 he did tell writer James Greenberg of his anger over the bad press the church regularly receives. 'The articles you've read have come from an absolute point of mystery and not knowing. They talk about how this religion dictates people's lives; it's the reverse of that. It doesn't dictate anything. The whole thing is not something that's directed towards dictating; it's actually directed toward conceptual thinking and independent ideas.

'It [Scientology] works for me. It's helped me be more me and do the things I want to do. I can't tell anybody what their path to enlightenment is. It's your own adventure. The whole thing is about self-discovery and deciding on your own what is real and true for you. It's not like Scientology wants a war with anyone. But it wants to get information out to people so they will be able to decide for themselves what they want.'

On the set of *A Few Good Men*, Tom insisted that his assistant, Michael Doven, be called 'the communicator' by all members of the crew. Doven, a Tom lookalike, wore the star's 'bat utility belt' complete with a cellular phone and water bottle. The basic *Dictionary of Dianetics and Scientology* describes a communicator as 'the person who keeps an executive's communication lines (body, dispatch, intercom and phone) moving or controlled. The communicator helps an executive free his or her time for essential income-earning actions, rest or recreation and prolongs the term of appointment of the executive by safeguarding against overload.'

Others members of Tom's personal staff have joined the church. His secretary has been listed in *Celebrity* magazine as having completed at least one Scientology training course.

Tom's sensitivity towards the publication of such information has sparked some unpleasant communications between his PR woman, Pat Kingsley, and a number of highly respected magazines in the USA. Before *Los Angeles* magazine published an article entitled 'No More Mr Nice Guy', writer Rod Lurie could only put certain points to Tom if he did it through Pat Kingsley.

Tom issued a statement through Kingsley that stated: 'I don't ask any employee or prospective employee what his or her religion is. Isn't that against the law? If not, why not?'

Tom's second wife, Nicole Kidman, was introduced to the church through her husband, who even admitted to Lurie that she 'learned Scientology from me and then investigated for herself'.

In 1992, Tom sparked an angry response from the Dyslexia Foundation of America when he was quoted as saying that the Scientologists had helped him cure his dyslexia problems. The Foundation was angry that Tom's statement implied that dyslexia could be cured as easily as a common cold. Its executive vice president, Joyce Bulifant, accused Tom of 'spreading misinformation'. She added: 'It would be nice if he understood the disease better.'

After his public outburst, Tom contacted Hollywood columnists Marilyn Beck and Stacy Jenel Smith to insist: 'I was diagnosed as dyslexic a long time ago, took remedial reading courses all through school. Then I was given *The Basic Study Manual*, written by L. Ron Hubbard. I started applying its principles, began reading faster, and that convinced me I had never been dyslexic.'

Simpson, an ex-Scientologist and producer of *Top Gun* and *Days of Thunder*, decided not to use a Scientology-developed sound system called Clearsound that Tom had been very impressed with soon after joining the church. Simpson put his foot down and refused to use the system, which Tom believes enhances and improves sound quality.

Interestingly, in early 1994 Simpson refused to get drawn any further into the furore over his one-time membership of the Scientologists and ignored three faxed messages and a number of telephone enquiries to his office in Los Angeles.

When *Los Angeles* writer Rod Lurie tried to press Tom, through Pat Kingsley, about the Simpson situation, the star simply said: 'Don Simpson's relationship to Scientology is his business, just as my relationship to Scientology is my business.'

There seems little doubt that Tom's own aversion to the media has been fuelled by the Church of Scientology's basic mistrust of the press. Reporters are deemed to be 'suppressive persons' and high-level members of the church have been given 'reporter training regimens' to learn how to handle themselves with journalists. One confidential memo instructs members on 'fending a suppressive TV interviewer' and refers to knowing how to be 'knowingly covertly hostile' and 'stalling for time'. There is also a section on 'bullbaiting', or 'training the student to outflow false data effectively'.

The church itself insists that it is not in any way obsessed by countering 'negative' publicity about the organisation. But founder L. Ron Hubbard, who died in January 1986, did produce a so-called Code of Honour that clearly stated: 'Do not give or receive communication unless you yourself desire it.'

The use of the controversial Clearsound system continued to be an issue throughout all Tom's films after *Days of Thunder* in 1990. Film-makers who have used the system claim that, while they are often impressed with the results, it still has enough kinks to make its use untenable. There is also the cost: standard sound rigs cost about $40,000, while Clearsound runs at around $120,000.

On *A Few Good Men*, director Rob Reiner used both Clearsound and a standard sound machine. A similar situation occurred on *The Firm*.

On guided tours held every Sunday at the Scientologists' desert retreat in Gilman Hot Springs, the woman who takes the tour refers proudly to member Tom Cruise and tells tourists that he used the Clearsound system 'on a number of his movies'.

However, while news of Tom's advocacy of Clearsound swept Hollywood, it should be pointed out, in fairness, that many have missed the point entirely. Tom seems to genuinely believe that his weakest point – his voice – can be improved by using Clearsound. As one movieland observer pointed out: 'Every actor in the world has a duty to himself to make sure that the best possible image of himself is projected on the screen. If Tom had elected to use some new system from a traditional source then this whole fuss would have died down years ago. Unfortunately, because it is linked with the Scientologists some people are not entirely happy about it.'

And there lies the basic problem about Tom's links with the Scientologists. However, members swear that Scientology rids them of their troublesome mental baggage, sharpens their focus and enables them to be in control of their own destiny.

By all accounts, Tom has progressed up the ladder of the church's hierarchy, having taken a number of bizarre 'courses' along the way. The 'Student Hat' course is a classic example. It features a section called 'word clearing', a simple technique to make sure you never skip over a word you don't understand. Many believe that Tom's difficulty during press interviews, when he was sometimes branded as a 'bad interview', was overcome thanks to that particular course.

It is not clear how much money Tom has donated to the church, but the organisation's 'courses' are expensive and completion of the entire programme can take a lifetime and cost as much as $400,000. It even costs between $3000 and $11,000 to use the controversial E-meter for twelve-and-a-half-hour sessions.

The most common entry to the Scientologists is through Dianetics, a mental 'science' formulated by L. Ron Hubbard and introduced to the world through his book *Dianetics: The Modern Science of Mental Health*. The book has sold huge numbers since its launch in the 1950s. However, Scientology's most basic recruitment tool is a 200-question 'free personality test'. After taking the test, one is told of 'flaws' in one's personality that can be cured by Dianetics.

In the early 1980s, Hubbard's wife and eleven others in the church went to jail for conspiring to break into federal offices and provoked accusations of being distinctly beyond the pale, maybe even dangerous. They were all sentenced to five-year prison terms for stealing thousands of official documents about Scientology.

Hundreds of writs have been issued over the years against and by the Scientologists. In 1986 a Milwaukee businessman and ex-member was awarded $30 million in damages after he charged that the church wrecked his business and drove him to a nervous breakdown when he grew disillusioned with the organisation and started to resist its teachings.

The church itself has its biggest base in California: a group of tall, powder-blue offices on the famous Sunset Boulevard and Berendo Street in East Hollywood, just a few miles from Tom's main home in Pacific Palisades. There is also the ten-storey L. Ron Hubbard Life Exhibition building on Hollywood Boulevard by the junction with Cahuenga. Swarms of Scientology officers – called Sea Orgs and often dressed in naval-style uniforms complete with ribbons and epaulettes – and students pour in and out of all the buildings every day.

Then there is the Celebrity Center – an aesthetic wonder, based in what used to be the Manor Hotel, a magnificent seven-storey turreted mansion built in 1927 in the style of a seventeenth-century château. During Hollywood's Golden Days it was a luxury pit stop for the likes of Clark Gable, Humphrey Bogart and Errol Flynn, with suites offering a magnificent view of LA. Now, however, it is home to the church's most publicised cause – the recruitment of the famous. It even features seminars like 'How to Make It as a TV Writer', 'Artists Revitalisation Workshop' and 'Success in the Music Industry'. Each Sunday there is a talent night, with an open mike providing sin-free karaoke sessions for members.

As one visitor explained: 'The famous names you read about being linked to the Scientologists are rarely there, but literally hundreds of would-be members turn up out of curiosity and in the hope they might spot a famous face.'

A large gold bust of founder L. Ron Hubbard perches at the side of the stage in the Celebrity Center and Sea Orgs often exhort the audience by proclaiming: 'Go out and raise the tone scale of this planet.'

Andre Tabayoyon, a former member of the security personnel at the Scientologists' base camp at Gilman Hot Springs, who left the organisation in 1993, explained that most of the church members were only allowed to talk to Tom 'if he talked to us. That was the rule. He had to originate the communications.'

Tom seemed more withdrawn when he visited the Gilman Hot Springs base camp with Nicole Kidman, said Tabayoyon, adding that Mimi Rogers never visited that camp after her divorce from Tom.

After his divorce from Mimi, Tom tended to go to the base camp at Gilman Hot Springs. Visitors to the camp say that Tom and David Miscavige were 'always in huddles together'.

Tom uses the same apartment whenever he visits the complex and keeps his own Mercedes and two trial bikes on the property.

Tom and Nicole always arrive at Gilman Hot Springs – known as 'Gold' to Scientology members – by private helicopter. One visitor described their arrival as being 'like something out of a James Bond movie. All these armed security guys surrounding the craft within seconds of it landing and then the couple are whisked away by car for the short journey to the apartment complex.'

In an annex of the Celebrity Center at the base camp, Tom enjoys gourmet cuisine in a dining area shaped like the court of King Arthur, complete with a tacky-looking replica Round Table. He often plays on the tennis courts with church leader David Miscavige. They were built for around $80,000 for the use of special members like Tom and other celebrities.

The base camp – about one mile wide and six miles long – also features a man-made lake with a single yacht bobbing on the water. At the edge of the lake is a sculptured waterfall, which, with the desert in the background, makes a truly bizarre sight.

Gilman Hot Springs is a tiny community on highway 79 just off the main road seventy miles from Los Angeles and about forty miles west of Palm Springs. Before World War Two it was as big a holiday resort as Palm Springs, but today armed guards on motorbikes patrol the site constantly. When I joined a tour of the compound one Sunday afternoon in April 1994, I was stopped three times and asked who I was.

The centre also features a golf course, soccer pitch and a film studio. Walkways shared by pedestrians and motorbikes link a series of buildings on the site. Minor staff are dressed in blue trousers, light-blue shirts and ties, but

Top: The $400,000 house, in the most exclusive area of Louisville, where Tom's grandparents on the Mapother side of his family lived until their deaths.

Bottom: The modest rented house on Cardwell Way, Louisville, where Tom befriended neighbour Bill Lewis.

Top: Tom with his first wife Mimi Rogers.

Bottom: The well secured – and carefully hidden – entrance to Tom's vast Pacific Palisades mansion, near Los Angeles.

Top: Tom in his classic *Top Gun* pose.

Bottom: The smoothest of barmen, in the movie *Cocktail*.

The dingy hole-in-the-wall club on Hollywood's sleazy Sunset Strip, where Tom met an Asian girl during the making of *Losin' It*.

The nondescript entrance to Tom's vast apartment in one of New York's trendiest districts.

The significant others in Tom's life – ex-wife Nicole Kidman, and new flame
Penelope Cruz.

Top left: Penelope Cruz was brought up in this crumbling block of council flats in the Madrid suburb of Alcobendas … a far cry from the £1 million house (*bottom*) on this exclusive gated community on the outskirts of Madrid – although she rarely visits because she spends most of her time with Tom in Los Angeles.

Top right: This was the disco where a teenage Penelope first dated boys and soon gained a reputation as a fun-loving girl.

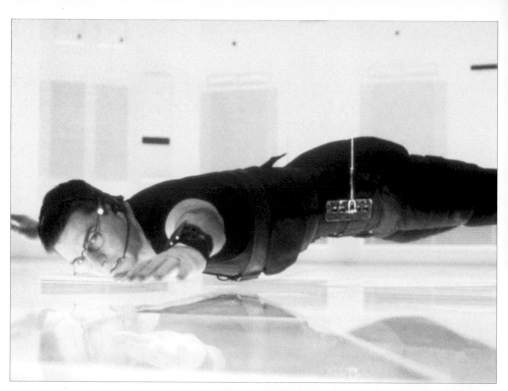

Top: Mission impossible? Then there's only one man for the job…

Bottom: Tom with fellow Hollywood great Steven Spielberg at the launch of *Minority Report*.

a number of officers wear medallions as if they have been in battle somewhere. I noticed one statuesque blonde in three-inch heels clipping along looking terribly officious in her full naval-officer-style regalia. Security guards wear brown and some are armed. Every entrance also has electronically operated fencing pierced with spikes. Women with short, tidy, neat hairstyles and a frightened look in their eyes walk constantly from building to building.

When I visited they were constructing yet another new building, to be a sound studio. All the tourists were prevented from taking photographs and an armed motorcyclist shadowed the tourist party virtually all the time the group was in the compound.

There is even a bizarre, clipper-shaped building on the edge of the base camp that looks like a ship moored in the desert sand. It is a very eccentric place.

At Gilman Hot Springs, Tom and other celebrities are personally looked after by David Miscavige and other senior Scientology officials.

Nicole Kidman claimed she was into Scientology even before she met Tom, despite what he has said publicly.

Tom's relationship with David Miscavige – the man who took over as leader of the Scientologists after L. Ron Hubbard's death – is the subject of much discussion in Hollywood. Miscavige drives an expensive Lexus limousine and is described as the head of the church. His wife is number two in the organisation; the couple have no children.

At a dinner party given in honour of Tom and Nicole after their wedding, Tom sat next to CAA super-agent Michael Ovitz, and on his other side was Miscavige. Nearby were two full tables of Scientologists. According to one report, the Scientologists around Tom were 'like they always are – very direct, very attentive, very protective – hovering over Tom. And shaking a lot of hands.'

Miscavige also flew out to the location where Tom was filming *Far and Away* to help the star celebrate his birthday, and regularly called in at Tom's private apartment at Gilman Hot Springs.

Screenwriter Bob Dolman attended a story meeting before filming of *Far and Away* began with director Ron Howard at the base camp. He was flown in from Los Angeles by private helicopter and later described the compound as 'so security-conscious, so military – there was a car waiting for the helicopter, people wearing brown khakis'. Dolman says it was made very obvious that Tom and Miscavige are very good friends.

Miscavige stoutly defended his good friend Tom when he responded to Rod Lurie's article in *Los Angeles* magazine by writing: 'Your report portrays me as visiting the set to lobby for use of Clearsound and getting kicked off the set and told to "f— off" by Don Simpson. Yet the facts are:

'1. I never lobbied for the use of Clearsound.

'2. I was never kicked off the set.

'3. I was never told to "f – off" by Simpson or anyone else.

'4. Any meeting I did have was prior to shooting and as a friend of Tom who happened to know about sound.

'Your reporter's intentions were clear: make it seem like there is a Scientology connection (thus Clearsound) and that the church gets involved with Tom's affairs and that some falling-out between Simpson and Scientology had something to do with the later relationship between Tom Cruise and Don Simpson – at least in regard to 'Top Gun II' – and the clear indication of that is Don Simpson kicking me off the set! Sound convoluted? Well, it is, and it's also maliciously false.'

Emilio Estevez, Tom's best man at his wedding to Mimi Rogers, was reported to be a target of a Scientology recruitment attempt. He did not join the organisation and told *Premiere* writer John Richardson that he supported his magazine's efforts to produce an 'informative' article about the church and its behaviour.

After Richardson's lengthy article appeared, lawyers representing the Scientologists sent dozens of letters complaining about the story he had written.

The journalist praised Pat Kingsley's skills as a PR person. 'She is a very good publicist.' But he added: 'Her line to everyone who asks her anything about this question [Scientology] is that it is not American to question someone's religion, which is ludicrous. Religious freedom does not mean that suddenly freedom of the press stops. Pat was just giving statements. It is her job.'

Richardson said he gained a firm impression that Tom Cruise is extremely involved with the Scientologists. 'He has allowed them to use his face on posters. He is definitely a member and from everything that I was able to determine very close to Miscavige.'

Tom himself admitted to *Premiere*: 'I have gained a lot from Scientology. I know how I can help people from my own personal involvement and study of the subject.'

The actor refused to even refer to the *Premiere* article as an interview because he only agreed to the questions being asked through Kingsley as a form of 'fact checking'. The magazine even had to present Tom's reaction in a separately laid-out position in the middle of the main article, under the heading 'Cruise Control' and with a letter to the editor from Pat Kingsley which stated: 'I got Tom Cruise to answer the questions and I offer them to you on one condition. The condition is that you use the questions exactly as they were asked and use the answers exactly as they were given. We have agreed that if any changes are contemplated by *Premiere* we can then withdraw all of the material and nothing can be printed without our specific approval. With that in mind I send these sheets on to you and would appreciate hearing from you once you have an opportunity to look at them.'

Premiere decided to accept the conditions and most of Tom's replies were fairly dull. However, he did state: 'I have no idea why my religion, or anybody's, would be the subject of an article in *Premiere* and that is why I have refused to participate in any interview. I make movies. And when *Premiere* wants to talk about the movies I make, I have been and will continue to be willing to discuss such at length.'

Tom went on to say: 'Not one of these questions has anything to do with that... The Church of Scientology doesn't run my life or career. By being asked to answer these questions I'm perceived as having to defend my religion or Church and by having to deny accusations a false impression is created. This is not what freedom of religion is about... I shouldn't be subjected to an inquiry... Likewise, my Church shouldn't be subjected to press disparagement because I'm a member. My work speaks for itself ... and as far as *Premiere* is concerned that should be the end of the matter.'

John Richardson believes Scientology seems to be a way of thinking that helps you get confidence and helps you overcome your doubts more so even than most religions.

'It is well suited to the kind of temperaments that many actors have. There are a lot of strange experimental things in Los Angeles and I think it is a combination of things; the receptivity of people in the arts to new ideas, combined with the specific character of Scientology, combined with the way that once you become involved in Scientology it becomes a world filled with people who think a certain way. It is a total experience.

'The question is, why are the Scientologists so interested in Hollywood? Why do they have the Celebrity Center? Why did L. Ron Hubbard specially say let's find celebrities? I find that a little unusual for a religious organisation.'

After publication of the *Premiere* article, the magazine was flooded with letters from Scientologists insisting that they had been deeply offended by its tone, and the church even paid out tens of thousands of dollars to publish a sixteen-page booklet, entitled 'Premiere Propaganda', denouncing the article.

Eventually the magazine published a 2000-word response to the article submitted by the Scientologists after church spokeswoman Leisa Goodman claimed that: '*Premiere*'s reporter was not interested in writing a fair story on the church. Instead, he went out of his way to seek individuals who he could use as a vehicle for his animus against Scientology.' The Scientologists believed that *Premiere* decided to publish their lengthy reply because the magazine had been confronted with its own 'appalling use of journalistic ethics' and was 'forced to realise that the church was due a far fuller response than a mere letter to the editor'.

Even journalists who have written about Tom's involvement are very sensitive about talking publicly about their articles. John Richardson insisted that his lawyer read every one of the quotes used in this book because he feared the Scientologists might pursue him legally. 'This is a legally dangerous area. I know that reporters do not like this, but can you run these quotes by my lawyer before you run this? They are very litigious,' he said.

Countless stories have appeared in both Britain and the USA over the years concerning parents' desperate efforts to get their children home from Scientology centres. In Britain, membership of the religion was considered reason enough to bar foreigners from entry into the country until a few years ago.

Other ex-members claim that the church actively encouraged its members to try to interest famous names like Tom. Lisa Halverson explained: 'Sometimes uniformed personnel would come into the course room and ask us to write down names of what they call in Scientology "opinion leaders", heavy hitters of some sort in whatever sphere of activity they might be – in business, politics, and arts and entertainment.'

Scientology leaders claim that the organisation's continuing bad press often comes from psychiatrists who are angry that the church is encroaching on their turf. They cite their fight against psychiatry and drug abuse as evidence of the beneficial side of the religion. 'We're helping celebrities,' said one official. 'We service them – to be more capable, to be more ethical, to be more able... Scientology celebrities are successful, and they're not messed up!'

Little clues of the teachings of the Scientologists occasionally slip out in press interviews given by Tom. In an article in *Entertainment Weekly* he said: 'I look at certain people that aren't doing well and say, "Well, who's around him? Do they want to see this person do well?" And often I might find one person that really doesn't want to see this guy succeed.'

However, most of the time he is very defensive about his membership of this organisation. 'He feels he has been misunderstood,' explained writer Stephanie Mansfield, who met Tom for an interview with *GQ* magazine.

By early 1997, some of Tom and Nicole's closest friends were saying that Nicole was growing increasingly frustrated and bored by her husband's involvement with the Scientologists. One said: 'Nicole doesn't like the commitment to it because she feels they should be spending all their spare time together as a family, not at some Scientologists' seminar or whatever.'

Nicole herself has refused to criticise her husband's continual attendance at Scientology events. But one ex-church member said: 'I saw her at a couple of events at the Celebrity Center and she looked bored rigid. It certainly doesn't seem to be her kind of scene.'

With no family problems and a remarkably functional background, maybe Nicole simply didn't have the right kind of emotional baggage to get swept up by Scientology. As that former member explained: 'She seems a sweet person who just isn't particularly complicated and that's a bit of a minus point when it comes to the Scientologists.'

As for Tom himself, there are those who say that there is absolutely no way he will walk away from the Scientologists. One friend said: 'They have helped him throughout his career. He will not turn his back on them.'

It seems that, whatever else Tom does in his career, he will stay close to Scientology.

24

Ask not what your country can do for you: ask what you can do for your country.

JOHN F. KENNEDY

When Ronald Reagan was elected President of the United States, he proved what many had suspected for a long time: if your face fits, then the ultimate American dream can come true. Reagan forged such a strong link between Hollywood and Washington that he opened up the political floodgates to prove that anyone handsome and presentable could become the world's most powerful leader.

And when Bill Clinton took over at the White House, ties between the showbiz glitterati and politics seemed to get even closer, with two Hollywood producers acting as the new president's closest advisers and a host of other showbusiness 'link-ups'.

So when Tom Cruise said recently, 'I do believe in the American dream. I think we're in trouble right now, there's no question about it. This country needs a boost,' it was deemed to be significant in Hollywood terms.

Tom has never openly said that he harbours ambitions to one day become President of the United States, but many inside moviedom believe he will one day turn his back on Hollywood to pursue the ultimate job. He is young enough to spend at least another ten years at the top of his profession – Reagan did not even think seriously about entering politics full time until he was well into his forties, several years older than Tom is now.

It has to be said, of course, that Tom's political beliefs are a million miles away from both the Reagan philosophy and that of many of his relatives back in Louisville. He has some very strong opinions about his home country and where things have gone wrong. Over the past few years he has let it be known that he is 'very concerned' about the future development of the United States. Friends have urged him to make his opinions heard more clearly and he is starting to realise that, when he speaks on any subject, people are prepared to sit up and take notice.

As with every other aspect of his life, Tom has quietly and carefully learned more about politics, social issues, even foreign affairs. If he did take the leap it would not be a Clint Eastwood-style stab at being mayor of a small town; it would be the real thing.

One Hollywood associate claims it is an open secret in California that Tom is looking beyond just being a movie star. 'He has healthy political aspirations. There is no doubt about it.'

Almost ten years after the success of *Top Gun* there is little doubt that the movie's right-wing, gung-ho ideals are far removed from Tom's real political opinions. If there is ever a sequel of the movie, then it will almost certainly be a much more sensitive, issue-led project. Tom said: 'Some people felt that *Top Gun* was a right-wing film to promote the Navy. And a lot of kids loved it. But I want the kids to know that's not the way war is – that *Top Gun* was just an amusement-park ride.'

The flip side to *Top Gun* was *Born on the Fourth of July*, a movie with a profound message that war was a waste of human life and effort. It seems that during the making of that movie the beliefs of director Oliver Stone rubbed off on Tom to a certain degree. Stone, a passionate anti-war convert following his own experiences in Vietnam, indirectly had a great influence on the young actor. Tom carefully absorbed many of the relatively left-wing opinions that flew around the set and chose to follow the aspects that appealed to him.

Tom saw *Born on the Fourth of July* as a film that started in an era when there was a real sense of the flag and country, and of loyalty to the Pledge of Allegiance. He referred to it as a time of 'blind commitment' to the government of the day. And he told *Playboy* magazine in an interview in January 1990 that Americans 'had no business' being in Vietnam. 'The country [USA] became impotent and embarrassed.'

Born on the Fourth of July was definitely a turning point in Tom's political beliefs. As he told *Playboy*: 'I heard the other day that President Bush said that we should forget about Vietnam and move on into a new era. No! Let's never forget Vietnam! Never! The second we forget Vietnam, we are going to make the same mistake again. That's an important lesson. History shows that we always forget. We didn't pay attention to the French; let's remember Vietnam and become better because of it. Let's not send our men to fight in a poor peasant country for no reason. It meant nothing to us. It had no value. It only killed off a generation of young men.'

Fortunately, Tom still believed in the American dream, but he recognised that it was in trouble and needed a big boost.

Around the same time as his encounters with Oliver Stone and Ron Kovic on *Born on the Fourth of July*, Tom became heavily involved in fighting the destruction of the rain forests in Brazil. Soon, like any good politician, he was referring to that particular situation, and he told *Playboy*: 'You have to bring Brazil in and have it become part of the team. You can't point a finger at Brazil and say, "Why the fuck are you letting everybody take – how many football fields is it a day? – of the rain forests?" I want to understand it more. I want to see it. I want to make sure there is air to breathe when my children are my age. It's one of the most important issues that this world has to face right now.'

Trips to Brazil with Mimi followed Tom's initial burst of interest. But by the early 1990s the subject seemed to have been replaced by a keener involvement in issues closer to home.

In Hollywood, close friends and associates were noticing Tom's increasing interest in politics. All of them recognised that the actor had what it takes to make the leap to Washington and they have all quietly encouraged him ever since.

Tom's own political hero in recent years has been one-time Californian Governor Jerry Brown, a left-of-centre liberal Democrat who masterminded a controversial tax programme to help the poor and needy throughout the state when he tried to win the Democratic presidential nomination that eventually went to Bill Clinton. Tom is full of admiration for Brown because he is known as a blunt, honest speaker prepared to attack any political friend or foe if he disagrees with a certain policy.

'Tom sees himself in that Jerry Brown mould,' says one Hollywood observer. 'He is interested in the under-dog, the guy in the street who is battling against all the elements just like he and his mom and sisters had to do when they were together.'

Speaking about Brown, Tom told writer James Greenberg: 'He attacks the press, he attacks Clinton, he attacks Bush, he attacks big business. He says whatever is on his mind because no one's telling him what to do.' Tom is particularly concerned about the future for the children of America and he told Greenberg: 'I look at the young faces in schools and it's so important to keep them dreaming, to educate them and give them purpose and responsibility.'

Tom has been careful not to squander his fortune. He could easily live the rest of his life very comfortably without ever acting again. This is not to suggest that he has in any way lost the will to act. Nothing could be further from the truth. But, as a meticulous planner, he is definitely looking to the future.

Tom was among the celebrities who jetted into Little Rock, Arkansas, for the huge party given to celebrate Bill Clinton's win in the US presidential race. Although there were a lot of things about Clinton that Tom did not agree with, he certainly felt they were on the same side. Some saw Tom's presence as yet more evidence of his eventual intentions. In his own classic way, he was learning, observing, taking in the atmosphere in preparation for what might turn out to be the biggest role of his entire life.

In 1993 Tom started to take a much closer interest in politics in New York, where he still considered he had his strongest ties. He observed the mayor's election campaign in November of that year with great intrigue and even nailed his flag firmly to the Democrat mast by holding a number of highly confidential meetings with the then mayor, David Dinkins. Tom is known to have been sorely disappointed when right-wing Republican Rudy Giuliani eventually won the election.

One of the other reasons why Tom may gradually begin to pursue his political ambitions is that his long-held desire to direct movies came to fruition in 1993 – and by all accounts it was a very low-key affair, considering his status as the world's most famous movie star.

Tom had always been convinced that movie-making was primarily a director's medium and that was why so many actors, including Kevin Costner, Mel Gibson and, to a lesser extent, Arnold Schwarzenegger, had tried their hand at directing, with very differing results.

'A director has to have a vision ... that he has great taste in performance, the ability to tell a story, and that he is going to create interesting characters in telling that story and use those characters to tell the story,' reckoned Tom. With these strong opinions in mind, he directed an episode of *Fallen Angels*, a series of half-hour *films noirs* co-produced by Tom's director on *The Firm*, Sydney Pollack. Although there was no doubting that Tom held his own in the impressive field of *Fallen Angels* directors, who include Steven Soderbergh, Jonathan Kaplan, Phil Joanou and fellow actor-turned-director Tom Hanks, his episode did not exactly set Hollywood ablaze.

Tom picked *The Frightening Frammies*, described as a 'first-class story' and penned by classic crime writer Jim Thompson. Series producer William Hornberg explained: 'Tom loved the main character, this hapless con-artist. And it's a love story between two people who are always conning each other and who end up wary but together – he liked that.'

Having cast Peter Gallagher and Nancy Travis, Tom put a call through to Isabella Rossellini and asked her if she wanted to play the femme fatale. Rossellini, whose first name inspired Tom and Nicole to call their daughter Isabella when they adopted her in early 1993, was incredibly flattered and accepted immediately.

Producer Hornberg admitted, rather surprisingly, that Tom was 'a little self-conscious' during filming of the short film. 'You know, "Here I am, the star, giving you your directions," but he went into it with the appropriate sense of humour.'

Tom proved a little terse on the set, barking at actors to repeat their lines if he thought they got them wrong. Rossellini said later: 'I don't think I could take it from another director because I would feel diminished. But because he was an actor, I could take it from him. I felt he was on my side.'

One of Tom's biggest problems was adjusting to the sort of penny-pinching required on a $700,000 budget as opposed to the $30-million variety he was more used to. The schedule allowed for only a six-day shoot and insiders on the set said that Tom found it quite a strain and eventually he went into 'blitzkrieg mode' in a desperate bid to get the film completed in time.

Tom worked for scale on *Frightening Frammies*, which meant he received a fee of approximately $70,000. Articles published at the time of the shoot suggested Tom had equipped himself adequately, but he knew that all these comments were worthless until the film was completed and out on the *Showtime* cable channel in September 1993.

The *New York Daily News* proclaimed the film to be 'full of twists and turns, yet Cruise leaves room for his actors to add their own touches – and his eye for composing scenes, while never too showy, demonstrates a feel for, as well as an appreciation of, the classic *film noir* techniques.'

But Tom later admitted he had found the entire directing experience far from easy and voiced his delight at having chosen a relatively simple debut project as opposed to directing something as heavyweight as *The Firm*, which had briefly been suggested to him.

The summer of 1993 was definitely a time of consolidation for Tom. He not only learned to relax a little – thanks mainly to Nicole and their adopted baby daughter Isabella – but he also began to socialise more in Hollywood. One weekend he and former basketball star Magic Johnson rounded up some pals for a friendly game of softball at Palisades High School, near the Cruise mansion. Tom played second base for one team; Magic pitched for the other. As Nicole watched from the sideline, Cruise's team won 12–11.

When Tom accepted the Actor of the Decade award at the twenty-ninth annual Chicago International Film Festival, it marked yet another significant step for the still relatively young star. Previous winners included such luminaries as Orson Welles, François Truffaut, Sophia Loren, Jack Lemmon and Oliver Stone.

Co-host of the awards, Londoner John Russell Taylor, commented that Tom represented 'the great American hero of his generation, in a league with such screen idols as Gary Cooper, James Stewart and Tyrone Power'. Clips from many of Tom's previous films were shown and a host of celebrities paid tribute to Tom in person, while there were telegrams from other big names like Jack Nicholson and Paramount chief Sherry Lansing.

Nicole's standing as a star in her own right was enhanced when she hosted the American comedy show *Saturday Night Live*. At home, Tom played house father with true relish. While Nicole was rehearsing one day, he took Isabella, then aged ten months, with his sister Lee Anne to see the Big Apple Circus on the grounds of Manhattan's Lincoln Center. Paparazzi popped up everywhere within minutes of Tom's arrival and then Isabella threw a tantrum and Tom could do nothing to stop her crying, so he and his sister beat a hasty retreat.

Nicole's obvious contentment at home with Tom and baby Isabella still tended to be regularly disrupted by her unfortunate inability to sleep well at night. Often Tom would stir in the early hours to find his wife sitting downstairs watching television. On such occasions the couple would play a round of backgammon before returning to bed. Beneath that bubbly exterior, Nicole was obviously a bundle of nerves.

The couple often found themselves so busy that they paid a professional wardrobe designer called Kate Harrington to go and buy them clothes in New York if they got stuck in Los Angeles because of some project or other. Kate met the Cruises through her work for famous photographer to the stars Herb Ritts, whom the couple usually insist does their pictures for them for any publicity. On at least three occasions in 1993 she was paid $1000 a day to fly from California to New York to go on a shopping spree on behalf of her multi-millionaire clients Tom and Nicole. 'Sometimes she would spend as much as $20,000 on a few clothes for the couple without batting an eyelid,' explained one close associate. Often Tom would reject half the clothes Kate brought back, but no one seemed worried about the enormous waste of money.

In January 1994 Tom was approached by his old friend Harold Becker, who directed him in *Taps* and Nicole in *Malice*, to consider a role that might well help to fuel his involvement in politics. *City Hall* is described as a *Network*-type drama set in city government. Bo Goldman, who wrote the Oscar-winning *Scent of a Woman* with Al Pacino, penned the script. Hollywood observers expected that Tom's fee for this project could top $20 million, putting him in a league of his own when it came to per-picture deals.

There seemed to be no stopping Tom, still only in his early thirties, married to a beautiful wife and the father of a young child. On the surface, his life seemed to be perfect. But the star was still fighting demons of self-doubt that would continue to drive him further and faster than any other actor in Hollywood history.

25

*A lie can travel halfway around the world
while the truth is putting on its shoes.*

MARK TWAIN

Once upon a time in Hollywood, everybody told lies. With so much
valuable product to shield from public attention, the studio bosses
wanted it that way; and the stars were happy when whoppers were told on
their behalf. So the scandals came and went more or less unnoticed. When one
of Jean Harlow's husbands was murdered, MGM's chief of police simply
sealed off the lot until the studio press agents were ready with their version of
what happened.

Meanwhile, as Nathanael West demonstrated in his classic 1939 novel
The Day of the Locust, the tabloid reality of Los Angeles (lynchings,
murder, sex crimes, explosions, car wrecks, love nests, fires and so on) kept
the crowd in the front row busy. Nobody expected to be told the truth about
their idols.

When the stars went freelance in the sixties, everyone expected things to
change. They didn't. Instead, Hollywood became an even more secretive
place, where privacy and wealth predominate and comfortable lies are told
easily. 'It's a joke being here. If I was in Detroit, I'd be able to find out about
cars; if I was in New York, I'd know about the mob, or about money. But
in Hollywood you just can't find out anything about the stars,' said one
Tinseltown reporter.

If Tom Cruise could have his way, that's how it would stay for ever. The
actor has become increasingly sensitive to any publicity he receives. That

means 'authorised interviews' are about all anyone can get with the most famous box-office star on the globe. Such interviews involve Tom making himself available to the media in the run-up to a film, usually in a plush hotel suite or his publicist's office. For many journalists who have interviewed Tom over the past ten years, such antechambers have become synonymous with bowing to the star's demands. In short, they feel the system is humiliating.

Interviews can only be arranged through Tom's personal PR, Pat Kingsley, a woman who believes that publicity people, not editors, should choose magazine covers. Tom has never denied that he looks on journalists as obstacles or liabilities and he carefully scrutinises every single writer's credentials before giving anyone an audience.

The restrictive contracts that Kingsley now demands every journalist should sign before she allows them to interview Tom have caused a lot of bitterness and resentment. Writers who break the rules have been denied access to Tom and banned from subsequent press conferences or movie junkets. Newspapers and magazines that have published hostile copy have been admonished by Kingsley on Tom's behalf.

The Cruise control system kicked in with the press junket for *Far and Away* in 1992. Typically, print, radio and TV people are flown to a hotel, usually at the film company's expense, where they meet the stars at tables of about ten reporters, answering innocuous questions like: 'How was it to work with your wife?'

This time, however, Tom and Nicole demanded that reporters sign contracts stipulating which publications these stories would appear in and when they would run. The contract also stated that anything Tom said could only be used in conjunction with *Far and Away* and could not be mentioned in regard to any other Cruise article or project. In other words, the content of the interviews would be the sole property of Tom.

At the Cannes Film Festival in May 1992, two journalists were escorted out of a press conference after refusing to sign similar agreements with Tom's PR people. At a junket for *A Few Good Men* in November of that same year, the same old contracts were pulled out for journalists to sign. The ever-faithful Pat Kingsley approached Columbia about putting the contracts on their letter-headed notepaper, but the studio refused. This time, when reporters flew in for the gathering, Tom was nowhere in sight. Instead, most journalists found a letter awaiting them at their seats, explaining that he had to leave town early to be on the set of *The Firm*. Tom ended the note by saying: 'I look forward to the opportunity to speak with you again in the future.' Really?

The same situation occurred just before *The Firm* was released, although Tom did do some American television interviews, but only after each journalist had once again signed a contract that this time also stipulated that his interview could only be used during the cinema release of the movie.

Even when Tom does give the very occasional public statement he tends to look irritated, especially when the questioners come round to his looks or religious beliefs. His replies are usually abrupt and short and his body language soon makes it clear if he does not like the tone of a question.

Examples of Tom's obsessive quest for secrecy are wide-ranging. On the set for the shooting of *Far and Away*, extras were cautioned against talking to the stars. Tom and Nicole spent much of their time holed up in their customised Bluebird mobile home, complete with king-sized bed and satellite TV.

When the Cruises rented a five-bed, six-bath, 7500-square-foot wooden house at the end of a private dirt road while filming in Montana for *Far and Away*, the owner, Mike Overstreet, his wife Linda and their fifteen-year-old daughter Shara temporarily moved into a nearby apartment, telling friends they were having the house redecorated. The written agreement with Tom's people had stipulated that any news of their stay at the house would in effect make the contract null and void.

There was also the most incredible amount of small print in all of Tom's movie deal contracts, which completely restricted photography of him – even if it was for personal use. During *Far and Away* Tom and Nicole posed for a cast picture with a hundred-odd extras, with promises that each would get a copy. Then they were unable to authorise its release. 'It left a real bitter taste in everyone's mouth,' said one crew member.

Even Jeff Bayers, Tom's best friend from his days in Louisville, had been carefully briefed by the ever-self-protective star about not helping writers who contact him about their friendship. 'I don't feel comfortable talking about Tommy unless I get his permission. I really don't want to give much detail until I get Tommy's permission,' explained Jeff nervously. He also insisted that Tom Cruise had made him promise not to hand over any of his photos of the two of them together when they were kids in Kentucky. 'He has asked me not to hand any out. He is concerned with his image,' said Jeff ominously.

Mr Jarratt, the father of Tom's wrestling captain at school in Glen Ridge, proudly took hundreds of photographs of the team in action and would often appear a few days after a match to offer the other team members copies of the pictures. Years later, after Tom's career had taken off, his wrestling coach Angelo Corbo went to the Jarratts to try to find some old photos. He was told that he could not have any because a representative of Tom Cruise had contacted Mr Jarratt and requested that he not distribute the photographs. It seems that the star's obsession with privacy even reaches back as far as his days as an innocent high-school pupil.

'I wish I'd got my hands on some of the shower-room photos, then I'd be a millionaire by now,' joked Corbo.

Tom became very agitated when he encountered author Larry Wolfe Horwitz, who was about to publish a book entitled *New York Star Walks*, which featured star's addresses and where 'they hung out'. The actor bumped into Horwitz at the famous Russian Tea Rooms in New York and told him: 'I'm not too excited by the idea.' Tom then proceeded to tell the author horror stories about stargazers and nutcases who had loitered near his vast apartment on East 13th Street in the past. It obviously grated with him that anyone would actually publish the full address of one of his homes.

Respected showbusiness reporter Stephanie Mansfield interviewed Tom for *GQ* magazine's December 1992 issue in an article headlined 'Tom Cruise from the Neck Up'. The first stage of the interview went off without incident, but when Tom had further contact with Mansfield to answer a few more questions, the warmth and camaraderie of that first meeting were replaced by white-hot anger because Tom had discovered that the writer had dared to call one of his old girlfriends from Glen Ridge High School. Further questions about his family and details of his parents' divorce brought an angry response: 'That's really nobody's business.' Then he snapped at Mansfield: 'We're supposed to be discussing a movie.' He was referring to *A Few Good Men*, which was about to be released at the time. Finally, before hanging up on Mansfield, Tom added bitterly: 'Whatever you want to say is what you've got to say.'

Then Tom called back. 'Look, I just would have appreciated it if you had told me,' he said, his voice still edgy and tinged with condescension. 'It doesn't matter what these people say about me – people I knew for a very short time in high school. They knew me, but not really. I didn't go to that place and disclose my innermost feelings. The people who knew me were my sisters.'

'Well then,' asked Mansfield, 'how about I talk to them?'

'You wanna talk to my sisters? No! They don't want to do interviews! They're not interested in it.'

Tom told the somewhat surprised Mansfield that her attempts to interview people from her past were akin to 'a covert operation. It's just, like, rude. It's just a courtesy to tell me first. That's just common decency. It's not a matter of doing it. It's just a courtesy.'

Within hours of that second interview, she says, she got a call from Pat Kingsley. Mansfield explained, 'I am certain I am not Pat Kingsley's favourite interviewer at this point. I think that she has to understand that as a reporter you are doing your job and she has to respect that, but she has her job to do to, which is to protect him.'

'It was all kind of silly,' she said later. 'I think he felt somehow that his privacy had been invaded. Despite the row, she said grudgingly: 'I sort of liked him. He's a kid. Not too bright. He is not very educated but he is an okay guy, I guess.'

Mansfield's original interview had been at the plush Bel Air Hotel in Los Angeles, and Cruise had, at that stage, been charming and congenial. She has her own theories as to why he turned nasty during the second interview. 'He is very young and this is his life. A lot of other people had a life before acting, but Cruise never did. He was very successful at a very young age and this is his life.

'He is not spontaneous. You can see the wheels turning almost robotically when he is asked a question. I think he is very wary of the press. That's the control. He has to protect that image because it is all he's got.'

Mansfield believes in retrospect that she would have achieved a more satisfying, revealing portrait of Tom if she had insisted he conduct the interview driving 'or doing something. It would have been more revealing.' She said that Tom is 'very manipulative. He knows what he wants,' and added, 'He has a switch-on smile. Tom Cruise created himself. Tom Cruise is a creation, so he naturally would be upset if people looked into his background. I remember feeling it was forced and carefully practised.'

She thinks it is a shame that Tom is so overprotective. 'He is a wonderful actor. He was wonderful in *Born on the Fourth of July*.'

I felt sad for him, ultimately. It was a very sad experience.'

Reporter Roger Fristoe, who has worked on the *Louisville Courier-Journal* for more than fifteen years, had an even tougher time when he tried to put together a piece on the town's local boy made good. The article was to be a follow-up to a story he wrote in 1983, when he interviewed Tom on the telephone before publicity agents advised him to stop giving such off-the-cuff interviews.

'It was like a steel curtain had dropped. Everything seemed fairly favourable when I first tried to do the follow-up piece. We wanted to do a cover story on our magazine that would elaborate on what I had originally written and be a more in-depth piece.'

Andrea Jaffe was Tom's PR woman at the time and at first she assured Fristoe that an interview could be arranged. She even told the journalist that she should be back in touch with a date for a meeting. 'I waited and waited for the call to confirm this, but it never came,' explained Fristoe. Then *Top Gun* came along and Tom leapt into the superstardom bracket, and Andrea Jaffe stopped returning Fristoe's calls.

'So I wrote her a letter. I kept pursuing it but started getting these very frosty letters in return. It would be something from her assistant that would say, "Ms Jaffe is aware of your interest in her client Tom Cruise and will get in touch with you when she feels it is appropriate" or something like that. But she never did. I kept a file in the hope that some day it would work out, but in the end I gave up,' explained Fristoe.

Another, even more innocent, victim of the protective publicity shield that surrounds Tom was retired grandfather Warder Harrison. The Louisville-based former real-estate broker was trying to put together a history of Kentucky and all its famous residents in 1990, so he wrote a letter to Tom's then agent, Paula Wagner at CAA in Los Angeles, asking if he could mention Tom's name in the book. It was an act of courtesy on the part of Harrison.

The letter he got back from the mega-powerful agents at CAA shook the pensioner. A brief note advised Harrison that 'Mr Cruise is unwilling to consent to your request. He has always been very protective of the use of his name, likeness or personal information and will take whatever steps are available to maintain his privacy.'

Harrison was astounded by what was a complete overreaction to a simple request to mention Tom's name in a history book. But, afraid of the big guns at CAA, he dropped the matter entirely.

Then, a couple of years later, he saw Tom and Nicole on the *Oprah Winfrey Show* and felt obliged to try another request to use Tom in his book, which had still not been published. As a professional genealogist and at one time commissioned by the Sons of the American Revolution to prepare the genealogy of President Reagan, he felt that perhaps they would look kindly on his letter asking them to reconsider their earlier decision. Harrison's only request to Tom's agent was a current photograph to use in the book.

The reply, dated 29 May 1992, sounded even more sinister than the previous one. This time a Lawrence Kopeiken wrote back on behalf of Paula Wagner and Tom's publicist Pat Kingsley. The letter stated: 'Mr Cruise has not changed his mind regarding this project... Mr Cruise will take whatever steps are available to maintain his privacy.'

'I did not understand it,' explained Harrison. 'If anything, I was going to embellish his image. I was saying what a fine gentlemen he was and what kind of bloodline he came from. It was harmless stuff. I was not writing anything derogatory about him. It seemed so strange. Tom Cruise is something else.'

Tom himself genuinely believes his attitude is just part of the job. He said: 'I think people who say I'm a control freak haven't worked with me. I expect a lot, I have very high standards, as do the people I work with. It's not a matter of control, it's a matter of contributing to the picture.'

Tom's influence over press interviews was only the tip of the Cruise iceberg, it seems.

Besides his problems with Gene Hackman's agents over top billing on *The Firm*, Tom also demanded power of veto over advertisements in all his movies after *Top Gun* because he was annoyed that a lookalike was used to promote the home-video version of *Top Gun*. Studio insiders say that Tom's contracts for each movie role he undertakes now grant him 'more influence over the entire production than anyone has ever seen'. However, it must be said that Tom and *Rain Man* co-star Dustin Hoffman did make an exception to that rule when they allowed a Buick advertisement to run before the video version of *Rain Man* on condition that a portion of the fee for the commercial was donated to the Autism Society of America.

Tom's sensitivity to revealing any secretive aspects of his life can be summed up by a comment he made to one writer: 'There are no secrets. Sometimes you walk along a beach, looking for a piece of sand. Sometimes it's right in front of you. You don't have to dig. The sand is the sand – do you know what I'm saying?'

Just four miles from Tom's secluded home in the hills overlooking Pacific Palisades, his former wife Mimi Rogers was finding that life without the world's most famous movie star had certain distinct advantages.

The beautiful actress had, as they say, gracefully slipped into the background following the break-up and divorce from Tom. But in fact that eighteen-month period was more like the lull before a storm. For Mimi had been deeply hurt by some of the rumours flying around Hollywood about her and Tom and why their marriage fell apart. Ludicrous gossips claimed that he was gay and she was a lesbian. Others spoke of a sexless marriage between two people who were never suited in the first place. In fact, Tom and Mimi had genuinely loved each other for the first two years of their relationship. Then they gradually discovered they had opposing priorities.

By the beginning of 1993 Tom must have been thinking that his first marriage was well and truly in the shadows and destined to stay there for ever. Within weeks of the separation in January 1990, Mimi had been given a sizeable house in Brentwood, a wealthy LA suburb that separates Bel Air from Pacific Palisades, plus a settlement rumoured to be worth $2–3 million.

Mimi turned down dozens of lucrative offers to tell all about her marriage to Tom, partly because she did not want to air her dirty linen in public and also because, as part of the divorce settlement, she had made certain 'agreements' about not talking about her former husband.

In one brief reference to her successor, Nicole Kidman, Mimi said she felt sorry for the young Australian actress: 'All of a sudden her name is never mentioned without his. No matter what the article is, it's "Tom Cruise's wife, Nicole Kidman". That is it! You're never again mentioned without that name and that's hard. I am waiting for the moment when I don't have to talk about that fucking name any more. I've had it welded on to mine for years now.'

That was the full extent of Mimi's references to any personal aspects of her marriage to Tom. She did not feel she could complain about the marriage because she had truly loved Tom until the association with him became too much to handle. She felt genuinely sorry for Nicole because she was now having to take the heat much more than Mimi ever did. She knew what a burden that could be and could not help feeling relieved. All Mimi now wanted was for that Cruise tag to disappear completely.

So, when Tom picked up an issue of *Playboy* magazine in March 1993, he must have got quite a surprise. For there, spread across the page in glorious colour, was his former wife with nothing on other than a sequinned bathing cap and a pair of stilettos. Other photographs further inside the seven-page article revealed Mimi to be a very well-built, sexually active woman approaching her forties but still as proud of her body as ever. One particularly erotic shot showed her grasping her own breasts as her nipples protruded through a skimpy white see-through vest.

For good measure, there was also a still photo taken from *The Rapture*, a highly controversial, recently released movie about a sexually promiscuous woman, showing Mimi being caressed by another woman and a man at the same time. Suddenly Mimi had come of age. No longer Mrs Tom Cruise, she was making a mark on Hollywood in her own sweet way.

The photos in the *Playboy* piece were only the tip of the iceberg. The accompanying interview, conducted by respected writer Michael Angeli, mentioned the rumour mongers who claimed that Tom and Mimi divorced because she liked to go out and party and he preferred to stay at home. 'Is that the story?' Mimi asked Angeli. 'That I was bored with that child and threw him over, chewed him up and spat him out? Shall we let that be the story? Because here's the real story.

'Tom was seriously thinking of becoming a monk. At least for that period of time, it looked as though marriage wouldn't fit into his overall spiritual need. And he thought he had to be celibate to maintain the purity of his instrument. Therefore it became obvious that we had to split.'

It was sensational stuff from Mimi after a silence of almost three years. And there was more to come.

Angeli then asked pointedly: 'What about your instrument?'

'Oh my instrument needed tuning,' purred Mimi.

Then she went on to say: 'Finances aside, divorce just sucks. I thought as part of my settlement I would get my age back.'

Mimi even tackled the rumours about her being a lesbian by explaining that the gossip had started because she used to go out to bars with her best friend, actress Kirstie Alley, and they would get drunk and flirt with each other. Mimi talked liberally about men's 'dicks', having threesomes and how penises look silly on screen.

The article must have infuriated Tom, but behind it lay Mimi's frustration at what she perceived to have been a time in her life when she completely lost her own identity. She was simply Mrs Tom Cruise and she did not like it one bit. The fact that she received in the region of $200,000 for the photo spread and interview was hardly important. 'It can be frustrating to have your work kind of passed over as being irrelevant. And that's what happened to a certain extent,' Mimi insisted. She said she agreed to the controversial article and photographs because 'I am a big fan of nudity and art.'

After the *Playboy* interview hit the newsstands, Mimi frantically tried to withdraw the clear implication of her quotes that Tom was incapable of making love during their brief marriage. She appeared on US television to say her claims in the article were merely a joke.

Mimi told host Jay Leno on the *Tonight Show*: 'I came up with what I thought was a ridiculous story about how we split up because Tom was thinking of becoming a monk and needed to be celibate. I was kidding. It was a joke.'

She even took the trouble to write to *Playboy* to suggest that her remarks were 'totally playful and completely in jest'. *Playboy* said it stood by the article entirely. Mimi was discovering that the confidentiality clauses in her divorce settlement were being strictly adhered to by Tom's lawyers.

The *Playboy* piece had another infuriating knock-on effect as far as Tom Cruise Inc was concerned. Newspapers around the world picked up on the story and put their own spin on Mimi's words, with the result that dozens of highly personalised articles appeared talking about 'celibate Tom' and interpreting Mimi's quotes as meaning that the world's number-one sex symbol was not interested in sex. It was great tabloid fodder, and very hurtful to Tom.

Things came to a head in late 1993 when, during an interview for *Movieline* magazine, writer Stephen Rebello asked Nicole Kidman if her husband was gay. Kidman, smart enough not to even bristle at the suggestion, replied: 'Really? Well, ummmm, he's not gay to my knowledge. You'll have to ask him that question.' Earlier in the interview she had described Tom as 'the best lover I've ever had. He's a very sexual guy.'

As if to reiterate the point, the couple requested tickets for a theatrical production of Terrence McNally's *Lips Together, Teeth Apart* in New York, and made it clear they didn't want the press or anyone tipped off. Then the two lovers proceeded to kiss and cuddle and whisper sweet nothings in each other's ears throughout the performance. 'Anyone sitting behind them had a hard time watching the play,' said one theatre-goer.

Every now and again the couple would pop up in public with an ever-so-loving display of matrimonial bliss. On Easter Sunday 1993 they astonished movie-goers at the Century City Mall in West Los Angeles by queuing up for the reduced-price afternoon matinee of *This Boy's Life*, starring Robert De Niro and Ellen Barkin. After splashing out the princely sum of $3.75 for their bargain cinema tickets they took their seats near the front and shared a huge bucket of popcorn. Tom had his head on Nicole's shoulder and she had her arm around him the entire time.

Just before Christmas 1993 Tom turned down an extraordinary $2-million offer from a Swiss businessman who wanted the star to spend two hours at his daughter's twenty-first birthday party.

One highly unlikely movie role that Tom was linked with was *The Saint*. According to Hollywood observers, the actor was approached by controversial producer Bob Evans, former husband of Ali McGraw, who asked if he would star in the movie version of the sixties British TV series that made Roger Moore famous.

Some of the tabloids had a lot of fun running photographs of six-feet-two-inch Roger up against five-feet-nine- inch Tom with articles that suggested the younger actor was too short for the role. In fact, Tom's height never became an issue because he turned down the role.

Meanwhile Nicole's career was going from strength to strength. In late 1993 she completed her part as the conflicted heroine in Jane (*The Piano*) Campion's film of the classic Henry James period piece *The Portrait of a Lady*.

However, her role as Tom's wife was definitely proving rather more demanding. Nicole came face to face with her predecessor, Mimi Rogers, when they bumped into each other outside the Hollywood premiere of the Australian film *Strictly Ballroom*. Nicole had arrived first in a black stretch limousine which was followed, seconds later, by Mimi in her own car. Tom was not at the premiere. Witnesses said the two Mrs Cruises glared momentarily at each other and then walked off in opposite directions.

Nicole was then stopped and asked to pose for photographers outside the premiere while Mimi gave TV interviews just a few feet away. At no time did either woman acknowledge the other.

At the 1994 Oscars, Tom awarded his old mentor Paul Newman with the Jean Hersholt Humanitarian Award. The two men embraced warmly and it was clear to the hundreds of millions of people watching the ceremony across the world that Tom and Paul had kept up a very warm and touching friendship since the shooting of *The Color of Money* eight years earlier. Tom rounded off the evening by smooching with Nicole, who was wearing a $5000 black dress from Valentino, at the after-show event held at Morton's restaurant in Beverly Hills. Sporting a few days' growth of beard for his part in *Interview with the Vampire*, Tom seemed relaxed and happily planted a kiss on his wife's neck for the cameras.

Tom also proved he did have a sense of humour when he put on a bra and red stilettos to collect the Man of the Year award from Harvard University's Hasty Pudding theatrical group. He put on the heels after jokes about his reputation for not wanting to share a stage with anyone taller. Tom was then given a bra with a Harvard insignia on each cup. He insisted after the ceremony that the awards had 'nothing to do with the fact I just played two Harvard grads' in *The Firm* and *A Few Good Men*.

On the property front, Tom was carefully and quietly expanding his empire. In addition to the apartment in New York, worth approximately $5 million, and the $15-million house in Pacific Palisades, he decided that it was time the couple purchased a 'country home'. They had fallen in love with Telluride when they were married there on Christmas Eve 1990, so it was no great surprise when they bought a seventy-seven-acre estate in the same Colorado town just two years later for a reported $2.5 million. Locals were told that, within weeks of the purchase, Tom was having architects planning out the construction of a vast mansion and two guest houses on the estate, which is next door to a spread owned by Sly Stallone.

About six months later, in a secretive property transaction, Tom is believed to have bought a vast ranch in New South Wales, Australia, although this has never been officially confirmed. The reports were refuelled when, at an awards ceremony in early 1994, Tom let slip that he and Nicole were looking for a play to do together in Australia. For once in her life, Nicole gave her husband a scornful look and reprimanded him when he blurted it out. She put her foot down and scolded him: 'You told the press!'

'Sorry, honey,' he replied sheepishly.

Nicole had made no secret over the years of how much she had missed Australia and buying a bolt hole down under seemed a sensible way of giving her an opportunity to fly back there whenever she wanted to see her mother, father and sister.

After the disappointing box-office performance of *Far and Away*, Tom and Nicole sensibly decided to pursue their own individual movie projects. For some strange reason, the public did not appear to like watching the couple together on the big screen. The real-life chemistry that obviously existed between them did not really translate. Many Hollywood observers speculated that Tom's tens of millions of female fans did not like seeing him alongside the woman who, in reality, had him to herself.

Both Tom and Nicole burst into fits of giggles when they read reports in some of the tabloids claiming that they had agreed to play Prince Andrew and Fergie in a movie about the royal couple's trials and tribulations. It seemed that the rumours got going when some bright spark worked out that Nicole and Fergie were both redheads so that made the actress top contender for the role.

While they laughed off reports of playing royalty on the big screen, Tom and Nicole were fast gaining a reputation as Hollywood's newly crowned king and queen. In San Francisco, Tom spent $3000 a night staying in a luxurious hotel suite – and still insisted on providing his own sheets.

In France in September 1993, Tom left Nicole and Isabella in Paris and flew down by private helicopter to Deauville for the annual film festival, where he was guest of honour. The trip was scheduled to last only ten hours but an entire floor of the five-star Regency Hotel was cordoned off for his use. A large crowd of French fans gathered outside the town's casino, where the thirty-one-year-old star was expected for a press conference. Most were disappointed because Tom was hidden behind a wall of beefy minders as he made the mere fifty-yard journey by limousine from the hotel to the casino.

As one half of Hollywood's most glamorous couple, it was not surprising when Tom helped raise $50,000 for an AIDS benefit by planting an autographed kiss on a piece of cardboard. Lathered in lipstick, Tom's imprint brought in a price approaching $1000.

Tom was ranked number eighteen in the *Entertainment Weekly*'s 'top 100 in Hollywood' list for 1994, leaping from the previous year's ranking of number thirty-one. The magazine suggested that his power and influence inside Tinseltown had been considerably increased by the success of *The Firm* and *A Few Good Men*.

Besides agreeing not to appear with Tom on the big screen, Nicole started to let it be known through her agents at CAA that she was interested in some meatier roles, especially since her husband had also begun changing direction with *Interview with the Vampire*. In early 1994 she beat Meg Ryan to the part of a sociopathic housewife who hires her teenage boyfriend to kill her husband in *To Die For*, directed by Gus Van Sant, the controversial character behind such films as the drug-riddled *My Private Idaho* and *Drugstore Cowboy*.

On the personal front, without realising it, Tom managed to avoid meeting America's most controversial so-called shock-jock Howard Stern, whose radio show is listened to by at least twenty million people every morning. The fearsome Stern admitted that even he felt too uncomfortable to approach Tom when he visited the Monkey Bar in Los Angeles, because he was always making fun of the actor's squeaky-clean image on his radio show.

One role that Tom might live to regret turning down was the lead in brilliant young director Quentin Tarantino's award-winning *Pulp Fiction*. The movie won the Best Film category at the Cannes Film Festival in May 1994 after John Travolta revived his career by stepping into the part, first offered to Tom, of a charismatic hitman hooked on heroin.

The time had come for Tom to sit back and take stock of his career. Perhaps there would be opportunities in the fresh pastures that lay ahead.

26

Hollywood can keep the Oscars.
The only reward I want is a baby.

TOM CRUISE

To the outside world, Tom and Nicole seemed like the world's most perfect couple. They shared good looks, success and their fair share of good fortune, or so it seemed. But there was one aspect of their marriage that was putting them both under immense strain: their desperation to have a child.

The first two years following the wedding seemed like an extended honeymoon for the couple. To all their friends and family it was apparent that their love was growing by the day. They took romantic holidays in faraway places and were frequently seen smooching in cinemas and shopping malls in West Los Angeles. It all seemed as if the fairy-tale romance was set to last for ever and ever.

Tom even commissioned the interior decorators who had already completely redesigned the couple's mansion in Pacific Palisades to build a nursery for the children they intended to have.

In private, however, away from the public appearances and the snatched paparazzi shots, Tom and Nicole were fighting a lonely battle to become parents. For Tom, it was the second time he had faced the stark reality of not being able to become a father. During his marriage to Mimi Rogers, the couple had reportedly had dozens of fertility tests and spent tens of thousands of dollars on specialist advice as to how Mimi could become pregnant.

Said Tom shortly after the break-up with Mimi: 'I have cried tears of frustration over the past year. I would love to have kids. I would turn down an Oscar to see my boy at a baseball game or my girl at a song recital.'

During a visit to London for the royal premiere of *Far and Away*, in the summer of 1992, Tom and Nicole were seen purchasing baby clothes at the Laura Ashley store in the King's Road, Chelsea.

Almost every week a new rumour about Nicole being pregnant surfaced and the constant speculation was starting to get the couple down. In 1992 Nicole's publicist Nancy Seltzer demanded a retraction from *Parade* magazine in America for claiming Nicole was about to give birth. Tom and Nicole had spent the best part of two years ignoring the stories, but the gossip was starting to make them feel uncomfortable about not being parents. By the end of that year they were getting increasingly frustrated. Nicole was not pregnant.

He had steadily gained complete control of his business and personal life but here was something that he could not influence. After ten years of getting more or less what he wanted, mother nature was getting in his way. In any case, he had turned thirty and had already told many friends that he had no intention of being an elderly father.

In early December 1992 the couple felt they could wait no longer and filed papers for adoption in Palm Beach, Florida, one of the few states where a biological mother can't change her mind and try to regain custody after giving a child up for adoption. The paperwork stipulated that they were waiting for a baby from a 'broking' company, a children's home or even through a private financial agreement with the natural mother.

Under local laws Tom and Nicole were required to be residents of Palm Beach, but there was no record of their having owned a home there. It later emerged that they got around this problem by renting a huge house in the same street as Donald Trump's ludicrously over-the-top Mar-a-Lago beachside estate.

Tom was incensed by the hundreds of stories sparked by the news of his and Nicole's intended adoption. For a few days, in classic PR style, his publicist, Pat Kingsley, steadfastly denied that the adoption papers even existed. Then, at the end of December, when it became clear that the press hounds would not be deterred, Tom ordered his Palm Beach lawyer, Weston Sigmund, to withdraw the papers. He insisted to friends that stories of jealousy and the clinical manipulation of the adoption system were far from the truth.

In fact, Tom and Nicole could have continued trying for a lot longer. They simply recognised that their desperation might lead to problems in their own relationship. In any case, adoption was becoming all the rage in Hollywood, with people like Kirstie Alley and Michelle Pfeiffer heading the long list of celebrities who had arranged to take delivery of a child.

Tom's decision to order the adoption papers to be withdrawn was a heartbreaking one for the couple, but they were angry that the papers' existence had been made public by the Palm Beach records office. Tom's lawyers complained of a blatant breach of confidence and told Chief Circuit Judge Daniel T.K. Hurley that Tom and Nicole had suffered an irreparable invasion of privacy and were robbed of an opportunity to become parents. In fact, Tom and Nicole instructed their lawyers to secretly continue the adoption process.

At first representatives of the couple tried to strike a deal with a surrogate mother in Florida, but that plan was abandoned when it was pointed out that the identity of the real parent would be certain to leak out because the scandal-hungry US tabloids would pay a king's ransom for such information. There were also fears that the couple could become blackmail victims if someone decided to threaten to release the information if Tom did not hand over a fortune.

Tom was discovering that being the world's hottest box-office movie star certainly had its drawbacks, but all these obstacles made the couple realise that they both had a deep desire to give an unwanted child the sort of life most of us can only dream about. Tom's team of lawyers and advisers suggested that adopting – rather than surrogacy – would be a much more sensitive way of handling the situation.

'In my marriage to Nicole, I have learned to be sensitive to someone else's feelings, that life isn't all about me. When you're married, "me" has to become "us",' he told one acquaintance at the time.

Nicole left a very carefully laid trail of confusion over the entire baby issue by insisting publicly that she was not ready to start a family. 'There is plenty of time for that later. Tom and I have only just settled into each other's ways,' she said in the summer of 1992. 'We both realise that we are too selfish in our marriage and our careers to worry about the responsibilities that parenthood brings.' She was understandably concerned about her career. It had just started to get going and she was being offered movie roles without Tom, which proved to a sometimes cynical Hollywood that she could carry a film without her famous husband. After *Days of Thunder* and *Far and Away* some had been saying that Nicole could only get decent parts if Tom came along for the ride as well.

Tom actually felt indebted to Nicole for making him happier than he had been at any other time in his life. But he, more than her, felt the need to make their partnership into a complete family. All the heartbreak and anguish caused by the break-up of his first marriage and that of his parents had made him even more determined.

Nicole was under additional pressure from the constant speculation that she was pregnant. She explained: 'It's true. People do that. One woman walked up to me recently and said loudly to her friend: "Of course she's pregnant – look at that little belly."' Nicole then added a comment that must have brought a wry smile to the face of her predecessor, Mimi Rogers: 'I'm never sure whether people are interested in me because I'm a movie star or because I'm married to Tom.'

And there lay the couple's dilemma. Nicole wanted to pursue her career to prove she was an actress in her own right, while Tom was more concerned with making sure she got pregnant. In the end they reached a compromise and visited an adoption agency in Palm Beach.

The adoption was formalised in the second week of January 1993, and the couple became parents to a nine-pound girl they decided to call Isabella Jane Kidman Cruise. The child's married mother already had two children, but she was so poor that she could not afford to look after a third.

From the set of *The Firm* in Memphis, Tom rushed to the hospital in Miami where the baby was born, while Nicole flew in from Los Angeles. Both were shaking with nerves as they looked down at the baby for the first time as she lay asleep in a cot. Nicole leaned down and gently picked her up, tears welling in her eyes. Then she held her close. Tom looked on in awe. This was going to be the biggest test of character he had ever faced.

Tom's lawyers drew up a complicated series of legal agreements to prevent the child's parents from later staking any claim on Tom's multi-million-dollar fortune. There was also the difficult question of whether the baby would be entitled to inherit the same as any subsequent natural children that might be born to the couple or Tom in any later marriage. In litigation-crazy America, every precaution had to be taken to prevent the adoption issue from ever turning ugly.

Before taking delivery of Isabella, Tom and Nicole added a nanny and a nurse to their permanent staff back in Pacific Palisades.

The strangest rumour of all concerned the candid photographs of the couple with their baby that appeared in the *National Enquirer*.

As if to contradict the entire *Enquirer* situation, Tom's lawyers answered the rumours in March 1993 by requesting an injunction to prevent an Australian magazine from running photographs of baby Isabella. The couple feared that the pictures might be seen by the birth mother, who apparently remained unaware of the adoptive parents' identities. 'Isabella doesn't have to be public, too. We want to do everything we can to make her life as normal as possible, like our childhoods,' insisted Nicole.

Within a week of the adoption, Tom was moved to speak about the joys of parenthood while at the Golden Globe awards ceremony in Los Angeles. 'Becoming a father is the greatest thing that has ever happened to me. I have longed for a child for so long. Now that I have little Isabella, I look at her and thank God every day for giving me such a precious gift. I adore her to death and I hope I will love and protect her to my dying day – I am ecstatically happy.'

Tom even emphasised: 'Isabella comes before everything – career, films, business, everything. The baby and Nicole are the most important things in my life. Becoming a father makes you realise what it is all about.'

Nicole was just as overwhelmed and poured out her feelings to one associate: 'We chose to call the baby Isabella not because it has any family connections but simply because we both love the name.

'She has turned our world upside down. We thought we had everything, but having a child makes you put everything into perspective. I cannot even begin to describe the change that has come over Tom. I always knew he would be a loving father, but seeing him with our little girl makes me pinch myself.'

The first night little Isabella was in the house in Pacific Palisades, Tom even got up in the middle of the night to feed her. Friends said that he seemed to 'loosen up' and become a much warmer person after the couple adopted their baby. Having the child made Tom reflect even more on his own childhood and the lessons he learned from that sometimes painful experience.

Isabella seemed to be the icing on the cake for Tom and Nicole. At the Golden Globe awards the couple could barely keep their hands off each other as they spoke to journalists. They stroked each other, touched hair and kissed tenderly. They also held hands constantly.

Nicole, barely recognisable after straightening her normally curly red hair and dying it blonde for her latest movie role, even admitted that the couple had been trying to conceive 'for so long that we are making the most of Isabella now'.

Within weeks of Isabella arriving at her new home, Nicole was starting rehearsals for her starring part alongside Michael Keaton in *My Life*, with shooting scheduled for Los Angeles and Chicago.

Nicole was particularly attracted to the role in *My Life* because it was a poignant drama about a young woman who is expecting her first child and then discovers her husband has cancer. She relished the prospect of playing a pregnant person on film and insisted to everyone she met that she and Tom would definitely be having children of their own eventually.

By the time *The Firm* toppled *Jurassic Park* from the top of the US box-office ratings in July 1993, Isabella was seven months old and Tom, despite a back-breaking schedule, insisted that neither he nor Nicole was going to be an absentee parent. 'Nic and I were never going to have a child and disappear off to work every day to leave her with a nanny. I mean, what kind of way is that to treat a child?' Admirable words spoken with utter intent, no doubt. However, when a multi-million-dollar movie rests on your performance it does not leave much time for a home life, although it has to be said that, during the late spring and most of the summer of 1993, Tom made a remarkable effort to be with Isabella whenever possible. He and Nicole adored getting up early and taking the baby out in her three-wheel pram, specially adapted so that Tom could jog as he pushed it. Rumours even circulated that they had decided to adopt a second baby because they so enjoyed parenthood. But these turned out to be false, fuelled by the couple's open admission to friends that they still hoped to have children of their own and the fact that they had to appear in a Florida courthouse in July 1993 to finalise the adoption process, which had started back in January.

One of the most unlikely public appearances by Tom and Nicole and Isabella came when the threesome visited the well-known British pub the King's Head, in Santa Monica, just five miles from their home in Pacific Palisades. Locals could not believe their eyes when the couple walked in and ordered a plate of bangers and mash each. The pub is the favourite drinking spot for more than a dozen British tabloid journalists based in the LA area. 'Talk about walking into the enemy camp. We could not believe it when he came in and sat down. Maybe nobody told Tom that the King's Head is Santa Monica's equivalent of Fleet Street-by-the-sea,' said one veteran tabloid reporter.

Meanwhile Nicole seemed to be working non-stop. Tom flew from Los Angeles to Boston every other weekend to see her and Isabella while she was making *Malice* with handsome Alec Baldwin. In the *Star* tabloid one report claimed that Tom showed up unannounced on the set of the movie to watch some of his wife's passionate clinches being filmed for a scene and then declared: 'Some of those kissing scenes are a little too strong – and a little too long!' The article went on to insist that Tom also added: 'A kiss shouldn't take a minute and a half – ten seconds is more like it!' Apparently, Alec Baldwin snapped back: 'Sorry, but Kim [his girlfriend Kim Basinger] is away for five days.'

Malice was directed by Harold Becker, the helmsman who had given Tom his chance in *Taps* all those years earlier. Reviews of the film were mediocre, but Nicole's acting skills were given some praise. *Movieline* described it as 'a wicked thriller that dances on the grave of the ordinary murder mystery'. Nicole was, said the magazine, 'unsuspecting, but push her in the wrong direction and you get a Nicole Kidman never seen on-screen before: ruthless, confrontational and angry as hell'.

Tom managed to persuade Nicole to take enough time off to fly to Australia with him to show Isabella off to all Nicole's relatives. He even sneaked in a few visits to some of the finest properties in the Sydney area as he was secretly contemplating buying a home in Australia. The high point of the trip, which coincided with the fortieth Sydney Film Festival, was a three-hour voyage in Sydney Harbour with some of Nicole's family on the yacht *Sea Gypsy*.

Tom and Nicole took turns to hold Isabella and enjoyed a tasty lunch from a hamper as the baby's nanny stayed out of sight in a cabin. Nicole dabbed some suntan lotion on the child to ensure she did not get burnt.

In August 1993 Tom told *Hello!* magazine that he had started to learn how to relax, thanks to Nicole and Isabella. 'For a long time before I met Nicole, I always put my career ahead of everything. Now we do everything together. Nic just makes it feel fun to be around her. The littlest things she'll do will get to me.

'She'll say, "Oh, a little tense today? The world's treating you a little rough." When she does that you realise things aren't so terrible."

However, that same month Tom discovered that taking your family on holiday can prove a little tiresome if you happen to be one of the world's most famous people. The happy couple hired a yacht and went cruising with their baby daughter off the Mediterranean island of Sardinia. But the local paparazzi got so intrusive that Tom begged local police to help him deter the lensmen. The police proved so vigorous in their pursuit of the dozens of photographers that a few days later Tom hired one of them as the family bodyguard for the rest of the holiday, at a cost of $1500.

The incidents with the paparazzi reminded him of how risky it was to not always have bodyguards, especially in Europe, where terrorism seemed more of a problem. The couple were proud of the fact that they tried to get out into the real world as often as possible, as was proven by their frequent appearances in shopping malls and restaurants in Los Angeles. In London, during the making of *Interview with the Vampire*, Tom even hired a top doctor to 'babysit' Isabella in case she got ill. The couple recruited senior registrar Jane Deal from the paediatric ward at St Mary's Hospital in Paddington to make sure that instant medical attention was on hand if their baby daughter fell ill. Tom paid Jane $200 an hour plus a weekly retainer of $700.

Tom and Nicole's decision to become parents had brought with it a number of unforeseen problems.

27

*For vampires, physical love culminates
and is satisfied in one thing, the kill.*

VAMPIRE LOUIS IN INTERVIEW WITH THE VAMPIRE

After completing *The Firm*, Tom realised that his career had reached a watershed. At the age of only thirty-one, his roles seemed predestined, his salary was stuck in the $15 million-a-picture range and his movies were virtually guaranteed to deliver a huge box-office success on the opening weekend. But Tom actually feared that the parts he had so far been playing to perfection might be wearing a little thin.

Hundreds of millions of movie-goers around the globe still adored the routine: pushy kid matures to manhood over the course of a ninety-minute movie. That familiar wink, smile and expression of mild bewilderment had become his calling card. Tom wanted to be stretched further. He wanted to go beyond the expected roles of a megastar and venture into unknown territory. So far, he had not put a foot wrong.

However, at the urging of Hollywood's two most awesome powerbrokers, CAA chief Mike Ovitz and record-company boss and movie producer David Geffen, Tom decided to enter that highly dangerous movie terrain called character depiction. And the project his two mentors encouraged him to take on was to prove the most controversial move of his entire career.

Interview with the Vampire was first published as a novel in 1976 and gained cult status as probably the greatest vampire book since Bram Stoker's classic *Dracula*. Author Anne Rice updated her version for a morally ambiguous age and the result was that her vampire was not just evil incarnate but was burdened with a conscience that haunted his every waking hour.

And that was precisely what happened to Tom after he was offered the role of Rice's chief vampire, Lestat de Lioncourt. He found himself haunted by controversy surrounding his decision to take the part and was plunged into self-doubt – not helped by the fact that the character he had agreed to play was known to millions of Rice fans as tall, blond, European and androgynous.

Even more significant than that was the fact that Tom's part meant he would be playing a villain for the first time in his life – a sallow mass murderer, an after-hours fiend who sinks his teeth into every man, woman and child he meets.

Tom insisted publicly that he was not in the least bit concerned that what Oliver Stone so rightly called his 'Wheaties-box' image would clash with his ability to play Lestat. 'I just couldn't resist the role. Besides, he's not a bad guy, he just has villainous aspects to him. From his point of view, he's right. He's really a terribly lonely character.'

In many ways Tom could have been describing himself, apart from the 'villainous aspects'. In fact, he wanted to be 'badder'. He wanted to show audiences that he was capable of a much wider range of human emotions.

And the role of the vampire would stretch him to breaking point. Lestat is an amoral solitary supervampire who voyages through time and space feasting on flesh. In *Interview with the Vampire* he coldly turns Louis Pointe du Lac, played by the then up-and-coming Robert Redford lookalike Brad Pitt, into a vampire because he likes the company and is envious of Louis's impressive home. Later, still bored and lonely, Lestat persuades Louis to 'adopt' a five-year-old girl and turns her into a vampire as well.

Tom first heard of the project when David Geffen contacted him in December 1992 while Tom was holidaying in Australia with Nicole. Geffen, the king of Hollywood's so-called 'velvet mafia', had gained billionaire status after the mega-sale of Geffen Records a few years earlier. But his influence on Tom went way back to the success of *Risky Business*, the movie that helped to launch Tom's career more than any other. Geffen had backed the movie financially and played the main producer's role. Tom had never forgotten how supportive Geffen had been and kept in touch with him throughout the following ten years.

Geffen came to have an increasing influence on Tom's career moves in the late eighties. He looked on Tom as a star whom he had helped steer to the top and the two men had a special affinity for each other, fuelled by Tom's eternal gratitude to Geffen for helping him land that all-important part in *Risky Business*.

When Geffen called Tom about *Interview with the Vampire*, the actor immediately took notice and, as he later admitted, 'got very excited'. Tom told

Geffen that he had read the novel when he was a teenager and loved it. (For a kid with dyslexia, Anne Rice's book must have taken a hell of a long time to read!) By the end of their conversation Tom was convinced that Lestat was going to be his next role. It was a decision that would turn into the most controversial, headline-hitting storm to hit Hollywood in 1993.

Tom immediately called his production company in Los Angeles and asked them to get hold of every one of Anne Rice's novels, and on his return to California he began the first stage of his homework for the role. He 'busted ass' reading every one of her books and tried to come to terms with the decadent lifestyle of the eighteenth-century French aristocrat turned vampire Lestat. Then he took piano lessons from teacher Margie Balter, who was recommended to Tom by his co-star in *The Firm*, Holly Hunter, who got Best Actress Oscar in March 1994 for her portrayal of a dumb woman in *The Piano*. Margie's comment on her new pupil Tom was not that surprising: 'He's very smart and very focused.'

While on a visit to Paris to cruise round museums as part of his research, Tom visited Versailles to get the feel of the period furniture and fashions. He also went on his most stringent-ever diet-and-exercise regime in order to lose twelve pounds to take on Lestat's gaunt physique. Then he had his hair streaked blond, his eyebrows flecked with gold and his newly grown locks parted in the centre. The transformation was under way.

But what Tom did not expect when he told David Geffen he wanted the role was the frequent and unflattering attacks on himself by a furious Anne Rice, who believed that Geffen and the movie's director, Neil Jordan, had committed a cardinal sin by casting the all-American hero in the part of her most sick and twisted vampire. She was incensed.

Rice publicly lashed out at Tom for being too short and having a voice that was too high. She complained bitterly to the *Los Angeles Times* that he was no more her Lestat 'than Edward G. Robinson is Rhett Butler'. The author, who herself looks a little like a coiffed Morticia Addams, stirred up such an angry response to Tom's casting as the vampire that protesters would turn up at her book signings across America with placards demanding: 'No Tom Cruise! No Tom Cruise! No Tom Cruise!' Dozens of petitions were raised calling for a boycott of the movie.

Spurred on by her readers, Rice embarked on a one-woman crusade to embarrass Tom, the movie's main backers Warner Brothers and David Geffen. To cheering crowds at her public appearances, she cursed Tom for allegedly butchering her script, sanitising the sexual content to accommodate his so-called clean-cut image and being one of the worst examples of bad casting in Hollywood history. Addressing an audience of around a thousand people on Halloween Night 1993, she said: 'I wanted to call David Geffen and say, "How the hell could you do this?"'

Rice's fans vented their outrage in classic terms. 'Tom Cruise is the man you take home to Momma. Lestat is the man you don't want Momma to know about,' said one. 'Cruise is a nice American boy not an evil European.'

Some Hollywood regulars likened the miscasting of Tom in *Interview with the Vampire* to such classic movie mistakes as Clark Gable's attempt to portray Irish nationalist Charles Parnell in *Parnell* and Spencer Tracy's performance in *Dr Jekyll and Mr Hyde*. What all these so-called experts failed to realise was that Tom's image was being decanted into the role because Warner Brothers actually required his radiant charisma to defuse a potentially repellent portrayal and so draw customers to the ticket booth.

Tom was wounded by the fury of the reaction against him. Normally carefully shielded from the press by the overprotective and highly professional Pat Kingsley, he had been caught completely off guard by Anne Rice's wrath. 'When it first hit, it really hurt my feelings, to be candid about it,' he admitted. 'Her venom hurt.'

But what really shook Tom was when he started to get calls from Hollywood friends and acquaintances asking him what was going on. 'Nobody could see what the big deal was,' he said. Initially Tom had hoped to meet Anne Rice, just like he had handled Ron Kovic for *Born on the Fourth of July*. This was now completely out of the question. 'You don't usually start a movie with someone not wanting you to do it. That's unusual,' said Tom.

America's best-known gossip columnist, Liz Smith – always a stout defender of Tom even when she had been the last to be told of his wedding to Mimi Rogers years earlier – wrote in her widely read column that she was 'disappointed' with Rice for attacking the casting of Tom. 'You'd think that stretching oneself artistically was some sort of crime!'

Smith continued: 'Tom Cruise is an actor – a good actor – and he will undoubtedly approach his role as the vampire Lestat with as much commitment as he has devoted to his other projects. This is exciting and daring movie-making; the most exciting thing, actually, to have happened in Hollywood in ages.'

Even Paula Wagner, the former CAA agent who was Tom's agent until January 1992, when she formed the production company with him, sprang to his defence. 'None of this is new. After *Taps* people were convinced Tom was a brilliant young character actor. At first, no one would even see him for *Risky Business*. People had much the same reaction when Tom was cast as Ron Kovic. Two years later he received an Academy Award nomination.'

Tom's Hollywood friends and associates were rallying behind their favourite star and countering Rice's 'troublemaking' stance over his casting with great defiance. Reading between the lines, they were telling the author that she had no chance of changing things, and their response proved that Tom did have the backing of Hollywood for the role as Lestat.

The other player involved in the controversy over *Interview with the Vampire* was CAA boss Mike Ovitz, the single most influential agent in Hollywood history and the man who had helped to steer Tom's career in recent years. So disturbed was he by the public reaction against his number-one client that he issued a statement: '*Interview with the Vampire* will stand on its own intrinsic quality, which, given the talented people involved, will likely be very high.'

However, there were others in Tinseltown who genuinely feared that Rice's very public campaign against the movie version of her book might seriously damage the $50-million film before it was even completed. By now many Hollywood observers were dubbing the movie *Cruise's Coffin*, *Geffen's Grave* and *Fangs a Lot*. Industry publications began to predict that it could be one of the biggest bombs of all time.

Then there was talk of a curse on the entire project, a rumour further fuelled by the untimely death of actor River Phoenix just a few days before he was due to join the cast in the role of a young reporter. The twenty-two-year-old actor died after consuming a cocktail of drugs at a Hollywood nightclub owned by fellow star Johnny Depp. Christian Slater stepped into Phoenix's role.

Just days after filming began, a number of death threats were made against Tom. Security was stepped up and a secret tunnel was constructed between Tom's trailer and the film set so that he could walk to work without being exposed to any of Anne Rice's overzealous fans who might, it was feared, take a pop at him in retaliation for his casting.

Behind the scenes, David Geffen – ever the protector of his carefully nurtured project and his favourite star – was starting to feel very bitter about Rice's campaign against the movie. 'Anne is a difficult woman at best, and what her motives are remains somewhat beyond me,' he said. 'But for her to attack this movie for her own self-importance, when she has been paid $2 million [in rights] and stands to make a lot more money selling her books, is just capricious. It lacks kindness. It lacks discretion. And it lacks professionalism.'

In fact, behind Tom's casting lay a complex web of Hollywood power playing that provides interesting evidence that he was by no means the first choice for the role of Lestat. Initially Geffen had, with Rice's blessing, pursued Daniel Day-Lewis to star as the ultimate vampire. The actor kept them waiting for six months before turning down the role on the basis that it was yet another costume drama. Rice pushed for John Malkovich, having already conceded that the actor she had originally based the character of Lestat on – chunky Rutger Hauer, famed for his performance in *Blade Runner*, among many other movies – was perhaps too long in the tooth at forty-nine. Another name mentioned was Jeremy Irons.

Then in stepped Irish director Neil Jordan, fresh from his extraordinary success with *The Crying Game*. He pronounced Rice's suggestions too old and clichéd. Tom's name now came into the frame. It is not known if it was Jordan or Geffen who chose him. Although the decision for such creative aspects of a movie are usually left to the director, in Hollywood, where a star's name can make or break a film, it is often the powerbrokers like Geffen who actually decide.

Anyhow, Jordan defended the decision, insisting: 'Sometimes when you go the opposite way from what people expect, you get the best results. Every casting choice is a leap and if it works, it's because the actor makes it fit his own skin.'

Leaving aside the controversy over the casting, the most extraordinary aspect behind Tom's decision to star in *Interview with the Vampire* is the blatantly perverted, downright kinky elements of the movie. In the book there are scenes of Lestat and a five-year-old girl cuddling in a manner which can only be described as paedophilic. David Geffen insists that Tom did not demand any changes to the script's sexually explicit ingredients, which also include homosexuality on the part of Lestat. If this is the case, it was the first time since the disastrous *Losin' It* that Tom had not interfered with a script.

'He has not had any input into this script whatsoever,' said Geffen angrily. The mega-rich producer then hit out at the rumours that Tom was concerned about the film's gay elements, stating: 'Any homophobia being alleged against Tom is an outrage and a bald-faced lie.'

Tom himself admitted: 'There's a lot of biting going on. It is a very erotic picture. The hard part is learning to bite someone in a different way each time. Each kill has to tell the story of that relationship.'

Meanwhile director Jordan tried to elicit some sympathy for Tom by pointing out that for him 'there is a huge amount on the line – money, reputation, everything'.

On the shoot itself, a series of beautiful young actresses were recruited to play the parts of some of Lestat's victims. Anouk Fontaine was given a juicy role on the strength of a single press shot. The nineteen-year-old brunette from London gushed: 'When I'm down on the set I'm totally in awe of what's going on. I have to keep running back into my room.'

Another recruit was British model Sarah Stockbridge. The beautiful blonde twenty-seven-year-old landed the part after years of modelling some of the most outrageous fashions for cult designer Vivienne Westwood. Young Irish actress Susan Lynch was similarly cast as the numbers of beautiful young women being recruited for the movie increased by the day.

On 15 October 1993 Tom was awarded the Actor of the Decade prize at the Chicago International Film Festival. Looking very gaunt and blond, he asserted: 'I'm terribly excited to be working with the cast.' But he was still concerned about the way things were going. 'I hope to prove a lot of people wrong,' he added.

The casting of handsome Brad Pitt, aged twenty-five, as Tom's co-star in the 'good guy' role of Louis, sparked further reports of problems on the set.

Pitt said: 'People are gunning for us. So what? The way I see it, I'm going to give some good performances and probably some bad performances, but I'm going to try my hardest on every one. I can't see there's much else I can do or should do. I also try to ignore the controversy and hype.'

In fact, Pitt had nothing whatsoever to lose from being cast opposite Tom. Having Tom on the picture would take the pressure off his shoulders and put it on to Tom's. Pitt was also savvy enough to know that Tom's name on the titles could add tens of millions to the box-office takings and that would mean a fatter fee for the young actor.

At one stage Tom insisted that the movie's producers hire an 'eyebrow person' to make sure that his vampire-look, gold-flecked brows were carefully maintained. Reports from the set claimed that Neil Jordan was, by this stage, 'sitting back and watching the whole scene looking miserable and uncomfortable'.

A report by British showbiz columnist Baz Bamigboye in the *Daily Mail* claimed that Tom was attending 'dailies' – where the previous day's footage is screened for the movie's executives – every day with Jordan and often suggested that scenes be reshot.

During filming at the Oak Alley Plantation in New Orleans, staff members were forced to sign agreements not to speak to anyone, including their own family members, about the cast and crew's presence. Rumours circulated Hollywood that even David Geffen's own employees had been persuaded to sign similar contracts.

Tom and Nicole rented a palatial three-storey antebellum Grecian-revival mansion on Audubon Place in the distinctly upmarket Garden District of New Orleans. It was just a few miles from Anne Rice's own gothic palace, but, not surprisingly, Tom and the author did not meet.

Besides his customary early-morning jogging, Tom occasionally played soccer with neighbourhood kids inside the gated, guarded community of just thirty houses. He also took Isabella out in her pram.

In the middle of all this came comments from two other actors whose names had been in the frame for the lead role. Daniel Day-Lewis gallantly tried to cool the controversy over Tom's casting by saying: 'I find it upsetting. These people are trying to make a film as well as they possibly can with the choices there are. It's absolutely horrendous to me that they're having to deal with my name thrown in the mix.' Rutger Hauer was less diplomatic: 'I can't quite see Tom Cruise as Lestat. But it's not the first time that someone got a part that I would have been much better for.'

Precious few photos of Tom with his vampire look were revealed in the media during the movie's production. But the paparazzi did manage to snatch a few shots and they showed the star with sunken eyes, a long wig and heavy white make-up. Some said he rather resembled an early Alice Cooper.

During filming in London, Tom and Nicole rented 42 Chester Terrace, one of the Regency gatehouses leading into Regent's Park. Early risers spotted him jogging through the park at 4 a.m., wearing a waterproof hooded top, President Clinton-style gloves and tracksuit bottoms. Sometimes, usually when it was a little warmer, Nicole would take her turn on the streets of London with her trainer in tow. After the couple vacated it, the property was put up for sale for £1.5 million.

Despite rumours to the contrary, Tom and Neil Jordan became very good friends during the shooting of *Interview with the Vampire*. The intense Irishman, who had astonished Hollywood with the success of *The Crying Game*, had tasted Hollywood before during the late 1980s and found it distinctly not to his liking. But this time around he decided to play Tinseltown at its own game.

On New Year's Eve 1993 Tom and Nicole even flew back to their beloved Dublin, where they had enjoyed so many romantic nights together during the making of *Far and Away*, to attend a private party thrown by the director at his home in Dalkey, just outside the city. The couple joined in some classic Irish folk dancing and Tom was said to even have supped half a pint of Guinness.

While in Ireland, Tom and Nicole checked out a few properties in the area with a view to buying a home in the Emerald Isle. Maybe Tom was planning to relinquish his Hollywood crown if *Interview with the Vampire* ended up being a disaster.

28

*It's hard to say what are the peaks, because
like anybody else, you have your good days and
your bad days. Right now I feel I'm in a groove.*

TOM CRUISE

Interview with the Vampire got an enthusiastic response from audiences when it was eventually released in the United States in the spring of 1994 and it went on to take a reasonable $80 million at the US box office. But movie critics insisted the horror flick did not achieve what Tom had intended, because his performance was overshadowed by his younger, handsome co-star, Brad Pitt. Tom refused to concede that his role in the film had been only a moderate success.

'It wasn't a failure, but it didn't really prove anything as far as Tom's career was concerned,' explained Hollywood producer Rupert Maconick, who has followed the star's career closely since Tom arrived in Tinseltown.

At least the row with *Interview with the Vampire* author Anne Rice reached a satisfactory conclusion when she did a complete about-turn after seeing the film, even proclaiming Tom's performance as impressive. But all the Hollywood praise in the world could not make up for the fact that Tom's role as a bloodthirsty vampire proved little about his acting abilities.

To the outside world, Brad Pitt insisted that working with Tom had been a pleasurable experience.

When the movie was first released Tom even made an effort to keep his flowing hair and grunge look intact. It was as if he was trying to prove to his millions of fans that he had changed. He believed he had pulled off that dark role with great style and no one close to him was going to disagree.

Back at their house in Pacific Palisades, Tom took over the role of father and mother to Isabella as Nicole was working round the clock on two back-to-back movies. Tom was seen at nursery-school parent meetings, out in the shopping malls and generally acting the role of enthusiastic parent throughout Hollywood. In all he took almost five months off work. It gave him a chance to recharge his batteries and consider his next move.

Beyond *Interview with the Vampire*, Tom had a niggling feeling that now he needed to return to more traditional pastures and he turned his attention back to the *Mission: Impossible* project that he had been quietly nurturing for three years.

His first significant step was to revamp his image by cutting the flowing locks and goatee beard he had been sporting for almost a year. His new role as disavowed agent Ethan Hunt was tailor-made for him thanks to dozens of rewrites of the original script of the movie. Hunt's impossible mission was to sift through the web of betrayal and double-double-cross to determine just who the good guys are in this movie, which was loosely based on the hit TV series of the late sixties and early seventies.

By the autumn of 1994, Paramount had green-lighted the movie on the basis of Tom's commitment to it. A brief involvement with Andrew Lloyd Webber's film remake of *Sunset Boulevard* was quashed when the impresario told pressmen that he believed Tom was too short for the lead role. The moment it became clear that *Sunset Boulevard* was not a Tom Cruise project, the star channelled all his efforts into *Mission: Impossible*.

Tom saw this as a complex action-adventure film which was the perfect vehicle for his return to the mainstream. For the first time ever, he was the main producer of a project, thanks to his earlier efforts to develop the project through his own production company. His first task was to hire a top-class director to helm the movie.

But finding a truly exceptional director can prove rather difficult for stars of the magnitude of Tom, since most Hollywood auteurs tend to shy away from working with big celebrities because of the inevitable interference from the star performer. Tinseltown was filled with horror stories about big-budget star vehicle movies which had been ruined for those very reasons. A number of big names turned down *Mission: Impossible* and Tom was starting to discover that a producer's job was not as easy as it appeared. Then Tom lucked out when he managed to persuade director Brian De Palma to come aboard. It was a brave move on the part of both men.

De Palma's previous efforts included classics like *Carrie* and *Dressed to Kill*, with Michael Caine. He had also directed the disastrous *Bonfire of the Vanities*, with Tom Hanks. But, having recently completed the relatively well-received *Carlito's Way*, starring Al Pacino, De Palma was considered a reasonably safe bet by Paramount. *Mission: Impossible* rapidly pushed forward into production towards the end of 1994, starting with a three-week shoot in Prague, followed by at least four months of complicated studio work at London's Pinewood Studios. The budget was already creeping towards $60 million.

In Prague, Tom assembled with co-stars, including Emmanuelle Béart, Jon Voight and Henry Czerny, at a number of tough locations in the forests surrounding the Czech capital. In freezing conditions, De Palma – a notoriously meticulous director – kept his cast waiting for hours between set-ups. Tom realised he had embarked on a difficult project and there was a long way to go yet.

In the middle of all this, Tom and Nicole secretly adopted a second baby. Tiny Connor Antony was born on 6 February 1995, and taken home by the Cruises less than two weeks later. He had been adopted from a single black mother who lived on the east coast of America. A carefully orchestrated news blackout prevented any further details about the child being revealed to the world.

Tom was particularly delighted to have adopted a son because he felt that now he had a complete family around him for the first time in his entire life. He even admitted to anyone who would listen that he'd rather see his son playing in a football game than win an Oscar. His priorities were definitely changing. He believed that bringing up a family would free him from the dogged, single-minded mentality that had seemed to dominate his professional and personal life up until that point. It was time to get a real life and start to lead a more normal existence.

And, as one Hollywood observer pointed out, by adopting the children, the two stars had created the family they had both longed for and shown the world their commitment to racial harmony.

To begin with, home for Connor tended to consist of stretch limos and aeroplanes. At less than a month old, he travelled with Nicole to join Tom on the Prague set of *Mission: Impossible* and a few weeks later the entire Cruise clan moved into a vast four-storey, double-fronted house in London's Holland Park, from where Tom travelled to Pinewood each day. The rent on that property was $15,000 a week, and it came complete with an entire gym in the basement, plus an indoor swimming pool and seven bedrooms.

On Tom's days off, he and Nicole would proudly walk through nearby Kensington Gardens with Isabella and Connor in tow. In London, they managed to dispense with bodyguards most of the time and were delighted to discover they could walk into any of the nearby pubs, order a cold glass of beer and not even be given a second glance by the staff and fellow customers. Tom had been surprised by the friendly, relaxed atmosphere when they lived in London during the *Interview with the Vampire* shoot the previous year, but life in swish Holland Park seemed even more laid-back than the period in the Regent's Park house. He had imagined hordes of paparazzi popping out of every bush and their every move being reported in the tabloids. But the reality was that people respected his privacy, a pretty remarkable feat when one considers that his neighbours included such famous individuals as John Cleese and Virgin boss Richard Branson.

Meanwhile Nicole was still insisting in public that she wanted to be a natural mother herself.

But Tom's relaxed demeanour at home was not reflected in his attitude on the red-hot *Mission: Impossible* set at Pinewood, which was to double for the CIA headquarters in Virginia, a Bombay prison, Waterloo Station and the French end of the Channel Tunnel.

As the weeks progressed on the mega-budget shoot, crew members began to wonder if the entire production was about to self-destruct. With his powerful dual role of leading man and producer, Tom was regularly screaming and shouting. 'They're not happy babies. It's going pretty badly and Tom is not being at all cool,' one crew member told the *Daily Mail*. The newspaper claimed that Tom 'blows his stack every half an hour'.

The full-scale arguments between Tom, quietly spoken director Brian De Palma and other *Mission: Impossible* associates continued to ring round the set. The main causes of these clashes were the film's ever-escalating budget and various problems over the script, which was being rewritten virtually every day of the shoot. At one stage two writers were kept on standby on the set at a cost of $100,000 a week, just to help beef up the storyline if Tom wasn't happy with it.

Crew members pointed out that none of them would be working on such a massive production if Tom had not decided to star in it. There remained a genuine enthusiasm for the movie, with great hopes being pinned on one particular scene that involved a helicopter chasing a train through the Channel Tunnel.

But all the most stunning action sequences in the world could not hide the fact that Tom was once again presiding over an unhappy set.

Princess Diana took her son Prince William on a secret visit to the set. She spent two hours at Pinewood chatting with Tom while the young prince was taken on a tour of the vast studio.

Tom and the Princess were even able to talk knowledgeably about the area near his house in Holland Park, which happened to be a stone's throw from Diana's home at Kensington Palace. The Princess scribbled down the names of two eateries where the actor could be guaranteed good food and privacy, and a lot of warm smiles were exchanged.

Crew members sensed that Diana – about to be divorced from Prince Charles – was even vaguely flirting with the Hollywood star and at one stage a rumour went round the set that she had given him one of her private phone numbers. In fact, she was simply writing down the names of those restaurants.

One weekend Tom even got one of his assistants to arrange for him to go flying in a Russian Yak aircraft at an isolated airfield at North Weald, Essex. After being greeted by half a dozen men who ushered him into a small hut, he emerged ten minutes later looking like an original *Top Gun* pilot before clambering into the rear seat of the aircraft.

The two-seater, from the Russian company Yakoviev, which makes everything from acrobatic planes to passenger jets, was airborne just ten minutes before bad weather forced it to land. But for Tom it provided a brief escape from the pressures of the *Mission: Impossible* shoot.

In the middle of their extended stay in London, Nicole flew to Cannes to attend the film festival in late May 1995. It was a significant development because she went alone and still managed to grab headlines across the globe by turning up for the premiere of her recently completed movie, *To Die For*, in a stunning long dress virtually split to the hip. The movie – a black comedy about an ambitious TV presenter – received rave reviews from the arthouse crowd at Cannes.

There was absolutely no mention of the missing Tom when Nicole told reporters she never doubted her ability to play the part: 'I told the director that he should give me it because otherwise he'd be standing in the way of destiny.'

The hectic publicity demands at Cannes were in sharp contrast to her low-profile stay in London. But it proved beyond doubt that Nicole had arrived as a star in her own right. In the early summer of that year further proof of this came when Nicole returned to the couple's main home, in Pacific Palisades, to help promote her role as Dr Chase Meridian in *Batman Forever*. The publicity circus surrounding the movie was vast and as Tom toiled away at Pinewood, Nicole found herself being hailed as the biggest female star in Hollywood after Demi Moore.

With Val Kilmer replacing Michael Keaton as the caped crusader there had been some speculation that this second Batman sequel might flop at the box office. But in fact it took even more money than its predecessor, *Batman and Robin*, and Nicole was hailed for her role, which many believe greatly contributed to the film's financial success.

Batman Forever was particularly significant for Nicole because it further marked her coming of age in Hollywood. No longer was she Mrs Tom Cruise. The backbiters who had claimed she only got good roles because of her husband's influence were having to eat their words.

Nicole celebrated her independence by posing naked in a bubble bath for *Vanity Fair*, with just a pair of stilettos and a glass of champagne for company. It was a pure Hollywood vamp look and Tom had absolutely no say in it whatsoever.

Nicole even revealed some highly intimate thoughts to the magazine, including her determination to one day give birth to children, as opposed to adopting them. She angrily hit back at claims that their marriage had been arranged. 'I take offence if people say I would marry into a marriage of convenience. I think that's very sexist because they're saying, "She married for fame and money." It's bullshit.'

Asked her opinion of why Tom has been the subject of constant speculation about being gay, Nicole added, 'He's mighty fine-looking and he's worth having a fantasy about'.

A few weeks later, as if to reiterate her position, Nicole even made a wager to one journalist that she would bet all the money the couple had earned in Hollywood (estimated to be in the region of $80 million) if anyone could prove Tom was either gay or had a secret mistress. The outburst astonished some Hollywood observers but Nicole was desperate to come up with some kind of ploy to end the rumours once and for all. She even snapped at the journalist, 'You marry for love. We're both heterosexual. I did not marry for convenience.'

Back in London, Tom was approached by the producers of *Interview with the Vampire* to consider starring in a sequel to the movie, which actually made more money outside America than at the US box office. It seemed that European and Japanese audiences were particularly impressed by the film. But Tom – well aware of his somewhat muted performance in the movie – turned them down flat, even when they upped their offer to an extraordinary $25 million.

But one sequel he is seriously considering is *Rain Man 2*. Dustin Hoffman has already voiced an interest and the original writer of the movie, Barry Morrow, is currently constructing a new story featuring those same two lovable characters.

In the middle of shooting the complicated action scenes for *Mission: Impossible* at Pinewood, Tom's old friend Emilio Estevez turned up on the set, having landed a cameo role in the movie. Tom and Emilio talked over old times and even hit a few pubs in London on a day off filming at Pinewood. But Tom drew the line when Emilio suggested a trip into the capital's seedy red-light district of Soho.

For Tom, it was an all-too-rare evening out with an old buddy. Most of the faces from his past had faded into the background long before he married his first wife, Mimi Rogers. But Emilio had remained in touch with him throughout. Tom considered him an uncomplicated, undemanding friend with absolutely no ulterior motive.

That evening Tom said some fairly candid things to his old friend. He even conceded that his biggest problem in life was that there were so few people he could truly trust. And he was painfully aware that those numbers would continue to shrink even further as his fame increased.

The only answer was to once again immerse himself in his work. With that in mind he poured all his energies into ensuring that *Mission: Impossible* was an incredible success.

29

*Art is not a handicraft, it is the transmission of
feeling the artist has accumulated.*

LEO TOLSTOY

In late 1997 Tom and Nicole had a rare disagreement about a starring role
in a remake of the Hitchcock classic *Psycho*. Tom was adamant that he
didn't want Nicole to take the part but when pushed for an explanation all he
could reply was, 'I just don't want you to do it, Nic. That's all I can say.'

Nicole was furious and refused to accept her husband's reasoning without
a more substantial response. The row went on for weeks and culminated in
front of friends at a cocktail party in the Beverly Hills home of one of
Nicole's agents.

One witness who was present at the gathering later recalled: 'When the
agent asked Nic if she had made up her mind about *Psycho*, Tom turned on her.
"The mere fact that I don't want you to do it should be enough to discourage
this damn thing," he said.

'"Well, it's not," snapped back Nicole. "I have to have more than that to
go on, Tom. You know me. Full disclosure."

'Tom then took a deep breath and plunged in. "Okay, look, it's the nudity,
Nic. Okay? There's too much of it. Too many scenes, even, to use a body
double. And then there's that awful murder scene in the shower. Do you want
Bella to one day see you killed on the screen like that? Even I can't take it,
and I'm an actor. It would be awful for me."

'Everyone at the gathering stopped talking. Nicole looked stunned by her
husband's honesty in front of so many people. Then he continued: "I love

you, Nic, more than I even tell you. Is that honest enough for you? Is that full disclosure for you?"

'Tom then turned and smiled sheepishly as he realised the deathly hush that had filled the room. Then he announced he was leaving "so that you can all recover".

'Nicole left with Tom, but they returned five minutes later, hand in hand, smiling and engaged in animated conversation. "Well, I'm definitely not doing the movie," Nicole then announced. As if by way of explanation, she later told a friend: "Everybody has a way of being in this world, and Tom has his. Sometimes he can be coaxed into sharing. I love it when that happens because that's when I get to see the real Tom."'

A few months later at a small dinner party in the private back room of a famous London restaurant, Tom and Nicole kept friends and colleagues highly entertained by outlining some of the more fun aspects of working for legendary director Stanley Kubrick, on a highly controversial project called *Eyes Wide Shut*. The couple hoped that the movie would help define them as the most successful couple in Hollywood history, but they both knew what an enormous risk they were taking.

Tom had reached a critical career point, one that could be compared to stepping into the headlights of an onrushing Porsche. Others at the dinner that night included British celebrity couple Jude Law and his actress wife Sadie Frost. Many years later Nicole's friendship with Jude would spark unfounded rumours.

Those who attended vividly recall Tom's rapt attention and the overwhelming sensation that they were being 'worked' by Tom, who was at his charismatic best. His smile was as magnetic as ever. As one who met him during that long stay in London for the filming of *Eyes Wide Shut* later recalled: 'Tom can be dazzlingly, gorgeously sincerely insincere.'

'For a sex symbol, he's curiously sexless,' added one of Tom's London companions. But then love scenes were never his strong point. Hence Tom and Nicole's virtual obsession with doing *Eyes Wide Shut*. They saw it not only as an expression of their love for each other, but as proof to the world that they really did know and understand the true meaning of the word 'romance'. While in London, the couple engaged in yet more energetic public displays of affection between walks in the park with their two adopted children.

In those early days of shooting *Eyes Wide Shut*, Tom and Nicole stayed at the Dorchester Hotel on London's Park Lane. They often filmed six days a week and were told to expect the shoot to continue for at least six months. The couple's future projects were soon stacking up like Jumbos at Heathrow.

During one promotional interview at the Four Seasons hotel, Nicole said,

'You know, we are both very private people and we don't like to discuss what we do late at night in bed – although,' she giggled, 'it's very, very good.' She went on: 'I suppose because my husband is very famous, our marriage is under great speculation and people just love stories. But look, believe me, Tom and I are heterosexual. We love each other very much. The gossip just gets boring after a while.'

Nicole had been haunted for some years by a remark made by Tom in which he claimed he wanted to be with Nicole 'twenty-four hours a day'. Was that true? asked one interviewer. 'Yeah,' she said with a grin. 'I'm addicted to him.' Then she added: 'Before I met Tom, I was never going to get married,' and laughed. 'Never!' And Nicole was without doubt making great strides in her own career. The 1997 release of Jane Campion's adaptation of Henry James's *Portrait of a Lady* was yet another notch on her belt of impressive, serious movie roles.

Back in London, Tom and Nicole's shooting of *Eyes Wide Shut* continued to spark great media interest. The disgraced architect of the then Tory Government's National Health Service reforms, Dr Clive Froggatt, was hired to advise Tom on his drug-taking role in the movie. The doctor had recently been fired from his prestigious job after a conviction for using heroin.

Throughout Tom and Nicole's long stay in London there were constant concerns about the security of the couple. They moved from house to house in the suburbs north of the city, near to where Kubrick had insisted on making *Eyes Wide Shut*. At one stage they were reported to be renting a vast, gated property in Moor Park, Hertfordshire, for £15,000 a week.

Around this time Tom sat down for a rare one-on-one interview with journalist Benjamin Svetkey at the Dorchester Hotel to help promote his traditional Hollywood blockbuster *Jerry Maguire* in the middle of the couple's seemingly never-ending *Eyes Wide Shut* filming schedule. Tom and Nicole were working fourteen-hour days with Kubrick and the strain was already beginning to show. Tom admitted to Svetkey: 'You work on a scene and you work on it and work on it. He'll do twenty takes – that's not unusual. You are not leaving until he gets it right. It's intense but, as an actor, that's exactly what you want.'

However, in the middle of all this intensity, Tom still had to do his day job, promoting *Jerry Maguire*. The film, which had earned him an Oscar nomination as Best Actor, was a classic Tom performance, full of cocky charm and boyish charisma, with a tang of dark desperation thrown in for good measure.

Tom himself described his character as 'playing a guy on the ropes'. Now almost thirty-five, Tom believed that the Maguire role was a mid-career breakthrough after years of playing irresistible smoothies. As critic Svetkey explained: 'Watching Cruise in this film, it's as if the kid who strummed air guitar in his underwear in *Risky Business* has finally grown up and got a real job.'

This was how Tom himself explained it: 'To be honest I never thought of it in those terms. I just related to the character emotionally. I meet these people and I wonder what their lives are like. Is this the person they want to be? That's what appealed to me about Maguire. Jerry's one of those guys I've always wondered about.'

Tom was honest enough in London to admit to Svetkey he'd had a few spats with *Mission: Impossible* director Brian De Palma the previous year. 'We had one bad argument on the phone. I don't even remember what we were fighting over. But suddenly we started yelling at each other and we hung up on each other. Nicole came in laughing, saying, "What was that about?" So I called De Palma back and said, "Brian, we just had our first fight." We were both exhausted and under a lot of pressure. It was no big deal. It was just one of those things.'

Meanwhile Tom's co-star in *Jerry Maguire*, Renee Zellweger, was full of praise for Tom. 'His acting is so good it was almost bizarre,' she explained. 'You'd look into his eyes and he'd really be there, he'd really be in love with you. You could see it in his heart and soul ... and then the director would yell, "Cut." Tom would leave the set and you'd have to go into therapy for six months.'

But throughout his long stay in London, Tom was more interested in talking about the legendary Stanley Kubrick and the making of *Eyes Wide Shut*. 'This stuff about Kubrick being difficult is overplayed,' he told one associate. 'I don't know how he works with other people, but I can tell you he doesn't have to push buttons on me or Nic to get a performance. He is intense, that's true. But he's also very funny. The guy is sixty-eight and has amazing energy. I see how he directs my performance. He's just stunning. Stunning!'

Tom went on: 'Nicole and I talk about this so much at night. When we're seventy years old, sitting on the front porch, we'll be able to look back and say, "Wow! We made this movie with Kubrick!" We know it may take a long time to finish, but we don't care. We really don't.'

Nicole wholeheartedly agreed with Tom. 'Nobody's had a nervous breakdown yet,' she said, giggling. 'Stanley has been incredibly generous to us. He deals with Tom and me separately – and when you see the film you'll understand why.'

Both Tom and Nicole refused to reveal details of the plot of *Eyes Wide Shut*, but she did offer one tasty titbit: 'When people see the film, they'll have a field day analysing our relationship.'

Back in Hollywood, Tom's trusted former agent and now head of his production company, Paula Wagner, had been acquiring the film rights to several new novels. There was also talk of a reunion with Oliver Stone for a movie about Alexander the Great, plus another project with Rob Reiner, director of *A Few Good Men*. There were also plans for a *Mission: Impossible* sequel.

And throughout all the stress and strains of working on *Eyes Wide Shut*, Tom continued to be blithely oblivious to the complexities of his own personality. Rob Reiner claims: 'He has no idea how people perceive him. It's one of his most endearing qualities. He forgets he's a star. He just goes along like a normal person.'

Nicole agreed wholeheartedly with that assessment at the time: 'Yeah. I take him to a party and I'll find him standing in a corner by himself. He assumes people don't talk to him because they aren't interested. I have to explain it's because they're too nervous to come over.'

Then the shooting schedule of *Eyes Wide Shut* started to slow down to a snail's pace. As one of Nicole's closest friends during her long stay in London explained: 'Stanley Kubrick took twice as long to make the film because he insisted on briefing Tom and Nicole separately. At one stage Kubrick explained the precise details of a specific sex act to Nic and then Tom came bursting in demanding to hear what he was saying and he had to be ushered away. It led to many furious rows. Tom started to get paranoid and believed that Nic was telling Kubrick intimate secrets about their love life.'

Others noticed evidence of tension between Tom and Nicole. Perhaps all was not well between the couple?

Around this time an article was published in London's *Guardian* which tried to seriously analyse Tom's undoubted appeal to gay men and concluded that it relied on more than just physical allure. Gay writer Christopher Kelly admitted he first fell for Tom when he stripped to his underwear in that notorious scene in *Risky Business* in 1983. As Kelly explained to his readers: 'My admiration for him as a performer is entirely bound up in my desire for him as a sexual persona. In fact, he's grown as an actor by exploiting the very things – a classic face, a perfect body, a predilection for roles in which sexuality is explored – that have also made him a gay icon.'

With *Eyes Wide Shut* still under wraps, there was a lot of expectation riding on Tom the performer. As Kelly added: 'If you allow yourself to be turned on by Tom Cruise, you can begin to see how far he's come.'

This article represented an important development for Tom because while it blatantly flagged his heterosexuality it also pointed out that many of his films had appealed to both a straight and gay audience.

Kelly even interpreted a scene in *Risky Business* which would have gone over the heads of many movie-goers. Kelly states: 'In *Risky Business*, Cruise imagines himself alone with his dream girl – the music swells, they begin making out. And then sirens, flashing lights and a curious mob of neighbours outside interrupt them. The next shot has Cruise lying in bed, with a sheet covering his lower body and his hand beneath it. The joke is that this is a masturbatory fantasy gone awry – and yet Cruise doesn't play it for laughs.' Kelly also insisted that Tom was blatantly unafraid to portray men completely overwhelmed by their own sexuality.

But there was undoubtedly more to Kelly's assessment than a few double entendres and camp moments. Tom's boy-next-door good looks – high, even-tempered cheekbones, big nose and sparkling eyes, combined with that big, bright smile – all attract gay interest. As Kelly added: 'There's something terribly prissy about Tom Cruise's body – as if he spends too much time working on it, trying to make it look perfect.'

And Tom's gay fans were naturally delighted when clips of *Eyes Wide Shut* started to be screened in cinemas across the world in 1999. One ninety-second sequence showed Tom standing with Nicole naked before a mirror, kissing and fondling her to the insistently nervy beat of Chris Isaak's 'Baby Did a Bad, Bad Thing'. Then came a thirty-second trailer in which the kissing scene was intercut with other shots of Tom and Nicole attending a swanky social event.

It was virtually impossible to tell what was actually going on in any of the clips, but Tom and Nicole's presence continued to generate a mountain of hype by keeping audiences guessing about just how sexually explicit the film would be.

Critics were already beginning to wonder if *Eyes Wide Shut* would turn out to be Tom's biggest mistake or most brilliant masterstroke.

But could he really pull it off – the big role in a movie by a legendary director? Not many people wanted to see him stumble and certainly not on such a grand scale. But then again, Tom knew there were plenty of other more traditional projects in the pipeline.

At one stage while the couple were living in their rented house in Regent's Park, Nicole suffered from acute insomnia and they were sleeping in separate rooms. Part of the reason was put down to Tom being a loud snorer.

But it was a lack of communication while the couple were in London that seems to have been the basis of their problems. Nicole later explained: 'We would go round and round in circles, never getting a solution to anything.' That's when, according to Nicole, Tom demanded to be left alone with his demons. He wanted his own space constantly.

By the summer of 1998 Tom and Nicole had been working pretty well constantly on *Eyes Wide Shut* for more than a year and the movie still wasn't finished. Many in Hollywood were starting to question the wisdom of

Kubrick and how much longer he could prevent Tom and Nicole from pursuing other future projects.

Respected film writer David Gritten summed it up when he wrote: 'Even by the notorious standards of Hollywood excess, this is a tale that stands out: director Stanley Kubrick's new film, *Eyes Wide Shut*, started shooting on 4 November 1996. And it isn't over yet. That makes it the most interminable Hollywood production in memory: longer than *Lawrence of Arabia*, longer than *Cleopatra*. Also, until the reclusive Kubrick finally decides to complete shooting, he is essentially keeping his leading man in Britain, where *Shut* is being made.'

It was an extraordinary chain of events not helped by Kubrick's obsessive quest for total secrecy surrounding the project. Co-star Alan Cumming inadvertently let slip to one friend that the famed director took five whole days to shoot one scene. The budget for *Eyes Wide Shut* was originally $55 million, but by the middle of 1998 it was said to be topping the $100-million mark.

As Gritten pointed out: 'If another director were involved it would have been deemed to be out of control.' It was widely believed that backers Warners were tolerating the situation because of the talent involved – Cruise, Kidman and Kubrick.

Warners' London-based executive Julian Seniro had even happily admitted before shooting began: 'He'll do his thing and when the film's ready, when it's shot, edited, the music's put in and there's about a week to go before release, then we'll probably get to see it.'

The truth was that Kubrick was a master at cutting himself off from the world. Even when reporters delivered handwritten notes to his palatial home north of London they failed to get a response from the supposedly great auteur. Yet interest in the film's progress was assuming cultish proportions and one could even browse numerous websites devoted entirely to the subject.

Just days after shooting of *Eyes Wide Shut* finally wrapped, Kubrick collapsed and died from a heart attack. His death shook Tom and Nicole to the core. Tom later described it as one of the worst events of his life. 'It was a moment of real loss and pain that I hadn't felt in a while. I mean shock – absolute shock. And Nic had never had anyone pass away on her that she had been close to, ever. That was a very difficult time. Here's this dear friend that you've lost – and immediately life is making you put it into perspective. Whereas when you're a child, if your parents are divorced, that's your whole world.'

Tom had never forgotten the unhappy times of his life, even though most of that had happened when he was very young. He later admitted he suffered painful misery at times. 'I would have moments of that, days of that, but I've not been a depressed kind of person. That's not who I am.' He still considered his beloved mother to be the person who prevented that life of depression from taking over. 'For her the cup was always half full. Always. And I loved her for it. She had that kind of impact on us. Things were tough.'

When *Eyes Wide Shut* finally made it to the big screen it was a disaster. It had been billed as the most keenly anticipated movie of the decade. But most critics soon agreed that it only worked if you didn't take it too seriously.

Peter Bradshaw, writing in the *Guardian* on 10 September 1999, summed it up perfectly: 'Stanley Kubrick's extraordinary last testament has effortlessly attained one of the criteria of a certain type of classic. This genre being best described as Manhattan porn gothic. It has left the global critical community uneasily aware of the possibility that it is not a masterpiece, but rather a grotesque, preposterous flop that embarrassingly damages one of the most unimpeachable reputations in world cinema.'

Bradshaw also speculated on just how much Tom and Nicole knew about what was really happening on Kubrick's set. He said: 'Cruise and Kidman are white-bread white folks but their prissy, uptight blandness is something which is all too plausible in this context – in fact, it is debatable how far the actors themselves realised how objectionable Kubrick was occasionally making them appear, particularly with touches such as Tom Cruise's black gloves, fastidiously worn outside.'

Even worse, the late and once-great Stanley Kubrick seemed to have damaged his own reputation as a cinematic genius – even after his own death. As Bradshaw added: 'Kubrick's last film works only if its satirical, mischievous quality is fully appreciated; as an essay on the nature of sexuality it is vulgar and pretentious, but taken as a bizarre, hallucinatory black comic fable about married life, it is plausible and enjoyable. The technical and visual command of the movie is captivating – but it is minor Kubrick.'

Many agree that things were never quite the same for Tom and Nicole after they completed shooting *Eyes Wide Shut* with Kubrick. The movie's difficult theme, combined with the gruelling work routine, left them both completely drained.

Tom always insisted that his marriage came out of *Eyes Wide Shut* even stronger, but to many observers that wasn't how it seemed. As one London associate later recalled: 'There was a lot of arguing when they were in that large house in Regent's Park. Nicole was throwing things around and felt she was at the end of her tether.'

When the couple were spotted at London's swish Met Bar in late 1999, Tom was up at the bar while his wife was sitting in a far corner. They were surrounded by friends and hangers-on but never once did they acknowledge each other.

Eventually Nicole got up to dance with a male friend. 'Oh nice,' muttered Tom, his face tightening. 'Real nice.' He threw some money on the bar and left.

After the sheer exhaustion of *Eyes Wide Shut*, Tom decided to take on an arthouse role in *Magnolia*. The result was impressive – a stomach-turningly creepy so-called sex guru called Frank Mackey. And it worked well for Tom as he was even nominated for a Best Supporting Oscar. Playing a slimy motivational speaker who gives unhappy bachelors seminars on how to seduce and destroy was not difficult for an actor as accomplished as Tom. His character even called men to arms and ordered them to 'respect that cock, conquer that cunt'. Many said that Tom brought the part to life brilliantly.

Tom's next classic Hollywood hit was *Mission: Impossible 2*. His mother even dropped in to see her son in a scene where he was rappelling down a cliff about a hundred feet off the ground. As Tom swung straight into the camera so that his face literally bounced off the lens, his mother said, 'Oh, sweet Lord Jesus! Sweet Lordy Jesus.' Then she stood up and looked as if she was about to have a heart attack. Tom later explained: 'But she's always up for anything. Like when I took her skydiving for *Days of Thunder*.'

Mission: Impossible 2 was to earn more than £60 million in its first five days of release in the USA. This not only placed Tom back on top of the movie world's earnings league, but it also proved that all his riskier ventures had done absolutely nothing to damage his standing as the globe's biggest movie megastar.

The film was nothing more than a daft, carefree action flick, but many reckoned it was a lot better than the original *Mission: Impossible*, thanks to the skills of Hong Kong's favourite action director, John Woo. Few doubted that the *Mission: Impossible* franchise would head onwards and upwards, spawning numerous sequels.

Tom insisted he made such blatantly commercial movies because he enjoyed the process. Those close to him pointed out that making the two *Mission: Impossible* films was a picnic compared with the stress and strain of *Eyes Wide Shut*. Others reckoned that the film personally cost Tom more than $100 million in lost fees for movies he had to turn down because of the extraordinary length of the shoot in Britain.

Yet both Tom and Nicole said nothing to distance themselves from the *Eyes Wide Shut* debacle. Their loyalty to the memory of Kubrick and his failure of a film was impressive. By now Tom was about to celebrate his thirty-seventh birthday, yet many still saw him as that perfect example of the American boy next door. It was frustrating for Tom the actor because he had undoubtedly come a long way since those early days back in the heady 1980s.

And, despite the apparently strong bond between Tom and Nicole, observers were still quick to predict that they might not remain in love for the rest of their lives. As one writer explained: 'The marriage may not last; unions of actors have a hard time in real life. But they strike me as a couple who are both devoted to the idea of doing what they believe in.'

But at least a few were predicting that despite the recent problems with Kubrick, Tom had yet to reach his acting peak. As one critic wrote: 'I suspect he's going to get better yet, and be honoured some day for having kept that rare, 20th-century faculty – of being likeable for its own sake – alive and well.'

In late 1999 Tom was confident enough to openly reflect on his relationship with ex-wife Mimi Rogers during an interview with director and friend Cameron Crowe for a US magazine. 'Before Nic I was dissatisfied, wanting something more. And listen, that's not because of Mimi either; it was just two people who weren't meant to work, and it wasn't what I wanted from my life. I think you do go on different paths. But it wasn't Mimi's fault, do you know what I mean? It's just the way it is. It's just the way life is. I really do wish her well. I know that she's got a family; I haven't seen her in years. It's funny – we never talk, you know? You're with someone, you spend that kind of time, and then that doesn't happen... I feel weird about that.'

Tom even talked openly about Nicole's old boyfriends. He told Crowe: 'Nic always has her old boyfriends – "Hi, hi, hi", you know? And I realise that's a good thing. She's just got a lot of friends; I mean we've got a lot of friends now. As I say, you marry an Australian, you basically marry a country. It's not just an individual, you have to understand – it's the country, and it's a social country.'

But behind Tom's words lay a constant problem between him and Nicole. While she enjoyed the company of many friends, especially back in Australia, he found it difficult to trust people in general and was appalled by the bluntness and drinking culture that still existed 'down under'. Tom started to resent some of Nicole's closest pals and that was beginning to create problems between the couple.

One of Nicole's friends – and the one Tom most disliked – was a tough-talking, rough diamond of an actor called Russell Crowe, who was hardly known outside his native Australia at the time. However, there was a mighty buzz about Crowe becoming the next big action hero in Hollywood and that in itself irritated Tom, who considered him to be a bit of an upstart, to say the least.

Meanwhile Tom and Nicole's tenth anniversary together was fast approaching. In his interview with Cameron Crowe there were no signs of any impending problems between the couple. Tom described Nicole as 'fantastic at balancing that stuff', meaning kids and work, but he made a point of saying that his life was simply 'pretty powerful, especially with the kids'. References to their love for each other were not particularly apparent.

But Tom resolutely insisted that all his childhood demons were safely stored away. 'There's a certain point when whatever your folks did, now it's your responsibility to deal with it. My relationship with my father, my parents, it was different from those of my friends. Somehow it helped mould me. You get a choice: you can either let it cave you in, or you can use it and move on and learn from it.'

And Tom's method in choosing a movie role had not changed since the day he arrived in New York as a penniless youngster. As he told Crowe: 'I do this weird thing. It's strange. Before I start something I literally create a barrier for myself – "I can't do it." It's a game I've played since I was a little kid. I just look up and, boy, there's Everest. "I don't think I can do it" – and for some reason that fuels me like nothing else. That's when I become obsessed with it, to the point where I've got to get it right. I've got to do it.'

In the autumn of 1999 Tom managed a mini-vacation with the couple's two children, Connor, five, and Isabella, seven, on a forty-foot-plus fishing boat called *Alibi*, for a trip through the ocean off the coast of Sydney, Australia. Meanwhile Nicole was staggering through the shooting of *Moulin Rouge*, in which she even managed to break a rib during a dancing sequence. The holiday turned into a bit of a disaster, with the vessel's motor conking out and a near miss with a jet ski. There was also the little matter of the boat hitting a reef. Then Tom threw an entire barbecue overboard when the flames roared a little high and he feared for Connor's safety. Moments later, Tom donned a full rubber suit and snorkel and dived overboard to retrieve the barbie.

Later Tom openly admitted what a disastrous holiday it had all been, with him being the main victim. It was a rare confession of failure. Tom and the children ended up spending some months in Sydney while Nicole was finishing *Moulin Rouge* with Aussie helmsman Baz Luhrmann. Tom took to travelling across the city late at night in a black BMW at high speed. And his wife's home town soon became a familiar and welcoming place for the Cruise entourage, although Tom still felt a relative stranger because he found it so difficult to relate to her friends.

Beneath the veneer, he was still the same old workaholic, deadly serious operator who continued to regulate his work according to schedules, calendars and documents that he kept in a folder called 'Battle Plans'. Being in laid-back Australia didn't really suit his temperament.

Yet Tom was still happy to tell anyone who'd listen that he felt on top of the world. The *Mission: Impossible* franchise was personally making him hundreds of millions of dollars. Then came the public reaction to that arthouse debut in *Magnolia*, which had given his reputation a definite edge. It was Tom's final scenes in that movie, in which he sobbed at the bedside of his character's long-lost dying father (played by Jason Robards) which hit him the deepest, as they so accurately mirrored his last visit to his own father's dying bedside.

Tom opened up to friend and *Jerry Maguire* director Cameron Crowe about how he really felt while filming those death scenes in *Magnolia*. He said: 'You just lose yourself – it is exhausting. You're tired emotionally. I was exhausted, Paul was exhausted, Philip was exhausted, Jason was exhausted... I think he was a little exhausted, because he's got to be there, and the first thing I heard was, "You cocksucker... You fucking cocksucker" [laughs]. You know what? He never once came out of character. It's just a very fine balance when you're doing those scenes, because you're out there on the edge, and there are things you can't necessarily be responsible for when you go out to those places.'

Tom was reluctant to admit that the scene related to the death of his own father but he did say: 'Well, I think anyone that understands the dynamic of that... You know, it's a character but it does have elements... But it is a character.'

Amazingly, the start of Tom's career now predated Madonna, *Ghostbusters*, the Brat Pack and *Miami Vice*. He was proud of linking up with many of Hollywood's finest directors, but ultimately he was completely his own man. No one could tell him what to do and which roles to take. Tom was in control of his own destiny.

By this time he was in the habit of making a point in conversational terms by using a fist to demonstrate a particular aspect of his life. Tom felt that fist perfectly demonstrated the unity and showed the world that he'd take no notice of all the gossip and innuendo that had constantly surrounded his professional and personal life for more than twenty years.

In January 2000 Tom picked up the prestigious Golden Globe for his role in *Magnolia*. Now he wondered if an Oscar was beckoning. As he told one associate, 'It would be real fun to win an Oscar but I never let myself expect too much. I mean, I expect a lot from myself with my work – that's why I don't sleep when I'm working on a picture; you can't help but become obsessed at times with it.'

Tom genuinely believed that he still had a lot more work to achieve in Hollywood terms. He knew he'd learned much over the previous two decades. People had always told him to wait until his thirties and the roles would get better and deeper, but then Tom had reached that age and realised there was even more to achieve.

He'd enjoyed producing and starring in *Mission: Impossible 2* – which involved scriptwriting and financial aspects of the movie – just as much as appearing simply as an actor in *Magnolia*, which he considered was nothing short of a 'gift' from director-writer Paul Thomas Anderson. As Tom later explained: 'I'd read a lot of different scripts and thought: "Well, I'd like to see this, but..." With *Magnolia* I thought: "This could be wild. I mean, I could really fail here! I could really fuck this up, make a total ass of myself. This could be a real pie in the face, you know? I'm gonna do it [laughs]."'

Tom later confessed that he was extremely nervous about allowing his mother to see his role in *Magnolia*. 'It wasn't the nature of the language – I mean, my mother's an elegant woman – but the emotional aspect of it. I wanted her to see it, but I didn't want her to see it [for the first time] the night of the premiere. So I called Paul [Thomas Anderson] and said, "Listen, let me screen this for my mother." So Jack [Tom's stepfather] came with her and that was a pretty powerful experience, sitting next to my mother and Jack, who will never hesitate to yawn if he doesn't like something. But he loved it; he was really moved by it, and he sat through the entire film without fidgeting.'

Tom and stepdad Jack's relationship had been a rocky one at times. But Tom never forgot the fact that Jack had loaned him £850 to get set up in New York before he started work as an actor, and Tom was proud of paying him back the money 'with interest' after getting his first big pay cheque for *Taps*.

Throughout his career Tom had become renowned as someone who would not take percentages as part of his salary. His attitude had always been 'you pay by the hour'. He explained to Cameron Crowe: 'Percentages are a scam, an absolute scam. People get a lawyer, and how much do you pay a lawyer? Ten, fifteen per cent. You have a manager, they want fifteen per cent. And then you have an agent. I try to tell these people – everyone I meet – especially these guys who are just starting out. "What do you do with your lawyer? Why pay him five per cent? Your agent negotiates the deal; what's your lawyer going to do?" "My lawyer can help negotiate." "Well, pay him $125, because that's how 'difficult' it is to negotiate your deals. There is only a limited amount of money you're going to earn, and you're either going to earn, and you're either going to get it or you're not."'

Tom still also firmly believed that his success was definitely wrapped up in his commitment to the job. 'If people are only interested in the fame celebrity of it, you can see how those lose their way. You don't know what movie is going to be a hit. You don't. The celebrity stuff can be fun at times, but it's just the pleasure you get out of creating a scene, of having a movie that just works, whether it's *Mission: Impossible* or *Magnolia*.'

During his interview with Cameron Crowe, Tom once again didn't hesitate to tackle those gay rumours that had haunted him for so many years. He explained: 'People say: "Your ex-wife said this, how do you respond to that?" I say: "Do you want to know something? I don't believe Mimi ever said stuff like that. I just don't believe it, and I'm not even going to buy into that." There's someone that sits down and creates it and just tries to ... keep it going, whatever it is. I remember going to a new school, you'd get in a fist fight, first day. Some of the worst fist fights I've had, you talk to the guy afterwards as to why: "You're dating my girlfriend." "I mean, I don't even know who your girlfriend is."'

Tom never forgot how a man approached him at a convention in Chicago many years earlier and told him, 'I've been telling my friends for years that I know you. Would you come over and say hi to them and pretend?' Tom told the man: 'No. And you really shouldn't tell people that you know me, because I don't know you.'

Tom was deeply frustrated by fans coming up to him in the street and asking him if he remembered certain people. Initially he'd been polite and pretended to think about the question, but by now he was turning them all down flat. And that was a clear extension of his attitude towards all the rumours flying around about him. Tom explained: 'I just don't believe the rumours unless I absolutely know for certain. Now my mother and people are hip to this: they know not to buy into it. But so many things are printed about my wife, my children, my friends. I mean, there was a point when I took legal action. After we won we gave the money to charity.'

Back at home in Pacific Palisades, Tom and Nicole agreed to bring in private tutors for their two children following a number of death threats to the family which began in 1997. While such threats were commonplace in Hollywood, Tom was extremely disturbed by them and insisted to Nicole they should be taken out of school. But in the end Tom won on the basis of the perceived threat to the Cruise family's security, although Nicole did later tell one close friend that she was never entirely clear on where that threat actually came from.

Tom also insisted publicly that he and Nicole wanted more children. He told Cameron Crowe: 'I think we'll probably have some more kids. We'll just have to see. I've always wanted a big brood. Yeah – at least an infield, you know? I've gotta work on Bella's pitching, though [laughs].'

Tom then decided to team up with Steven Spielberg to make *Minority Report*. Just days later the world's most famous movie director was rushed into hospital to have a kidney removed.

Tom saw the shock news on a TV bulletin and immediately phoned Spielberg's people. The director then rang from the hospital.

'Tommmm – it's Steven.'

'What the hell? Hey man, you okay?'

'Ah, I'm fine. Had you going, huh, Tom?'

As Tom later admitted: 'He had me going. Nearly gave me a heart attack.'

Cruise and Spielberg working on a movie together. It sounded like a recipe for Ego Wars.

30

Life itself is a very humbling experience.
So that keeps you honest.

TOM CRUISE

Evidence that all was not well between Tom and Nicole came when the couple attended a film premiere in late 2000. Nicole cut away from Tom outside the movie theatre to greet some fans leaving her megastar hubby standing all alone. Eventually he walked across to her and literally dragged her into the premiere with a grim expression on his face. Nicole was heard to say: 'My fans mean everything to me. If I want to shake hands with them, I bloody well will.'

'What are you talking about?' asked Tom, genuinely perplexed.

Clearly the incident meant nothing to him, but it deeply disturbed Nicole. And it wasn't helped when Tom also added with a grin: 'Oh, Nic. Stop being so melodramatic. I'm thinking we should go home and go to bed. Maybe we can stop for a cheeseburger on the way. What d'you say to a cheeseburger, Bubba [one of his many pet names for Nicole]?'

Then, in early December, Nicole was spotted by a friend sitting alone in the bar of Fix, a nightclub in the Kirkton Hotel, in Darlinghurst, Sydney. Nursing a Diet Pepsi, Nicole was engrossed in writing what appeared to be a long handwritten letter. As her friend approached she looked up and managed a faint smile before taking off her orange-tinted rectangular glasses. Her blue eyes seemed moist, her face puffy and pinker than usual. She quickly folded up the paper and put it in her handbag before explaining that Tom was with the kids.

'Are you okay, Nic?' asked her friend.

'Not really,' she replied wearily.

'It's Tom, isn't it?' responded her friend, who, along with many of the couple's friends, had noticed something was wrong with their marriage, but no one could actually put their finger on the problem.

'Oh well, you know Tom,' Nicole said. 'He's so... so,' she struggled to get the words out. 'Deep,' she concluded. 'Who knows what he's saying.'

As her friend later recalled: 'It was as if she was trying to tell us something was wrong but didn't know how to express herself. I was very distressed and worried about her from that moment onwards.'

Those problems may have stemmed from the sheer intensity of making *Eyes Wide Shut* with Stanley Kubrick. Some of the couple's friends say that Tom was never able to handle Nicole in the same way after that movie role. The film had clearly touched nerves and made both feel uncomfortable about certain aspects of their marriage.

Another time Nicole was said to have thrown a silver-framed photograph of the two of them – a present from Tom – against a wall. That's a measure of how frustrated she felt. And, from the autumn of 2000, these arguments worsened. Soon Nicole was claiming to friends in Australia that the couple's only real conversations were when they spoke about the children. Ten-hour drives from the resort of Byron Bay to Sydney would be punctuated by long hours of silence between the couple.

Then, towards the end of the year, Tom and Nicole accompanied friends, including Russell Crowe, to Float, a New York nightclub. At about 2.30 a.m., Nicole, who'd had a couple of drinks, began doing a sexy mock striptease for Tom.

Dressed in a black and white sleeveless leather dress, she beckoned to Tom, who responded with a sexy smile. He then walked over and pinned her against the wall and kissed her passionately. It was almost as if they wanted the world to know how incredibly in love they were with each other.

In late December, Tom and Nicole ignored the cracks in their marriage by hosting a Hollywood party to renew their wedding vows. Nicole was stick thin and dressed in a black silk dress with sequinned white top with beaded fringe, her red hair piled high atop her head. To those present they looked like the happiest couple in the world. But behind the smiles, tensions were growing.

Cut to mid-January 2001, and an Italian restaurant in Santa Monica, California. A waiter later recalled: 'They seemed in an intense mood. Nicole talked a lot, seeming to ask a lot of questions, gesticulating a lot. Tom seemed distant, his expression blank. If anyone came over to their table, they brightened up. But if you observed them long enough, you'd see they were not happy at all. I overheard them say, "Now you see, that's what I mean, Tom. There you go again. Enough is enough."'

A week later, on 21 January, Tom and Nicole attended the Golden Globe Awards together, but later that evening they left in separate cars.

Then, on 7 February, Tom's attorney relayed a shocking demand to Nicole – he was filing for divorce. She was perplexed. Why didn't he try and talk it over with her? As Nicole's old friend Australian director John Duigan pointed out: 'Even though there were strains in the marriage the actual final breach was sudden and jarring.'

Over the following days Nicole hid herself away in the couple's Pacific Palisades mansion with their two children. Two days after Nicole received the lawyer's communication, her mother, Janelle, and sister Antonia flew in from Sydney to offer support.

Janelle was mystified by the break-up since she'd always looked on Tom as virtually her son. She kept saying: 'Tom likes me, let me talk to him. Let me find out what's going on.' But it was impossible.

Not even Nicole could get in touch directly with Tom. He was shielded by an army of lawyers and agents. When Nicole was yet again refused contact with her husband she hurled a vase against the wall of the sitting room. Her mother and sister found her huddled in a corner crying when they rushed into the room. She knew her marriage to Tom was about to become Hollywood history.

Stories about the tragic decline and fall of Tom and Nicole's marriage quickly surfaced. Popular showbiz biographer J. Randy Taraborrelli even claimed that Nicole had suffered an ectopic pregnancy when she was carrying Tom's baby just before the couple married in Colorado in 1990. It was that tragedy, he said, that sparked the couple's decision to adopt two children.

Then, on 16 March 2001, Nicole had another, even more tragic miscarriage at home in Pacific Palisades. She immediately phoned Tom with the news. He was sad for her, relatively supportive – and did send her some flowers. But his response was muted and detached in a way which had become his trademark since the divorce announcement.

Tom looked on Nicole's surprise pregnancy as more evidence that the couple no longer had the close relationship they had enjoyed for the previous ten years. One supposed friend told Taraborrelli: 'If anything, the miscarriage showed him that he had made the right decision. Either way, I think that Nicole would have lost.'

In fact, Tom had been agonising about the state of his marriage for at least two years before the separation announcement. True, Nicole could be a bit of a nag and certainly quite moody if she was tired after working on a gruelling film schedule. Friends claimed she sometimes lashed out at Tom and at such times would say he was not affectionate enough to her, not understanding enough, either.

But it was clear from some of Tom's friends and advisers that he didn't want his life spiralling out of control any more. That was when he made the decision to separate. Nicole had not done anything particularly harmful. He'd heard rumours about her nightlife in London when she was appearing in the West End play *The Blue Room*, but that was nothing more than gossip and he, more than anyone, knew not to take much notice of such gossip.

By May 2001 the legal tussle between Tom and Nicole's laywers had really hotted up. It was reported that Nicole was demanding custody of both their children and twelve years' maintenance. In a ten-page document filed in an LA court, she stated that she was prepared to share the upbringing of Connor, now six, and Isabella, eight. It was the first official response by Nicole since the shock news of the marriage break-up three months earlier.

Nicole clearly stated she intended to continue working as long as it fitted around the children. She also emphasised that she'd prefer to live in Australia but was prepared to consider staying on at the couple's mansion in Pacific Palisades.

But, even more significantly, Nicole publicly confirmed that Tom was the father of the baby she'd lost just a few weeks after the couple's separation. In a document filed through her lawyers, Nicole stated: 'On Sunday, 4 February 2001, Cruise told Kidman he no longer wanted to live with her and that he wanted a divorce. This came as a shock to her. On 24 December last year the parties had happily celebrated their tenth anniversary with a group of friends. During the balance of December and thereafter the parties were intimate, in fact Kidman became pregnant but lost the baby through a miscarriage.'

Nicole even revealed in the document that she had begged Tom not to leave her and had suggested marriage counselling. But the document stated: 'Cruise said his decision was final and he departed their home.' Nicole also stated that she hoped both of them could keep gifts, including art and jewellery which they bought for each other.

Around this time Tom let it be known that he'd opted for such a quick divorce because he wanted a speedy split to help them both 'move on with our lives emotionally'. He wasn't exactly revealing the reasons for the split but at least he'd finally started to talk openly about the circumstances.

Tom wrote in a court declaration: 'Irreconcilable differences have arisen between Nicole and me. These differences have led to an irremediable breakdown of our marriage. I do not believe professional counselling or the assistance of any mental health professional, lapse of time or any other factor will change this breakdown.'

In the same official court papers – listed as number BD339413 – Tom's signature appeared under a declaration detailing in his own words why his marriage had crumbled. Tom said: 'Nicole and I were married on 24 December 1990. We separated in December 2000. The petition for Dissolution of Marriage was filed on 7 February. I am the petitioner in this action. I have personal knowledge of the facts. If called to testify to them, I could and would competently and truthfully do so.'

In the middle of all this divorce drama, Tom launched a £75-million lawsuit against a porn actor after the man claimed they'd had a gay affair. Tom's close confidant and lawyer Bertram Fields stated in court papers: 'Tom Cruise is not and never has been a homosexual.'

Magazines in France and Spain had alleged that Tom and Nicole's marriage had been wrecked by Tom's alleged relationship with Kyle Bradford, a gay porn star otherwise known as Chad Slater. Bradford immediately issued a statement saying he'd never even spoken to Cruise, let alone had sex with him. 'I can't afford to give Tom Cruise $100 million. Do you think I would be involved in porn if I was worth that sort of money?'

Bradford added: 'I can't tell you how upsetting all this has been. Suddenly my face is on every TV screen in America as a gay porn star – and my family didn't even know I was homosexual.'

Allegedly, Bradford had sold his story to an international magazine known as *Acustar* and a translation had later appeared in the Spanish and French magazines. Tom's defamation lawsuit also stated: 'Bradford concocted and spread a completely false story. It is unequivocally false. Bradford's statements are of a kind calculated to cause Cruise harm in his profession and his ability to earn. Because Cruise is a motion picture actor he is dependent upon worldwide public acceptance of his films.' Losing the respect and enthusiasm of a substantial segment of the movie-going public would cost Cruise very substantial sums.

The statement added: 'While he believes in the right of others to follow their own sexual preference, vast numbers of the public throughout the world do not share that view, and believing that he had a homosexual affair and did so during his marriage, they will be less inclined to patronise Cruise's films, particularly since he tends to play parts calling for heterosexual romance and action adventure.'

Bertram Fields added: 'Tom never had a homosexual or any other relationship with Bradford. He doesn't even know him. He is tired of the gossip and it hurts his children. And damn it, he's going to stop it.'

One of the magazines immediately printed a retraction and Fields vowed that any further repeat of the malicious gossip would provoke another writ from the megastar. 'We're very anxious to hear what this porn actor says under oath about this garbage story he's handing out.'

Meanwhile shock waves from Tom and Nicole's separation continued to rumble through Tinseltown. A date for the couple's divorce hearing had yet to be set but both were bracing themselves for yet more hurtful and highly personal stories trying to expose the supposed real reason behind the tragic split.

In the months following the separation, Tom confessed to some friends that he'd seriously wondered whether he'd made an awful mistake. Nobody dared mention his close friendship with a stunning young Spanish actress called Penélope Cruz.

You have to go back to 1998 and the private viewing by Tom of a couple of little-known Spanish films called *Abre los Ojos* and *La Niña de Tus Ojos* to mark the moment that beautiful actress Penélope Cruz first caught his eye. *Abre los Ojos* was directed by Spaniard Alejandro Amenabar, who went on to direct Nicole in *The Others*. *La Niña de Tus Ojos* was supposed to show the real depth of Penélope Cruz's acting talents but some of the steamy scenes featuring her having sex in a bath and later with another man showed Tom another side to the stunningly attractive young actress. He was so smitten by *Abre los Ojos* that he persuaded his old friend Cameron Crowe to agree to direct a US version – to be called *Vanilla Sky* – and splashed out hundreds of thousands of dollars on script development. Tom encouraged Crowe to cast Penélope in the same role she'd played in the Spanish version. The cast was set but could Tom resist the beautiful young actress he had swooned over on screen?

The official version of events is that Crowe visited Penélope on the set of *Captain Corelli's Mandolin* in the middle of 2000 and offered her the role. She then flew to New York and met Tom for the first time. She has always insisted that a relationship did not begin then.

Rumours of a romance with Penélope Cruz began to circulate within days of the divorce announcement. She was already the new face of Ralph Lauren and appearing with alarming regularity on the cover of such prestigious magazines as *Vogue*. There had even been tabloid reports about how Hollywood actor Matt Damon had dumped his girlfriend, Winona Ryder, after getting together with Penélope on the set of her US feature debut, *All the Pretty Horses*, in 2000. Then Nicholas Cage split with his wife, Patricia Arquette, after he shot *Captain Corelli's Mandolin* with Penélope on the romantic Mediterranean island of Cephallonia.

And all this came before she turned up as Tom's co-star in *Vanilla Sky*. Just a couple of months later Tom and Nicole's marriage fell apart. Penélope Cruz might only have left her native Spain a few years earlier, but by early 2001 she was getting more exposure than Nicole and Julia Roberts combined. And not all of it was positive.

Penélope was projected in the USA as a Latin femme fatale – five feet six inches tall, slender, curvaceous, with much-tossed dark tresses and large, sparkling brown eyes. She was almost the exact opposite of most female Hollywood stars of the previous two decades, with the possible exception of Jennifer Lopez and Catherine Zeta-Jones.

Yet Hollywood was quick to point out that her performances in a number of little-known European films were hardly noticeable. Even so, Penélope's director in *Captain Corelli's Mandolin*, John Madden, did manage to gush: 'She's an extravagant physical beauty. All the cliches apply: dark, mysterious, sexual, predatory. She has an astonishing physical charisma.'

But where exactly did Penélope come from in the first place? This author spent many weeks researching her background on the mean streets of Madrid's working-class district of Alcobendas. Her father was a car mechanic and her mother, Encarna, a hairdresser. Penélope was by all accounts a hyperactive little show-off from an extraordinarily early age.

Penélope was born in Alcobendas on 28 April 1974. Her family home was a cramped fourth-floor flat in the suburb's main street, half a mile from the bullring. It was sandwiched between a discount supermarket and a men's clothing store. She still calls her mother and father most nights from wherever she is in the world.

Spain was and still is an integral part of Penélope's life. She even insists she still dreams in Spanish. At four years old she was packed off to regular dancing classes by her parents.

It was clear that even by the age of five or six Penélope Cruz was an attention seeker. Her ballet teacher, Angela Garrido, recalls her standing at the front of her class in her tutu and announcing: 'One day I am going to be on stage – and I am going to be a star.' As Angela later said: 'It was blatantly obvious that she had a gift, something special. And her ambition was offset by a very sweet personality. She was almost timid but when she walked into my studio her eyes would light up. She came alive when she was performing. She wasn't a girl who talked much. When she did, it was always about dance, about a step she wanted to perform or about her ambition to become a ballet dancer.'

And, despite her parents' poverty, it really was a case of whatever Penélope wanted, Penélope got. Angela recalled: 'I remember her at five turning up in a brilliant white tutu. It would have cost about £60 and she would have quickly outgrown it, but nothing was too good for her.'

By then Penélope was already entertaining her family by re-enacting TV commercials. When she was eight she was posing as a model at her first communion. While the other little girls around her stood nervously for a group photo, Penélope turned her body sideways and posed with a pout on her lips. As her former headmaster, Juan Miguel Sánchez, explained: 'She had decided she wanted to be an actress and she never wavered. The Cruz family are full of talent. Her sister Monica is a professional dancer.'

Even as a young schoolgirl, Penélope exuded a disturbing sexuality and self-consciousness about her body. Señor Sánchez recalled: 'During a Spanish class I was trying to find a sentence to explain some grammar. I scanned the class and my eyes fixed on Penélope and I said, "Penélope is skinny." I hadn't meant anything by it, but Penélope went home crying and reported it to her mother. Her mum came to the school "to complain".'

Penélope's ballet teacher, Emilia Martín Rodríguez, was more impressed with the Cruz family. 'Penélope and her sister Monica were very close to one another, as were the whole family. Monica was the better dancer, while Penélope was the better actor, always playing up in class. Monica had a good body and presentation and Penélope was a real extrovert, with all the natural signs of an actress.'

So Penélope enjoyed dressing up in extremely grown-up outfits from a young age. As one childhood friend explained: 'It always made Penélope seem more sophisticated than the rest of us, but some of us were shocked at the way she would wear mini-dresses and stockings from such a young age. It was almost as if she was a mini-grown-up. She knew how to swing her hips from a young age and that was kind of disturbing in someone so young.'

Penélope later confessed to one Spanish journalist that she had her first love affair when she was just five years old. 'I was in love with a boy called Alfonisto and I have always had to be in love ever since. I need tranquillity and security from a man. That makes them much more attractive than anything physical. But I've had some periods of real suffering. When I was fourteen or fifteen I had some bad times. I was doing too much – studies, dance lessons, castings and work. I felt I was going to die. But it passed. It was the worst time of my life for big sufferings.'

At the age of fourteen Penélope discovered the joys of the opposite sex. Augustín López's family used to run a bar round the corner from the hairdressing salon where Penélope's mother worked. Augustín, now thirty, has never forgotten the handful of dates he enjoyed with the teenage temptress Penélope. 'Penélope was very mature for her age. She loved flirting with boys and was not afraid to show off her sexuality.

Augustín says that Penélope was a brilliant kisser. 'She'd been out with other people before we met. She seemed determined to leave Alcobendas and make it in the big wide world. But she also enjoyed eating lots of tapas and flirting with boys. She was so beautiful and still is.'

In Alcobendas, sexual awareness was a lot different from how it was in Tom's childhood. As one of Penélope's oldest friends explained: 'Here in Spain we are much more open about sex. There is no sense of embarrassment when talking about it.'

Another local boy who went on a couple of dates with Penélope when she was in her early twenties said: 'She gives the impression of being a shy, inexperienced little girl. Although we enjoyed every minute of our time together, she made it clear there was no future for us because she saw her life beyond Madrid.'

Penélope's big break came when she was just fourteen and was spotted by her future manager, Katrina Bayonas, at a talent contest where she beat three hundred aspiring young actresses. 'There was something magical about her, so powerful and magnetic, it literally took my breath away,' recalled Bayonas. 'I knew this girl was going, one day, to be one of the biggest stars in the world.'

So, soon afterwards, Penélope moved out of the family's very modest apartment and began studying dance full-time at a school in the centre of Madrid.

Back then, Penélope spoke with the Spanish equivalent of a strong cockney accent. One of her school friends later recalled: 'I was amazed when I bumped into her a couple of years ago. She sounded like a member of the Spanish royal family, not a tough little street kid from a poor Madrid suburb.'

Less than three years later – after leaving for the bright lights of Madrid's city centre – Penélope agreed to star in a film in which she was expected to perform outrageous nudity and sex scenes. Her movie debut in *Jamón, Jamón* included writhing naked on a bar table for much of the film. Many years later – after making her mark on Spain's relatively small movie industry – she pronounced that making love to a variety of men for the camera at the age of seventeen had caused her to have a nervous breakdown. 'I had a strong rejection of anything sexual or sensual for a while. I cut my hair very, very short and didn't do any more love scenes, not even kisses, for many years. When I was given the part I knew about the nudity. I was comfortable with that. But when I saw the film I was shocked. I found it very hard to deal with the fact that the whole world would be seeing me like that. It was a horrible breakdown. It was huge, the worst period of my life, and it lasted for a couple of months. I moved back in with my parents.' She added: 'I feel frightened sometimes with the reaction of men to me.' From then on, Penélope's mother read and vetted all scripts offered to her daughter.

Later, during the filming of some Spanish movies, Penélope became such a recluse that she refused to go out at night and would stay in her hotel bedroom sleeping. She later claimed she banned herself from socialising because she couldn't cope with the stress of being in the outside world.

When Penélope auditioned in 1995 for a part in *A Walk in the Clouds* with Keanu Reeves, she spoke just three words of English and was rejected for the part. She learned a severe lesson and set out with steely determination to speak English fluently. She also became a committed Buddhist in an effort to deal with the pressure and loneliness that seemed to come with acting and living in a big city away from her family.

More surprisingly, but a lot less worryingly, Penélope confessed to one

Spanish reporter at the time that she'd had a secret crush on Marlon Brando since she was a teenager. 'He is still very good-looking. Mmmm, so handsome.'

And along the way she enjoyed seven years as the live-in lover of Spanish rock legend Nacho Cano, whom she'd met when she was just fourteen years old. Cano later insisted that he did not make love to Penélope until she was sixteen but their relationship seemed to blossom from the moment they met. He was twelve years her senior. Penélope spent much of her time with Nacho Cano living in London and New York, as well as in Madrid.

In an interview with a Spanish journalist in 1996, Penélope let slip that she had been only fourteen when she met and fell in love with Nacho. 'I lied and said I was sixteen because I wanted to be in his video. It was my first real film project and I was desperate to get it. Two years later we fell in love. I still love Nacho very much and he taught me how to make love.'

In 1997 Penélope spent a year in London – a period of her life which she has always been intriguingly vague about. All she will admit is that she lived near Hampstead Heath with her boyfriend (presumably Nacho). She spent a lot of time going to auditions and once even dyed her dark hair peroxide blonde when a certain part called for it. 'I looked very, very strange,' she says. 'I felt like an alien.'

Penélope also had a one-year fling with industrial heir Enrique Sarasola, a member of Spain's Olympic equestrian team. But for her this was all mere training, because she knew the big time was beckoning.

An intense relationship with Czech film director Tomas Obermaier followed. That finished in the summer of 2000 after Penélope was photographed topless with Tomas on a Spanish beach and the photos appeared on the front pages of Spanish tabloids.

Penélope's international breakthrough as an actress came when she starred in legendary Spanish director Pedro Almodóvar's film *All About My Mother*, in which she played a nun made pregnant by an AIDS-infected transsexual. Typically, Penélope saw her raunchy role in the following terms: 'It was a very rich part: it has everything. She is like a lost bird. It was very intense but very good fun at the same time.' Shortly afterwards she landed her first Hollywood role, in *All the Pretty Horses*.

There is no doubt that within Spain's movie industry Penélope actively sought out fame and was extremely determined to make it in Hollywood. Says one who knew her well: 'Penélope is a weird combination of little-girl innocence and steely determination. Remember, she comes from a very poor background and she is determined to have everlasting success. She can be so sexy and yet so selfish. But I've seen men melt in her presence because you always feel with Penélope that she craves sex and attention. It is a heady mix.'

In Alcobendas, it's said that when Penélope left home aged fourteen she was penniless but when she came back after conquering Hollywood she was worth in excess of £20 million. Yet throughout all this success she remained close to her mother and father and admitted there were long periods in Hollywood when she missed them dearly. At one stage in 2001 Penélope ran up a £5000 phone bill in just four weeks because of the non-stop calls she made to her family in Madrid. Whenever she felt desperately lonely she flew back to Spain and spent weeks sleeping and eating with her family. Says one childhood friend: 'They are like her security blanket. She knows she is safe with them.'

And when she was back in Alcobendas, Penélope splashed out a fortune on gifts for her family. This included expensive designer clothes for her teenage brother Eduardo. She even flew him out to Los Angeles. She also continued to make hefty donations to a sanctuary for slum kids founded by Mother Theresa in Calcutta.

In many ways Penélope was a sexy, flirtatious Latin beauty who was like a whirlwind to many of Hollywood's younger male stars. Soon after arriving in LA, she was introduced to Russell Crowe, who'd just completed filming *Gladiator*. Predictably, Crowe was bowled over and later sent her a series of steamy love letters from a film location back in Australia. All she will say these days is that Crowe is 'loco!'. But one of Crowe's closest Hollywood pals said recently: 'Russell was head over heels in love with Penélope for a few weeks. They went on a couple of dates and he thought it was true love. But Penélope then started working on *All the Pretty Horses* and immediately replaced Russell in her affections with Matt Damon. Poor bloke never got a look in.'

In early 2001 actor Nicholas Cage helped Penélope and Tom convince the world they were not an item following Tom's shock split from Nicole. Cage flirted outrageously with Penélope at the London premiere of their movie *Captain Corelli's Mandolin*. Penélope was unable to keep a sensuous grin off her face every time she caught his eye across the after-movie party. As one onlooker later recalled: 'It was a brilliant performance but then they are both actors after all!'

No wonder Matt Damon and his best friend, Ben Affleck, nicknamed Penélope 'trouble' when they encountered her during her early days in Hollywood. Says one Hollywood source: 'Penélope had those two eating out of her hand at one stage. She was like a breath of fresh air compared with pale-skinned, anorexic, self-obsessed actresses in Hollywood. Here was a sexy, sassy firecracker with a sparkle in her eyes and an ability to swing her hips and attract glances from every man in the room.'

Shortly after the official break-up announcement, Tom's publicist Pat Kingsley publicly insisted there were no other parties involved. She told reporters: 'There is absolutely no third party. There is nobody else. I have had people ask if Nicole has gone with Ewan McGregor but she hasn't seen him since they stopped filming *Moulin Rouge* months ago in Australia. And people are asking about Tom and Penélope Cruz and that is certainly not true.'

Penélope told London's *Daily Mail*: 'I did not break up Tom Cruise's marriage. I am not having an affair with Tom Cruise. I am just one of his leading ladies in a film. He is a very nice actor, that's all.'

In March, at the 2001 Oscars, Tom watched with interest as Penélope sashayed across the stage on the arm of Spain's other big export to Hollywood, Antonio Banderas. She held on tightly to the handsome actor as they announced director Pedro Almodóvar as the winner of award for Best Foreign Film.

The previous June, Almodóvar had upset Tom by stating in a Spanish newspaper that he would never use Tom in a film. 'I would never use stars like Tom Cruise – ever! It's the star system and I don't like it. You have to give up ownership of the film to the studio,' said the director, completely unaware that this comment might later come back to haunt him.

In the early weeks of 2001 Penélope continued to insist there was no one special in her life. She told one reporter: 'Maybe because I am *not* dating anyone no one has criticised me. I have stepped off the relationship scene to come to terms with myself. Most of my adult life I've been someone's girlfriend. Now I'm happy being single.'

She did admit to the *News of the World*'s magazine *Sunday* in London that she'd suffered emotionally during this period and blamed her supposed determination to stay single on this fact. 'I am making time for me. I haven't been single for a while and I think it's been good for me.'

All this, plus a frantic work schedule which included filming *All the Pretty Horses* and *Captain Corelli's Mandolin*, did not help Penélope's health. She later explained: 'I worked all summer, then I went to Calcutta to make a documentary for a Spanish charity. When I returned to America I broke down – out of exhaustion and because of what I saw in India. Once I left, everything came out. Then I had two choices. I could go down, or up. So I quit smoking, started a healthier diet and began meditation again. Now my ambition is to be happy.'

Her agent before the romance with Tom blossomed admitted recently that Penélope was 'quite flaky'. Brandt Joel explained: 'A couple of times she was late for meetings I was taking her to. So one time I said, "I'll pick you up at one o'clock." She doesn't drive. And I picked her up at 1.30. I said, 'See how it feels?' She got it.' Punctuality was a near obsession for Tom.

Penélope even gave up smoking. She admitted to a friend that her craving for nicotine drove her close to a nervous breakdown. At one stage she even flew back to Madrid – to learn how to cook! Up until then she had been unable even to boil an egg.

Around the same time, a number of steamy still photos from Penélope's movie *Blow*, with Johnny Depp, were released. Depp made it clear he was enjoying a happy relationship with French actress Vanessa Paradis and they had a young child.

Penélope has never said much about her time playing opposite the handsome Depp, but she did admit recently: 'It was like a liberation to play the character, although the scenes were difficult and I had not to be self-conscious. I play a cocaine addict and Johnny plays a cocaine dealer. We had a lot of good times working together and laughed a lot. He is a wild one. If he feels like getting up at three in the morning and going out somewhere, then he will do it. I lost a bit of weight for the part in the opening scenes of *Blow* where I'm going crazy, but I always try to eat more because I like the way I look when I'm bigger.' Penélope took lactose powder as a substitute for cocaine throughout the film and always insisted she was firmly opposed to drug use. 'Drugs are the devil,' she said.

It wasn't until July 2001 that Tom actually officially confirmed he was having a relationship with Penélope. The news became undeniable after the couple spent a brief vacation at the same resort in Fiji as Nicole, who'd been there the previous week with her old friend (and one-time Penélope Cruz fan) Russell Crowe.

Penélope was then reported to have 'had a few dates' with Tom in LA. She also attended his thirty-ninth-birthday celebrations at the city's Buffalo Club.

On 8 August 2001 Tom and Nicole were officially divorced. Tom's attorney, Dennis Wasser, told newsmen: 'This will give them an opportunity to get on with their lives. There are a lot of issues to be resolved but we are hopeful that they can be resolved amicably. The first matter was to get the parties divorced. The second is the settlement.'

As one celebrity lawyer explained: 'Tom is obviously far richer and with the profits from the *Mission: Impossible* films he will be keen to keep as much cash as possible away from Nicole. It is standard in Hollywood for the main player to protect the assets they went into the marriage with. Much of the pair's wealth stems from Tom's shrewd marketing of his heart-throb image.'

That same month, both Penélope and Nicole began using Hollywood TV chat shows to talk about life with or without Tom. In some appearances they even chose spookily similar clothes and Nicole made a point of denying to one host that she had ever kissed Russell Crowe, although she openly admitted they were good friends.

Nicole even went on to describe how her perfect date would involve a lot of kissing, although she insisted: 'I'm not dating at the moment. I'm taking care of my kids. On a date I like to kiss, oh and have dinner, but I do like to kiss. I don't know what else I'd do on a date. I haven't been on a date for a long time.'

That summer, Tom and Penélope were even conveniently caught kissing for the first time in public by a paparazzo. The besotted pair made no attempt to hide their passion for each other on a shopping trip in Los Angeles. The snapper even managed to find a passerby, who later told a reporter: 'It was very passionate. They could not keep their hands off each other. They are obviously very much in love.' An hour later the two lovers were spotted walking into LA's swish Ivy restaurant wearing matching jackets.

Shortly afterwards Penélope Cruz signed a £5-million deal to promote Spanish sparkling wine. Tom even sanctioned the deal on the basis that the TV commercials would only be seen in Spain. Many of Tom's Hollywood friends and associates reported that Penélope was a very different person from Nicole. She loved dancing and would get up at five every morning, to sit cross-legged in various yoga poses in the garden of her new Beverly Hills home for at least an hour before showering and having breakfast. Explained one friend: 'She's a much more solitary person than Nicole. Penélope might be close to her family when she goes back to Spain, but out here in LA she has few friends and seems to enjoy her own company much of the time. I think Tom likes that because it's very similar to the way he wishes to run his life.'

Penélope's only addiction was to watching the classic movie *Dangerous Liaisons*, starring Michelle Pfeiffer. Penélope saw it more than twenty times and even accepted a role in another movie made by the same director, Stephen Frears, on the basis of her love of *Liaisons*. And she insisted to anyone who would listen that her affair with Tom had not started until after the filming of *Vanilla Sky* was complete. The description of her by the movie's director, Cameron Crowe, was fascinating: 'Penélope is three-quarters soft and one-quarter tough. She has a checks-and-balances thing going: the sweetness protects the toughness and the toughness protects the sweetness.'

Later Penélope went one step further. 'I'm more tough than sweet,' she said to one reporter before adding that it might be because she is Spanish and Taurus, a star sign known for its stubbornness. 'When I get too stubborn I can hurt myself. I say the truth to people and sometimes get myself into a place I can't get out of, focusing on the one thing. It doesn't happen often, but when it does it is not a nice thing because you feel trapped in an idea.'

In the summer of 2001 Penélope's mother, Encarna, confirmed in Spain that her daughter was dating Tom. She said: 'It's the same for me if it's Tom Cruise or anybody. As long as my daughter is happy, I'm not fussed about anything else. They are together – and there's no need for that to upset anybody.'

In those first few months of her relationship with Tom, Penélope was given special lessons on how to avoid being caught by reporters' questions about her personal life. She started referring to the 'red lights' whenever questions delved too deeply into her private business.

Penélope definitely didn't trust any outside stimulants. She never drank coffee and tea, insisting she didn't need 'the extra stimulation'. Just like Tom, she avoided reading negative newspaper stories about herself. One classic had her burning herself with an iron, after completing the filming of *Captain Corelli's Mandolin*, to mark the beauty of her experience starring alongside Nicholas Cage. The truth was, she burned herself by accident.

In Spain, Penélope upset the bullfighting traditionalists who still dominated opinion on the so-called sport in her country by signing a petition to stop it because of its cruelty. She ended up receiving death threats. Tom wasn't pleased about her involvement in such controversial issues. As one of his Hollywood associates explained: 'Tom doesn't like rocking the boat and he told Penélope that she had to learn to avoid getting involved in such heavy topics in the future.'

Also in Spain, Penélope's mother and her younger brother Eduardo lived in her £1-million mansion near Madrid while Penélope was travelling the globe. Her mother looked after Penélope's three cats and three dogs. But the actress still made a point of trying to get home every couple of months for at least a few days of peace and quiet. She said recently: 'My parents are both still very young, only forty-eight, because I was born when they were just twenty-one. So I can talk to them about everything and I even take my mother out dancing with me sometimes.'

But, following their own recent divorce, Penélope's parents admitted to local friends that they were worried about their eldest daughter. And Penélope herself admitted: 'Secretly they are worried. "Does Penélope want children?"' 'Someday, someday,' she told the interviewer in a faraway tone, 'I would love to have kids but I don't feel ready right now.'

In one foreign magazine interview, Penélope revealed intimate secrets of what she expected from men: 'A man must be a good kisser. The man I love must have a good sense of humour. And I only like a man if I feel truly connected with him.'

Penélope was learning how to be a professional photographer because she remained uncertain about whether she would remain an actress for ever. Already her pictures of Tibetan children in exile in Nepal had featured in an exhibition in Spain.

As director of *All the Pretty Horses*, Billy Bob Thornton, said of Penélope: 'She cares so deeply. I think it'll be her downfall. This is a long-winded way of saying that she's co-dependent, and it makes life pretty tough sometimes.' Penélope herself agrees: 'I know what he means. We're similar in some ways, about how we get obsessed with work, but I don't think you have to be suffering to give a good performance. I feel everything a lot, but I don't feel that has to be my downfall.' She added: 'I like to have my emotions aroused. If you do not have bad times then you cannot properly experience the good times.'

Penélope had been known to enjoy the occasional glass of wine, but eventually she gave up alcohol altogether. 'I reached a point once when I was so exhausted that I couldn't live like that any more. I wasn't doing anything bad to myself, only overworking, but that can take you to a place that is not good,' she explained to a Spanish journalist. 'Work can be your best friend or your worst enemy. I used to smoke for four years; that's when I decided to quit and to eat when I have to eat, to stop what I'm doing, even if it's twenty minutes, and to sleep, rest and take free time for myself.'

Penélope's only remaining vice was an addiction to sleeping. She often managed fifteen hours at a time. 'It's a family habit. Sleep is the best thing for happiness, beauty and everything. Once, my sister slept for three days straight. My own record is eighteen hours.'

Back in Hollywood, Tom and Penélope were now a fully fledged couple. As Penélope admitted: 'We don't hide that we are dating: there is nothing to hide. Things are going very well, but we wouldn't go into details about it, because that wouldn't be right.'

One interviewer then asked her: 'Are you happy?'

'Mmmm. Mmmm, very.'

'Are you in love?'

'Don't ask me any more,' she said, giggling nervously. 'You can write that I've nothing to hide, that we are dating, that things are going excellently, and there are no more details to give. I am sure everyone understands that.' But, beneath the sweet, girly exterior, lay determination.

Penélope Cruz had quickly bought into the entire Hollywood star system in accordance with her boyfriend's rules. She signed to the all-powerful Creative Artists Agency and all requests for interviews had to go through a series of PR doors, each one more firmly locked than the last. Even photographs had to be approved. Her rise to superstardom was being very carefully orchestrated.

Penélope admitted that she was 'always sad' whenever a film shoot ended because 'life is always easier when you're making a movie. You can forget about your problems and throw yourself into your character. I always find it sad when a film ends and I have to go back to all the day-to-day problems of life. It takes a while to adjust to the fact that the magic of being in a movie isn't there any more.' But then this is the same woman who admits: 'I like flirting. I like putting on a show. Like a lot of women I enjoy the game of seduction.'

Cameron Crowe later revealed: 'In this movie [*Vanilla Sky*] we really have this intense love story. So Penélope had to appear to truly fall in love. And Tom's character falls in love with her. You watch them portray going through that hideous, great, awful, intoxicating moment. Without it, we couldn't have a movie. The first time we screened the movie – just in-house – it was the kind of situation where at the end you get a reaction of "Wow! They really were in love."'

There remained one easy way to upset Penélope – mention Nicole Kidman.

When one Hollywood reporter asked what she thought of Nicole's latest hairstyle, Penélope snapped back: 'I don't give a fuck what she looks like. Why should I care? But I do sometimes get angry when I hear him talking about Nicole.'

Meanwhile Tom and Penélope were playing happy families with Tom's two adopted children. She insisted: 'There are no bad feelings in that area. But of course it's a sensitive topic. And we have to be very careful and very respectful. Tom loves his children and I respect him for that.'

But she did lose her cool about Tom's nickname for her – 'Lupe'. She explained: 'I keep telling him not to call me that. It's a joke name that I got when I was filming with Tom. Lupe is from Guadalupe and Guadalupe is not my name. But it has stuck. And even some of my best friends call me that now.'

Then Tom splashed out £100,000 on keeping a water-world theme park open just for him, Penélope and his two children. Tom and Penélope turned up at Raging Waters in California, amid tight security, with Connor and Bella and twenty of their friends. The party later departed by three privately chartered helicopters which flew them to the nearest airstrip, where a fleet of limos was waiting to whisk the family and friends home.

Christmas 2001 proved a very testing time for Tom and Penélope's relationship because Tom only revealed to his new love once they got to Sydney that he would be spending half the time with Nicole and the kids. Penélope later explained: 'I told him that I would leave him if he went ahead with his plan. When he did I got the first flight back to LA.'

Penélope then flew to Spain to shoot a film and many saw it as the beginning of the end. There were even rumours he had asked her to remove things from his home. But Penélope later insisted: 'I went to Spain to work and see my family. But my break has had an improving effect on my life, career and relationship.'

Newspapers in London and LA reported that Tom had ended his relationship with Penélope. It was alleged that Tom had called off their wedding plans and she was so upset she'd jetted back to her family in Madrid. One of her friends told a London-based journalist: 'Penélope's head is spinning. She doesn't know what's going on.'

Reports in the USA claimed that Tom tried to 'let her down gently'. Others alleged that the relationship had hit the rocks because 'Tom has so many other priorities at the moment'.

It was claimed that only a few weeks earlier, Penélope's father, Eduardo, had flown out to meet Tom to discuss the wedding plans. But others close to Tom claimed they knew nothing of a split.

However, within weeks the tabloids were claiming that Tom and Penélope were an item once again and that she was desperate to have his baby! Rumours of a sudden, short-notice wedding swept Tinseltown. But the marriage never materialised, although it seemed that Tom and Penélope had never broken up in the first place.

In late January 2002 Tom travelled to Madrid to meet Penélope's family in what was billed as a happy-go-lucky meet-the-family trip to Europe. In fact, it was carefully planned to coincide with the promotional tour for *Vanilla Sky*. As one of Penélope's oldest friends back in Alcobendas explained: 'Tom briefed all of Penélope's family on how to deal with the media. How they must never talk about him or Penélope otherwise it might endanger the happiness of their relationship. I heard that Penélope's father was quite upset because it seemed as if Tom's only reason for coming out to Spain was to ensure that her family did not cause him any embarrassment.'

At a large family party, Tom was said to have wowed guests with his flamenco dancing skills at Penélope's Madrid home, overlooked by one of the city's most notorious brothels. More than thirty close family and friends were invited to the party. Witnesses said that Tom and Penélope remained virtually glued together throughout the evening. If she got up he would pat his leg to get her to sit back on his lap.

Penélope wore a stunning black skirt and sweater to the gathering and guests (except for Tom) enjoyed smoked salmon, caviare, prawns, bacon and spicy chorizo sausages. Among the guests was Real Madrid soccer star Luis Figo, and after the party a chauffeur-driven car picked the couple up and dropped them at a swish Madrid hotel. Penélope's close family members were hurt that she wouldn't stay in her own house. As one lifelong friend explained: 'Penélope's mother and father were disappointed at how they were just whisked off to a hotel rather than staying with her family, but Tom seemed determined not to hang around too long and he was obviously in charge of the whole event.'

The promotional tour for *Vanilla Sky* proved extremely nerve-racking for Penélope, as she told a friend back in Madrid. 'I couldn't stand the way everyone wanted to know about Tom and not the film. Then they tried to compare the film to my other roles but that wasn't fair either. Everything I do means a lot to me because I'm an actress and you depend on the trust of others to be able to work.'

Back in LA, in April 2002 Tom threw a massive twenty-eighth birthday party for Penélope to cement their union. However, she was deeply hurt by criticism of the dress she wore to the party, and later explained: 'I wanted everyone to be in 1980s tacky style. The kind of style that comes from American soap operas like *Dynasty* or *Dallas*. I wore a hat with lace over the front and some stupid dress.'

Throughout the development of Tom and Penélope's relationship there were many diehard cynics who regularly pointed out that the publicity surrounding that romance had helped skyrocket Penélope from mediocre foreign movies to major Hollywood box-office success. Despite being panned by the critics, *Vanilla Sky* made more than $200 million worldwide.

In early 2002 Nicole and Penélope even held a secret 'summit' so that Nicole could make her acquaintance for the sake of the Cruise children. The meeting took place at a hotel in Bel Air, California, and both women behaved with dignity, according to one witness. Nicole later told friends that Penélope did seem intimidated by the older actress.

Nicole is even alleged to have told her: 'I may not be the person he wants to be married to, but I'm certainly the best person he could ever divorce because I'm not angry. I'm not bitter. Lucky for him.' Before leaving the summit, Nicole extended her hand to shake Penélope's but Penélope gave her an inappropriate hug, which appeared to annoy her.

Meanwhile Tom remained utterly loyal about Nicole whenever her name came up with Penélope. Says one friend: 'Tom is so used to protecting Nicole, he would never say anything to anyone – even Penélope – that would disparage her. That has to be tough for Penélope to accept.'

Some of Penélope's friends admitted that her relationship with Tom could be very tempestuous. 'But that's the way Penélope is. She is typical Latin. One minute loving, sexy and seductive. The next she can turn into a street fighter.'

It was even rumoured that Penélope had put a deadline on their 'courtship'. If they hadn't married by the time she turned thirty in April 2004 she might end their relationship. 'She's tough enough to do it if she has to,' says one friend.

However, it is believed there have been other deadlines in the past which have always been extended. 'She loves him very much and starts almost crying when she talks about him. But it is very difficult for her and who knows what the future might hold for them both?'

In March 2002 Penélope invested in a $1.6-million apartment in Manhattan without any financial help from Tom. Many of her friends believed she made the purchase to prove to him that she was not totally reliant on him and would live on her own if necessary.

Back in Madrid, Penélope's parents were reported to be unhappy at the prospect of their daughter marrying a man who'd been twice divorced. One alleged family friend told a notorious US tabloid: 'Penélope's father's Eduardo is tearing his hair out. He'd rather see his daughter marry a pauper in Madrid than walk down the aisle with Tom.' According to the report, Penélope's dad also told her: 'Find a nice Spanish guy and settle down with him. You'll be much happier.'

Tom admitted to close friends and colleagues that he was in no hurry to follow his first two failed attempts at matrimony. Penélope was in a romantic no-man's land. 'She's going nowhere. She needs Tom in every sense of the word and she'll be clinging on to him,' explained one friend from Madrid. 'Penélope is a needy girl. She's never really been without a man since she was fourteen years old and she's not going to let her biggest catch go.'

By the end of 2002 Penélope was regularly attending Church of Scientology events in LA. One of her pals told a reporter: 'She's really into it but she hasn't told many people because she believes that religion is a private matter.' One of her oldest childhood friends back in Madrid explained: 'Penélope has always been interested in slightly oddball religious beliefs, so I'm not surprised she has got into the Scientologists.'

Penélope also went out of her way to take regular breaks from work in order to be constantly at Tom's side. Some friends described it as her way of making sure their relationship didn't hit another rocky patch, as it had done at the end of 2001. One friend explained: 'The feeling I am getting is that Penélope wants to take the time off to spend some serious quality time with Tom. Since they got together they have been feeling the heat of the media glare and they want to be together to see how their future develops.'

Penélope was still coming to terms with the fact that although Nicole may have gone from Tom's life she was never far from his thoughts. In January 2003 Penélope was with Tom in Japan finishing work on a new action film, *The Last Samurai*.

Tom had delighted Penélope by giving her a £500 cashmere scarf fringed in leather as a love token. She wore it at dinner and looked stunning. But as they enjoyed that meal together, Tom's mobile phone rang and it was Nicole. As Penélope later complained to a friend: 'Always, it's Nicole. Just when you think she's not going to call, when you think you're so far away she could never find you, guess what? She calls.'

Penélope eventually managed to get Tom to agree not to answer his mobile during romantic dinners together, but getting used to being one of two women in his life has certainly not been easy for the young Spanish actress. She has told friends she remains convinced that one day Tom and Nicole will be reconciled, saying: 'I still think they are destined for one another. It's just a feeling I have when I'm with him, that he still loves her, that he is in pain — that he misses her. It's hard on me.'

That little outburst by the firecracker from Madrid got her into deep water with Tom, who was upset that she had even dared to utter Nicole's name. In Tom's mind that was crossing the boundary. Nicole's name was never to be uttered in public by any of his friends, and that included Penélope.

Meanwhile few doubted that the future of the relationship between Tom and Penélope rested entirely on Tom's shoulders. If he chose to turn it into a serious relationship, then so be it. But as one Hollywood associate pointed out: 'Penélope didn't exactly get off to a good start. In the Tom Cruise story, maybe she will be just a footnote.'

31

*A true believer and a half ...
a guy with a halo turned on at all times.*

Tom Wolfe, describing John Glenn
in The Right Stuff

Nicole slept badly for the first few nights of September 2001, and she later told friends it wasn't just to do with the shock of her recent divorce. In a number of disturbing dreams she saw visions of airliners crashing into high buildings. On the eleventh day of that month she realised the full significance of those dreams.

Nicole will be eternally grateful to have been with her two children in Los Angeles on the day terrorists struck on the east coast of America. She'd planned to take the children with her on business to New York, and they had been scheduled to leave on 10 September. But then she cancelled her plans, telling friends that she'd had a premonition that something would not go well for her in New York.

Subsequently, Nicole was horrified to see what happened to the World Trade Centre towers but has refused to discuss her premonition with anyone since the terrorist outrage. As she and the kids watched the tragedy unfolding, Tom rang. The couple had not talked directly since February. The result of that conversation was that they agreed to keep in closer contact for the sake of the children.

Following the terrorist outrages of 11 September, Tom had a long, hard think about certain issues. He found himself torn between his belief in individual freedom and today's need for heightened security. 'It's so strange that we trust each other so little that we have got to the point where we have to have fingerprinting and ID. You look at terrorism today and I've got to tell you, it's a tough thing. I don't know what the hell to do. I certainly don't want to get on an aeroplane or think about my family or friends getting on one with the potential of what occurred on that day.

'I also believe in freedom of speech and thought and I think the less governmental control the better, yet we are in a situation where people are so irresponsible that human life holds such little value to them. It's just crazy. Look what's going on – it's unbelievable. It's shocking. It's terrifying.'

Contact between Tom and Nicole started to become more cordial. Nicole admitted to one friend that they had to be 'more mature. For the sake of the children.' Yet when Tom sent flowers and a note to congratulate Nicole on her outstanding acting performance in *Moulin Rouge*, she put the display in a guest room and never looked twice at it. As the film's director, Baz Luhrmann, pointed out: 'Nicole Kidman embodies more than anyone I have ever known the catchline of *Moulin Rouge*: "The show must go on."'

Nicole's friends believe that Tom's lukewarm reaction to her miscarriage showed that he really wasn't the man she thought he was. As she explained: 'If people look at my life and see that, yes, I have had hard times and times that seemed so crushing, but that I went on – and that maybe they can do the same in their own lives – that's good.'

Ultimately, both parties acknowledged that there was something wrong with the marriage because neither was entirely happy. But would they one day look back at its conclusion with the response that it could so easily have been saved from the divorce courts?

Nicole had long since proved beyond doubt that the show must go on. Caught by photographers leaving her lawyer's LA offices where she'd just signed the documents ending their ten-year marriage, she threw back her head and let out a scream. Her message to the world was clear: 'I'm a free woman.' Yet behind this magnificent performance lay a complicated mind. Out in the real world she quipped: 'What an excellent, excellent morning,' before driving to Beverly Hills and buying a £25,000 Fendi fur coat. 'I deserve this damn coat,' she explained to one friend with a nervous giggle.

Less than a mile away, Penélope Cruz was moving into the vast mansion being rented by Tom and his entourage. Tom and Penélope even vacationed together at the Cruise family ranch in Telluride, Colorado – the same house in which Tom and Nicole had married in 1990. Tom and Penélope were also spotted lunching at Sofio's, Nicole's favourite restaurant in the mountain resort. Penélope, dressed in figure-hugging tight blue jeans and a pink blouse unbuttoned low enough to reveal her push-up bra, was seen kissing Tom passionately.

Later the two walked hand in hand across the street to a clothing store called Telluride Trappings and Toggery. 'This would look perfect on you,' said Tom as he picked out a slinky black Calvin Klein negligee with matching panties, costing £350.

'Oh, Tommy,' Penélope purred, according to witnesses. 'This is pretty, isn't it?'

News of Tom and Penélope's Telluride love-in was soon relayed to Nicole in Hollywood in an email from a friend. She was hurt but knew there was little point in doing anything other than continuing her dignified silence. But she must have been infuriated when Penélope was reported to have invaded a Beverly Hills toy store with bodyguards and Tom and Nicole's two children. The Spanish actress encouraged the children to buy anything they wanted. As one of Nicole's friends later said: 'Nic would have been appalled that they were being spoiled by this woman.'

Nicole was convinced that Tom and Penélope would not last long. She even told one associate: 'I'm sure she's a sweet girl. But, really, does she have the resources to handle Tom Cruise? I think not.'

Tom and Nicole eventually agreed that Tom should keep the 280-acre estate in Telluride, as well as his prized aeroplanes, including a $28-million-plus Gulfstream IV jet. The couple also agreed joint legal and physical custody of their children, who would live alternately with each parent. They would share important decisions on the children's religious and educational upbringing and both children would continue to be educated at schools in Sydney and Los Angeles.

At $250 million, Tom's net worth was estimated to be twice that of Nicole and it has since been claimed that Nicole was given a settlement worth in excess of $75 million. As she said to Tom in LA after a meeting between them and their lawyers: 'When you think about what's happening in the world these days, we really are so blessed.'

'Yes, Nic,' Tom replied, pulling closer to her as she spoke. 'That we are.'

Nicole then kissed Tom on the cheek before pulling abruptly away. In many ways she still loved him. The sudden look of heartbreak on her face said it all. For the first time since the separation announcement, the reasons for the divorce didn't seem to matter. Now it was time for both of them to start a new life.

'Goodbye, Tom,' Nicole finally said. 'Nice to see you again.'

'You look great, Nic,' Tom observed with a sad smile. 'Really great.'

Just then Nicole stopped, turned round and faced her ex-husband one last time. 'I do look rather smashing, don't I?' she said. Then, as she swept grandly out of the room, she added with a good laugh: 'Eat your heart out, won't you?'

Nicole still tortured herself with thoughts of how she might have been able to save their marriage. She kept wondering why she hadn't seen the signs that it was over sooner. But ultimately, she concluded that she would never get Tom back and there was a seething anger at the way she had simply been removed from his life.

That was when she was heard to say: 'How dare he do this to me? I loved him, I trusted him. How dare he?' As one friend explained: 'What was wrong with him? That's what people in Nicole's life were asking about Tom. He had been the dearest, sweetest, most honourable person, so fine and good. We wondered what had gone wrong.'

Meanwhile Nicole continued attending movie openings and other functions looking as if she was the happiest person in the world. Would it really be that easy to come to terms with life without Tom?

It wasn't helped by the endless appetite for photos of Tom and Penélope together, especially when Nicole got to England to promote *Moulin Rouge*. The new couple appeared in photos to be 'deliriously happy'. And Tom with Penélope seemed so similar to Tom and Nicole. Nicole even told one friend she found it 'disturbing and nasty, so insensitive to everything – even the good things'.

Then it was on to Paris for more promotional work on *Moulin Rouge*. By this time Nicole was extremely despondent because other aspects of her failed marriage were coming back to haunt her. For example, the realisation that they would never have any more wedding anniversaries.

Then in a hotel in France, a new Nicole was born. She later explained that was the night she decided that she could be a woman who was really free in her life. For the first time in her adult life she could do whatever she wanted.

Nicole even became friendly with handsome thirty-seven-year-old Fabrizio Mosca, head of Hollywood film company Miramax's Italian operations, during a promotional tour for *Moulin Rouge*. They found themselves both staying at the same hotel in Venice, the Cipriani, and Mosca accompanied Nicole to all the city's film festival events that November.

Nicole confided in Fabrizio that she didn't know what to do with her wedding ring. Should she keep it with her at all times or put it in a vault? Fabrizio suggested going to a pier and tossing it into the sea. While watching it disappear she could 'bless the experience as complete'.

Nicole totally rejected the idea on the basis that the ring had such great sentimental value to her. Instead, she gave it to a friend in Sydney for safe keeping. Fabrizio then began trying to advise Nicole on everything from the colour of her dresses to the type of wine she ordered. Not surprisingly, their romance never got off the ground.

Then came reports of a romance with top British singer Robbie Williams. Their remake of Frank and Nancy Sinatra's hit 'Somethin' Stupid' was to top the UK charts that Christmas. Rumours of a romance persisted but Nicole had no intention of dating Williams since she knew there would have been a media frenzy. In any case, she told a friend, Robbie was more like a girlfriend. 'He makes me laugh but that's all,' she said.

A rumoured romance with *Moulin Rouge* co-star Ewan McGregor was similarly dismissed as nothing more than tabloid gossip. The reality was that Nicole was far from ready for any kind of public relationship with another man. She hadn't yet completely fallen out of love with Tom. But she did admit she'd harboured fantasies about Ewan McGregor, telling one friend: 'In my fantasy, he treats me the way I haven't been treated in an alarmingly long time. And afterwards I go to sleep nestled in his arms, which is where I awaken the next morning. Then, we have a romantic breakfast in bed – which he prepares, serves and takes away.'

Nicole knew nothing would ever happen with Ewan McGregor, who was happily married with a young family. But her secret fantasies seemed to perfectly illustrate just how starved of love she felt in the aftermath of her divorce from Tom.

Nicole told all her friends and associates that she was getting on with her life and had put the divorce behind her. At a lunch at Orso's restaurant in Beverly Hills she told a friend: 'Our lives just got so hectic. The kids and our careers. We managed our relationship into a ditch by staying busy, by avoiding intimacy. Maybe he found Penélope more fun and exciting. I really don't know...'

But some of Nicole's friends present that day remained appalled that Tom was flaunting Penélope Cruz around town. Nicole tried to maintain a dignified silence. Then a smile came across her face and she suddenly exclaimed: 'Oooh, I am just so furious at that ... that...' She seemed lost for words. 'That little shrimp.' Everyone at the table burst into laughter.

Newspapers across the globe interpreted Nicole's divorce agreement with Tom as a 'definite moral victory' for the actress. It also emerged that her breakthrough in the divorce negotiations had come when she used DNA samples to prove she had miscarried Tom's child shortly after their separation. Tom and Nicole even sorted out ownership of several pieces of jewellery, including Nicole's £355,000 diamond wedding band, a £28,000 pair of matching earrings and a £17,000 emerald necklace.

Then Tom turned up on the front pages of most of the tabloids in a set of raunchy photos which showed him in tight black leather trousers and even tighter T-shirt getting a lift on the shoulders of fellow actor and *Jerry Maguire* co-star Cuba Gooding Jnr at his thirty-ninth-birthday party at the Buffalo Club in Los Angeles. With his head freshly shaved, Tom brought admiring glances from both men and women. Other guests included Rob Lowe, Emilio Estevez, Ben Stiller and Neve Campbell. Director Cameron Crowe helped Tom blow out the candles on his vast chocolate cake. Tom's beloved sister Lee

Anne acted as hostess and greeted all the guests. Comedian Jim Carrey roared up on a Harley-Davidson motorbike. And there in the background was Penélope Cruz in a stunning red dress deliberately keeping a low profile while Tom and his mostly male friends performed for one lucky, hand-picked photographer allowed into the club.

Nicole certainly had the guts not to try to avoid certain issues following her divorce from Tom. When appearing on David Letterman's chat show on US TV she even managed a dig at her pint-sized husband, telling the host: 'At least I can wear high heels now.' Nicole was certainly true to her word – but she didn't find her three-inch heels particularly comfortable at the best of times. That night she slipped them off and ended the evening in bare feet.

In the middle of all this, Nicole even attended the same film premiere as Tom but managed to steer clear of him. It was the LA opening of her new film, *The Others*, which Tom had produced. Tom turned up alone while Nicole managed to waltz into the auditorium with a girlfriend on each arm and ended up chatting and laughing in a corner. Nicole, dressed in a sexy backless black corset and a clinging black and silver skirt, smiled broadly for the cameras as she posed with close friends actresses Naomi Watts and Rebecca Rigg and the director of *The Others*, Alejandro Amenabar.

To Tom's credit, he did not try to avoid the topic of his divorce from Nicole and the fact she was attending the same gala night. He told newsmen: 'We're here, we love what we do. We feel privileged to be doing something that we enjoy doing. Tonight is a celebration of a picture we all worked very hard on. The performance Nic has given is flawless.'

Tom vanished through a back exit as soon as the screening ended. Nicole left five minutes later and was driven to the after-bash at the Mondrian Hotel, where she quickly found a table in the corner of the restaurant. As one onlooker later reported: 'Nicole appeared to be having a brilliant time. She didn't seem in the slightest bit bothered that Tom failed to appear. She was smiling and laughing all evening.' Nicole left at 1 a.m. and was driven back to the family mansion in Pacific Palisades.

All Tom could do was stand back and watch after his movie with Penélope – *Vanilla Sky* – was mauled by the critics. In the USA it took $81 million, while most Tom Cruise movies achieved around $250 million.

Yet Tom continued to retain an iron grip on all the media coverage of him. At movie premieres he demanded that print journalists – who might dare to ask impertinent questions – were kept away from him altogether. That left him able to work the crowd without anyone asking him how he felt about Nicole's professional successes since the end of their marriage.

At one *Vanilla Sky* party in London only three other celebrities attended, despite Tom's supposed star power. Those celebs were actor Timothy Spall, who appeared in the film with Tom and Penélope; comedian and actor Eddie

Izzard, who was starring in a play next door; and British children's TV presenter Dani Behr. The entire event cost in excess of £500,000 but the significance of its failure may have been lost on Tom.

In May 2002 Nicole was briefly romantically linked with *Spiderman* star Tobey Maguire. The tabloids enjoyed a field day speculating about the relationship because Maguire wasn't much taller than Tom. The *Daily Mail* reported: 'The actor appears to have caught a rather willing Miss Kidman in his web. The couple have met three times in the last three days, enjoying intimate dinners out and a visit to Mr Maguire's Los Angeles home.'

One onlooker who saw the couple out together in LA remarked: 'She was constantly smiling and they seemed to have a definite rapport. But even in her flat heels she was slightly taller than Maguire. He was on his best behaviour, opening the car door for her and affectionately clasping her arm.'

The fact that Nicole was nine years older than her new friend seemed to make little difference to their friendship. As another witness reported when the couple were spotted out in an LA diner: 'At one stage Tobey leaned over and pinched her behind. She looked surprised but then started to laugh about it. She certainly wasn't upset.'

Then Tom starred in *Minority Report* – his long-awaited collaboration with Steven Spielberg. He played one of the most flawed and troubled heroes of his career, as well as asking tricky questions about the moral dilemmas of a society that has made an art of surveillance. Tom perfectly summed up his feelings towards the movie when he said: 'Personally, I think of it as a summer film for grown-ups. There's action, sure, but there's also a great twisting, turning story.'

Tom's character, John Anderton, is a drug addict, but Tom had no reservations about playing such a person. 'Definitely not. I'm interested in playing all different kinds of characters and it works for the story, it's what the character needed.'

But it was the chance to work with Spielberg that most attracted Tom to the lead role in the film. The two had first been introduced by David Geffen on the set of *Risky Business* almost twenty years earlier, so Tom had no doubts about sending him a screenplay he had developed of *Minority Report*. 'He's the master. So when I sent him the original script for *Minority Report*, I still didn't know it would happen. I wondered what he was going to say, and I was so excited when he said he would do it.'

Working with Spielberg proved a unique experience for Tom. He later explained: 'Steven's always bouncing ideas around, coming up with new ways of doing things. There's a sequence in the film with all these mechanical spiders and I guess I thought it would all be storyboarded and planned in advance. But he uses that sort of stuff as a starting point and the speed at which he thinks of new ideas is dizzying to me.'

Tom had thrown himself into even more work since the break-up of his marriage to Nicole. He was dubbed the world's hardest-working actor, but was, intriguingly, reluctant to try his hand at directing again. And for the moment he deliberately steered clear of predictions for the future.

In June 2002 Tom turned up in London for the premiere of *Minority Report*, already No. 1 at the US box office. He happily posed with co-stars, including beautiful blonde British actress Samantha Morton as well as chatting with many of the three thousand fans gathered outside the venue in the West End. Tom worried his army of security guards by insisting on spending more than an hour talking to the crowd, signing autographs and even using their mobile phones to call their friends. Penélope Cruz was nowhere to be seen.

The 3rd of July 2002 was a very significant day for Tom because it was when he turned forty. Maybe, he started to think to himself, it was time to reassess his life. On the eve of that birthday Tom gave an insightful interview to one journalist in which he talked relatively openly about both Nicole and his new love. He insisted he still had no regrets about divorcing Nicole and made a point of professing his love for Penélope. 'Of course I love her,' he said. 'I wouldn't be with her if I didn't. She's a wonderful girl. When you're in a relationship you have a good time, enjoy each other's company and live your life. I am very happy in my relationship and I have no regrets about what happened in the past.'

Tom was speaking on the eve of flying out to New Zealand for a gruelling nine-month shoot on an epic movie called *The Last Samurai*. He even paused to ponder the question of whether Nicole had broken his heart. 'Has my heart been broken?' he mused. 'I think that's part of life when your heart gets broken, and of course you have losses and disappointments. It's really about how well you deal with them. People deal with adversity in different ways. Some people, it hits them and they just can't get up, while others can. Of course I've been through lots of things in my life.'

And Tom said: 'What happened between Nic and I is very personal and is only between us.'

But at least Tom and Nicole were now back in proper contact – for the sake of the children. Tom explained: 'As a parent, you're always concerned about your children and the divorce hasn't changed anything as far as my love and concern for them go. And I know Nic feels that also. You want the best for them and you know what life is like. You know life deals out what it's going to deal out and I want the children to be strong enough and smart enough to be able to make the right choices.'

Penélope Cruz was naturally Tom's guest of honour at his fortieth birthday party, but, typically, he told her in advance not to get him a surprise present. 'I don't want anything in particular,' said Tom. 'I feel very happy with everything. I'm pretty simple like that.'

Tom even told one friend that since his divorce from Nicole he had learned to appreciate the most simple things in life. 'To relax, I like to go for hikes and all that stuff.' Tom's dream birthday treat was to take a few days off filming and head for the wilds to climb a mountain alone. It was a typical Tom idea – something that used to frustrate Nicole because it so often involved his being alone.

And turning forty didn't really hold many fears for Tom, either. 'I hadn't thought a lot about it until recently. When I think back on my life it's amazing how things have turned out. I feel very proud. I remember being a young actor, wondering what it would be like when I was forty, fifty and sixty and hoping I would still be working. I could not have anticipated something like this happening.'

If anything, Tom had become even more focused on his work since the split from Nicole. When he wasn't with Penélope, he was usually up at dawn, reading scripts and then making breakfast for the two children. That was often followed by a gruelling seventeen-hour day.

Tom prided himself on getting away with five hours' sleep three or four times a week. The rest of the time he needed at least seven hours. But when actually making a movie he was usually up at 4.30 a.m., taking phone calls, reading lines, and when the kids were not with him he preferred to work seven days a week.

Tom still relished the pressure that came with the fact that huge-budget movies were riding on his ability to pull in the fans. 'I love the pressure. It's not something that's ever bothered me. It's part of making films every day.'

The only downside to all this glitz and glamour, according to Tom, was the paparazzi. 'Before you go out you have to think whether you want to face the paparazzi or not,' he explained to one reporter in July 2002. 'Things have changed so much over the past five or six years. You used to be able to go in a restaurant or even a movie and every now and then a guy might come up and ask for an autograph or a picture. It's very different now. But I still go out to movies and go to restaurants for dinner. I'll go to an Inn and Out [a popular chain of hamburger restaurants] or I'll go to McDonald's for a double cheeseburger.'

Tom began throwing himself into a whole variety of hobbies. His renowned stamina was being put to good use for skydiving, scuba diving and flying his own Pitts Special S-2B stunt plane – he'd gained his pilot's licence back in 1994.

He regularly made a point of describing Penélope as a 'wonderful girl' but still refused to reveal the real reason behind the break-up with Nicole. Work was his definite priority. 'I want to keep pushing, see what's going to happen next. The more you work the more confidence you gain, and yet every time I start a new project I get nervous and have that thing in my stomach.'

Some time after Nicole's split with Tom, her mother, Janelle, told her: 'Don't be a porcupine.'

Nicole later explained: 'Sometimes it may feel safer to act like a porcupine because you can't hurt a porcupine. Why, you can't even get close to one. But you can't hug a porcupine, either. I want to be open to people in my life. I want to be hugged.'

It was not until the winter of 2002 that Nicole finally plucked up the courage to take a photo of Tom, Isabella and Connor out of her wallet, replacing it with just a shot of the children. Nicole admitted to her closest family and friends that she remained terrified of what lay ahead.

In November of that year Tom was reported to be seriously considering buying a £5.5-million apartment in central London, just a short distance from where Madonna had just splashed out a fortune on a home for her and her husband Guy Ritchie.

A few years earlier Tom and Nicole had splashed out on other properties in the London area but this planned purchase was significant because Tom intended sharing the apartment with new love Penélope. The property featured full air-conditioning, six bedrooms, three with bathrooms and two with *en suite* shower rooms. But most important to Tom was the high-tech security system, with CCTV cameras permanently whirring outside the front door and a resident porter on call twenty-four hours a day. Even its location opposite the Chinese Embassy ensured that armed police patrols passed the front of the building every ten minutes day and night.

There was little doubt that Tom was trying extra hard to win over his fans in the wake of his divorce from Nicole.

Tom couldn't help but notice the way Nicole was given ovations wherever she went. And how she competed against herself in the Oscars' Best Actress section for *Moulin Rouge* and *The Others*. He was quite sensitive about how his former wife was hogging the limelight. Not even a masterful PR campaign to put Tom on the cover of all the most prestigious magazines, including a ludicrously flattering cover interview for *Vanity Fair*, Hollywood's favourite in-house journal, helped his profile. The article was accompanied by supposedly raunchy photos of Tom stripped to the waist and the whole package was supposed to put him in the running for an Oscar for his *Vanilla Sky* performance. It failed.

Nicole was playing the Hollywood power game to perfection. She remained sweet and wistful whereas Tom was chippy about anything relating to his private life. She summed it up perfectly when she told one friend: 'It's amazing the way my life has twisted and turned. I used to take my hat off to a woman who is a single mother and now that person is me.'

Occasionally Nicole even tearfully told journalists that she still believed in love but had not yet found a steady relationship to replace Tom. Some were saying that there had been nothing like it since the peak years of Prince Charles and Princess Diana. Yet again, it was the lady who held all the trump cards.

Tom continued trying to promote his wonderful new lover. '[Penélope's] incredibly romantic, and yet real, you know? She's beautiful. She's a very skilled actress but has an effortless quality about her,' he gushed. 'She's a lovely person and I'm enjoying the time I spend with her. We started off as friends and then began talking on the phone and spending a lot of time with each other. And that's how it should be. Relationships like this evolve; you enjoy each other and see where it goes.' Many pointed out that it didn't exactly sound like a passionate relationship.

Nicole had much time to think about what might have been if Tom had come to her and confronted their marriage problems before demanding a divorce. She concluded that one important issue ultimately divided them – she came from a family where people argued in front of each other and said what they felt. Tom's mother took the opposite view – 'Don't rock the boat. It's nicer to just be nice.'

As a result Tom never let Nicole know how he really felt. There was a classic breakdown of communications. End of story. As one of Tom's relatives recalled recently: 'Once Tom said: "If I want to change toothpaste, Nicole wants to know why, and whether I'll ever go back, and what it may mean for our future if I don't." He's the type of guy who has trouble with intimacy, whereas Nicole always wants to delve deep into what's going on.'

Then, in February 2003, Nicole got a career boost when she collected a prestigious Bafta Best Actress award for her latest role, as Virginia Woolf in *The Hours*, with many tipping her for Oscar honours. It was just reward for a low-paid role in an arthouse movie whose success was propelling Nicole further up the A-list ladder and increasing her desirability as a leading lady.

After winning the award in London, Nicole told her favourite tabloid journalist, Baz Bamigboye: 'I'm astounded at how well the film has done. I thought of *The Hours* as this small art film that would probably get lost amongst everything.'

Then Nicole for once dropped her guard and opened her heart to Baz about her family life. 'There was a time when part of me didn't really want to take on too many projects because I had other priorities like my marriage and my family,' she said. 'I didn't always feel I could experiment as much as I can now. I feel more confident. Also I find with two children that are older, that sort of allows me a bit more time to devote to making films.

'The children go, "Get out of our hair, Mum," so they don't need you every five minutes and they spend time with their father. In any case, I'm a pragmatist and I won't always be offered these opportunities. Work while you can, I say.'

Tom's attitude towards his children was, he insisted, a reaction to his own childhood. He insisted he wouldn't make the same mistakes. 'It's fun discovering who my children are and also having to discipline them, telling them what line they can't cross for their own safety and education. I think I've lost more sleep over that than anything else. For me now my life is sleep, work, kids and family and time for Penélope.'

Yet still in the background was the Church of Scientology. Tom continued to insist it had helped him overcome all his personal ups and downs. He said: 'Life pounds you, it doesn't matter who you are or how much money you have. I became a Scientologist seventeen years ago and it helped me alleviate stress and fear. It also gave me tools to cope and find out who I am.'

As to the future, it was impossible to predict where Tom's career or personal life was heading.

For Nicole, the emotional damage was far from healed. In an interview in Los Angeles in March 2003 she made it clear she was still 'getting my feet on the ground. There's grief and loss. You have to deal with it. It was like a small death to me. I wouldn't go back to that place and time. I lost a baby, everything. It was not a good time.'

Nicole even hinted that rumours of a love affair with British actor Jude Law were wide of the mark and that in truth someone – she wouldn't say who – had been in love with her, although she did not return that love. In other words, someone had been besotted with her. Nicole explained: 'They wouldn't have been getting me. It would have been a catastrophe. They would have been getting a damaged person and they don't want that.'

She then insisted: 'I'm very committed and intense and passionate. So I'm not going to dabble. I love, I fall in love. I have not fallen in love.'

No doubt the saga of Tom and Nicole will rumble on for years to come.

EPILOGUE

The whole star process can be destructive.
The pressure is unbelievable. There's pressure
to get to the top and to stay on top. There's fear
of losing stardom. People who go into this
business often just look at the rewards.
They don't realise what they're getting into.

BEVERLY HILLS CLINICAL PSYCHOLOGIST DR EUGENE LANDY

Tom Cruise must not look back on his old self with the ache of longing that he always imagined he would feel when he reached his thirties. Hopefully, he probably felt a slight cringe and a great sense of relief that his hyperactive twenties were over. His late thirties proved his youth was completely over. They also marked the beginning of that true adulthood promised to every twenty-one-year-old.

'Youth is overrated,' said one Hollywood starlet once. For Tom, his thirties meant waving goodbye to a troublesome first marriage, the occasional love affair and an addiction to the highs when things were going well with no care or consideration for the abject misery of the lows.

Tom's twenties coincided with the 1980s – a decade of youth culture that he found himself a part of. In that ten-year span, achievement was the name of the game, but even that was not enough; with every attainment, there were bonus points for each year that stood between him and the big three-O. The term 'young film star' ceased to mean an actor under the age of forty-five, and was now applied to Tom and his fellow Brat Packers, all under twenty-five in those days.

Tom – like everyone else of his generation – undoubtedly had a long list of things he wanted to achieve by the age of forty. But when that birthday – 3 July 2002 – came and went he realised that it had nothing to do with lowering his expectations. Instead he had started to appreciate there was no value in being the most successful movie star on the planet for his age – you're either brilliant or you're not. The irony is that once Tom freed himself from the pressure of his own expectations, he actually kicked his career into a new gear.

The trials and troubles of Tom's twenties were, in a sense, a necessary evil, a rite of passage in the journey towards self-knowledge. A lot of his confidence grew as he got older because he felt a huge relief at having survived and then thrived in Hollywood. Tom had come through a lot of emotional and personal problems unscathed. He had gained a new sense of purpose in life. Tom finally discovered his own values because he had tested them out in his twenties. That meant making decisions became even easier.

There was also a commonly held belief that Tom's looks would adjust in his late thirties. Certainly he'd started to develop a more lived-in appearance, as in movies such as *Interview with the Vampire*. Tom reacted to the end of his trademark good looks and boy-next-door appearance by taking on meatier, more mature roles, by contrast with the matinee idols of yesteryear, who held on to their youth far too long and ultimately paid the price – failure.

In the second half of the nineties Tom even adopted a grunge-style look which defied his tuxedo image and sent a sharp message to his fans that his materialistic ideals were a thing of the past. His fee might have leapt up beyond the $20-million mark, but he wanted the world to know he was a regular sort of guy who cared about people.

But one of the disadvantages for Tom of entering early middle age was that he was actually expected to reveal more of his inner self, which he certainly did in *Jerry Maguire*. Many TV chat shows have an unwritten rule to avoid featuring celebrities not yet in their early thirties because younger people simply don't have enough to talk about. Now those same programmes – and in turn their audiences – expect Tom to 'come out' and prove he's attained new maturity. This notoriously private star has already actually bowed to the pressure.

Perversely, it seems that only as time has gone by has Tom truly learned to relax, to realise that there is no hurry to achieve fresh goals in his life. As he actually manages to do this, a new character is emerging, a character with the true charm and relaxed demeanour of one of those old-time stars upon whom he has modelled himself so carefully.

It seems that Tom Cruise has already been crowned the real King of Hollywood.